THE EUROPEAN UNION SERIES

General Editors: Neill Nugent, William E. Paterson, Vincent Wright

The European Union series is designed to provide an authoritative library on the European Union, ranging from general introductory texts to definitive assessments of key institutions and actors, policies and policy processes, and the role of member states.

Books in the series are written by leading scholars in their fields and reflect the most up-to-date research and debate. Particular attention is paid to accessibility and clear presentation for a wide audience of students, practitioners and interested general readers. The series consists of four major strands:

- general textbooks
- the major institutions and actors
- the main areas of policy
- the member states and the Union

Published titles

Michelle Cini and Lee McGowan
Competition Policy in the European Union

Renaud Dehousse
The European Court of Justice

Wyn Grant
The Common Agricultural Policy

Justin Greenwood
Representing Interests in the European Union

Alain Guyomarch, Howard Machin and Ella Ritchie
France in the European Union

Fiona Hayes-Renshaw and Helen Wallace
The Council of Ministers

Simon Hix
The Political System of the European Union

Simon Hix and Christopher Lord
Political Parties in the European Union

Brigid Laffan
The Finances of the European Union

Janne Haaland Matláry
Energy Policy in the European Union

John McCormick
Understanding the European Union: A Concise Introduction

John Peterson and Elizabeth Bomberg
Decision-Making in the European Union

John Peterson and Margaret Sharp
Technology Policy in the European Union

WITHDRAWN

Forthcoming

Simon Bulmer and Drew Scott
European Union: Economics, Policy and Politics

Ben Rosamond
Theories of European Integration

Richard Sinnott
Understanding European Integration

•   •   •   •

Simon Bulmer and Wolfgang Wessels
The European Council

David Earnshaw and David Judge
The European Parliament

Neill Nugent
The European Commission

Anne Stevens
The Administration of the European Union

•   •   •   •

David Allen and Geoffrey Edwards
The External Economic Relations of the European Union

Laura Cram
Social Policy in the European Union

Wyn Grant, Duncan Matthews and Peter Newell
The Greening of the European Union?

Martin Holland
The European Union and the Third World

Malcolm Levitt and Christopher Lord
The Political Economy of Monetary Union

Anand Menon
Defence Policy and the European Union

James Mitchell and Paul McAleavey
Regionalism and Regional Policy in the European Union

Jörg Monar
Justice and Home Affairs in the European Union

John Redmond and Lee Miles
Enlarging the European Union

Hazel Smith
The Foreign Policy of the European Union

Mark Thatcher
The Politics of European High Technology

Rüdiger Wurzel
Environmental Policy in the European Union

•   •   •   •

Simon Bulmer and William E. Paterson
Germany and the European Union

Carlos Closa and Paul Heywood
Spain and the European Union

Phil Daniels and Ella Ritchie
Britain and the European Union

Other titles planned include

The History of the European Union
The European Union Source Book
The European Union Reader
The Political Economy of the European Union

•   •   •

Political Union
The USA and the European Union

•   •   •   •

The European Union and its Member States
Reshaping the States of the Union
Italy and the European Union

The Political System of the European Union

Simon Hix

St. Martin's Press
New York

THE POLITICAL SYSTEM OF THE EUROPEAN UNION

Copyright © 1999 by Simon Hix

St. Martin's Press, Scholarly and Reference Division, 175 Fifth Avenue, New York, N.Y. 10010

First published in the United States of America in 1999

This book is printed on paper suitable for recycling and made from fully managed and sustained forest sources.

Printed in Great Britain

ISBN 0–312–22535–0 clothbound
ISBN 0–312–22536–9 paperback

Library of Congress Cataloging-in-Publication Data
Hix, Simon.
The political system of the European Union / by Simon Hix.
p. cm. — (European Union series)
Includes bibliographical references and index.
ISBN 0–312–22535–0 (cloth). — ISBN 0–312–22536–9 (pbk.)
1. European Union. I. Title. II. Series.
JN30.H5 1999
341.242'2—dc21   99–21956
                                                              CIP

To Beth

Contents

List of Tables and Figures

Tables

Figures

Preface

The idea for this book first came to me in 1991, while I was studying for an MSc in West European Politics in the Government Department at the London School of Economics and Political Science (LSE). The LSE is a rare institution in that it has separate departments of International Relations (IR) and Government. At the LSE, research and teaching on European Integration and the European Community (EC) institutions was traditionally the preserve of the IR department. But, in the early 1990s, with the single market and the new EC policy competences in the Single European Act and the Maastricht Treaty, the Government Department started to become interested in teaching and researching EC politics and government. At that time, however, there was not much theoretical literature from this perspective. 'Neo-functionalism' and 'intergovernmentalism' are theories of European integration, and are hence limited when applied to government and politics. Those interested in the day-to-day workings of the EC had to be content with mainly empirical and inductive literature, under the umbrella of 'EC studies'. As students of government, we desperately sought a theoretical text on the government, politics and policy-making of the emerging European-level political system.

Then, in 1994 I found myself in Washington, D.C., working as a freelance consultant on European Union (EU) affairs while trying to finish my doctoral thesis for the European University Institute, in Florence. One of my most enjoyable assignments while in Washington was running a series of sessions on 'How the European Union Works' for some officials in the US State Department. I needed a book about the EU that could speak to people who were primarily interested in the policy-process of the EU, and were eager to compare it to the American system of government. Alberta Sbragia's edited book, from a project for the Brookings Institution, came the closest (Sbragia, 1992). However, I still felt that a monograph would be the best vehicle for achieving a coherent and comprehensive text.

I subsequently set about planning and writing the book when I returned to academia in 1996, first at Brunel University in West London, and then 'back home' in the Government Department at the LSE. This process turned out to be easier than I had feared. Since the early 1990s there had been a huge increase in the number of political scientists trying to approach the EU as an emerging 'political system'. The result was an explosion of theoretical and analytical literature on EU government, politics and policy-making. This new research appeared for the first time in comparative politics journals (such as *Comparative Political Studies* and *West European Politics*) and general political science journals (such as the *European Journal of Political Research* and the *American Political Science Review*), as well as in the specialist EU studies publications (such as the *Journal of Common Market Studies* and the *Journal of European Public Policy*). I consequently decided that the task should be to provide an extensive review of this new research, while highlighting how these approaches are connected to general issues in political science.

The result, I hope, is that this book will satisfy several interests. First, it can be used as a teaching tool on EU government, politics and policy courses, particularly for advanced undergraduates or graduates. For introductory courses, the book may be used as a companion volume to an introductory text on the EU, such as Dinan (1994). Second, the book should be a guide for those involved in political science research on the EU, particularly within the fields of comparative politics and comparative public policy/public administration.

This book would not have been possible without the encouragement and support of friends, family and colleagues. I wish to thank my publisher, Steven Kennedy, and Vincent Wright, of Nuffield College, Oxford, who provided invaluable encouragement throughout the writing of this book. I would also like to thank my colleagues at the LSE who read and commented on various draft chapters: Damian Chalmers, Keith Dowding, Patrick Dunleavy and Christopher Hood. A special note of gratitude goes to Matt Gabel, who read almost the entire book and provided numerous suggestions for improving the text and ironing-out inconsistencies. I am thankful to my students at Brunel and the LSE, who have had to suffer my often strange and incomprehensible thoughts about the EU, and have given me invaluable feedback on my ideas for the book, particularly Jan Meyer-Sahling. Also, my ideas in this book have been shaped profoundly by my friends and 'fellow travellers' in the international political science community, particularly Karen Alter, Cees van der Eijk, Mark Franklin, Maria Green Cowles, Kris Deschouwer, David Farrell, Liesbet Hooghe, Hussein Kassim, Amie Kreppel, Chris Lord, Howard Machin, Giandomenico Majone, Peter Mair, Gary Marks, Anand Menon, Andrew Moravcsik, Mark Pollack, Herman Schmitt, Tapio Raunio, Alberta Sbragia, Roger Scully, Paul Taggart, George Tsebelis, Helen Wallace, William Wallace, Paul Webb, Antje Weiner and Steve Wolinetz. And, I would really like to thank the people in the EU institutions who have taught me so much about the EU, especially Pete Brown-Pappamikail, Richard Corbett, Francis Jacobs, Mike Shackleton and Martin Westlake.

Finally, I am deeply indebted to my parents, Godfrey and Maureen Hix, without whose emotional and financial support over the years I could never have been able to do the job of my dreams. However, the person who deserves the greatest thanks is my wife and best friend, Beth Ginsburg. She has been by my side since the beginning, enduring my single-mindedness and my self-doubts, and offering support and counsel at every stage. Beth, I dedicate this book to you.

SIMON HIX

Abbreviations

ACP	Africa, Caribbean, Pacific Group	EPP	European People's Party
AER	Assembly of European Regions	ERA	European Radical Alliance
		ERDF	European Regional Development Fund
ASEAN	Association of Southeast Asian Nations	ERM	Exchange Rate Mechanism
AWGI	Ad hoc Working Group on Immigration	ERT	European Round Table of Industrialists
BEUC	European Office of Consumer Unions	ESCB	European System of Central Banks
CAP	Common Agricultural Policy	ESF	European Social Fund
CC	Consumers' Committee	ESPRIT	European Strategic Programme for Research and Development in Information Technologies
CCC	Consumers Contact Committee		
CCP	Common Commercial Policy	ETUC	European Trade Union Federation
CEEP	European Centre of Public Enterprise	EU	European Union
		EUL	European United Left/Nordic Green Left
CEMR	Council for European Municipalities and Regions	EUROCHAMBRES	Chambers of Commerce and Industry, Association of
CFSP	Common Foreign and Security Policy		
CIS	Commonwealth of Independent States	EUROPOL	European Police Office
		FIFG	Financial Instrument for Fisheries
COPA	Confederation of Professional Agricultural Organizations	GATT	General Agreement on Tariffs and Trade
CoR	Committee of the Regions	IEN	Independents for a Europe of Nations
COREPER	Committee of Permanent Representatives	IGCs	intergovernmental conferences
CRE	Commission for Racial Equality	ILO	International Labour Organization
DG	directorates-general	JHA	justice and home affairs
EC	European Community	NAFTA	North American Free Trade Area
ECB	European Central Bank		
ECHR	European Court of Human Rights	NATO	North Atlantic Treaty Organization
ECJ	European Court of Justice	OCA	optimal currency area
ECSC	European Coal and Steel Community	OECD	Organization for Economic Cooperation and Development
EDC	European Defence Community	ONP	open network provision
		OSCE	Organization for Economic Cooperation in Europe
EEC	European Economic Community		
		PES	Party of European Socialists
EFTA	European Free Trade Area	QMV	qualified-majority voting
ELDR	European Liberal, Democrat and Reform Party	TABD	Transatlantic Business Dialogue
EMS	Economic and Monetary System	UN	United Nations
		UNICE	Union of Industrial and Employers' Confederations
EMU	Economic and Monetary Union		
		UPE	Union for Europe
EP	European Parliament	VERs	Voluntary Export Restraints
EPC	European Political Cooperation	WTO	World Trade Organization

Chapter 1

Introduction: Explaining the EU Political System

The EU: a political system but not a state
How the EU political system works
Actors and institutions: the basics of modern political science
Theories of European integration: the neo-functionalist legacy
Structure of the book

The European Union (EU) is a remarkable achievement. It is the result of a process of voluntary economic and political integration between the nation-states of western Europe. It began with six states, now involves 15, and will soon incorporate 20 or even 25. Also, it began as a coal and steel community and has evolved into an economic, social and political union. Moreover, European integration has produced a set of governing institutions at the European level much like any other multilevel political system. But, this book is not about the history of 'European integration', as this story has been told at length elsewhere (see for example Dedman, 1996; McAllister, 1997). Nor does the book try to explain European integration and the major 'turning points' in this process, as this too has been the focus of much political science research and theorizing (for example Moravcsik, 1998; Sandholtz and Stone Sweet, 1998). Instead, the aim of this book is to understand *how the EU works today*. How is governmental power exercised? Under what conditions can the Parliament influence legislation? Is the Court of Justice beyond political control? Why do some citizens support the central institutions while others oppose them? How important are political parties and elections in shaping political choices? Why are some social groups more able to influence the political agenda than others? Are policies to govern the single market deregulatory or reregulatory? Who are the winners and losers from budgetary and redistributive policies? Will Economic and Monetary Union work? Have policies extended and protected citizens' rights and freedoms? And, how far are the central institutions able to act with a single voice on the world stage?

We could treat the EU as a unique experiment. However, these are questions that can be asked of any multilevel democratic political system. And, the discipline of political science has developed a vast array of theoretical tools and analytical methods to answer exactly these sorts of questions. Instead of a general theory of how political systems work, political science has a series of mid-level explanations of the main processes in all political systems: such as public opinion, party competition, interest group mobilization, executive and judicial discretion, legislative bargaining, economic policy-making, citizen–state relations, and international political and economic relations. Consequently, the main argument of this book is that to help understand how the EU works, we should use the tools, methods and cross-systemic theories from the general study of government, politics and policy-making. In this way, teaching and research on the EU can be part of the political science mainstream.

This introductory chapter sets the general context for this task, explaining how the EU can be a 'political system' without also having to be a 'state'. It then introduces the key interests, institutions and processes in the EU political system, and the connections between these elements. The chapter subsequently reviews some of the basic assumptions of modern political science, and finally it briefly discusses how this conceptual framework differs from the main theories of European integration.

The EU: a political system but not a state

Gabriel Almond (1956) and David Easton (1957) were the first to develop formal frameworks for defining and analysing political systems. Most contemporary political scientists reject the 'functionalist' assumptions and grand theoretical aims of these projects. Nonetheless, Almond and Easton's definitions have survived (see for example Keman, 1993). Their essential characterizations of democratic political systems consist of four main elements:

1. There is a stable and clearly-defined set of institutions for collective decision-making and rules governing relations between and within these institutions.
2. Citizens and social groups seek to achieve their political desires through the political system, either directly or through intermediary organizations like interest groups and political parties.
3. Collective decisions in the political system have a significant impact on the distribution of economic resources and the allocation of social and political values across the whole system.
4. There is a continuous interaction ('feedback') between these political outputs, new demands on the system, new decisions, and so on.

The EU possesses all these elements. First, the level of institutional stability and complexity in the EU is far greater than in any other international regime. The basic institutional 'quadrangle' – the Commission, the

Council, the European Parliament (EP), and the European Court of Justice – was established in the 1950s. However, successive treaties and treaty reforms – the Treaty of Paris in 1951 (establishing the European Coal and Steel Community), the Treaty of Rome in 1957 (establishing the European Economic Community and the European Atomic Energy Community), the Single European Act in 1986, the Maastricht Treaty in 1992 (the Treaty on European Union), and the Amsterdam Treaty in 1997 – have given these institutions an ever-wider range of *executive*, *legislative* and *judicial* powers. Moreover, these institutional reforms have produced a highly-evolved system of rules and procedures governing how these powers are exercised by the EU institutions. In fact, the EU probably has the most formalized and complex set of decision-making rules of any political system in the world.

Second, as the EU institutions have taken on these powers of government, an increasing number of groups attempt to make demands on the system – from individual corporations and business associations, to trade unions, environmental and consumer groups and political parties. The groups with the most powerful and institutionalized position in the EU system are the governments of the EU member states, and the political parties that make up these governments. At face value, the centrality of governments in the system makes the EU seem like other international organizations, such as the United Nations and the Organization for Security and Cooperation in Europe. But, in the EU, governments do not have a monopoly on political demands. As in all democratic polities, demands in the EU arise from a complex network of public and private groups, each competing to influence the EU policy-process to promote or protect their own interests and desires.

Third, EU decisions are highly significant and are felt throughout the EU. For example:

- EU policies cover virtually all areas of public policy, including market regulation, social policy, the environment, agriculture, regional policy, research and development, interior affairs, citizenship, international trade, foreign policy, defence, consumer affairs, transport, public health, education and culture.
- In fact, the EU sets over 80 per cent of rules governing the exchange of goods, services and capital in the member states' markets.
- The primary and secondary acts of the EU are part of the 'the law of the land' in the EU member states, and EU law is supreme over national law.
- The EU budget may be small compared to the budgets of national governments, but several EU member states receive almost 5 per cent of their national gross domestic product from the EU budget.

- The EU regulatory policies and Economic and Monetary Union have a powerful 'indirect' impact on the distribution of power and resources between individuals, groups and nations in Europe.

In short, EU outputs affect the 'authoritative allocation of values' (Easton, 1957) and influence 'who gets what, when and how' in European society (Lasswell, 1936).

Finally, the political process of the EU political system is a permanent feature of political life in Europe. The six-monthly meetings of the heads of government of the member states (in the European Council) may be the only feature of the system noticed by many citizens. This can result in the impression that the EU operates through periodic 'summitry', like other international organizations. However, the real essence of EU politics are the constant interactions within and between the EU institutions in Brussels, between national governments and Brussels, within the various departments in national governments, in bilateral meetings between governments, and between private interests and governmental officials in Brussels and at the national level. As a result, unlike other international organizations, EU business is conducted in multiple settings on virtually every day of the year.

What is interesting, nevertheless, is that the EU does not have a 'monopoly on the legitimate use of coercion'. As a result, the EU is not a 'state' in the traditional Weberian meaning of the word. The power of coercion, through police and security forces, remains the exclusive prerogative of the national governments of the EU member states. But, the early theorists of the political system believed that a political system could not exist without a state. As Almond (1956, p. 395) points out:

> . . . the employment of *ultimate*, *comprehensive*, and *legitimate* physical coercion is the monopoly of states, and the political system is uniquely concerned with the scope, direction, and conditions affecting the employment of this physical coercion.

Nevertheless, some contemporary social theorists reject this conflation of the state and the political system. For example, Bertrand Badie and Pierre Birnbaum (1983, pp. 135–7) argue that:

> . . . the state should rather be understood as a unique phenomenon, an innovation developed within a specific geographical and cultural context . . . Hence, it is wrong to look upon the state as the only way of governing societies at all times and all places.

In their view, the state is simply a product of a particular structure of political, economic and social relations in western Europe between the sixteenth and mid-twentieth centuries, where a high level of centralization, differentiation, universality and institutionalization was necessary for government to be effective. In other words, in a different environment, government and politics could be undertaken without the classic apparatus of a state.

This is precisely the situation in late-twentieth-century Europe. The EU political system is highly decentralized and atomized, is based on the voluntary commitment of the member states and its citizens, and relies on sub-organizations (the existing nation-states) to administer coercion and other forms of state power. In other words, European integration has produced a new and complex political system. This has certainly involved a redefinition of the role of the state in Europe. But, the EU can function as a full-blown political system without a complete transformation of the territorial organization of the state – unlike the evolution from the city-state to the nation-state in the early-modern period of European history.

How the EU political system works

Figure 1.1 shows the basic interests, institutions and processes in the EU political system (the arrows indicate the direction of connections: complete arrows indicate a strong/direct link, and non-continuous arrows indicate a weaker/non-direct connection). At the base of the system are the EU *citizens* – the nationals of the 15 member states. EU citizens make demands on the EU system through several channels. In national elections, citizens choose governments, who subsequently represent these citizens in the Council. In European elections, citizens choose political parties, whose members sit in the EP. By joining political parties and interest groups, citizens provide resources for these intermediary organizations to be involved in EU politics. By taking legal actions to national courts and the Court of Justice, citizens influence the development and enforcement of EU law. And, as a result of these links, public office-holders take note of 'public opinion' when defining their preferences and choosing actions in the EU policy-making process.

There are two main types of 'intermediary associations' connecting the mass public to the EU policy process. First, *political parties* are the central political organizations in all modern democratic political systems. Parties are organizations of like-minded political leaders, who join forces to develop a common political agenda, seek public support for this agenda, and capture political office in order to implement this agenda. Political parties have influence in each of the EU institutions. National parties compete for national governmental office, and the winners of this competition are represented in the Council. European Commissioners are also partisan politicians: they have spent their careers in national party

Figure 1.1 *The European Union political system*

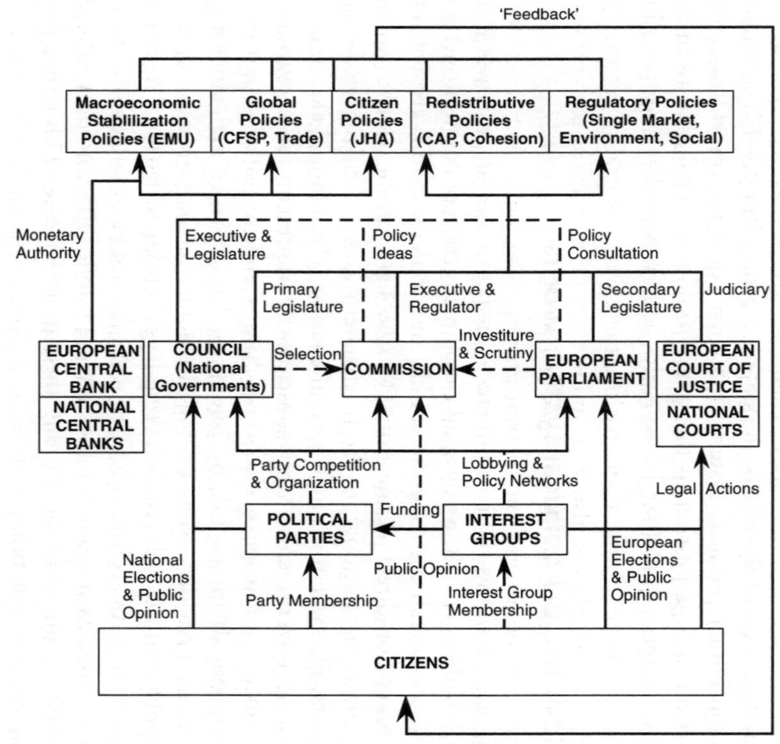

organizations, owe their positions to nomination and support from national party leaders, and usually seek to return to the party-political fray. Members of the EP (MEPs) are elected on (national) party platforms and form 'party groups' in the EP, to structure the political organization and behaviour in the Parliament. And, in the main party families, the party organizations in each member state and in the EU institutions are linked through the 'transnational party federations'.

Second, *interest groups* are voluntary associations of individual citizens or other private actors, such as trade unions, business associations, consumer groups and environmentalist groups. These organizations are formed to promote or protect the interest of their members in the political process. This is the same in the EU as in any democratic system. National interest groups lobby national governments or approach the EU institutions directly, and similar interest groups in different member states club together to lobby the Commission, the Council working groups, and the EP. Interest groups also give funds to political parties to represent their views in national and EU politics. In each policy area, public office-holders and representatives from interest groups form 'policy networks' to thrash out policy compromises. And, by taking legal actions to national courts and the Court of Justice, interest groups influence the application of EU law.

Next are the EU institutions. The *European Commission* is composed of a political 'college' of 20 commissioners (one from each member state and two from the five largest member states) and a bureaucracy of 26 directorate-generals. The Commission is responsible for initiating policy proposals and monitoring the implementation of policies once they have been adopted, and is hence the main executive arm of the EU. The *Council* brings together the governments of the member states, and is organized into several sectoral councils of national ministers (such as the Council of Agriculture Ministers). The Council undertakes both executive and legislative functions: it sets the medium and long-term policy agenda, and is the dominant chamber in the EU legislative process. The Council usually decides by unanimity, but uses a system of qualified-majority voting (QMV) on a number of important issues (where the votes of the member states are weighted according to their size and a large majority is needed for decisions to pass). Also, each government in the Council chooses its members of the Commission, and the governments collectively nominate the Commission president.

The other chamber in the EU legislative process is the *European Parliament*. The EP is composed of 626 MEPs, who are chosen in European-wide elections every five years. The EP has various powers of legislative consultation, amendment and veto under the EU's legislative procedures: the consultation procedure, the cooperation procedure, and the co-decision procedure. The EP can also amend the EU budget. The EP scrutinizes the exercise of executive powers by the Commission and the Council, and it votes on the Council nomination for the Commission president and the full Commission college (the investiture procedure), and has the power to throw out the Commission with a vote of censure.

The judicial authority of the EU is composed of the *European Court of Justice* (ECJ) and the national courts. The EU also has an independent monetary authority, the European System of Central Banks, composed of the *European Central Bank* (ECB) and the central banks of the member states in Economic and Monetary Union.

These institutions produce five types of policy outputs:

1. *Regulatory policies* – these are rules on the exchange of goods, services and capital in the single market (where the cost of policy implementation is not borne by the EU institutions), and include the creation of the single market, the harmonization of national standards, European-wide environmental and social policies, and competition policies.
2. *Redistributive policies* – these policies involve the transfer of resources through the EU budget from one social group or member state to another, and include the Common Agricultural Policy, socioeconomic and regional cohesion policies, and research and development policies.
3. *Macroeconomic stabilization policies* – these policies are pursued in Economic and Monetary Union, where the ECB manages the money supply and interest rate policy, while the Council pursues exchange rate policy and cooperation on fiscal and unemployment policies.
4. *Citizen policies* – these are rules to extend and protect the economic, political and social rights of the citizens of the EU member states, and include cooperation in the field of justice and home affairs (JHA), common asylum and immigration policies, police and judicial cooperation, and the provisions for 'EU citizenship'.
5. *Global policies* – these are aimed at ensuring that the EU acts with a single voice on the world stage, and include trade policies, external economic relations, the Common Foreign and Security Policy, and defence cooperation.

Regulatory and redistributive policies are adopted through *supranational* (quasi-federal) practices: where the Commission has a monopoly on policy initiative; legislation is adopted through bicameral procedures between the Council and the EP, and QMV is often used in the Council; law is directly effective and supreme over national law and the ECJ has full powers of judicial review and legal adjudication. In contrast, citizen and global policies are mainly adopted through *intergovernmental* procedures: where the Council is the main executive and legislative body; decisions in the Council are usually made by unanimity; the Commission can generate policy ideas but its agenda-setting powers are limited; the EP only has the right to be consulted by the Council; and the powers of judicial review of the ECJ are restricted. On the other hand, macroeconomic policies are adopted through a mix of supranationalism and intergovernmentalism, where the ECB is an independent and powerful federal monetary authority (rather like the United States Federal Reserve), but the Council of Economic and Finance Ministers (EcoFin) is the collective 'economic government' of EMU, and the EP plays an important scrutiny role but cannot enforce its wishes on the ECB or the Council.

Finally, there is a '*feedback*' between policy outputs from the EU system and new citizen demands on the system, and so on. However, this feedback loop is relatively weak in the EU compared to other political systems. EU citizens gain most of their information about the EU from *national* newspapers, radio and television rather than any *European* media channels, and the national media are focused on national government and politics rather than on European-level politics. Consequently, national elites are the main 'gatekeepers' of EU news: deciding which information is important, and how these should be 'spun' in the national setting. Only social groups who have direct contacts to the EU institutions, such as farmers and some business groups, are able to circumvent the filtering of EU information by national elites.

Table 1.1 contains some basic socioeconomic and political data about the EU member states, and their representation in the EU institutions. Suffice is to say at this stage that no member state is either physically, economically or political powerful enough to dominate the EU. In a sense, every member state is a minority in the EU political system.

Actors and institutions: the basics of modern political science

Political science is the systematic study of the processes of politics and government. The modern discipline dates from the end of the nineteenth century, when people like Woodrow Wilson, Robert Michels, Knut Wicksel, Lord Bryce and Max Weber first developed tools and categories to analyse political institutions, such as bureaucracies, governments, Parliaments and political parties. In the interwar period, a 'behavioural revolution' sought to replace this focus on the structural features of politics with 'methodological individualism' (Almond, 1996). This method seeks to explain political outcomes through the interests, motives and actions of political actors (such as elites, bureaucrats, voters, political parties and interest groups) rather than through the power of institutions and political structures (such as constitutions, decision-making rules, and social norms). However, the 1980s and 1990s have seen a return to institutions: under the

Table 1.1 *Basic data about the EU member states*

| Member state | Date joined | Socioeconomic data | | Political data | | Representation in the EU institutions | | |
		Pop'n 1996 (mil.)	GDP/ Head, 1996 (ecu)	Main political parties and votes in last Parliamentary election (%)	Territorial structure	Votes in Council under QMV	Commissioners	MEPs
Austria	1995	8.1	28 200	Social Democrats 38 Christian Democrats 28 Extreme Right 22	Federal	4	1	21
Belgium	1952	10.1	26 000	Social Democrats 26 Liberals 25 Christian Democrats 24	Federal	5	1	25
Denmark	1973	5.3	31 400	Social Democrats 36 Liberals 24	Unitary	3	1	16
Finland	1995	5.1	21 600	Social Democrats 28 Liberals 20 Conservatives 18	Unitary	3	1	16
France	1952	58.3	26 200	Conservatives 30 Socialists 24	Regional	10	2	87
Germany	1952	81.8	29 000	Social Democrats 41 Christian Democrats 28	Federal	10	2	99
Greece	1981	10.5	8 600	Socialists 42 Conservatives 38	Unitary	5	1	25

Country	Year			Parties				
Ireland	1973	3.6	15 400	Conservatives (FF) 39 / Christian Dem's (FG) 28	Unitary	3	1	15
Italy	1951	57.3	20 000	Centre-Left Alliance 41 / Centre-Right Alliance 37	Regional	10	2	64
Luxemb.	1951	0.4	43 300	Christian Democrats 30 / Socialists 25 / Liberals 19	Unitary	2	1	6
Netherl.	1951	15.5	25 200	Liberals 27 / Christian Democrats 23 / Labour 17	Unitary	5	1	31
Portugal	1987	9.9	10 200	Socialists 44 / Conservatives (PSD) 34	Unitary	5	1	25
Spain	1987	39.2	14 300	Conservatives 39 / Socialists 38	Regional	8	1	64
Sweden	1995	8.8	25 000	Social Democrats 36 / Conservatives 23	Unitary	4	1	22
United Kingdom	1973	58.7	19 600	Labour 43 / Conservatives 31 / Liberals 17	Unitary	10	2	87
Total EU		372.7	16 641			87	20	626

Source: Eurostat (1997), Elections Around the World (http://www/agora/stm/it/elections/election/htm).

label of 'new institutionalism'. As a result, many contemporary political scientists – for example, in both 'rational choice institutionalism' and 'historical-institutionalism' – try to integrate theories and assumptions about both actors and institutions in a single analytical framework (see for example Shepsle, 1989; Thelen and Steinmo, 1992; Hall and Taylor; 1996).

Starting with *actors*, a common assumption in theories of politics is that political actors are 'rational' (for example Dunleavy, 1990; Tsebelis, 1990). This means that actors have a clear set of 'preferences' about what outcomes they want from the political process. For example, party leaders want to be reelected, bureaucrats want to increase their budgets or to maximize their independence from political interference, judges want to strengthen their powers of judicial review, and interest groups want to secure policies that increase the well-being of their members. Furthermore, actors act upon these preferences in a rational way: by pursuing the strategy that is most likely to produce the outcome they want. So, party leaders will position themselves close to the key voters, bureaucrats will try to increase the size of the public sector, judges will make rulings that strengthen the rule of law, and interest groups will lobby those office-holders that are most likely to be decisive in the bargaining process.

But, actors do not form their preferences and choose their strategies in isolation; they must take account of each other's interests and expected actions. 'Strong' rational choice theories assume that actors have perfect information about the preference-ordering of the actors in the system, and consequently that actors can accurately predict the result of a particular strategy. Nevertheless, the perfect information assumption is often relaxed, which allows for 'unintended consequences' of actions and policy deci-sions. In either approach, political outcomes are seen as the result of 'strategic interaction' between competing actors. Sometimes this strategic interaction results in an outcome that is the best of all the possible outcomes for the actors involved. This is said to be an 'optimal' outcome. But very often actors are forced to pursue strategies that do not lead to the best outcome – as in the famous 'prisoners' dilemma' game (see Chapter 4). When this happens, the result is said to be 'sub-optimal'.

Turning to *institutions*, which include both formal institutions such as constitutions and rules of procedure, as well as informal institutions such as behavioural norms and personal and collective ideologies (North, 1990), these institutions are 'constraints' on actors' behaviour. For example, one case of a formal institution is the term of office of a public office, which restricts the office-holder to a particular 'time horizon', and hence leads the office-holder to not take account of the possible long-term effects of strategies or outcomes. In addition, institutions determine the likely pay-offs from particular actions, and hence which is the best strategy to achieve a particular goal. As a result, institutions can produce particular outcomes ('equilibria') that would not occur if the institutions were absent or were changed (Riker, 1980). When this happens, the outcome is said to be a 'structure-induced equilibrium' (Shepsle, 1979).

However, if actors think they are more likely to be better off under a different set of institutions, they will seek to change the institutional arrangements. As a result, actors have preferences about a whole range of political institutions, and act upon these 'institutional preferences' in the same way that they do on their primary political goals. The process of 'institutional choice' is hence no different from strategic interaction over policy outcomes (see for example North, 1990; Tsebelis, 1990). In both cases, there is an existing structure of preferences and institutions, but in the institutional choice game the outcome is an 'institutional equilibrium' rather than policy equilibrium (Shepsle, 1986).

In sum, the basic theoretical assumptions of modern political science can be expressed in the following 'fundamental equation of politics' (Hinich and Munger, 1997, p. 17):

Preferences × Institutions = Outcomes

'Preferences' are the personal wants and desires of political actors; 'institutions' are the formal and informal rules that determine how collective decisions are made; and 'outcomes' (public policies and new institutional forms) result from the interaction between these preferences and institutions. This simple equation also illustrates two further basic rules of politics:

- if *preferences change*, outcomes will change, even if *institutions remain constant*; and
- if *institutions change*, outcomes will change, even if *preferences remain constant*.

Politics, then, is an ongoing process. Actors choose actions to maximize their preferences, within a particular set of institutional constraints and a particular structure of strategic interests, but, some actors change their preferences, for example as new politicians come to power. Or, actors collectively decide to change the institutions. In either case, actors pursue new actions, which leads to new policy or institutional equilibria, which lead to new preferences, and so on.

These assumptions can easily be applied to the EU. As we discussed above, there are a number of actors in the EU system: national governments, the supranational institutions, political parties at the national and European level, bureaucrats in the national and EU administrations, interests groups, and individual voters. To explain how the EU works, we must understand the interests of all these actors, their strategic relations *vis-à-vis* each other, the institutional constraints on their behaviour, their optimal policy strategies, and the institutional reforms they will seek to better secure their goals.

Theories of European integration: the neo-functionalist legacy

Many other contemporary scholars of the EU describe it as a political system (for example Attinà, 1992; Andersen and Eliassen, 1993; Quermonne, 1994; Leibfried and Pierson, 1995; Wessels, 1997a), and some early scholars of the European Community (EC) have argued that European integration was creating a new 'polity' (for example Lindberg and Scheingold, 1970). However, few contemporary theorists try to set out a systematic conceptual framework for linking the study of the EU political system to the study of government, politics and policy-making in all political systems. The conceptual framework in this book is not the same as a single theoretical approach that explains everything about the EU. Thankfully, the 'grand theories' of the political system died in the 1960s, to be replaced by mid-level explanations of cross-systemic political processes. As discussed, an underlying argument in this book is that much can be learned if we simply apply these cross-systemic theories to the EU. This is a very different project to much theorizing about the EU, which has tended to seek 'grand theories' of *European integration* rather than mid-level propositions about specific elements of the EU policy process. Nevertheless, these 'integration theories' make certain propositions about the day-to-day workings of the European political system (cf. Hix, 1994, 1998).

The first and most enduring grand theory of European integration is *neo-functionalism* (see for example Haas, 1958, 1961; Lindberg, 1963, Lindberg and Scheingold, 1970, 1971). First developed by Ernst Haas, the basic argument of neo-functionalism is that European integration is a deterministic process, whereby 'a given action, related to a specific goal, creates a situation in which the original goal can be assured only by taking further actions, which in turn create a further condition and a need for more, and so forth' (Lindberg, 1963, p. 9). As part of the wider 'liberal school' of international relations (IR), neo-functionalists believe that the driving forces behind this 'spillover' process are *non-state actors* rather than sovereign nation-states. Domestic social interests (such as business associations, trade unions and political parties) press for further policy integration to promote their economic or ideological interests, and the European institutions (particularly in the Commission) argue for the delegation of more powers to 'supranational' institutions to increase the European institutions' influence over policy outcomes.

However, neo-functionalism's failure to explain the slowdown of European integration in the 1960s, and the subsequent strengthening of the 'intergovernmental' elements of the EC, led to the emergence of a starkly opposing theory of European integration, known as *intergovernmentalism* (for example Hoffman, 1966, 1982; Taylor, 1982; Moravcsik, 1991). In line with the 'realist school' in IR, intergovernmentalism argues that European integration is driven by the interests and actions of the European nation-states. In this interpretation, the main aim of governments is to protect their geopolitical interests, such as national security and national 'sovereignty'. In addition, decision-making at the European level is a zero-sum game, where 'losses are not compensated by gains on other issues: nobody wants to be fooled' (Hoffman, 1966, p. 882). Consequently, against the neo-functionalist 'logic of integration', intergovernmentalists see a 'logic of diversity [that] suggests that, in areas of key importance to the national interest, nations prefer the certainty, or the self-controlled uncertainty, of national self-reliance, to the uncontrolled uncertainty of the untested blunder' (*ibid.*, p. 88).

These two approaches have been two great monoliths at the gate of the study of European integration since the 1970s. Subsequent generations of researchers have been forced to learn and repeat these approaches virtually by rote, and to explain how their own theories relate to these dominant frameworks, usually by siding with one or the other. However, two recent integration theories have successfully adapted these frameworks and gone some way towards developing a new dichotomy in the study of European integration.

First, Andrew Moravcsik has developed a theory he calls '*liberal-intergovernmentalism*' (Moravcsik, 1993, 1998). Liberal-intergovernmentalism divides the EU decision process into two stages, each of which is grounded in one of the classic integration theories. In the first stage there is a 'demand' for European integration from domestic economic and social actors, and, as in neo-functionalism and the liberal theory of IR, these actors have *economic* interests and compete for these interests to be promoted by national governments in EU decision-making. In the second stage, European integration is 'supplied' by intergovernmental bargains such as Treaty reforms and budgetary agreements. As in intergovernmentalism, states are treated as unitary actors and the supranational institutions have a limited impact on final outcomes. In contrast to the classic realist theory of IR, however, Moravcsik argues that state preferences are driven by economic rather than geopolitical interests, that state preferences are not fixed (because different groups can win the domestic political contest), and that inter-state bargaining can produce positive-sum outcomes.

Second, Paul Pierson has proposed a theory of European integration derived from the *historical-institutionalist* school in political science

(Pierson, 1996; cf. Sandholtz and Stone Sweet, 1997; Fligstein, 1998). This theory works through a three-step model. At time $T0$, a set of institutional rules is chosen or a policy decision is made (by the member state governments), on the basis of the structure of existing preferences. At time $T1$, a new structure of preferences emerges under the conditions of the new strategic environment: the changed preferences of the member states, the new powers and preferences of the supranational institutions, and the new decision-making rules and policy competences at the European level. And, at time $T2$, a new policy decision is adopted or a set of institutional rules is chosen. As a result of this model, decisions at time $T0$ 'lock' the process of integration into a particular 'path'. In addition, and in fundamental opposition to Moravcsik's theory, actors have imperfect information in this model: at $T0$ national governments are unable to predict their preferences at $T1$, or to predict the impact of their decisions on the influence of supranational institutions on policy outcomes at $T2$. As a result, policy choices and institutional reforms tend to produce profound unintended consequences.

By making assumptions about how the EU works, these integration theories share some analytical propositions with the cross-systemic theories of government, politics and policy-making. Neo-functionalism's analysis of preference formation in the domestic arena are similar to pluralist theories of interest group behaviour and party competition (see Chapters 7 and 6), and its propositions about the behaviour of supranational institutions are much like theories of discretion by executive agencies (see Chapter 2). Intergovernmentalism's analysis of inter-state bargaining shares the same assumptions as theories of decision-making under unanimity rules (see Chapters 8, 9, 10, 11 and 12). In particular, the two later integration theories consciously use general theories of politics and government. Moravcsik applies theories of domestic preference formation from the study of international political economy (see Chapter 5), and in his approach to intergovernmental bargaining he uses transactions-costs theories of decision-making and non-cooperative game theory (see Chapters 2, 3, 4, 8 and 9). Pierson, on the other hand, uses *inter alia* theories of agency and judicial discretion (see Chapters 2 and 4) and theories of structure-induced equilibrium in legislative bargaining (see Chapter 3).

Structure of the book

The rest of the book introduces and analyses the various aspects of the EU political system. Part I looks at EU *government*: the structure and politics of executive power and public administration (Chapter 2); political organization and bargaining in the EU legislative process (Chapter 3); and judicial politics and the development of an EU constitution (Chapter 4). Part II turns to *politics*: public opinion and political cleavages (Chapter 5); the role of parties and elections and the issue of the 'democratic deficit' (Chapter 6); and the organization and influence of interest groups (Chapter 7). Part III focuses on *policy-making*: the regulation of the single market (Chapter 8); redistributive policies through the EU budget (Chapter 9); economic and monetary union (Chapter 10); citizens' rights and freedoms (Chapter 11); and global economic and security policies (Chapter 12). In an effort to create a link with the rest of the discipline, each chapter begins with a review of the general political science literature on the subject of the chapter. Finally, in Chapter 13, the underlying arguments and issues in the book are brought together in a short *conclusion*.

PART I

GOVERNMENT

Chapter 2

Executive Politics

As the EU has evolved, the governments of the EU member states have delegated significant powers of political leadership, policy implementation and regulation to the Commission. The result is a 'dual executive' in the EU, where the Council and the Commission share the responsibilities of 'government'. Sometimes this institutionalized separation leads to deadlock, as in other 'dual-executive' systems (Blondel, 1984). However, consensus and stability are secured through a division of labour, with the Council governing the long term and the Commission governing the short term, and through highly developed mechanisms to manage Commission discretion, such as 'comitology'. To help understand how this came about and how it works we shall first explore some theories of executive powers, delegation and discretion.

Theories of executive power, delegation and discretion

In classic constitutional theory the legislature decides, the executive enacts, and the judiciary adjudicates. However, modern 'government' does more than simply implement law. In fact, governments have two different types of executive power: *political*, the leadership of society through the proposal of policy and legislation; and *administrative*, the implementation of law, the distribution of public revenues, and the passing of secondary and tertiary rules and regulations.

In some systems all these powers are concentrated in the hands of one set of office-holders. However, in many systems, such as the EU, executive tasks are divided between different actors and bodies. One way of

21

conceptualizing the relationships between different executive actors is 'principal–agent' analysis. In this approach, the 'principals' – the initial holders of executive power – decide to delegate certain powers to 'agents'. Put another way, principals 'demand' certain tasks, which agents 'supply'. The eventual division of power is located where the demand for and supply of executive tasks meet. This framework was originally developed to analyse the relationship between the US Congress (principals) and the US presidency and the federal bureaucracy (agents). But, a similar relationship exists between the EU governments and the European Commission (Pollack, 1997a).

When delegating responsibilities to agents, principals might like the agents to exercise these powers in a neutral fashion. However, agents have interests and policy preferences of their own, which derive from several sources. First, once a bureaucracy or a regulatory agency has gained a degree of autonomy, it becomes the target of lobbying by private interest groups. Interests who are the subject of the bureaucratic actions of the agency have an incentive to 'capture' the agency (Lowi, 1969), and moreover, the head of an agency can be tempted by inducements offered by interest groups, such as a well-paid job or senior position in the relevant industry when his or her term of office runs out.

Second, public officials are interested in increasing their influence in the political process. In classic public-choice theory, public officials are 'budget maximizers' (Niskanen, 1971). They seek larger budgets to increase their own salaries, employ more staff, secure more patronage or increase their profile and reputation. Moreover, agents are in competition with each other to secure limited public resources, so they deliberately overestimate their budgetary needs and oversupply policy outputs (by spending as much as possible) to prevent 'downgrading' relative to their competitors. The result is ever-larger claims by bureaucracies for public resources.

Third, an alternative view is that bureaux prefer to 'shape' their own destiny (Dunleavy, 1990). Different bureaux have different budgetary needs: delivery agencies, which provide direct entitlements and subsidies, can distribute more benefits with larger budgets, whereas regulatory agencies only need to cover personnel, research and administration costs. Moreover, within each agency senior and mid-level officials have different incentives. Mid-level officials may seek more resources to dispose, but senior officials will have few personal benefits of larger budgets. In fact, a larger budget usually means more pressure. Instead, senior officials are primarily interested in securing policy influence, job security and freedom from direct line responsibilities. Rather than maximizing budgets, there-fore, senior bureaucrats (and particularly in regulatory agencies) will seek to maximize their independence from control and their opportunities to determine policy outcomes.

The implications of these theories are the same: agents have the desire to move from the principals' original policy intention. A key issue, then, is how far are agents able to do this (cf. Weingast and Moran, 1983; Epstein and O'Halloran, 1998). The problem for principals is that the delegation of power often results in 'bureaucratic drift' – where an agent is able to use its 'policy discretion' to move final policy outcomes closer to its ideal position. This phenomenon is illustrated in Figure 2.1 which represents a two-dimensional policy space in which there are three governments with 'ideal policy preference' at points A, B, and C on the two dimensions. The Commission has an ideal policy preference outside the 'core' of inter-governmental preferences (shown by the triangle). The governments agree on a piece of legislation inside their 'policy core', at position X. The Commission is responsible for implementing this legislation. Through this implementation, the Commission is able to shape the final policy outcome: moving the eventual policy away from X towards its ideal policy preference. In fact, the Commission can move the final policy as far as position Y. Governments A and B prefer this policy outcome to the original deal (since Y is closer to their ideal preferences than X), and consequently they have no incentive to introduce new legislation to overrule the Commission, and will oppose any attempt by government C to take such action. However, governments A and B will block any moves further towards the Commission's ideal point, as any policy in this direction would be less attractive to these two governments than position Y. The result, then, is that the Commission has discretion to change the original policy outcome, within the constraints of the preference structure of the legislators.

Nevertheless, principals can limit bureaucratic drift. First, they have several powers at their disposal to monitor the behaviour of agents (see for example McCubbins and Schwartz, 1984). For example, they can gather information on the performance of the agent, and force the agent to disclose information in public hearings, a strategy known as a *'police patrol'* oversight procedure. But the extra costs of information-gathering might outweigh the benefits of delegating the responsibilities. Alternatively, principals can use private and public interest groups to do the monitoring for them. Interest groups that are the subjects of an agent's actions possess special expertise and information on the actions of the agent, and also, if the agent is captured by a particular interest, competing groups will inform the principals. As a result, principals can simply sit back and wait for complaints before acting, an alternative strategy known as a *'fire-alarm'* oversight procedure.

Figure 2.1   *Bureaucratic drift by the European Commission*

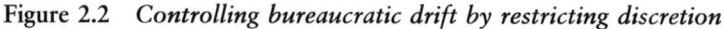

Figure 2.2   *Controlling bureaucratic drift by restricting discretion*

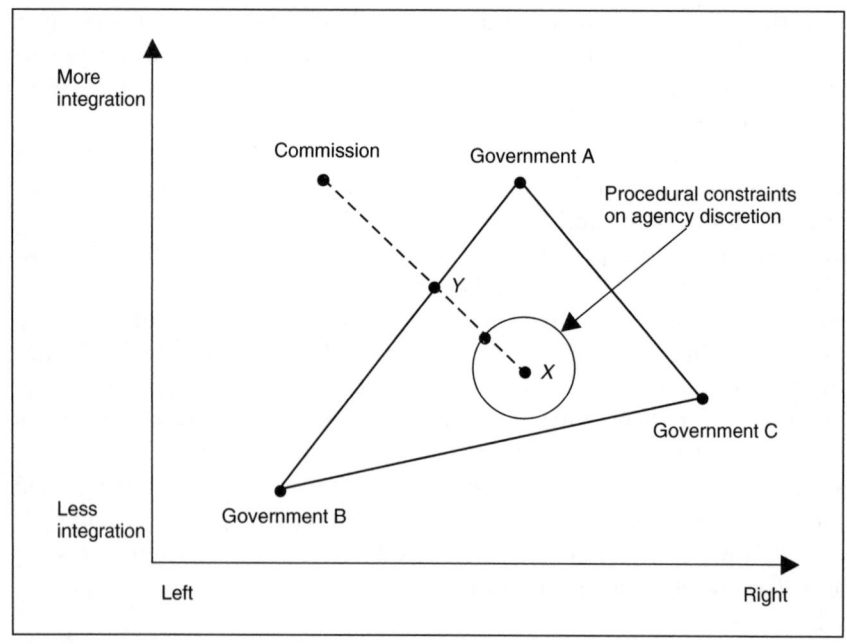

Second, principals can design rules and procedures to minimize agent discretion (Moe, 1989; Kiewiet and McCubbins, 1991; Horn, 1995). For example, rules can be established that specify how an agent must behave before reaching a decision (such as listening to both sides of the debate), how an agent relates to other administrative and political officials, and how an agent's deliberations should be reported to the media.

The result of these controls is a restriction of the ability of an agent to move from the original policy intention. This is illustrated in Figure 2.2. As in Figure 2.1, the governments agree on a legislation at X, but to constrain the discretion of the Commission to move the policy outcome, the governments introduce a set of procedures defining how exactly the Commission shall go about its job. The result is some drift towards the Commission's ideal point, but only to Z instead of Y.

In sum, certain executive tasks and institutional configurations give more powers to executive agents than others (Horn, 1995). As a result of successive treaty reforms and secondary legislation, executive power in the EU is shared between the Council and the Commission (cf. Lenaerts, 1991). Principal–agent analysis helps us conceptualize the tension between the Council and the Commission.

Government by the Council and the member states

As discussed in Chapter 1, the Council is composed of ministers from the EU member states' governments'. Possessing both executive and legislative powers, the Council is the 'decision-making centre' of the EU (Wessels, 1991). The organization and operation of the Council in exercising legislative power is tackled in the next chapter, whilst in this section we focus on the executive powers of the Council, which it exercises in four main ways:

1. In treaties and reforms, the Council sets the long-term policy goals of the EU and delegates powers to the Commission for the pursuit of these goals.
2. The European Council (of heads of government) and certain other councils set the medium-term policy agenda.
3. The member states are responsible for implementing EU legislation through their own bureaucracies.
4. The EU governments manage the day-to-day administration of EU policies in cooperation with the Commission through the 'comitology' system (see below).

The first two on this list relate to the *political* aspect of executive power, whereas the third and fourth relate to its *administrative* aspect.

Treaties and treaty reforms: deliberate and unintended delegation

The signing of treaties and their subsequent reform are the result of careful bargaining and agreement between every member government in 'inter-governmental conferences' (IGCs) (Moravcsik, 1998), where the require-ment of unanimity tends to produce 'lowest common denominator' agreements. However, the process of European integration has proceeded because governments place different emphasis on different issues; and are hence prepared to 'lose' on some issues in return for 'winning' on the ones that are more important for their national interests. The resulting 'package-deals' have gradually added new competences to the EU and delegated increasing executive powers to the Commission.

For example, the Treaty of Paris of 1951, which established the European Coal and Steel Community (ECSC), was essentially a deal between France and Germany. In return for fostering German reconstruc-tion and reindustrialization, France sought a framework for planned production and distribution in its own coal and steel industry. To secure these aims, the member governments delegated certain powers to a new supranational body – the High Authority, the precursor of the Commis-sion. Robert Schuman and Jean Monnet were the brains behind this idea. Common production and distribution of coal and steel could be governed through meetings of ministers of the member governments, but Schuman and Monnet argued that such intergovernmental arenas would suffer from procrastination, indecision and disagreement, as each government would defend its own interests. They consequently proposed that decision-making efficiency could only be guaranteed by delegating the responsibility for generating policy ideas and for the day-to-day management of policy to a supranational body (Haas, 1958, pp. 451–85; Monnet, 1978). This combination of intergovernmental decision-making and policy initiation and management by a supranational executive – the so-called 'Monnet method' – was the model for future treaties.

The Treaty of Rome, signed in 1957, established the European Econo-mic Community (EEC) and the European Atomic Energy Community (Euratom). In the EEC, the bargain was between the German goal of a common market and the French goal of protection for agricultural products, through the Common Agricultural Policy (CAP) (Lindberg, 1963). Again, to achieve these aims the EEC treaty delegated policy initiation in the common market and administration of the CAP to the Commission. A further innovation of the Treaty of Rome was a legislative procedure that made it easier for the Council to accept a Commission proposal than to overturn it. This rule allowed the new supranational executive significant 'agenda-setting' powers in the establishment of rules governing the common market.

The package in the Single European Act (SEA), signed in 1986, centred around the economic goal of establishing a 'single market' by 31 December 1992 in return for new social and environmental 'flanking policies' (cf. Hoffman, 1989; Moravcsik, 1991; Garrett, 1992). This time, however, the Commission had played an important leadership role by detailing how the single market could be achieved and by preparing the treaty reforms (Sandholtz and Zysman, 1989; Dehousse and Majone, 1994). The reward was new responsibilities for the Commission: to initiate over 300 pieces of legislation to establish the single market; to propose and implement common environmental, health and safety and social standards; to prepare the reform of the structural funds; and to draft a plan for economic and monetary union (EMU). Moreover, to enable the single market programme to be implemented by the 1992 deadline, the decision-making rules of the European Community (EC) were amended to strengthen the agenda-setting powers of the Commission – through more qualified majority voting in the Council and a new legislative procedure (the cooperation procedure, see Chapter 3). Finally, the SEA also introduced provisions for intergovernmental cooperation in foreign policy, known as European Political Cooperation (EPC), but in this area the governments decided that executive authority would remain with the Council.

The Treaty on European Union (the Maastricht Treaty), signed in 1992, institutionalized the Commission's plan for EMU. In return, more funds were promised for 'cohesion policies', EU social policy was strengthened, new health, education, transport and consumer protection policies were added, and EU 'citizenship' was established (cf. Moravcsik, 1993; Sandholtz, 1993). The Commission was again delegated the responsibility of initiating legislation and managing these policies. However, the Council refused to delegate executive powers to the Commission in two new 'pillars', which were separate from the main EC pillar: on justice and home affairs policy (JHA), to pursue the goal of the 'free movement of persons' between the EU member states; and common foreign and security policy (CFSP), which replaced EPC.

Finally, the main innovation of the Amsterdam Treaty, signed in 1997, was the transfer of the provisions for establishing the free movement of persons to the EC part of the EU Treaty. The governments accepted that the JHA provisions in the Maastricht Treaty had failed, partly due to the lack of political leadership, and to resolve this the governments again agreed to delegate policy initiation rights in this area to the Commission (but also allowing policies to be initiated by the member states). However, similar arguments about the lack of development of CFSP did not result in new Commission powers in this field. Instead, the governments delegated responsibility for policy ideas and the monitoring of CFSP issues to a new 'task force' located in the Council secretariat.

In other words, the development of the EU treaties is a story of selective delegation of political and administrative powers by the governments to the Commission. However, treaty reform is a blunt instrument. When signing treaties, governments cannot predict the precise implications of treaty provisions and new decision-making rules, or exactly how the Commission will behave when granted new powers. For example, few member states understood the implications of the new decision-making rules in the Treaty of Rome and the Single European Act (Tsebelis and Kreppel, 1998). Moreover, in the above discussion of the theories of executive power, once certain powers have been delegated through this mechanism, they are unlikely to be overturned in subsequent treaty reforms as at least one member state will feel that they benefit from Commission discretion. As a result, there are inevitable 'unintended consequences' of this selective delegation that will allow bureaucratic drift by the Commission (Pierson, 1996).

Political leadership by the European Council and the Council

The main executive roles of the European Council and the Council are to set guidelines and objectives for the Commission, monitor the work of the Commission in the implementation of these guidelines, delegate short-term responsibilities to the Commission, execute CFSP, JHA and EMU policies, and adopt new policy competences for the EU (under article 308 [ex 235]). To highlight a contrast with the Council's legislative powers, Hayes-Renshaw and Wallace (1997) describe these executive powers as 'political rather than legal decisions'.

The highest authorities in the EU political system are the 'summits' of the EU heads of government. These meetings have been held since the Paris and Rome Treaties, but formally became part of EU decision-making only in 1975, in the form of the European Council. European Councils are where final agreements and compromises are reached on treaty reforms. In addition, as article 4 [ex D] of the EU Treaty states: 'The European Council shall provide the Union with the necessary impetus for its development and shall define the general political guidelines thereof'. Werts (1992) consequently describes the European Council as the 'Provisional European Government' (cf. Bulmer and Wessels, 1987, pp. 132–46; Johnston, 1994). The European Council meets at least twice a year, usually at the end of each presidency of the Council. The presidency of the Council rotates every six months between the member-state governments (see Chapter 3).

The European Council takes a central political leadership role, guiding the work of the lower meetings of the Council and the Commission, and setting the medium-term objectives of the EU. An example of this are the variety of decisions made at any European Council meeting, such as the Luxembourg European Council of 12–13 December 1997. As set out in the 'Presidency Conclusions', the Luxembourg European Council:

- agreed a two-speed strategy for EU enlargement to central and eastern Europe, resolving an internal EU dispute over which states should join first;
- adopted a resolution on economic policy coordination in EMU, resolving a dispute over the relative powers of EcoFin and the 'Euro-X' committee, of the finance ministers of the states participating in EMU;
- adopted a declaration on food safety, setting out a series of principles to guide the Commission's development of its green paper on food legislation;
- agreed that the Social Affairs Council would adopt common employment policy guidelines for 1998 on 15 December 1997;
- asked the Internal Market Council to agree as soon as possible on the action plan on the review and implementation of the single market;
- reviewed the Commission's work in preparing the reform of the EU budget;
- reviewed the work of the Agriculture Council in preparing the reform of CAP;
- reviewed developments in justice and home affairs, and urged the remaining governments to ratify the Convention setting up a European Police Agency;
- reviewed the work of the General Affairs Council on an EU strategy towards the Middle East peace process;
- reaffirmed that the EU will push for further liberalization of world trade in the next round of trade negotiations in the World Trade Organization; and
- adopted a declaration on the fiftieth anniversary of the UN Declaration of Human Rights, reaffirming the EU's commitment to uphold human rights.

Only the first two issues were really resolved at the level of heads of government. All the other issues were prepared and agreed in lower meetings of the Council and in the Committee of Permanent Representatives (COREPER) (see Chapter 3). Nevertheless, the formal approval of the European Council in these areas confirmed the highest level of political commitment on all these issues.

Lower meetings of the Council also exercise executive power. This is particularly true in the CFSP and JHA fields, in the meetings of the General Affairs Council and the Justice and Home Affairs Council, respectively. In these areas, the right of policy initiative remains with the member states, with the government holding the Council presidency. Executive powers on these issues have not been delegated to the Commission due to the political sensitivity of these issues (see Chapters 11 and 12). This is also true on a number of issues relating to EMU, where the Council of Economic and Finance Ministers (EcoFin) is effectively the 'economic government' of the EU, as Dominique Strauss-Kahn, the French Finance Minister, once described it. The other councils (such as the Agriculture Council, the Internal Market Council and the Environment Council) are generally responsible for legislative rather than executive acts (see Chapter 3).

In exercising executive powers, the general practice in the Council is to decide by 'consensus' (as close to unanimity as possible): under these rules, each government can block an initiative that is against its interests. This is a classic 'power-sharing' arrangement, where stable government is secured in deeply divided societies through the participation and agreement of each societal group in executive decisions (Lijphart, 1977; Taylor, 1989) (see Chapter 5).

Administrative 'fusion': national coordination of EU policy

The civil services of the member states play a central role in the pre- and post-legislative stages of EU policy-making. In the drafting of legislative initiatives, national officials are members of 'expert' and 'consultative' committees set up by the Commission, and national civil servants are also involved in scrutinizing Commission proposals in COREPER working groups. And, following the adoption of legislation, national civil servants monitor the implementation of EU legislation in 'comitology' committees (see below). In fact, Wessels and Rometsch (1996) estimated that over 25 000 national officials were involved in the EU policy-process in 1994.

Furthermore, national administrations are responsible for the 'coordination' of EU policy-making. Civil servants prepare 'national' responses to Commission proposals and their government's positions in the Council, and they are also at the front-line of the implementation of EU legislation. Nevertheless, each national administration organizes its coordination and implementation of EU policy in a different way. For example, in Germany a State Secretaries' European Committee was set up in 1963 and the Cabinet Committee on European Policy in 1973 to coordinate the federal ministries' involvement in EU policy-making (Wessels, 1996). However, the involvement of the EU in policy competences of the German *Länder* governments has undermined the ability of Bonn to centrally control German responses in the EU policy process (Goetz, 1995). Also, the involvement of national administrations in both the initiation and implementation stages of the EU policy process and at the European and national levels creates coordination problems for national governments (Wright, 1996). The continuous nature of the EU policy process presents constant demands on national administrations, and responses on one level of the EU system, or at one stage of the EU policy process, are inherently linked to responses at another level and at a later or former stage. Sometimes, administrations can use this to their own advantage. Governments can invoke 'problems back home' when opposing a policy initiative or an implementation measure in comitology, while claiming that 'Brussels made us do it' when enforcing unpopular measures on domestic constituencies. Nevertheless, the result tends to be a highly unsettled policy environment in most member states, with often inconsistent policy responses by national governments.

The growing interaction of national administrations in the day-to-day running of EU government led Wolfgang Wessels to develop what he called a 'fusion thesis' (Wessels, 1992, 1997). At an empirical level, European integration has lead to a 'fusion' between administrative responsibilities at the European and domestic levels and between the member states. The fusion thesis is also a theory of European integration: national administrative elites have played a crucial role in promoting the development of the EU. European integration increases civil servants' inability to respond to societal transformation and globalization, and administrative elites have designed the EU system to give themselves powerful executive and legislative powers, beyond the control of national parliaments.

In sum, national governments, both in the Council and at the domestic level, possess key executive functions in the EU. Wessels (1997) describes this as a 'third way' between pure intergovernmentalism (where no powers are delegated to supranational institutions) and pure federalism (where powers would be concentrated in a separate federal executive). However, the EU could also be thought of as a form of 'executive federalism', where the governments of the sub-units play a dominant role in the political system: both in the initiation and adoption of legislation at the federal level; and in the coordination and implementation of federal policy at the lower level (for example Frowein, 1986). Moreover, as in executive-federal systems, the EU governments are in constant competition with the other holders of executive power at the central level: the Commission.

Government by the European Commission

The European Commission has several responsibilities:

1. to develop medium-term strategies for the development of the EU;
2. to draft legislation and arbitrate in the legislative process;
3. to represent the EU in bilateral and multilateral trade negotiations;
4. to make rules and regulations, for example in competition policy;
5. to manage the EU budget; and
6. to scrutinize the implementation of the Treaty and secondary legislation.

To fulfil these responsibilities, the Commission is organized much like domestic governments: where a 'core executive' (the College of Commissioners) focuses on the political tasks (in other words, 1, 2 and 3 on the list); a bureaucracy (the directorates-general (DG)) undertakes legislative drafting, administrative and some regulatory tasks (2, 4, 5 and 6 on the list); and a network of quasi-autonomous agencies fulfils regulatory tasks (especially 6).

A cabinet: the EU core executive

At the political level, the 20 EU commissioners (one from each of the ten smaller and two from each of the five larger member states) form the College of Commissioners. The College meets at least once a week, and meetings are chaired by the Commission president. As far as possible, the College governs by consensus, but any commissioner may request a vote. When votes are taken, decisions are made by an absolute majority (11 out of 20), with the Commission president exercising the deciding vote in the event of a tie. This absolute majority rule means that abstentions or absentees are equivalent to negative votes. Voting is usually by a show of hands (so, not by secret ballot). The results of votes are confidential, but how each commissioner voted is recorded in the College minutes, and on high-profile issues this information is often leaked from somewhere in the Commission bureaucracy. Nonetheless, the commissioners are bound by the standard principle of 'collective responsibility' (a key norm in most 'cabinet government' systems), which means that even if they were in a minority they must toe-the-line of the majority to the outside world.

The political leadership of the Commission operates along the lines of cabinet government in several other ways. The first is through the allocation of different portfolios to each commissioner, as shown in Table 2.1. The most high-profile portfolios are given to the Commission vice-presidents and the people who were commissioners in previous administrations. In the Santer Commission, for example, the commis-

Table 2.1 *The Santer Commission*

Name	Member State	Party	Portfolios
President:			
Jacques Santer	Lux.	CD	Secretariat-General; Forward Studies Unit; monetary policy (with de Silguy); CFSP (with van den Broek); institutional issues (with Oreja)
Vice-presidents:			
Sir Leon Brittan*	UK	Con	External relations (N. America, Australia, NZ, Japan, China, Korea, Hong Kong, Macao, Taiwan); Common Commercial Policy; WTO
Manuel Marín*	Spa.	Soc	External relations (Mediterranean, Middle East, other Asia, Latin America); development aid
Members:			
Martin Bangemann*	Ger.	Lib	Industry; information and telecommunications technology
Ritt Bjerregaard	Den.	Soc	Environment, nuclear safety
Emma Bonino	Ita.	RL	Fisheries; consumer policy; European Community Humanitarian Office
Hans van den Broek*	Net.	CD	External relations (central & eastern Europe, former Soviet Union, Mongolia, Turkey, Cyprus, Malta, rest of Europe); CFSP
Edith Cresson	Fra.	Soc	Science, research and development; human resources, education, training and youth
Franz Fischler	Aus.	CD	Agriculture and rural development
Pádraig Flynn*	Ire.	Con	Employment and social affairs; relations with Economic and Social Committee
Anita Gradin	Swe.	Soc	Justice and home affairs; EU Ombudsman; financial control and fraud protection
Neil Kinnock	UK	Soc	Transport, including trans-European networks
Erkki Liikanen	Fin.	Soc	Budget; personnel and administration; translation and computer services
Karel Van Miert*	Bel.	Soc	Competition policy
Mario Monti	Ita.	Con	Internal market; financial services; customs and taxation
Marcelino Oreja	Spa.	Con	Relations with EP; relations with member states (transparency); culture and audiovisual; IGC
Christos Papoutsis	Gre.	Soc	Energy and Euratom; small businesses; tourism
João de Deus Pinheiro*	Por.	CD	External relations (African, Caribbean and Pacific countries, South Africa), Lomé Convention
Yves-Thibault de Silguy	Fra.	Con	Economic and financial matters; monetary policy; credits and investments
Monika Wulf-Mathies	Ger.	Soc	Regional policies, Committee of the Regions, Cohesion Fund (with Kinnock and Bjerregaard)

Note: * = Member of the previous Commission.
Party affiliations: Soc = Socialist, CD = Christian Democrat, Con = Conservative, Lib = Liberal, RL = Radical Liberal.

sioners who were in the last Delors administration all hold key portfolios. Nevertheless, any commissioner is capable of making a name for themselves through hard work and skilful manipulation of the media, as Emma Bonino has shown with her highly-publicized missions to war-torn regions in Africa and Central Asia.

The Commission president is what Bagehot (1963 [1865]) called the 'first among equals', he or she decides which commissioner gets which portfolio in consultation with the individual commissioners and the governments who nominated them. The Commission president also prepares the annual work programme of the Commission, sets the agenda of meetings of the College, and is in charge of the Secretariat General (which oversees the work of the DGs). Moreover, the Amsterdam Treaty gave the Commission president new powers: a veto over the nomination of individual commissioners by national governments, and a responsibility to provide the general political leadership of the Commission.

However, the political impact of any 'first among equals' depends on their personal characteristics and policy ideas (cf. Jones, 1991; Rhodes and Dunleavy, 1995). Of the Commission presidents (shown in Table 2.2), Walter Hallstein and Jacques Delors have probably been most influential (Ludlow, 1991). Both had a clear vision of the political development of the Commission, sought a high-profile role for the Commission, and were willing to provoke opposition with prominent European leaders to achieve these goals. For Hallstein the goal was a federal union, which was adamantly opposed by De Gaulle. For Delors the goal was economic and political union and a 'social Europe', which was adamantly opposed by Thatcher (Drake, 1995). Jacques Santer, in contrast, was deliberately selected by the EU governments as a less ideological figure than Delors, and duly promised that the Commission should do 'less but better'.

A further aspect of cabinet government is the system of the commissioners' *cabinets*. These are teams of political advisors who are hand-picked by each commissioner. The *cabinet* system was imported from the French government system, although it exists in a more-or-less formalized way in most collective-governmental systems. These *cabinets* have four main functions: political antennae and filters for party and interest-group demands; policy advisors counterbalancing the advice of civil servants in the DGs; the mechanism for inter-commissioner coordination and dispute resolution; and supervisors and controllers of the work of the DGs responsible to the Commission (Donnelly and Ritchie, 1997). In all these tasks, the role of the *cabinets* has steadily increased (Cini, 1996, pp. 111–15). For example, in the Delors administration, the Commission president's *chef de cabinet*, Pascal Lamy, controlled the flow of commands from Delors to the other commissioners, and the flow of information back to Delors (Ross, 1994).

Table 2.2 *The Commission presidents*

Years	Name	Member state	Party	Position before Commission
1958–67	Walter Hallstein	Germany	Christian Dem.	Foreign minister
1968–69	Jean Rey	Belgium	Liberal	Economics/finance minister
1970–72	Franco Maria Malfatti	Italy	Christian Dem.	Public works minister
1972	Sicco Mansholt	Netherlands	Liberal	Agriculture minister
1973–76	François-Xavier Ortoli	France	Conservative	Economics/finance minister
1977–80	Roy Jenkins	UK	Socialist	Economics/finance minister
1981–84	Gaston Thorn	Luxembourg	Liberal	Prime minister
1985–94	Jacques Delors	France	Socialist	Economics/finance minister
1995–	Jacques Santer	Luxembourg	Christian Dem.	Prime minister

Finally, as in national cabinets, commissioners are partisan actors. Article 213 [ex 157] of the EU Treaty proclaims that:

> The Members of the Commission shall, in the general interests of the Community, be completely independent in the performance of their duties. . . They shall neither seek nor take instructions from any government or from any other body.

This principle of independence derives from Monnet's vision of an apolitical functionalist bureaucracy, to protect the collective interest of European citizens. Nevertheless, due to previous occupations, peer contacts, future aims and national media scrutiny, each commissioner tends to have significant links to partisan domestic constituents.

As Table 2.3 shows, commissioners are career politicians. Between 1967 and 1995, almost 80 per cent of commissioners had held at least one elected post before entering the Commission, and most had held a senior ministerial position in a national government. Also, these partisan affiliations are important in determining the overall direction of the Commission. The Commission has always been a grand 'coalition' of Socialists, Christian Democrats, Liberals and Conservatives (MacMullen, 1997). However, the political agenda of the Commission changes as the political colour of the Commission president and the partisan make-up of the College changes. For example, Delors' promotion of a 'social dimension' of the single market was clearly a Social Democratic agenda; and in the

Table 2.3   *Political careers of Commissioners, 1967–95*

Political offices held before entering the Commission	Number	Per cent
Governmental office		
Senior ministerial post (e.g. Prime Minister, Foreign Minister)	19	21.3
Other cabinet post	31	34.8
Junior government post	8	9.0
No ministerial office	31	34.8
Elected office		
Member of national parliament	59	66.3
Local government	21	23.6
Member of European Parliament	20	22.5
Senior party position	16	17.3
Regional assembly	6	6.7
No elected office	19	21.3
Total	89	100.0

Source: Calculated from data in Page (1997).

Santer Commission there have been divisions on several environmental and social issues between the nine Socialists and the other 11 more 'free market' Christian Democrats, Conservatives and Liberals.

The partisan affiliation of commissioners also impacts on their choice of portfolios. For example, as Table 2.1 shows, in the Santer Commission: Socialists are in charge of many of the classic social and welfare policies, such as environment, education and human resources, regional policies, energy, transport and culture; a Christian Democrat is in charge of agriculture; and Conservatives cover free trade, financial services and financial and monetary policies. Nonetheless, a Conservative (Flynn) also covers employment and social policy, which has traditionally been held by Socialist commissioners. Finally, these partisan features extend to other parts of the Commission administration: the members of the *cabinets* are often recruited from partisan contacts, and senior appointments and promotions in the DG are often determined by partisan affiliations and contacts (Hooghe, 1997).

A bureaucracy: the EU civil service

Below the College of Commissioners is the EU bureaucracy, composed of 25 DGs and several temporary offices. The DGs are the organizational equivalent of government ministries in domestic administrations, and they also fulfil many of the same functions as government ministries: of policy development, preparation of legislation, distribution of revenues, monitoring of legislative implementation, and advice and support for the political executive.

The DGs and other services in the Santer administration are listed in Table 2.4. The number of DGs has expanded as new competences have been delegated to the Commission (Fligstein and McNicholl, 1998), and moreover, each new Commission administration has reorganized the DGs to promote particular agendas. For example, as part of a drive to make the Commission more relevant to individual European citizens, the Santer administration created DGXXIV out of the old Consumer Policy Service.

Each DG has a responsibility for policy initiation and management in a particular policy area, and the DGs are broadly aligned with the policy competences of the commissioners. However, the division of competences between the DGs is at a lower-level of policy competence than in most national administrations. For example, the competences of DGs III (industry), IV (competition), XII (science, research and administration), XIII (telecommunications) and XV (internal market and financial services) would be combined in a single Ministry of Industry in most domestic administrations, under the leadership of a single minister. This often leads to competing policy positions of DGs under the same commissioner. This lack of policy coherence is also facilitated because most DGs have a particular 'administrative culture'. For example, DGV (employment and social policy) has a highly corporatist culture, with the formal involvement of the European peak associations for industry and labour (UNICE and ETUC) on many issues, whereas DGXIII (telecommunications) is more pluralist and focused on technical expertise and ideas (Cram, 1994; cf. Cini, 1997). Different administrative cultures also stem from the predominance of different national groups in senior positions in each DG (Abélès *et al.*, 1993). For example, many senior officials in DGVI (agriculture) are French, German and Irish, whereas in DGIV (competition) they are British and Dutch.

The Commission employs approximately 13 000 staff, and there is considerable variation between the DGs. The two largest are DGIX (personnel), with approximately 2600 staff, and DGVI (agriculture), with approximately 2000 staff (Cini, 1996, p. 105). Entrance to the Commission civil service is by competitive examination, the '*concours*', and promotion within the Commission is competitive. However, most senior officials in the largest DGs are 'parachuted-in' from national administrations, after protracted negotiations to decide which nationality gets which position. This has lead to discontentment amongst officials in posts immediately below these 'political appointments' (Spence, 1997).

Table 2.4   *The Commission bureaucracy*

No.	Title	Commissioner responsible
Directorates-general		
I	External Relations: Commercial Policy, N. America, Far East, Australia, NZ	Brittan
IA	External Relations: Europe and NIS, CFSP and External Missions	van den Broek
IB	External Relations: Mediterranean., Mid. East, Latin Am., S&SE Asia, N.–South coop.	Marin
II	Economic and Financial Affairs	de Silguy
III	Industry	Bangemann
IV	Competition	Van Miert
V	Employment, Industrial Relations and Social Affairs	Flynn
VI	Agriculture	Fischler
VII	Transport	Kinnock
VIII	Development	Pinheiro
IX	Personnel and Administration	Liikanen
X	Information, Communication, Culture, Audiovisual	Oreja
XI	Environment, Nuclear Safety and Civil Protection	Bjerregaard
XII	Science, Research and Development	Cresson
XIII	Telecommunications, Information Market and Exploitation of Research	Bangemann
XIV	Fisheries	Bonino
XV	Internal Market and Financial Services	Monti
XVI	Regional Policies and Cohesion	Wulf-Matthies
XVII	Energy	Papoutsis
XVIII	Credit and Investments	de Silguy
XIX	Budgets	Liikanen
XX	Financial Control	Gradin
XXI	Customs and Indirect Taxation	Monti
XXII	Education, Training and Youth	Cresson
XXIII	Enterprise Policy, Distributive Trades, Tourism and Cooperatives	Papoutsis
XXIV	Consumer Policy and Consumer Health Protection	Bonino
Other services		
Secretariat General		Santer
– Title VI TEU Task Force (cooperation on justice and home affairs)		Gradin
Forward Studies Unit, Inspectorate General, Legal Service, Spokesman's Service		Santer
Joint Interpreting and Conference Service		Santer
Statistical Service		de Silguy
Translation Service, Informatics Directorate, Security Service		Liikanen
Euratom Supply Agency		Papoutsis
European Community Humanitarian Office		Bonino
Office for Official Publications of the European Communities		Oreja
European Foundation for the Improvement of Living and Working Conditions		Flynn
European Centre for the Development of Vocational Training		Cresson
Joint Research Centre		Cresson

Page (1997, p. 136) points out that 'the most distinctive characteristic of the EU administration is its multinational character'. This produces specific cultures in each DG as well as different elite-groups, as senior officials of the same nationality prefer to do business with each other. Given this fact, however, Page argues that 'the evidence that . . . this creates an administration fragmented along national lines is very weak'. Despite the persistence of national identities, practices and cultures, Commission officials are self-selecting as they have made a conscious choice to make a career in the EU civil service. The result is an overriding pro-European ethic and a bureaucracy that is no more functionally and culturally fragmented, and divided between political and administrative appointments, than most public administrations.

A regulator: the EU quango(s)

A common feature of executive power in representative government is to use executive instruments to enforce legislation. For example, in the US and the UK these governments use 'orders' or 'regulations', in France they use '*ordonnances*', and in Germany they use '*Rechtsverordnungen*'. In the same way, the EU Commission can issue Directives, Regulations and Decisions without recourse to the EU legislative process. These 'executive instruments' are a traditional feature of representative government for two reasons. First, executives are given powers to act as surrogate legislators in areas where the legislature has neither the time nor the ability to take action. For example, executives are often allowed to act if a rapid response is needed, if technical knowledge is required, or if the issue is too low in salience for the political process to be involved. The Commission issues between 6000 and 7000 such instruments a year (mostly relating to the Common Agricultural Policy).

Second, executive agencies are given powers to deliberately prevent the involvement of parliamentary institutions in the making of rules and regulations. In certain circumstances it is often in the public interest for policy to be made by 'independent' executive agencies, as they have longer time horizons than elected parliaments or governments (Majone, 1991). These agencies can be independent competition regulators, such as competition authorities or regulators of privatised utilities, or independent central banks. The delegation of regulatory policies to such quasi-auton-omous-non-governmental-organs ('quangos') is a classic feature of Amer-ican government and has been growing at the domestic level in Europe (Majone, 1994).

In some respects, the Commission is such an agency (Majone, 1993b). For example, the Commission makes rulings under the competition and state aid sections and the Treaty and the Merger Regulation (see

Chapter 8). This is managed by DGIV (competition), which operates like a 'European cartel office'. The media consequently like to refer to Karel Van Miert, who is responsible for DGIV, as the EU's 'competition policy tsar'. Nevertheless, to protect competition policy from interference by national interests and the political aims of the Commission, many commentators advocate removing DGIV from the Commission bureaucracy and setting it up as a truly independent regulatory agency, along the lines of the German Federal Cartel Office (cf. Wilks and McGowan, 1995).

The Commission also oversees the work of a number of independent European agencies. These agencies, listed in Table 2.5, are set up by Council decisions on the basis of Commission proposals, and most had forerunners somewhere in the Commission bureaucracy. For example, the

Table 2.5   *Autonomous executive agencies of the EU*

Agency	Est.	Budget in 1997 (m.ecu)	Staff	Location
European Centre for the Development of Vocational Training	1975	14.4	81	Thessaloniki
European Foundation for the Improvement of Living and Working Conditions	1975	13.6	83	Dublin
European Environment Agency	1994	16.5	62	Copenhagen
Office for Harmonization in the Internal Market (Trade Marks and Designs)	1994	12.5	220	Alicante
European Monitoring Centre for Drugs and Drug Addiction	1994	6.3	31	Lisbon
European Translation Centre for Bodies of the EU	1994	0.3	34	Luxembourg
European Training Foundation	1995	15.4	130	Turin
European Agency for the Evaluation of Medicinal Products	1995	14.0	100	London
European Agency for Safety and Health at Work	1995	3.0	13	Bilbao
Community Plant Variety Rights Office	1995	n/a	15	Angers

Source: Web-sites of the agencies and data in Kreher (1997).
Note: n/a = not available.

European Agency for the Evaluation of Medicinal Products came from two comitology committees, the European Environment Agency came from one of the Commission's policy programmes (CORINE), and the Commission has proposed to set up a Food and Veterinary Office from a division in DGXXIV (consumer policy). But, others, such as the Office for Harmonization in the Internal Market, were set up as part of new EU policy regimes (Kreher, 1997, pp. 232–3). None of these agencies are full-blown regulatory authorities with powers to adopt and implement policies; their main responsibilities are to monitor the implementation of EU legislation and specific aspects of the single market. However, as their reputations develop, and through their control of the collection and supply of information, the EU agencies are likely to play a key role in the emerging 'regulator networks' linking national and European regulatory authorities (Dehousse, 1997; Majone, 1997).

The traditional image of the Commission is of a monolithic supranational bureaucracy with a single objective: to promote further European integration (see for example Coombes, 1970). In this section a somewhat different picture has been painted: of an executive organization which fulfils many of the traditional tasks of government, and which is politically and organizationally comparable to other public administrations. At the pinnacle there are partisan politicians in a classic 'cabinet government' system, who pursue individual and collective political objectives. Beneath the politicians there is a highly-developed bureaucracy and an emerging network of regulatory agencies, where the various administrative organs have different policy and institutional and organizational cultures.

Comitology: the interface of the EU dual-executive

The Commission is not completely free to shape policy outcomes when implementing EU legislation. The Council has designed an elaborate system of committees, known as 'comitology', where 'national experts' issue opinions on the Commission's proposed implementation measures. Under some procedures, comitology provides for a separation of powers where the legislators (the governments) can scrutinize the executive (the Commission); under other procedures, however, comitology has created a fusion of powers where the member governments enforce their wishes on the Commission, and hence exercise both legislative and executive authority.

The comitology system was established by a Council decision in July 1987. The decision (87/373/EEC) established three sets of committees – advisory, management and regulatory committees – and a set of rules governing their operation. Officially, the Commission lists 380 such committees, but if sub-committees and temporary committees are counted there may be as many as 1000 committees in the comitology system (Vos, 1997). The membership of the committees depends on their role: committees of national civil servants monitor the implementation of legislation; the Commission has set up temporary committees of representatives of private interest groups in areas where it feels wider consultation is necessary; and committees of scientists and 'experts' give advice on technical issues (*ibid.*, p. 213).

The committee procedures

Table 2.6 shows how the comitology system works. A basic guide to its operation is that as the number of the procedure rises, the autonomy of the Commission from national governments declines. Under the advisory committee procedure (procedure I), the Commission has the greatest degree of freedom; although it must take 'utmost account' of the opinion of the national experts, it can simply ignore their advice (although the committee can record its opposition to a proposed measure in its minutes). This procedure is used in most areas of EU competition policy, such as Commission decisions on mergers and state aids to industry. The management committee procedures are mostly used for the Common Agricultural Policy, and the more restrictive version (procedure IIb) is mostly used on non-agricultural issues, such as the implementation of the PHARE programme of aid to central and eastern Europe. The regulatory committee procedures were developed by the Council in the late 1960s to cover areas outside agriculture, where the member governments wanted more control over the Commission than under the advisory or management committee procedures (Docksey and Williams, 1997, pp. 136–7). These procedures are used in such areas as customs legislation, veterinary and plant health, and food. The more restrictive variant (procedure IIIb), the so-called 'safety-net' (or '*contre-filet*'), is usually used in the sensitive area of veterinary health, as in the decision by the veterinary committee on the European-wide ban on beef exports from Britain during the BSE crisis.

The basic difference between the management and regulatory procedures relates to the role of the committee as a 'gate-keeper' of the Council. As Steunenberg, Koboldt and Schmidtchen, (1996, p. 340) point out:

> Whereas in a management committee procedure a qualified majority is needed to open the gates [refer the decision to the Council], in the regulatory committee procedure the committee must be able to form a qualified majority to keep the gates closed.

In other words, under the management committee procedures it is easier for national experts to approve the Commission's proposed implementa-

Table 2.6 *How comitology works*

Procedure	Operation of the procedure (In all procedures, the Commission must consult the relevant committee of national experts on the proposed implementation measures)
Advisory committees	
Procedure I	The Commission must take the 'utmost account' of the committee's opinion, but the Commission is free to enact the measures regardless of their opinion.
Management committees	The Commission can enact the measures *unless the committee opposes* the measures by QMV, in which case the matter is referred to the Council, and either:
Procedure IIa	the Commission may enact the measures, but the Council has one month to annul or modify them by QMV; or
Procedure IIb	the Commission must defer enactment of the measures until the Council either rejects or modifies them by QMV, or fails to act within three months.
Regulatory committees	The Commission can enact the measures *only if the committee supports* the measures by QMV, otherwise the matter is referred to the Council, and in a set time period either:
Procedure IIIa	('net') the Council can reject the measures by *QMV* or modify them by unanimity, but the Commission can enact the measures if the Council approves them by QMV or fails to act; or
Procedure IIIb	('safety net') the Council can reject the measures by *simple majority* or modify them by unanimity, but the Commission can enact the measures if the Council approves them by simple majority or fails to act.
Safeguard measures	The Commission must notify the Council of the proposed safeguard measures before acting, after which, either:
Procedure IVa	the Council may reject or modify the measures by *QMV*, but the *Commission can enact the measures if the Council fails to act* in a set time period; or
Procedure IVb	the Council may confirm, amend or reject the measures by *simple majority*, and *the measures are deemed revoked if the Council fails to act* in a set time period.
The Council itself	
'Procedure V'	In special cases, the Council reserves the right to exercise direct implementing powers itself.

Note: QMV = Qualified majority vote (see Chapter 3).

tion measures than to refer them to the Council ('open the gates'), whereas under the regulatory committee procedures the situation is reversed.

Finally, the 1987 comitology decision established two other procedures, under which the Council has final veto power. First, the Commission can take 'safeguard measures' to protect the interests of the EU or a member state, but must secure prior agreement from the Council. These procedures (procedures IVa and IVb) are usually used for issues under the common commercial policy, as in the signing of association agreements with non-EU states. Second, in specific cases the Council has the right to exercise implementing powers itself ('procedure V'). These have been used in highly sensitive areas, such as financial institutions.

Interinstitutional conflict

Given the different degrees of freedom of the Commission under each of the procedures, one would expect the Commission and the Council to be constantly in conflict over which procedure should be used for the enactment of each piece of legislation. However, in the most comprehensive study of the use of comitology procedures to date, Dogan (1997) finds that this is not completely true. For example, Dogan found that 29 per cent of all comitology procedures proposed by the Commission between 1987 and 1995 were under procedures where the Commission is weak (such as procedure IIIb), and, contrary to the Commission's rhetoric about the Council's opposition to the advisory committee procedure, the Council accepted 40 per cent of the Commission's proposals for use of this procedure. Dogan (*ibid.*, p. 45) consequently argues that 'the Commission is deeply implicated in the pattern of Council comitology preferment'. Nevertheless, these figures might also reflect the fact that the Commission is strategic in its choice of comitology procedures, and hence only proposes the advisory procedure in cases when it thinks it has a reasonable chance of getting this past the Council.

The European Parliament, on the other hand, has been highly critical of comitology. The EP argues that there is a lack of transparency as a result of the number of committees and in the use of the procedures, and that also by allowing the governments to scrutinize the executive powers of the Commission, comitology undermines the principle of the separation of powers whereby the EP should have the right to scrutinize the Commission. And, the EP claims that the procedures only allow for issues to be referred back to one part of the EU legislature (the Council) (cf. Corbett, Jacobs and Shackleton, 1995, p. 253; Bradley, 1997).

In 1988, under the so-called 'Plumb–Delors Agreement', the President of the Commission and the President of the EP agreed that the Commission would refer most implementing measures to the EP at the same time as they were forwarded to the comitology committee. However, the EP was dissatisfied with the operation of the agreement, and in July 1994 rejected a directive (on the application of open network provision to voice telephony) because the Council refused to change the proposed comitology procedure to a procedure more favourable to the Commission. Following this EP veto, the Council and the Commission agreed a '*modus vivendi*' with the EP, under which the Commission would send all measures to the EP and inform the EP of decisions in comitology, and the Council would 'take due account of the EP's point of view'. The *modus vivendi* was due to be reviewed by the Intergovernmental Conference that negotiated the Amsterdam treaty, but the IGC failed to reach an agreement on the issue.

In June 1997, the Amsterdam European Council nevertheless instructed the Commission to draft a proposal for revising the 1987 comitology decision. The Commission subsequently proposed that the system should be simplified (by reducing the number of procedures to four), more transparent (by defining the tasks of the committees more clearly) and more democratic (for example by referring issues back to both the Council and the EP) (European Commission, 1998c). However, an agreement on the reform of comitology will be the product of long and drawn-out negotiations between the Commission, the Council and the EP.

Overall, Joerges and Neyer (1997) argue that comitology is a unique political process, where the Commission and national experts work together to solve policy issues in a 'non-hierarchical' and 'deliberative' policy style. The technical nature of EU legislative and executive actions requires a high degree of scientific expertise. The comitology system also removes bureaucrats and experts from national settings, and promotes collective identities in each 'policy community'. However, the involvement of scientific experts and private interests in the process of policy implementation and regulation is a common feature of most public administration systems. And, on high-profile policy issues, conflict does emerge between the Commission and the national experts, and between experts from different member states. For example, during the BSE crisis each member of the veterinary committee was under considerable pressure to support their government's position.

Democratic control of the EU executive

In most systems, the political and administrative roles of the executive are legitimized in different ways. The *political leadership role* is usually legitimized through electoral competition for political office and control of the political agenda. In presidential systems, the head of the executive is directly elected, whereas in parliamentary systems the executive is accountable to a parliamentary majority (see for example Lijphart, 1992). In contrast, the *administrative role* is usually disconnected from electoral and parliamentary majorities, which enables bureaucrats and regulators to serve the 'public interest' rather than the interests of a particular political majority (Majone, 1996, pp. 284–301). Instead, civil servants and regulators are usually held accountable through the principle of 'ministerial responsibility' (where ministers are accountable for the actions of the civil servants under their responsibility), and the right of public access to documents and information (for example, through a Freedom of Information Act).

Political accountability: selection and censure of the Commission

In the collective exercise of political leadership in the Council, the governments can claim legitimacy via national general elections (see Chapter 7). However, the legitimacy of the political leadership role of the Commission is more problematic. Until 1994, the Commission president was chosen by a collective agreement between the heads of government, in the European Council. The Commission president was regarded as one post in a package-deal between governments on the heads of a number of international agencies, such as the secretaries-general of the World Trade Organization and the North Atlantic Treaty Organization. This was more akin to selecting the head of an international organization than to choosing the 'first among equals' in a political cabinet.

However, the Maastricht Treaty introduced a new procedure (article 214 [ex 158]), where the term of office of the Commission was aligned with the term of the EP. Also, the EP would now be 'consulted' on the governments' nominee for Commission president, and the full Commission would be subject to a vote of approval by the EP. However, the EP interpreted the meaning of 'consultation' as a right to *vote* on the nominee for Commission President. Consequently, in July 1994, in the first ever 'Commission president investiture vote' in the EP, Jacques Santer was ratified by the EP as Commission President by a margin of only 12 votes (Hix and Lord, 1995). In addition, following the nomination of the individual commissioners, the EP introduced 'Commission hearings', where the nominees had to give evidence to the EP committee covering their portfolios (consciously modelled on US Senate hearings of the nominees for the US president's cabinet). Finally, once the committee hearings were complete, the EP took a second vote on the Commission as a whole. The Amsterdam Treaty reformed article 214 to formally institutionalize this EP interpretation.

Since the Treaty of Rome, the EP has had the right to censure the Commission as a whole by a 'double majority': an absolute majority of MEPs and two-thirds of votes cast (article 201 [ex 144]). Motions of censure have been proposed on several occasions, but none has ever been carried. The EP usually fears that throwing-out the Commission would backfire, as governments and the public would accuse the EP of acting irresponsibly. Also, before the new investiture procedure there was nothing to prevent governments from reappointing the same commissioners. Above all, however, the EP is aware that the Commission, as a fellow supranational institution, is more often an ally against the Council than an enemy. In practice, then, the EP right of censure is more like the right of the US Congress to impeach the US president than of a domestic parliament in Europe to withdraw majority support for a government, and so can only be exercised in extreme circumstances.

However, in 1998 and 1999, the EP became more confident in its use of the threat of censure. In 1998, with widespread public disapproval of the Commission's handling of the BSE crisis, the EP successfully used the threat of a censure motion to force the Commission to reorganize its handling of food safety issues. Similarly, in January 1999 the EP demanded that the Commission answer the high-profile allegations of financial mismanagement, nepotism and cover-up (the Commission had sacked an official who had leaked a report on fraud and financial mismanagement). On the eve of a censure vote, the Commission president promised an independent committee to investigate the allegations and fundamental administration reform of the Commission, including a new code of conduct, rules governing the appointment and work of the *cabinets*, and restrictions on 'parachuting' political appointees into top administrative jobs. As a result, the censure motion was narrowly defeated: with 232 MEPs in favour of censure, and 293 opposed (mostly from the PES and EPP groups).

Consequently, the procedures for selecting and deselecting the Commission are a hybrid mix of the parliamentary and presidential models. The Maastricht and Amsterdam Treaties injected an element of parliamentary government by requiring the Commission to have the support of a majority in the EP before taking office; and the right of censure allows the EP to withdraw this support. However, in the process of selecting the Commission president, the member governments are the equivalent of a presidential 'electoral college', over which the EP can only exercise a veto. The EP cannot propose its own candidate. And, once invested, the Commission does not really require a 'working majority' in the EP. The right of censure is only a 'safety-valve', to be used in the event of serious political or administrative failure by the Commission.

This design reflects a conscious effort by the governments to maintain their monopoly over who holds executive office at the European level. The EP has gained a limited role in the investiture procedure because governments needed to address the 'democratic deficit' (see Chapter 6). Hypothetically, the Commission could be chosen via a parliamentary model, with a contest for the Commission president in EP elections and the translation of the electoral majority into support for the Commission (as has been proposed by Jacques Delors). Or, a presidential model could be adopted through some form of direct election of the Commission president. However, neither model will come about until the governments perceive that the benefits, such as the need to give the Commission a greater degree of legitimacy, outweigh the costs of losing their right to choose the holders of the other branch of the EU executive.

Administrative accountability: parliamentary scrutiny and transparency

The administrative and regulatory tasks of the Commission and the Council are subject to parliamentary scrutiny in much the same way as domestic bureaucracies and regulatory agencies. The Commission president presents the annual Commission Work Programme to the EP; commissioners and civil servants in the DGs regularly give evidence to EP committees; and certain EP committees have introduced a 'question time' of the commissioner responsible for the policy competences they follow. The president-in-office of the Council also presents their six-monthly work programme to the EP. Government ministers from the member state holding the presidency often appear before EP committees (Corbett *et al.*, 1995, p. 257), and the president of the European Central Bank and the heads of the EU agencies appear before the EP committees on a regular basis.

The EP also has a highly-developed system of asking oral and written questions to the Council and the Commission (Raunio, 1996b). As in national parliaments, these questions enable members of the EP to gain information, force the executive to make a formal statement relating to a specific action, defend their constituency interests, and inform the Commission and Council of problems with which they might be unfamiliar. In 1995, the EP asked 3217 questions of the Commission and 444 of the Council. The full texts of the questions and the answers by the institutions are published in the EU *Official Journal*.

Unlike most national administrations, however, there is no system of 'ministerial responsibility' in the EU. Individual commissioners are often blamed for inconsistencies in a DG in which they are in change, or for lack of action in a policy area for which they cover, but no procedure exists for forcing individual commissioners to resign. And, the Commission has not developed a culture whereby a commissioner or a senior official in the Commission administration would resign out of a sense of obligation. Since the early 1990s, the EP has argued for the right to censure individual commissioners. And, in January 1999 the EP held separate 'votes of no-confidence' in two commissioners (Edith Cresson and Manuel Marin) who were in charge of administrative divisions and budgets where fraud and nepotism had been alleged. Although these motions had no legal force, there was considerable pressure on these two Commissioners from the media and several governments to resign if the EP passed these motions by a simple majority. In the event, the motions were defeated. The experience also raised the issue of the need for greater individual and collective *political* responsibility for *administrative* irregularities, and the possibility of institutional reform to allow the EP to remove individual commissioners to achieve this goal.

Nevertheless, since the early 1990s the Commission has been eager to promote 'transparency' in its administrative operations. In February 1994, the Commission unveiled a 'transparency package', as a result of which the annual work programme is published in October instead of January, which allows the EP and Council to debate the draft before the final adoption of a full legislative programme in January. In the initiation of legislation, the Commission makes more use of Green and White Papers, public hearings, information seminars and 'consultation exercises'. And, a new code of conduct was introduced which commits the Commission to make public any internal document, except minutes of Commission meetings, briefing notes, the personal opinions of its officials and documents containing information that might 'damage public or private interests' (Peterson, 1995b, pp. 478–81). The Commission also submits draft legislative initiatives to national parliaments, so that their committees on EU affairs can scrutinize the legislation before their government ministers address the legislation in the Council.

Officially, the Council supports more openness of EU decision-making, and in October 1993 the Council signed an interinstitutional 'Declaration on Democracy, Transparency and Subsidiarity'. However, both the Commission and the EP accuse the Council of hypocrisy. First, a majority of member states oppose the Commission's efforts to promote public access to EU documents; many national governments are eager to prevent private interests and the media learning more about what they sign-up to in the EU legislative and executive processes. And, second, the Council is reluctant to open itself to public scrutiny. The Amsterdam Treaty (article 207 [ex 151]) specifies that:

the Council shall define the cases in which it is to be regarded as acting in its legislative capacity, with a view to allowing greater access to documents in those cases. In any event, when the Council acts in its legislative capacity, the results of votes and explanations of vote as well as statements in the minutes shall be made public.

However, this allows the Council to remain highly secretive in its executive capacity, and also to define for itself when it is 'acting as a legislature'.

Explaining the organization of executive power in the EU

So, how can this division of executive responsibilities between the Council and Commission be explained? The answer is that the level and type of delegation to the Commission is at the point where the *demand* by the member governments for independent executive powers meets the *supply* of political leadership, administration and regulation by the Commission.

Demand for EU government: selective delegation by the member states

Having decided to create the single market, the EU governments have been faced with the problem of how and by whom the single market should be governed. The governments could undertake this task amongst themselves, by drafting and passing laws through intergovernmental arrangements and through cooperation between national regulators. However, it is in the collective interests of the EU governments to delegate governing responsibilities to the Commission for a number of reasons.

First, governments need someone to come up with legislative ideas (cf. Moravcsik, 1993, pp. 511–12; Pollack, 1997a, pp. 104–5). Governing a market of 370 million consumers and harmonizing/replacing 15 existing regulatory regimes requires legislative specialization. Each government could specialize in a particular area, just as national legislators specialize in parliamentary committees. However, this would enable each government to promote their special economic and sectoral interests and to supply limited information about alternative options to each other. To avoid this, each government could come up with separate proposals on every piece of legislation, but this would be extremely costly. Alternatively, governments could delegate legislative initiative responsibilities to an independent authority, who can be required to take account of diverse national and sectoral interests in the drafting of legislation, and can be charged with promoting the collective interests (the 'European interest') of the governments. The result of such delegation would be a significant reduction of 'transactions costs' of legislative initiative.

Second, governments also need an independent agent to execute and administer legislation once it has been adopted (cf. Moravcsik, 1993, pp. 512–14; Majone, 1996, pp. 72–4; Pollack, 1997a, pp. 102–4), and again, the governments could undertake this task through intergovernmental means with each government promising to implement legislation in their own systems. However, there would be an incentive to 'free ride'. For example, if a government implements an EU environment directive or opens part of their market to European competition, another government would benefit without having to enforce the same legislation in their own system. It would also be difficult for the member states to monitor each other's compliance with EU law. Hence, as long as the EU governments do not trust each other, it is also in their collective interest to delegate the monitoring of the transposition and implementation of EU legislation to the Commission.

Third, the need for independent legislative initiative and enforcement is compounded by the specific nature of market regulation as a policy tool (Majone, 1996, pp. 68–72). Regulation is heavily dependent upon scientific and economic knowledge but information is never complete, and regulators often have to rely on the subjects of regulation (private firms) for technical expertise. In addition, regulation consists of applying generally agreed principles to specific and ever-changing circumstances. The result is that in initiating and implementing regulations, policy-makers are forced to exercise 'policy discretion' when choosing between possible courses of action. Also, governments are reluctant to impose heavy costs on their own industries, and consequently governments will tend to use this policy discretion to 'blur the distinction between providing public goods for the citizens and engaging in policies designed to advantage the locality or the country at the expense of their neighbours' (Majone, 1996, p. 70). European governments have progressively delegated regulatory powers to independent institutions to avoid redistribution in favour of special interests (Majone, 1994). A supranational regulator, which is independent from any national or sectoral constituency, is less likely to use policy discretion to protect domestic firms.

Fourth, the delegation of certain initiative and implementation functions to a supranational agent is facilitated by the fact that governments are primarily interested in being re-elected. A classic assumption of political science is that political parties primarily seek to win and maintain government office (cf. Downs, 1957, and see Chapter 6). Governments in the EU consequently focus on the next general election, which is always only a few years away. With such short time-horizons, governments are less concerned about the long-term implications of the delegation of powers to the Commission than about how immediate decisions will affect their electorates and supporting interest groups. When popular decisions are made by the Commission, governments can claim that they 'brought home the bacon'. Conversely, delegation of unpopular decisions to the Commission enables governments to claim that 'Brussels made me do it'. This has been a popular claim in relation to EU rules on state aids and the privatization of public monopolies (Smith, 1997a).

In short, governments would like to maintain a monopoly on the collective exercise of executive power in the EU, but there are a variety of incentives for the delegation of particular short-term executive responsibilities to the Commission. However, to prevent 'bureaucratic drift' in the exercise of these functions the governments have an incentive to police the work of the Commission, and hence the comitology system has been established as a means of 'patrolling' the executive powers of the Commission (Pollack, 1997a, pp. 108–21), and the governments have maintained a monopoly on the nomination of the President and the selection of individual commissioners.

Supply of EU government: Commission preferences, entrepreneurship and capture

Just as the member states are selective about what they delegate to the Commission, the Commission is selective about what it supplies to the member states. First, the Commission has specific policy preferences: like any bureaucracy it has an incentive to promote its own power and organizational development. As discussed in the theoretical introduction, most bureaucracies try to maximize their budgets, but there are tight constraints on the ability of the Commission to do so. The EU budget is only 1.27 per cent of the total GDP of the EU member states, and the proportion of the EU budget on redistributive policies (such as agricultural and cohesion policies) is set by the member states. As a result, the Commission is prevented from expanding its budgetary capacity, but this has not prevented the Commission from developing its executive powers.

For example, the proportion of the EU budget spent on administration increased from 4.35 per cent of the total EU budget in 1985, to 4.8 per cent in 1994. Meanwhile, in the same period, the volume of legislation proposed by the Commission and the volume of direct executive instruments issued it increased dramatically. This is because the Commission is more interested in expanding its responsibilities and 'shaping' its own organizational design than increasing its budget (Dunleavy, 1997; Dunleavy and O'Duffy, 1998). The Commission is not a 'delivery agency', which provides public services such as health and education. Instead, the

Commission administration is composed of a variety of 'regulatory agencies' (which make rules for private actors), 'control agencies' (which pass on their budgets to other public bodies, as under EU cohesion policies), 'transfer agencies' (which pass on budgets to the private sector, as under the EU's development aid policies), and 'contract agencies' (which spend their budgets on private corporations, as under EU research and development policies). None of these types of public agencies is particularly interested in increasing its budget. Instead, they are interested in increasing their control over the policy agenda, and the staff within these agencies are eager to increase their profile within their own 'policy community' (for example, through more contacts with the private sector). As a result, the Commission does not pursue greater EU expenditure, but does seek more EU regulatory policies and greater involvement of private sector actors in the EU policy process. Majone (1996, p. 65) consequently concludes that 'the utility function of the Commission is positively related to the *scope* of its competences rather than to the *scale* of the services provided or to the size of its budget'.

Second, and linked to its preference structure, the Commission is a 'policy entrepreneur' (Majone, 1996, pp. 74–7; Pollack, 1997a, 1997c; Cram, 1997) – an actor who can set the policy agenda under certain circumstances. Policy entrepreneurs are particularly influential when there are information asymmetries, a high variation of actors across time and space, and where the preferences of the actors are underdetermined (Kingdon, 1984). The Commission does not have a monopoly on information and expertise. However, the Commission can drive the policy agenda by manipulating asymmetries between the member states and between different private interests and the lack of specification of member states' and private interests' preferences.

Third, like any agency, the Commission is susceptible to 'capture' by particular private interests. In an ideal world, in drafting policies and promoting issues, the Commission is simply the 'neutral arbiter' between competing private interests – this would be the classic pluralist model of government. Inevitably, though, some interest groups are more able to organize to influence the Commission than others (see Chapter 7) and the subjects of EU policies and regulations (such as private firms) have a particular incentive to mobilize to influence the EU policy process. For example, farmers have a vested interest to lobby DGVI (agriculture) to prevent reform of the Common Agricultural Policy. Similarly, multinational firms have a vested interest in securing a deregulation of social and environmental rules as part of the completion of the single market programme. The Commission can promote the involvement of 'public interests' in EU decision-making, such as consumer and environmental groups; however, in addition to specific incentives, private firms have significant resources at their disposal and can offer particular inducements to Commission staff, such as lucrative jobs outside the EU bureaucracy, and as a result private interests are more likely to mobilize to influence the Commission than public interests.

Conclusion: the politics of a dual-executive

The power to set the policy agenda and implement EU policies is shared between the EU governments (in the Council) and the Commission. Basically, the Council sets the long- and medium-term agendas, through reforming the EU Treaty and delegating political and administrative tasks to the Commission. In the areas where these executive powers have been delegated, the Commission has a significant political leadership role, and is responsible for undertaking the distribution of the EU budget, monitoring policy implementation by the member states, and making rules and regulations. This separation of powers has evolved through an interaction between the strategies of the Council and the Commission.

On the one hand, the EU governments have delegated powers to the Commission to overcome collective action problems, to reduce transactions costs, and to produce policy credibility. However, governments have been selective in this delegation. For example, the governments have limited Commission instruments to certain 'regulatory' issues, such as competition and agricultural policies, and they have maintained control of key executive powers, such as Treaty reform through IGCs, policy-making under the JHA and CFSP, long-term agenda-setting in the European Council and front-line policy implementation. Governments have also limited Commission discretion through the comitology system and maintained their monopoly over the selection of the commissioners.

On the other hand, the Commission has developed many of the characteristics of a supranational 'government'. At the political level, the College of Commissioners operates along the lines of cabinet government, with collective responsibility and the Commission president as the first-among-equals. Also, the commissioners are partisan career politicians with their own ideological objectives in the EU policy process. At an administrative level, the Commission DGs are quasi-ministries, and the Commission is at the heart of an emerging network of European regulatory agencies. Also, like national administrations, each service in this Euro-bureaucracy has its own administrative culture, institutional interests, policy objectives, and supporting societal groups. As a result, the Commission has powerful incentives and significant political and administrative resources to pursue an agenda independently from the EU governments.

The result is a system with strengths and weaknesses. The main strength is that the dual character of the EU executive facilitates extensive deliberation and compromise in the adoption and implementation of EU policies. This is a significant achievement for an emerging political system, and reduces the likelihood of system breakdown. However, there are two important weaknesses. First, the flip-side of compromise is a lack of overall political leadership. Dual-executive systems tend to be characterized by policy immobilism. Second, and linked to this issue, there is a problem of democratic accountability. There is no single 'chief executive', whom the European public can 'throw out'. The result is a political system that seems remote to most European citizens, as we shall see in Chapter 5.

Legislative Politics

The EU has a classic two-chamber legislature: in which the Council represents the 'states', and the European Parliament (EP) represents the 'citizens'. In contrast to many other legislatures, however, the Council is more powerful than the EP. Nevertheless, under the so-called 'co-decision' procedure, the EP and the Council are genuine co-legislators. Finally, despite the fact that the main actors in the Council are governments and the main actors in the EP are political parties, internal politics and political organization in the two chambers are very similar. To understand how this system works, we shall first look at some theories of legislative behaviour and organization.

Theories of legislative coalitions and organization

Contemporary scholars of legislatures are less interested in their functions than in explaining how legislative bargaining, coalition formation and organization works. One of the first such approaches was Riker's (1962) theory of 'minimum-winning' coalitions. Riker argued that legislators aim to have as much influence as possible in a winning coalition. The result is that coalitions are unlikely to include any group that is not necessary to reach a majority. Fewer coalition partners means fewer interests to appease in the distribution of benefits. But, if a party is 'decisive' in turning a minimum-winning coalition into a majority-winning coalition it can demand a high price for participating in a coalition. Hence, what actors want is to be 'pivotal' in the formation of legislative coalitions. The more likely an actor is to be pivotal, the more 'power' it will have in coalition bargaining (see for example Shapley and Shubik, 1954; Banzhaf, 1965). However, actors do not simply form coalitions with anyone: coalitions are easier to hold together if they are between actors with similar policy preferences. This is the basis of Axelrod's (1970) argument for the likelihood of 'minimum-*connected*-winning' coalitions: between legislators next to each other on a policy dimension. Hence, whereas Riker's theory is 'policy-blind', Axelrod's argues for a 'policy-driven' approach.

To study legislative behaviour in the US Congress, Mayhew (1974) adopted a similar policy-driven assumption. He argued that the primary goal of legislators is to gain reelection, but to achieve this goal legislators must secure policy outputs for their constituents. To secure these outputs, legislators try to 'exchange' votes with other legislators to form winning majorities. For example, legislators from agricultural constituencies will agree to back a proposal of legislators with manufacturing constituencies in return for their support in a future vote on an agricultural issue. This legislative-exchange is often called 'logrolling' or 'pork-barrel' politics because the result is usually a new policy initiative and/or increased public expenditure.

However, a fundamental problem with these policy-driven approaches is that vote-trading between legislators is inherently 'unstable'. This is illustrated in Figure 3.1, where three legislators (A, B and C) have different 'ideal policy' positions on the pro-/anti-Europe and left–right dimensions.

Figure 3.1   *Legislative instability in a two-dimensional policy space*

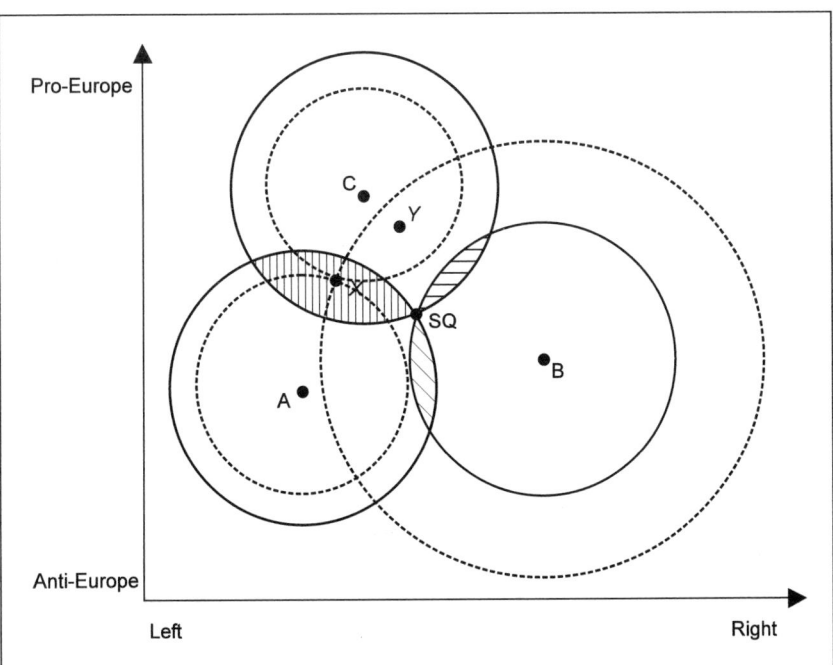

The current policy situation, the status quo SQ, is between the three legislators. The circles through SQ are the 'indifference curves' for each legislator: where any policy on these circles is equally as far from the ideal-policy of the legislator. Each legislator prefers a policy to SQ if it is closer to his or her ideal policy (inside the indifference curve). As a result, any policy in the shaded areas (the 'win-set' over SQ) is preferred by a majority of legislators to SQ. Consequently, legislator A can propose policy X, which A and C will vote for instead of SQ. But, legislator C will then propose policy Y, which both B and C will vote to beat X. And, legislator B will then propose SQ, which both A and B will support to beat Y, and so on, *ad infinitum*. The result is 'chaos': there is no stable policy ('equilibrium') is preferred by a legislative majority in two or more-policy dimensions (McKelvey, 1976).

This is a problem for majoritarian democracy. Thankfully, however, vote-cycling rarely occurs in practice, because institutional rules produce a 'structure-induced equilibrium' (Shepsle, 1979, Riker, 1980), as discussed in Chapter 1. For example, if different policy dimensions are tackled separately (a 'germaneness rule'), stable legislative majorities can be constructed on each dimension. For example, in Figure 3.1, legislators A and B form a stable majority that beats SQ on the pro-/anti-Europe dimension, and legislators A and C form a stable majority that beats SQ on the left–right dimension. This effect can be established through legislative 'specialization', for example in parliamentary committees. If each specialist committee 'controls the gates' on a particular policy issue, they can preclude the consideration of their policy issue when another issue is being discussed, and consequently prevent the issue-linkage that might result (see for example Shepsle and Weingast, 1987).

However, Krehbiel (1991) offers an alternative explanation of legislative specialization. He argues that although legislators try to get policies as close to their ideal position as possible, they are not certain of the precise relationship between legislative instruments and final policy outcomes. There is thus an incentive on behalf of all legislators to foster policy expertise through legislative specialization. From this perspective, legislative organization results from the need to acquire and disseminate 'information'. As a result, to facilitate legislative bargaining, specialized groups of legislators will be allowed to monopolise information and expertise.

Political parties are legislative institutions who also facilitate legislative stability. Why do political parties exist? This is obvious in systems where an individual legislator's chances of reelection are dependent upon cohesive legislative parties to turn their election promises into legislation. However, this is harder to explain in the US Congress and the EP, where election campaigns are not fought on the policy promises of the party leadership in the legislature. As with specialization, nevertheless, legislative party organizations exist to overcome collective action problems for individual legislators. For example, individual legislators are unlikely to obtain their own policy objects alone. Legislators could cooperate spontaneously, but each coalition would have to be negotiated separately. Hence, by establishing formal relationships binding individuals together, the 'transactions costs' of coalition-formation are reduced (Cox and McCubbins, 1993). Parties also help overcome information gaps (Kiewiet and McCubbins, 1991). With uncertainty about other legislators' preferences and the impact of legislative decision, legislators with similar policy preferences will benefit from institutional arrangements that divide information-gathering and policy expertise amongst themselves. The result is a 'delegation of tasks': backbench members provide labour and capital, and party leaders distribute committee and party offices and determine the 'party line' on complex legislative issues. And, once these organizational arrangements have been set up, the costs of leaving a legislative party for an individual legislator are high.

Finally, a further solution to the problem of legislative instability is bicameralism: the existence of two legislative chambers. With two legislative chambers, two different majorities have to be in favour of a proposal before it can become law, which consequently restricts the set of possible policy choices and so simplifies legislative bargaining (Riker, 1992; Tsebelis and Money, 1997). However, depending on how the procedures are organized, bicameralism can favour one chamber over another in the bargaining process. For example, if the lower house 'goes first', and the upper house is faced with a 'take-it-or-leave-it' situation, then the majority in the upper house will choose to accept the proposal if it is closer to their 'ideal preference' than the status quo. In this situation, the lower house holds 'agenda-setting power'. However, if disagreement will lead to the convening of a special intercameral committee (such as a 'conciliation committee'), the upper house is likely to reject the proposal from the lower house in the hope that it can achieve something closer to its ideal position in the bicameral negotiations.

In sum, there have been three 'generations' of formal legislative studies (Shepsle and Weingast, 1994). The first focused on the motives of individual legislators and the formation of coalitions in an institution-free environment. The second generation introduced institutions, such as committees, parties and bicameralism, to explain why legislative outcomes can be stable. And the third generation explained where these institutions came from. Together, these theories help us understand how the EU legislative process works: what coalitions are likely to form, why the internal Council and EP rules are organized the way they are, and who holds the most power under the EU legislative procedures.

Development of the legislative system of the EU

Despite its complexity, the EU legislative system is highly effective in developing, amending and passing laws. As Figure 3.2 shows, between 1986 and 1995 an average of 67 directives were proposed each year by the Commission, of which 56 were adopted by the EP and the Council. Also, more legislation was proposed and adopted in the early 1990s than in the late 1970s and early 1980s, largely due to the 300 or so pieces of legislation relating to the completion of the single market by the end of 1992 (see Chapter 8). Since then, the annual volume of EU legislation has fallen.

The EU legislative process has not always been so effective. The Treaty of Rome established that legislation would be adopted through interaction between the Council of national governments, the Commission and the EP, but the Treaty did not set out a single procedure governing this interaction. Rather, the type of procedure to be used was specified in each individual article (see Appendix A for the decision-making rules under each current Treaty article). However, there were two common rules that determined political outcomes: the role of the EP, and the voting rule in the Council – whether the Council decided by unanimity or the 'qualified-majority-vote' (QMV) system of weighted-voting.

However, the ability of the Council to make decisions by QMV was challenged in the mid-1960s. De Gaulle, the French president, strongly objected to the idea that majority voting would be used in a number of important areas after 1966, in the so-called 'third stage' of transitional development towards a Common Market. De Gaulle insisted that every member state should be allowed to veto legislation, even where the Treaty specified that QMV could be used, and in 1965 he provoked a crisis by withdrawing French representatives from the European institutions – the famous 'empty-chair' policy. The crisis was resolved in January 1966 by the so-called 'Luxembourg Compromise'. This was an agreement between the EU heads of government, establishing the principle that if a member state declares that 'a vital national interest' is at stake, the Council will make every effort to reach a unanimous agreement.

This Luxembourg compromise was not legally-binding, as it was not part of the treaties, but it ushered in nearly two decades of 'intergovernmental' bargaining. Any member state faced with being outvoted on a key issue could simply invoke the Luxembourg compromise and halt proceedings. For example, although the Treaty of Rome specified that after 1966 the liberalization of capital movements would be decided by QMV, the Commission did not initiate any proposals as it expected that at least one member state would claim a right to veto a directive (Teasdale, 1993, p. 570).

Figure 3.2 *Volume of EU legislation proposed and adopted*

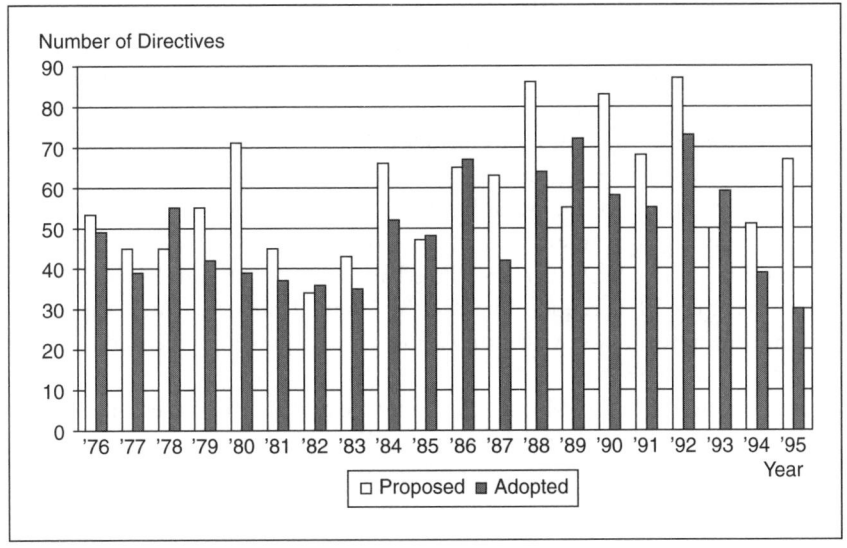

Source: Calculated from data in Golub (1997).

Nevertheless, from this intergovernmental beginning, by the mid-1990s the EU possessed a legislative system akin to bicameralism in many other political systems. The first major development was the 1980 'isoglucose' ruling by the European Court of Justice. The first direct-elections to the EP were held in June 1979, and between the dissolution of the EP before the elections and the reconvening of the new EP, the Council had adopted a piece of legislation without consulting the EP. In the ruling, the Court annulled the legislation on the grounds that when the Treaty requires that the Council 'consult' the EP, the Council cannot act before the EP has issued an 'opinion' to the Council. The Court argued that consultation of the EP is 'an essential factor in the institutional balance intended by the Treaty'. This does not allow the EP to force its opinions on the Council, as a national parliament could on an upper house. But, backed by the isoglucose ruling, the EP now had a 'power of delay'. For example, in 1989 the EP threatened to delay a Commission proposal to start the first phase of EMU on 1 July 1990 because the Commission would not accept a stronger role for the committee of Central Bank governors. Eager not to jeopardize the EMU timetable, the Commission accepted the relevant EP amendments.

The powers of the EP were substantially extended by three subsequent treaty reforms. First, in 1987, the Single European Act (SEA) introduced a new legislative procedure: the 'cooperation procedure'. This was the first procedure set out in a separate treaty article, to which other treaty articles referred (article 252 [ex 189c after Maastricht and article 149 after the SEA]). The procedure gives the EP a 'second reading', after the Council has adopted a 'Common Position', and reduces the ability of the Council to overturn EP amendments made in the second reading. The SEA applied this procedure to only 10 treaty articles, but these included most areas of the single market programme, specific research programmes, certain decisions relating to the structural funds and some social policy and environmental policy issues. This constituted approximately one-third of all legislation. The SEA also introduced an 'assent procedure', whereby the approval of the EP is required before the Council can act, which applied to association agreements with non-Community states and the accession of new member states.

Second, in 1992, the Maastricht Treaty extended the assent procedure and introduced a fourth legislative procedure, the 'co-decision procedure', which was also set out in a separate treaty article (article 251 [ex 189b]). This procedure introduced the rule that if the EP and Council disagree on a piece of legislation a 'Conciliation Committee' is convened, of equal representatives of the EP and Council. And, after the conciliation committee, the EP can reject the legislation outright. The co-decision procedure originally applied to most areas of internal market legislation that had been covered by the cooperation procedure, and several new areas introduced by the Maastricht Treaty, such as public health, consumer protection, education and culture.

Third, the Amsterdam Treaty, signed in 1997, reformed and extended the co-decision procedure: the reforms increased the power of the EP within the procedure and extended the co-decision procedure to most areas previously covered by the cooperation procedure.

Consequently, following the Amsterdam Treaty, the policy areas covered by the EU legislative procedures are as set out in Table 3.1. Most areas of regulation of the EU single market, such as environment policy, health and safety, social policy, and harmonization of standards are covered by the co-decision procedure, whereas the cooperation procedure is restricted to some limited provisions relating to EMU. However, one anomaly is that unanimity is still required under the co-decision procedure on the right of residence of workers, social security for migrant workers, and rules governing the professions. The consultation procedure, on the other hand, still exists in a wide range of areas. Finally, there are still several issues where decision-making is exclusively by the Council, without even EP consultation, such as on the Common Commercial Policy.

The result is that the EU has perhaps the most complex legislative system in the world. However, the Council and EP have adapted to this system, and both have developed sophisticated rules governing their internal organization to improve their scrutiny, amendment and adoption of legislation, and developed sophisticated strategies to maximize their influence *vis-à-vis* each other in the various stages of bicameral interaction.

Legislative politics inside the Council

As discussed in the previous chapter, the Council is composed of ministers from the governments of the EU member states – in other words, agriculture ministers in the Council of Agriculture Ministers, economic and finance ministers in the Council of Economic and Finance Ministers (EcoFin), and so on. The main goal of these governments is reelection to national government office. Consequently, if legislation in front of the Council threatens the interests of the key voting groups for the parties who make up the government, the government will seek to block the legislation. In this regard, governments in the Council are like legislators in any parliament: where potential benefits to the whole society are weighed against potential losses to individual constituents.

Nevertheless, there can also be conflicts of interests within governments in the Council, between the different ministers. These arise for two main reasons. First, in coalition governments (the case in most EU member states), ministers from different parties have different core electorates, and consequently a policy proposal before the Council could be beneficial to the supporters of one governing party but threaten the supporters of another. This leads to pressures for different ministers to take opposing positions in different Council meetings. Second, different ministerial portfolios have different functional support groups and fiscal interests. For example, whereas ministers in EcoFin have an interest to constrain public spending, ministers in the Social Affairs Council, the Regional Affairs Council and/or the Employment Council have an interest in EU outputs that increase public spending on their social programmes.

Agenda organization: the presidency, sectoral councils and committees

Despite the above, the Council has developed several mechanisms to coordinate the EU legislative agenda. First, the *Presidency of the Council* has evolved since the 1970s into the central coordinating mechanism of the Council agenda. The Presidency rotates every six months between the member governments in a prearranged system, originally by alphabetical order, but which was amended from 1998 to achieve a balance between large and small states. The rules of procedure of the Council set out the

Table 3.1   *Main policy areas covered by the EU's legislative procedures*

Procedure/Policy issue
(Commission initiative + QMV in the Council, unless stated otherwise)

Assent
  Economic and Social Cohesion: objectives and organization of the
    structural funds (unanimity)
  Institutions: uniform election procedure for EP elections (unanimity)
  Common Provisions: breach of human rights by m.state (initiative by
    1/3 m.st. or Com. + unan.)
  Enlargement: acceptance of new members states to the EU (unanimity)
  External Relations: international agreements/association agreements
    (unanimity)

Co-decision
  Principles: discrimination on the grounds of nationality
  Citizenship: right of residence (unanimity)
  Single Market: free movement of workers/right of establishment/
    harmonization of laws
  Single Market: social security for migrant workers/rules governing the
    professions (unanimity)
  Justice & Free Movement: rules on visas for non-EU nat's (5 years
    after Amsterdam Treaty)
  Transport: implementation of common transport policy/
    transEuropean networks
  Employment: certain measures for cooperation on employment
  Social Policy: sexual equality/health & safety/working conditions/
    worker consultation
  Education/Vocational Training/Culture: all areas
  Public Health/Consumer Protection: certain public health standards/
    all consumer protection laws
  Economic and Social Cohesion: implementation
  Research: adoption/implementation of framework programmes
  Environment: general environment policies/adoption of environmental
    action programmes
  Development Co-operation: all areas
  Financial Provisions: measures for countering fraud

Cooperation
  Economic & Monetary Union: surveillance of national economic
    policies/certain other provisions

Consultation

Principles: non-discrimination on grounds of sex, race, ethnicity etc. (unanimity)

Flexible Integration: authorization (unan. in the Euro.Council if 'vital national interest' threatened)

Citizenship: voting rights of EU citizens in EP and local elections (unanimity)

Common Agricultural Policy: all areas

Single Market: liberalization of services in the single market

Single Market: harmonization of indirect taxation (unanimity)

Justice & Free Movement: common visa list (initiative by a member state or Commission)

Justice & Free Movement: all other issues (initiative by a m.state or Commission + unanimity)

Competition Policy: rules applying to undertakings/state aids policy

Economic & Monetary Union: excessive deficit procedure

Employment: annual employment policy guidelines for member states

Common Commercial Policy: extension of policy to intellectual property and services

Institutions: appointment of Commission Pres./appointment of ECB officials (unanimity)

Police & Judicial Cooperation: all areas (initiative by a m.state/ Commission + unanimity)

Final Provisions: adoption of any measure not covered in the Treaty (unanimity)

No European Parliament involvement

Single Market: common customs tariff

Economic & Monetary Union: breach of excessive deficit/external monetary agreements

Employment: recommendations to member states

Common Commercial Policy: all areas

Education/Culture/Public Health: recommendations to member states

Common Foreign & Security Policy: implementation (Council initiative)

Common Foreign & Security Policy: decisions (Council initiative + 'constructive abstention')

Note: The Appendix contains an exhaustive list of the decision-making rules under each article of the Treaty. The budgetary procedure is dealt with in Chapter 9.

main tasks of the presidency as follows (cf. Hayes-Renshaw and Wallace, 1997, pp. 136–9; Westlake, 1995, pp. 45–6):

- to convene Council meetings, and announce the dates of the Council meetings seven months in advance;
- to draw up the provisional agenda for each meeting, including indicating the items on which any government or the Commission may request a vote;
- to chair the meetings of the Council and the meetings of the Committee of Permanent Representatives;
- to submit a six-month work programme;
- to sign the minutes of meetings and all decisions; and
- to represent the Council to the EP, the Commission and the outside world.

The government holding the presidency consequently has considerable control of the legislative agenda before the Council. Each government takes over the presidency with a particular list of policies it would like to see adopted, and these form a central part of the presidency's work programme and will be top of the agenda in all the key Council meetings. However, the presidency can only act on these issues if legislation is proposed by the Commission. On the other hand, if the government holding the presidency does not like a Commission proposal, the presidency can simply refuse to put it on the Council agenda.

Overall, member states treat their term of holding the presidency as an opportunity to pursue their own policy objectives. The result is the rolling addition to the Council agenda of specific national policy issues (Bulmer and Wessels, 1987; Kirchner, 1992). However, member states also like to be seen to have held 'good' presidencies, and not all member states are equally able to manipulate the agenda to the same extent. The member states that are most capable are those with ministries that are well adapted for dealing with European issues and have sufficient administrative capacity. This is often difficult for the smaller member states, but the larger member states also often have problems as their periods in the presidency tend to be taken up with domestic political developments and attempts to promote their own 'national agendas' at the expense of the overall Council agenda (see for example O'Nuallain, 1985; Kirchner, 1992). Hayes-Renshaw and Wallace (1995, p. 571) consequently conclude that where the presidency is concerned ' "medium-sized" member governments probably have a comparative advantage'.

Second, through *sectoral Councils* the Council agenda has become increasingly specialized. As Table 3.2 shows, until the mid-1980s the General Affairs and Agriculture Councils constituted almost half of all council meetings. In the 1990s, in contrast, with the rise of EcoFin, the

Table 3.2   *Frequency of sectoral council meetings*

	1975	1980	1985	1990	1995
General Affairs	16	13	14	13	14
Agriculture	15	14	14	16	10
EcoFin	8	9	7	10	9
Environment	2	2	3	5	4
Transport	2	2	3	4	4
Fisheries	–	7	3	3	4
Social Affairs	2	2	2	3	4
Justice and Home Affairs	–	1	–	1	4
Industry	–	–	6	4	3
Research	2	–	2	4	3
Internal Market	–	–	5	7	2
Development	3	1	2	4	2
Energy	2	2	3	3	2
Health	–	–	–	2	2
Budget	2	3	5	2	2
Education	1	1	1	2	2
Telecommunications	–	–	–	2	2
Consumer Affairs	–	–	1	2	2
Culture	–	–	2	2	3
Other	2	3	–	1	1
Total	57	60	73	90	79

Source: Annual Reports of the Council.

various Councils dedicated to the regulation of the single market, and the new activities of justice and home affairs ministers, this figure fell to less than one in three. Formally, the General Affairs Council (of foreign ministers) is still at the pinnacle of a hierarchy, where issues are referred if agreement cannot be reached at a lower level. However, the increased legislative volume and the time constraints of the legislative procedures limit the ability of the General Affairs Council to control decisions in lower meetings. Also, with the development of EMU, EcoFin has usurped some of the coordinating functions of the General Affairs Council on many macroeconomic and budgetary issues.

As a result, in terms of the organization of the EU legislative agenda, these meetings are the functional equivalent of the committees of a parliament: each having a specific policy domain. By delegating issues to meetings of ministers with shared functional and fiscal interests, and often with established *esprit de corps* (as in EcoFin), the potential for trading agreements between different policy sectors is increased. For example, to overcome a deadlock in the adoption of the single market programme, an agreement between internal market ministers on market liberalization can be traded-off with an agreement between social affairs ministers on minimum health and safety standards. However, the inevitable result is 'log-rolling' of the EU towards further integration.

Third, to facilitate pre-legislative agreement there is a network of *Council committees, working groups and the Council secretariat*. The Committee of Permanent Representatives (COREPER), with fixed members from the member states' office of 'Representations' to the EU in Brussels, is the real engine behind much of the work of the Council, and this is where the majority of issues are decided before legislation is even seen at ministerial level (de Zwaan, 1995; van Schendelen, 1996). COREPER meets each week at the level of member states' ambassadors to the EU (COREPER II) and 'deputies' (COREPER I). Hayes-Renshaw and Wallace (1995, p. 562) estimate that approximately 70 per cent of Council business is agreed in working groups of national officials below COREPER II. The EU Permanent Representatives then tackle about 15–20 per cent of business, which they hand up to Council meetings as 'A points' (in other words, already agreed but formally needing ministerial approval), which leaves the Council to focus on the 10–15 per cent of 'B points' that still need to be resolved.

Under COREPER there are various sectoral committees of specialist civil servants, such as the Special Committee on Agriculture (SCA), the Political Committee (covering Common Foreign and Security Policy), the Article 113 Committee (dealing with the Common Commercial Policy), and the Coordinating Committee on Justice and Home Affairs (the 'K.4 Committee'). And supporting these committees is the Council secretariat, with a staff of approximately 2000. Every day, between 300 and 400 officials from national bureaucracies attend meetings in the Council building (Hayes-Renshaw and Wallace, 1997, p. 70). The result is a growing institutionalization of patterns of interaction and bargaining, which is essential for the operation of a successful legislature. Nevertheless, one continuous problem for the Council is the high turnover of personnel at ministerial and working group level, and because of this the Council secretariat also plays a crucial role in securing continuity and institutional memory.

Voting and coalition politics in the Council

There are two basic voting rules in the Council:

- Unanimity, where each member state has one vote and legislation cannot be passed if one or more member states vote against the legislation.

- Qualified majority voting (QMV), where the votes are weighted according to the size of a member state's population, and a majority of 62 out of the 87 votes is required for legislation to be passed.

However, there is a quirk in the Council's voting rules relating to the issue of 'abstention'. Article 205(3) [ex 148(3)] of the Treaty states that, 'Abstentions . . . shall not prevent the adoption by the Council of acts which require unanimity', so that several member states can abstain and the legislation can still be carried. As a result, under unanimity an abstention is equivalent to support for a proposal (although an abstaining government can argue to its voters that it did not support the legislation). Under QMV, in contrast, an abstention is equivalent to voting against a proposal, as 62 votes are still required to carry the legislation. Consequently, as one of the Council's own publications points out:

> This sometimes results in the paradoxical situation where a decision for which a qualified majority cannot be reached . . . is taken more easily unanimously as a result of abstention by certain members of the Council who do not wish to vote in favour but who do not want to prevent the Act concerned from going through. (Council of the European Communities, 1990, p. 41)

Table 3.3 shows the number of votes each government has under the Council voting rules. Under unanimity, every member has an equal chance to be 'pivotal' – determining whether a coalition is winning or losing. Under QMV, although the larger member states have more votes, the system of weighting overrepresents the citizens in the smaller EU member states (cf. Felsenthal and Machover, 1997). Nevertheless, with more votes the larger member states are more than twice as likely to be part of a winning coalition than the smaller states (cf. Brams and Affuso, 1985; Hosli, 1995b; Lane and Maeland, 1995; Widgrén, 1995).

The member governments are acutely aware that changes in their voting strengths or the QMV threshold affect their relative power. For example, the level of the new QMV threshold was a key issue in the enlargement of the EU to Austria, Finland and Sweden in 1995 (Johnston, 1995, 1996; Garrett, McLean and Machover, 1995; Morriss, 1996; Garrett and McLean, 1996). Some member states argued that the 'blocking minority' as a proportion of all votes should be extrapolated from the old threshold, of approximately 30 per cent of total votes. However, the United Kingdom, Spain and Italy argued that enlarging the EU to three smaller and northern member states would alter the type of coalition that needed to be built to achieve a qualified majority. As a result, in the Ioninna Declaration of March 1994, the member states agreed to 26 votes as the blocking minority (30 per cent of all votes), but stipulated that 'if members of the

Table 3.3 Voting weights and voting power in the Council

	Population (000s)	Unanimous voting		Qualified majority voting		
		Votes	Power (proportion of cases where a member state is pivotal)	Votes	Power (proportion of cases where a member state is pivotal [Shapley–Shubik])	Citizens per vote (million)
Germany	81.7	1	100.0	10	11.7	8.2
United Kingdom	58.6	1	100.0	10	11.7	5.9
France	58.1	1	100.0	10	11.7	5.8
Italy	57.7	1	100.0	10	11.7	5.8
Spain	39.1	1	100.0	8	9.6	4.9
Netherlands	15.5	1	100.0	5	5.5	3.1
Greece	10.5	1	100.0	5	5.5	2.1
Belgium	10.2	1	100.0	5	5.5	2.0
Portugal	9.9	1	100.0	5	5.5	2.0
Sweden	8.9	1	100.0	4	4.5	2.2
Austria	8.1	1	100.0	4	4.5	2.0
Denmark	5.2	1	100.0	3	3.5	1.7
Finland	5.1	1	100.0	3	3.5	1.7
Ireland	2.6	1	100.0	3	3.5	0.9
Luxembourg	0.4	1	100.0	2	2.1	0.2
Total votes		15		87		
Required to adopt		15		62		
Required to block		1		26		

Council representing a total of 23 to 25 votes indicate their intention to oppose [an Act]. . . the Council will do all in its power to reach. . . a satisfactory solution that could be adopted by at least 65 votes' (cf. Westlake, 1995, pp. 93–4). Hence, if the governments in the minority insist, there is a *de facto* blocking minority of 23 votes (26 per cent) and a qualified majority of 65 votes (75 per cent).

But these calculations of relative power based on the absolute number of votes for each member state assume that all types of coalitions are equally as likely, but this is clearly not the case (Garrett and Tsebelis, 1996). First, several informal bilateral and multilateral alliances exist between governments with similar interests. For example, a Franco-German coalition – the so-called 'Paris–Bonn Axis' – has been at the heart of Council decision-making since the 1950s. Also, the Benelux states are more economically and politically integrated than any other grouping in the EU; the less-prosperous member states – Greece, Ireland, Portugal and Spain – often vote together to protect their interests in the single market and under the EU structural funds (a 'cohesion bloc'); and Denmark, Sweden and Finland have close economic and political ties and similar cultural and economic structures (a 'Nordic bloc'). Hosli (1996) consequently calculates that a Franco-German coalition and a 'cohesion bloc' are both pivotal in 24.5 per cent of cases, the Benelux is pivotal in 14.5 per cent of cases, and a 'Nordic bloc' is pivotal in 11.2 per cent of cases.

Second, coalitions are likely to form between governments with similar policy goals. Figure 3.3 shows the approximate policy location of the governments in January 1999 on the two main dimensions of EU politics (calculated from the locations of the parties in each government). The location of governments on the pro-/anti-Europe dimension, suggests that the United Kingdom, Denmark and the new member states would be the most isolated in Council decision-making. Moreover, the adjacent positions of France and Germany suggest that a Paris–Bonn axis could be easily formed on this dimension. Also, in this scenario, if the status quo (SQ) is less integrationist than the proposed legislation, Spain is pivotal in turning minority support into a winning qualified majority, and Sweden is pivotal in establishing unanimity (cf. Garrett, 1992).

However, the majority of Socialist and Socialist-led coalition governments in the EU in 1999 suggests that on left–right issues (such as the level of social protection in the single market), the centre-right governments in Spain and Ireland are isolated. Also, in this scenario, if the status quo (SQ) is relatively centrist (in other words, the continuation of existing national welfare regimes without any EU regulation), the Netherlands becomes pivotal in turning minority support for a proposal into a winning qualified majority. But, there is no unanimous coalition that can beat the status quo. If a Franco-German coalition is negotiated prior to a Council meeting, it is

Figure 3.3 *Policy location of Council members and winning coalitions, January 1999*

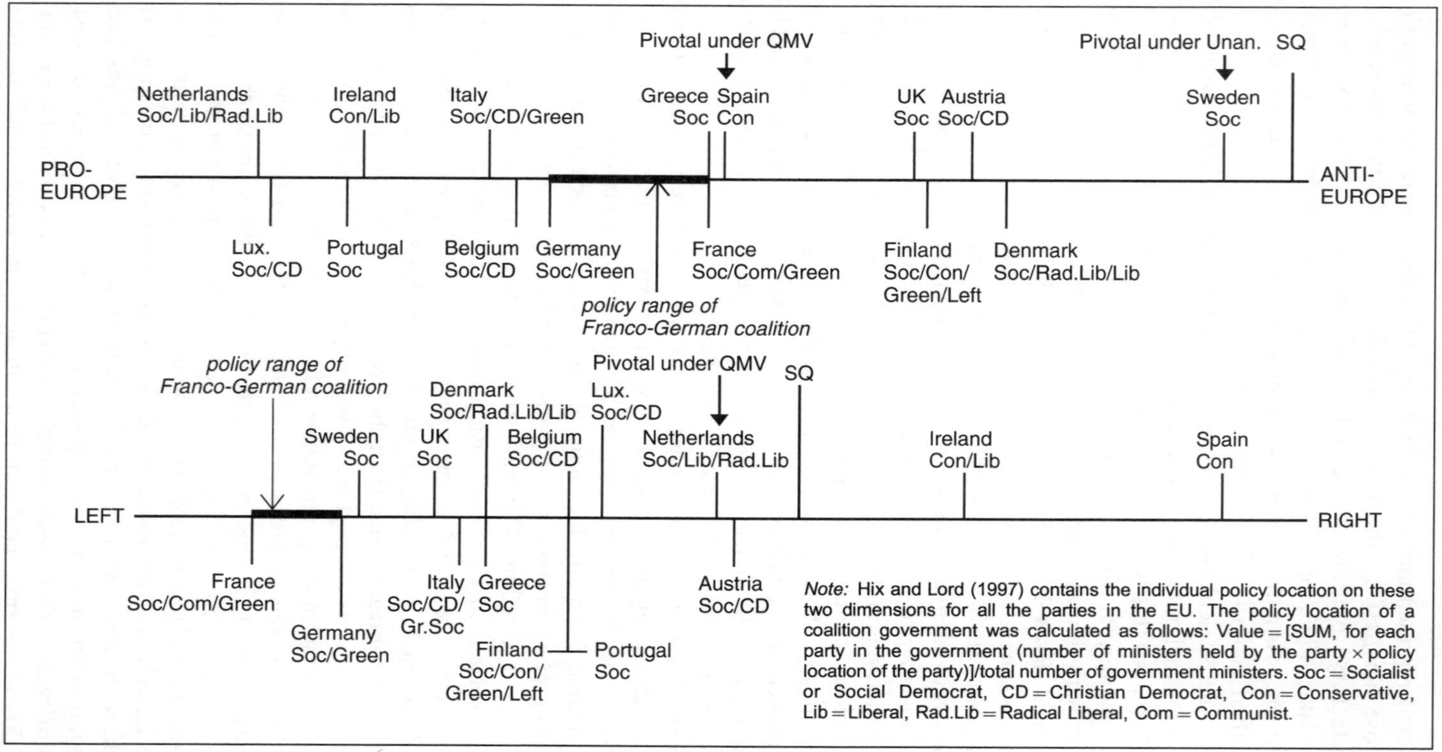

Note: Hix and Lord (1997) contains the individual policy location on these two dimensions for all the parties in the EU. The policy location of a coalition government was calculated as follows: Value = [SUM, for each party in the government (number of ministers held by the party × policy location of the party)]/total number of government ministers. Soc = Socialist or Social Democrat, CD = Christian Democrat, Con = Conservative, Lib = Liberal, Rad.Lib = Radical Liberal, Com = Communist.

Source: Calculated from data in Hix and Lord (1997).

unlikely to secure a qualified majority in the full Council. For example, this was the case in December 1998 when a Franco-German initiative on tax harmonization (a left-wing policy) was opposed by almost all the other governments.

Nonetheless, there is an underlying 'culture of consensus' in the Council, which ensures that the Council hardly ever acts by QMV even when it is allowed to under the provisions of the Treaty. Table 3.4 shows all the

Table 3.4 *Council voting records, December 1993–December 1994*

Votes	Number	Per cent
Votes with member states voting against		
1 member state voting against	20	7.7
2 member states voting against	9	3.4
3+ member states voting against	7	2.7
Total	36	13.8
Votes with only abstentions and the rest unanimous		
1 member state abstaining and none against	26	10.0
2+ member states abstaining and none against	2	0.8
Total	28	10.7
Uncontested/unanimous votes	197	75.5
Total legislative votes	261	100.0

Member state	Negative votes	Abstentions
Denmark	11	1
Netherlands	10	5
Germany	9	6
United Kingdom	7	14
Luxembourg	4	0
Greece	4	0
Italy	3	3
Portugal	3	3
Spain	2	7
France	2	3
Belgium	2	0
Ireland	1	2

Source: Calculated from data in Hayes-Renshaw and Wallace (1997).

legislative votes in the Council between December 1994 and December 1995. Of the total of 261 votes, on 86 per cent the Council either acted by unanimity or adopted positions by unanimity with one or more member states abstaining. Moreover, in the remaining cases three or more member states voted against a proposal on less than 3 per cent of the cases. Denmark had the highest number of negative votes, the United Kingdom preferred to abstain rather than veto, and the Netherlands and Germany were in opposition more times than the United Kingdom.

The fact that national governments are involved in adopting EU legislation as well as executing the legislation once it has been passed causes real problems of compliance under QMV. If a member state is in a minority in a vote it may be under pressure from domestic interests to oppose the legislation, and then also not to implement the legislation. The problem of compliance may in fact become more acute as voting records in the Council become more transparent (Hayes-Renshaw and Wallace, 1995, p. 575). It is unsurprising, then, that in most cases the Council would rather see no legislation adopted than risk undermining a delicate consensus. Nevertheless, it might also be the case that voting rules have an implicit impact on decision-making. For example, if a qualified majority is in favour of a proposal, there is pressure on the minority governments to concede to maintain consensus. As the Council admits: 'the relatively small number of decisions actually taken by a qualified-majority does not fully show the part played by qualified-majority voting as a factor for efficiency in the implementation of Community policies' (Council of the European Union, 1995, p. 11).

Legislative politics inside the European Parliament

Unlike the Council, the EP does not have a fixed seat; it holds most of its plenary sessions in Strasbourg, whilst the official seat of the EP secretariat is in Luxembourg. However, the bulk of the work of the EP is in Brussels, where an increasing number of plenary sessions are held, where the party groups and committees meet, and where the offices of the MEPs, the party group and committee secretariats are based. Despite this handicap, the EP operates like any parliament, organizing and mobilizing to influence EU legislation and the EU executive. However, the institutional design of the EU – the separation of executive and legislative power – means that the EP is more like the US Congress than most domestic parliaments in Europe. The EP does not form an EU government. In return, though, there is no EU government to enforce its wishes on its supporting majority in the EP.

MEP behaviour: reelection versus promotion and policies

Since 1979, MEPs have been elected in European-wide contests every five years. The main goal of MEPs is reelection, but public opinion surveys repeatedly show that less than 60 per cent of EU citizens know anything about the EP, and less than 5 per cent have an informed impression of what MEPs do. Also, European elections are not fought on European issues, the campaigns are by national parties and on national issues (see Chapter 6). Hence, an MEP's chance of *reelection* is not dependent upon his or her performance in the EP, but is determined by the popularity of his or her national party. Moreover, most EU member states use list-PR systems in EP elections, where national party leaderships determine the order of MEPs on the lists. Consequently, for most MEPs, the chance of standing as a candidate and being *reselected* is not determined by his or her party group in the EP, but by his or her national party leadership (Bowler and Farrell, 1993; Norris and Franklin, 1997).

Traditionally, a career in the EP was either a training ground for a job back in national politics, or a 'retirement home' at the end of a national career. Nevertheless, the 1989 and 1994 elections brought an increasing number of MEPs who plan either to stay in the EP for at least two terms, or to pursue a career in another EU institution or European-level organization (approximately 30 per cent of all MEPs, and approximately 60 per cent of British and German MEPs) (Scarrow, 1997).

MEPs interested in making a career in the EP are interested in two different types of goals within the EP. First, there are *office goals*, such as promotion to party leadership, a senior position in the EP (such as EP president), or a chairmanship of an EP committee. Second, there are *policy goals*: the pursuit of an MEP's ideological views or the interests of his or her constituents through the influence of the EP on the EU legislative and executive processes. Whereas reelection may not be dependent on performance within the EP, the ability to achieve these goals *is* dependent upon gaining promotion within the EP committees and the EP party groups, and on being able to form coalitions with other legislators to secure common policy aims.

In other words, MEPs face a dilemma. To secure reselection and reelection, MEPs must cater to national party interests; but to secure promotion within the EP and policy outputs from the EP, MEPs must cater to interests of committees and party leaderships within the EP.

Agenda organization: leaderships, parties and committees

Like most national parliaments, the EP determines its own organization and writes its own rules. The EP prefers to use formal Rules of Procedure rather than informal conventions and norms (probably because the EP is multilingual and formal rules reduce miscommunication and linguistic confusion). Through these rules of procedure, the EP has set up three main organizational structures to facilitate agenda-control.

First, there is the *parliamentary leadership*. The most senior offices in the EP are the president and the 14 vice-presidents. The EP also has three leadership bodies: the Bureau of the Parliament (consisting of the president and vice-president), the Conference of Presidents (consisting of the EP president, the leaders of the EP party groups and the chairman of the Conference of Committee Chairmen), and the Conference of Committee Chairmen. Together these committees involve all the senior figures in the EP. The Bureau deals with internal EP organizational and administrative matters, but is increasingly active on political issues and meets almost every week. The Conference of Presidents is traditionally where most political issues are tackled, particular as regards the relationship between the EP and the Commission and Council, and normally meets twice a month. The Conference of Committee Chairmen coordinates the committee agendas and tackles inter-committee demarcation disputes.

Second, the *EP party groups* are the central mechanisms for structuring debate and coalition-formation in the legislative process in the EP. After the enlargement of the EP in 1995, rule 29 of the Rules of Procedure set out how many MEPs are needed to form a party group: 29 from one member state, 23 from two member states, 17 from three member states, and 14 from four or more member states. The party groups have certain privileges: such as a significant secretarial and research staff and financial resources. Table 3.5 shows the seats of the party groups and their national memberships in January 1999. The Party of European Socialists on the centre-left and the European People's Party on the centre-right are the largest groups – commanding two-thirds of the seats between them. There are, however, several smaller groups that can be crucial in influencing the legislative behaviour.

The real relevance of the party groups relates to the way their leaderships determine most of the vital political issues in the EP: the choice of the EP leadership, the allocation of committee positions and *rapporteur* assignments, and the agenda of plenary sessions. As a result, if a national political party is not a member of a party group, it is unlikely to be able to secure any office or policy goals for its MEPs. And, national parties are more likely to secure these goals in the two larger groups than in one of the smaller groups.

These pressures have consequently facilitated a reduction in the number of EP party groups and a consolidation of the PES and EPP. Whereas EP elections increase party group fragmentation (because of national issues in the campaigns), the incentive structure within the EP reduces party group

Table 3.5 Seats in the European Parliament, January 1999

Member state	Party group									Total seats	Citizens per EP seat
	PES	EPP	ELDR	UPE	EUL	G	ERA	IEN	na		
Germany	40	47				12				99	826 000
UK	61	17	3		1	1	2	1	1	87	675 000
France	16	12	1	18	7		13	8	12	87	670 000
Italy	18	37	4	3	5	3	2		15	87	659 000
Spain	22	30	2		9		1			64	613 000
Netherlands	7	9	10	2		1		2		31	500 000
Greece	10	9		2	4					25	420 000
Belgium	6	7	6			2	1		3	25	404 000
Portugal	10	9		3	3					25	396 000
Sweden	7	5	3		3	4				22	400 000
Austria	6	7	1			1			6	21	386 000
Denmark	4	3	5					4		16	331 000
Finland	4	4	5		2	1				16	319 000
Ireland	1	4	1	7		2				15	240 000
Luxembourg	2	2	1				1			6	67 000
Total seats	214	202	42	35	34	27	20	15	37	626	
Per cent	34.2	32.3	6.7	5.6	5.4	4.3	3.2	2.4	5.9	100.0	

Note:
PES = Group of the Party of European Socialists (socialist/social democrat).
EPP = Group of the European People's Party (Christian democrat/conservative).
ELDR = Group of the European Liberal, Democrat and Reform Party (liberal).
UPE = Group Union for Europe (conservative).
EUL = Confederal Group of the European United Left/Nordic Green Left (radical-left).

G = The Green Group in the European Parliament (green).
ERA = Group of the European Radical Alliance (radical liberal/regionalist).
IEN = Group of Independents for a Europe of Nations (anti-European).
na = non-attached members (mostly extreme right).

Source: http://www.europarl.eu.int/members/en/default.htm

fragmentation between elections (Bardi, 1996). For example, in 1992 the European Democratic Group was disbanded after all its member parties (the British, Spanish and Danish conservatives) joined the EPP, and in 1996 Forza Europa was disbanded after its members (the Italian Forza Italia and allies) joined the UPE. Moreover, in 1992 the Italian ex-communists left the EUL to join the PES, and in 1994 and 1996, respectively, the French Parti Républicain and the Portuguese Partido Social Democrata left the ELDR to join the EPP.

The same pressures also ensure that individual MEPs try not to upset their party group leaderships. Also, individual MEP adherence to the party-group line in legislative voting is enforced through 'whipping' systems, where votes are designated 'one-line', 'two-line' and 'three-line' whips signifying the importance of the agenda item to the party group. (based on the system in the British House of Commons). The result has been a growing 'cohesion' of the major party groups in the EP, to levels that are almost as high as in some national parliaments in Europe and certainly higher than in the US Congress (see Chapter 6). Nevertheless, within the party groups the 'national delegations' remain powerful organizations, with the British and German delegations dominating the PES, and the German and Spanish delegations dominating the EPP. However, party-group leaders cannot really prevent a whole national delegation breaking from the party-group line.

Third, there are the EP *committees*. 'If the political groups are the Parliament's life blood, then its . . . committees are its legislative backbone' (Westlake, 1994, p. 191), and it is in the committees that the real scrutiny of EU legislation takes place. The committees propose amendments to legislation in the form of a report and a draft resolution, which are then submitted to the full EP plenary session in an almost 'take-it-or-leave-it' form. Amendments to the proposed committee resolutions can be made in the full plenary, but without the backing of a committee and the party-group support that goes along with this they are less likely to be adopted by the parliament. Consequently, in terms of the influence of committees on the legislative agenda, the EP is again more like the US Congress than most European parliaments.

Furthermore, the jurisdictional organization of EP committees is based around the need to specialize in the legislative process. Table 3.6 shows their jurisdictions for the 1989–94. MEP membership of these committees is correlated more with MEPs' interest-group affiliations and previous occupational experiences than with nationality or party affiliation (Bowler and Farrell, 1995). In fact many MEPs join committees with policy competencies close to the interests of their constituents or supporting interest groups – which suggests legislative specialization to secure distributional benefits. Nevertheless, other MEPs join committees because of their previous occupational experience – which suggests legislation specialization to secure information and knowledge. Either way, the design of EP committees facilitates log-rolling and legislative agreement in the full plenary session.

The importance of the committees has meant that committee chairmanships are prized offices for MEPs, and this is particularly the case in the committees with active roles in the EU legislative processes, such as agriculture, environment and economic and monetary affairs (as Table 3.6 shows). For example, Ken Collins (PES, UK), the chair of the Environment Committee between 1989 and 1999, was a key player in determining outcomes on several important pieces of environmental legislation (Judge, 1993; Judge and Earnshaw, 1994). However, the importance of the EP committees also produces incentives for the party group leaderships to influence committee assignments and agendas. At the beginning of each parliamentary term and again half-way through each term, the committee chairmanships are reallocated, and the party groups have established a system of allocating these posts in proportional to each party group's seats (using the D'Hondt counting system, which favours the larger groups). The actual portfolios each party group gets are then subject to inter-group negotiation, and the whole package is presented to the parliament as a whole. For example, Table 3.6 shows that in the 1989 parliament, the PES had eight committee chairs compared to the EPP's five. Following this 'carve-up' between the party groups, there is a similar negotiation within the groups over how the party groups' prizes are distributed between the national delegations. The party groups have also developed a system for influencing committee agendas and coordinating party policy across committees, through 'group coordinators' in each committee who meet regularly to discuss party-group strategies.

Coalition formation in the Parliament

There is no permanent coalition in the EP and, without a government to support, legislative coalitions form around each individual vote (again like the US Congress). Also, on many issues the EP behaves as if it is a single cohesive actor, with a single interest (to promote further European integration) in opposition to the interest of the other legislative chamber of the EU (the Council) or the holders of executive power (the Council or the Commission).

However, an informal 'grand coalition' between the PES and EPP is facilitated by the rules of the EU legislative process. In the adoption of opinions in the early stages of the legislative procedures, when voting on 'own initiative' reports and in adopting amendments to resolutions on legislation, the EP decides by a 'simple majority' of those present at the

Table 3.6 Work of the EP committees in the 1989–94 Parliament

	Chair 1989–92/1992–94	Number of Reports by Committees								
		A	B	C	D	E	F	G	H	Total
1. Foreign Affairs	EPP/PES	4		14	3		20	46		87
2. Agriculture	PES/EPP	201	2		10		4	10		227
3. Budgets	PES	33				54	15			102
4. Economic & Monetary Affairs	EPP	136	81	4	29		21	6	1	274
5. Research & Energy	PES	87	48		2		12	21		170
6. External Economic Relations	ELDR	63			1		16	38		122
7. Legal Affairs	EPP	49	40		11		7	11		118
8. Social Affairs	PES	42	18		9		12	7		88
9. Regional Affairs	G/EUL	7	2		20		7	29		67
10. Transport	ELDR/G	78	3	2	10		7	21	1	120
11. Environment & Consumer Protection	PES	119	51	1	4		1	45	2	223
12. Culture, Education, Youth & Media	EUL/PES	20	2		4		19	11		56
13. Development Co-operation	PES	23	1	10	1		19	18		72
14. Budgetary Control	ED/EPP	14			8	40	17	1	1	81
15. Institutional Affairs	EPP	4	1		4		25	10		43
16. Women's Rights	PES	2			2		7	15		27
17. Rules Committee	PES/ELDR						1		59	60
18. Petitions Committee	EPP								11	11
19. Civil Liberties & Home Affairs (est. 92)	–/ED	4					10	9		23
20. Fisheries (est. 94)	–									–
Temp. Cmte on German Unification	–	5	2				3			10
Special Committees of Enquiry	–						2			2
Temp. Cmte on the Delors II Package	–				1					1
Total		891	251	31	119	94	225	298	75	1984

Notes to Table 3.6
A = Reports under Consultation, Cooperation (1st reading) & Co-decision
    (1st reading).
B = Recommendations under Cooperation (2nd reading) & Co-decision
    (2nd & 3rd readings).
C = Reports under Assent procedure.
D = Consultation on non-legislative issues.
E = Budgetary reports.
F = Committee 'own initiative' reports.
G = Reports on motions for resolution (tabled by individual MEPs).
H = Other issues, including *inter alia* legal-base issues, reports on EP rules and
    petitions.
ED = European Democrats (British and Danish conservatives).
Source: Calculated from data in Corbett *et al.* (1995).

vote. However, according to the Treaty, final EP resolutions on EU legislation must be carried by an 'absolute majority' of *all* MEPs, not just of those turning out in the vote. This rule presents a problem for the EP as the average attendance in legislative votes is less than 65 per cent (cf. Scully, 1997a), and with a 65 per cent turnout a coalition of 77 per cent of all those voting is needed to carry legislation by an absolute majority. Nevertheless, in 1998 the party group leaderships agreed to new rules on the reimbursement of MEPs' expenses, which stipulate that in addition to being present in Strasbourg for plenary sessions, they must participate in the votes to claim their expenses. This has lead to a much higher level of MEP turnout. But, with still only an approximate turnout of 75 per cent, a coalition of 67 per cent (two-thirds) of those voting is still needed to pass legislation. This consequently encourages cooperation between the two largest groups.

Coalition politics in the EP is consequently shaped by whether a simple or an absolute majority is required. Under a simple majority procedure, the PES or the EPP can form majority winning coalitions with various combinations of the smaller party groups. Hence, as Table 3.7 shows, although the PES and EPP have the most power (in terms of the proportion of times they are pivotal for the formation of a majority-winning coalition), the smaller groups can also be pivotal on some occasions under simple majority rules. In contrast, when an absolute majority is required it is virtually impossible to construct a winning coalition without both the PES and EPP on board. Hence, in this situation, the PES and EPP are very powerful and the smaller groups are marginalized (Lane, Maeland and Berg, 1995; Hosli, 1997; Nurmi, 1997).

The centrality of a PES–EPP coalition is further illustrated if we consider 'connected' coalitions: between party groups next to each other in the

Table 3.7   *Party-group voting power under simple and absolute majorities*

	% of seats	Power under simple majority (proportion of cases where a party group is pivotal [Shapley–Shubik])	Power under absolute majority (proportion of cases where a party group is pivotal [Shapley–Shubik])
PES	34.2	30.2	50.3
EPP	32.2	25.5	39.5
ELDR	6.7	9.5	1.2
UPE	5.6	7.6	1.2
EUL	5.4	7.3	1.2
G	4.3	5.6	1.2
ERA	3.2	4.1	1.2
IEN	2.4	2.9	1.2
Non-attached Italian MEPs	2.4	2.9	1.2
Non-attached French MEPs	1.9	2.3	1.2
Non-attached Austrian MEPs	1.0	1.1	0.4
Non-attached Belgian MEPs	0.5	0.7	0.3
Non-attached British MEPs	0.2	0.2	0.1
Per cent (no.) of seats to win		50.2 (314)	66.8 (418)

policy space. As Figure 3.4 shows, on a pro-/anti-Europe dimension, where each party group favours different degrees of integration in an area where there is no existing EU regulation (hence the status quo is at the 'anti-Europe' end), the EPP is pivotal under both a simple and an absolute majority. In other words, all the party groups who are more pro-European than the EPP would support an EPP position against the SQ. Also, the PES and EPP are adjacent to each other on this dimension, so will find it easy to agree on a policy compromise.

However, on legislative issues that force the party groups to line up on a left–right dimension, the status quo is usually centrist (as without EU rules national welfare regimes will continue as before). In this scenario, the only simple majority that exists is amongst all parties to the right of the SQ, which makes the ELDR pivotal. Or, if the SQ is to the right of the ELDR,

Figure 3.4 Policy location of EP party groups

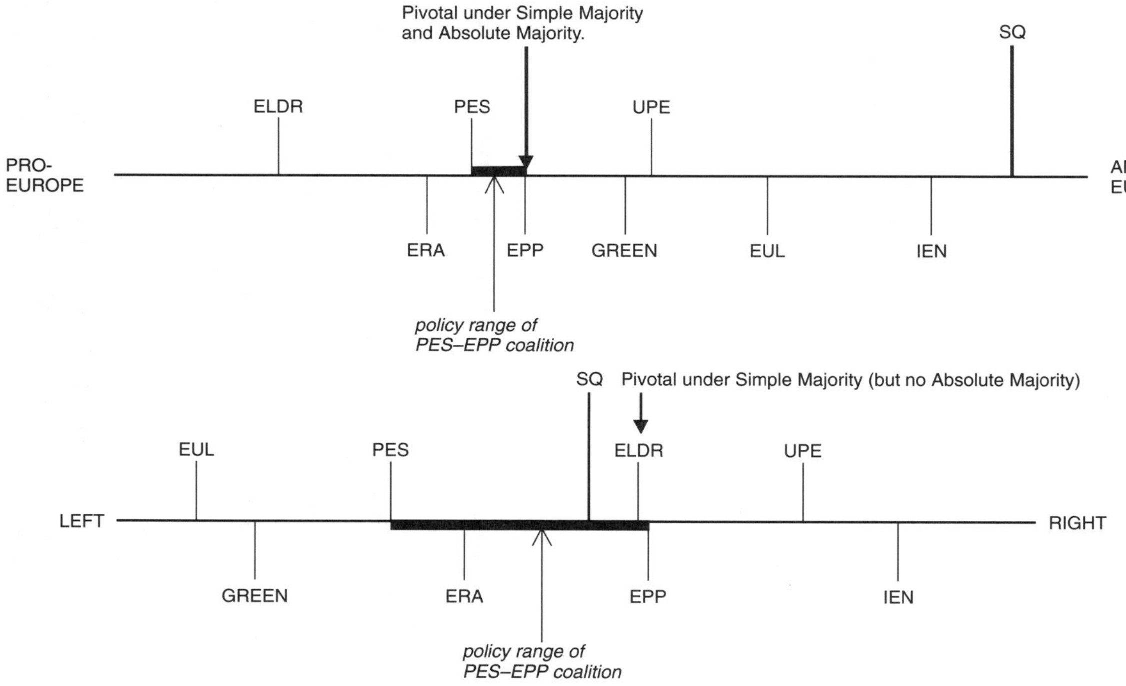

Pivotal under Simple Majority and Absolute Majority.

PRO-EUROPE

ELDR

EUL

PES

GREEN

ERA

EPP

UPE

GREEN

EUL

IEN

SQ

ANTI-EUROPE

policy range of PES–EPP coalition

SQ Pivotal under Simple Majority (but no Absolute Majority)

LEFT

GREEN

PES

ERA

ELDR

EPP

UPE

IEN

RIGHT

policy range of PES–EPP coalition

Note: Hix and Lord (1997) contains the policy location on these two dimensions for all national parties in the EU. As the internal decision-making of the EP party groups is by majority rule, with the party groups usually voting *en bloc*, the policy locations of each party group in the figure is the location of the *median* national member party in the party group, with the votes of each party group weighted according to its number of MEPs.

Source: Calculated from data in Hix and Lord (1997).

the ELDR is pivotal in constructing a majority EUL–G–PES–ERA–ELDR coalition. However, no absolute-majority coalition exists that beats the SQ, so that on this dimension the EPP and PES again have an incentive to organize prior to a legislative vote to secure an absolute majority, which would then be supported by the party groups between these two party groups.

Furthermore, Figure 3.4 shows the weakness of the IEN group in the EP. If coalition formation is a random process, between any parties that could reach a majority, then (as Table 3.7 shows) the IEN is as powerful as the UPE and twice as powerful as the other smaller groups. However, in a spatial analysis (as shown in Figure 3.5) the IEN is isolated on both dimensions of EU politics – at the anti-Europe extreme and on the extreme right. This makes the IEN group uncoalitionable, and hence much weaker than the ERA, G or UPE.

In sum, even without a common EP interest *vis-à-vis* the Council, an oligopolistic relationship between the two largest groups is enforced by the absolute-majority requirement, the current strengths of the party groups, and the policy location of the party groups on the left–right and pro-/anti-Europe dimensions. The PES and EPP must cooperate to ensure legislative coherence and protect their partisan interests and policy goals. But, counterfactually, with a simple majority in legislative votes and further consolidation of the PES and EPP (for example if the ERA and some of the EUL joined the PES, and if the UPE joins the EPP), alternative coalitions may begin to form. On left–right issues this would give significant power to the ELDR as the 'king-maker' of a winning-coalition.

Legislative bargaining between the Council and the EP

Figure 3.5 shows the EU legislative process in detail. The first stage is the proposal of legislation by the Commission: the Commission has the exclusive right to initiate legislation under most Treaty articles relating to the establishment and regulation of the single market (see the Appendix). The Commission submits the proposed legislation (a draft directive or draft regulation) to both the EP and the Council. In the *first reading* stage, the EP (in full plenary) and Council adopt positions on the legislation. The EP adopts an opinion, which normally involves a series of amendments to the Commission text, most of which are suggested by the EP committee that 'reported' on the legislative proposal.

The Council then examines the Commission proposal and the EP text, and decides whether to accept or reject the EP amendments. Under the *consultation* procedure, either the Council can adopt an Act, by QMV or unanimity (depending on the Treaty article, see the Appendix), or it can refuse to make a decision, in which case the legislation falls. Under the *cooperation* and *co-decision* procedures, the Council agrees a *Common Position* (CP) by QMV which usually involves a series of amendments to the Commission proposal, most of which are suggested by the government holding the Council presidency.

Under the cooperation and co-decision procedures, the legislation then goes to a *second reading* stage. Under both procedures, the EP has three months to decide whether to amend, accept or reject the Council's CP, acting by an absolute majority. If the EP fails to act, the legislation is deemed accepted by the EP. However, the Amsterdam Treaty introduced two changes to the EP second reading under the co-decision procedure. First, if the EP accepts the CP at this stage, the Act is then signed into law by the President of the EP, without waiting for subsequent reapproval by the Council. Second, if the EP rejects the CP at this stage, the law falls (whereas under the Maastricht Treaty co-decision procedure the EP had to declare an 'intention to reject', and the legislation then passed back to the Council).

The Commission then decides whether to accept or reject the EP amendments before resubmitting the legislation to the Council. The Council then has three months act. Under the *cooperation* procedure, the Council acting by QMV can *either* adopt the legislation into law if the EP made no amendments, *or* can adopt the EP amendments accepted by the Commission. But, the Council needs unanimity to overturn an EP second-reading rejection of the legislation or to reject EP second-reading amendments accepted by the Commission. Under the *co-decision* procedure, the Council must accept *all* the EP amendments for the legislation to be passed at this stage – by QMV for those accepted by the Commission, and by unanimity for those rejected by the Commission – otherwise, the Council must convene a *Conciliation Committee*.

Thus, if the EP and the Council do not agree after the second reading, a *Conciliation Committee* is convened: with 15 members from both the Council and the EP and a non-voting representative of the Commission. Within six weeks the conciliation committee must adopt a *Joint Text* (JT), by a QMV of the Council representatives and a simple-majority of the EP representatives. Under the Amsterdam Treaty reforms, if the conciliation committee fails to reach an agreement the legislation falls (whereas under the Maastricht co-decision procedure, the procedure could continue to a third stage).

Finally, following the adoption of a JT in the conciliation committee, under the co-decision procedure the legislation goes to a *third reading* in the Council and the EP, where the two institutions each have six weeks to decide. Under the reforms of the Amsterdam Treaty, the Council must confirm the JT by QMV and the EP must confirm the JT by an absolute

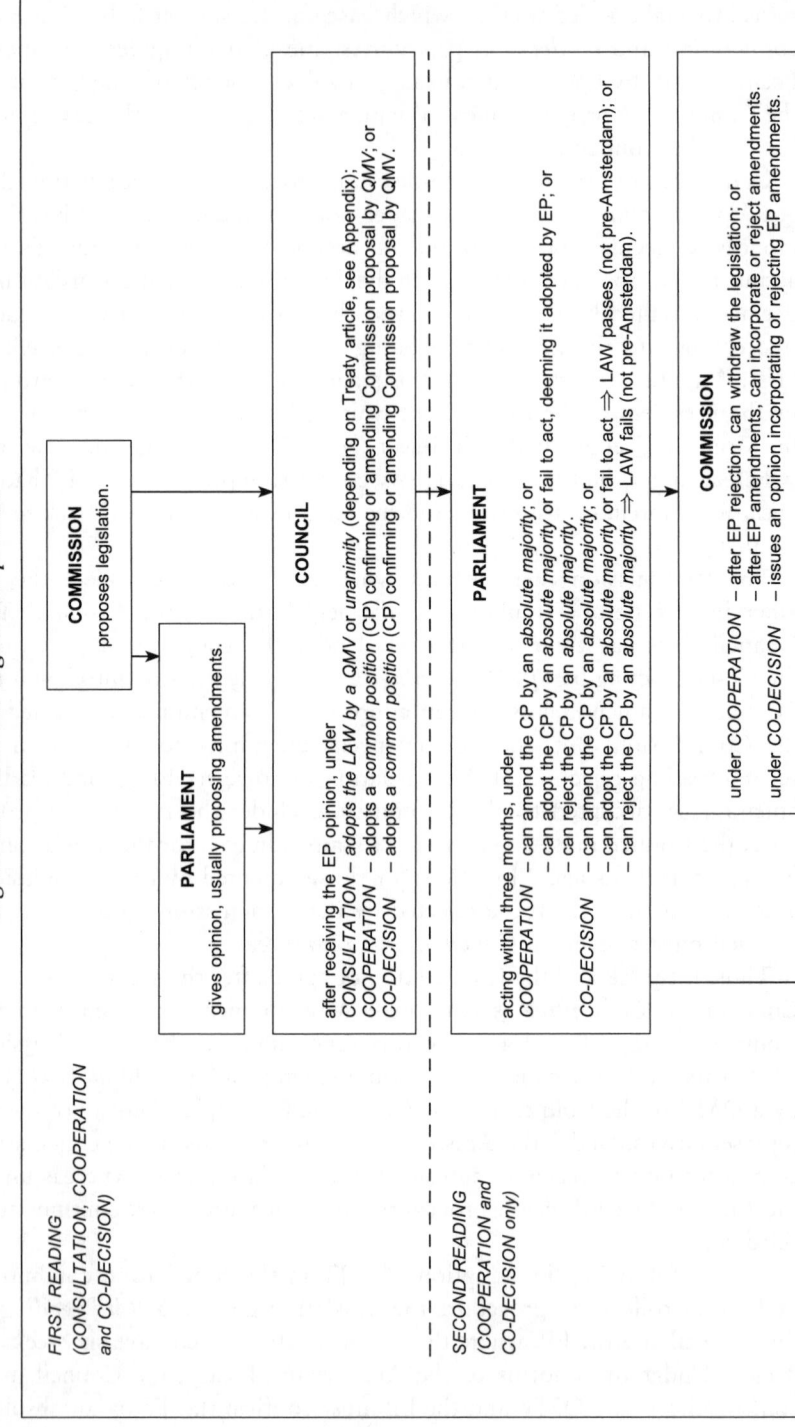

Figure 3.5   The EU legislative process

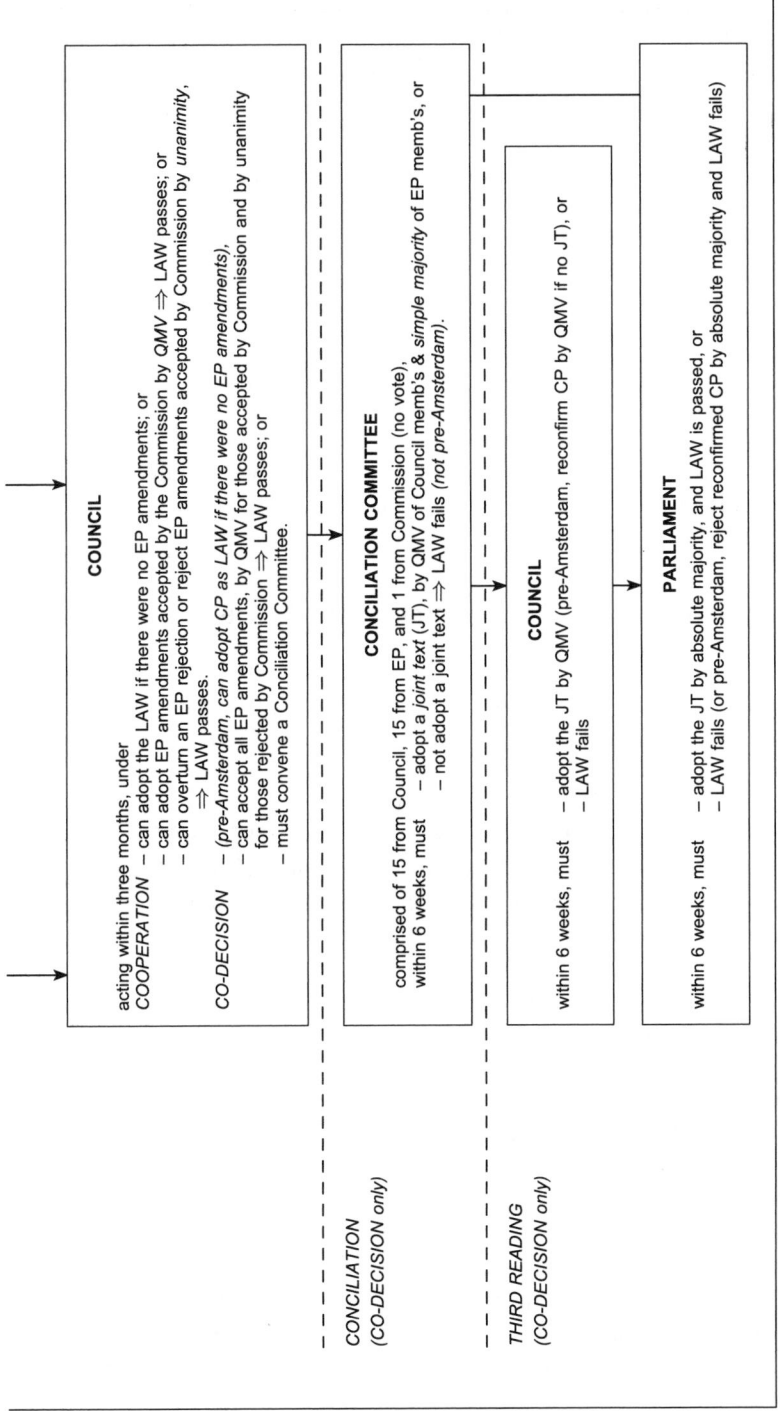

COUNCIL

acting within three months, under

COOPERATION – can adopt the LAW if there were no EP amendments; or
– can adopt EP amendments accepted by the Commission by *QMV* ⇒ LAW passes; or
– can overturn an EP rejection or reject EP amendments accepted by Commission by *unanimity*, ⇒ LAW passes.

CO-DECISION – *(pre-Amsterdam, can adopt CP as LAW if there were no EP amendments)*,
– can accept all EP amendments, by QMV for those accepted by Commission and by unanimity for those rejected by Commission ⇒ LAW passes; or
– must convene a Conciliation Committee.

CONCILIATION (CO-DECISION only)

CONCILIATION COMMITTEE

comprised of 15 from Council, 15 from EP, and 1 from Commission (no vote), within 6 weeks, must
– adopt a *joint text* (JT), by QMV of Council memb's & *simple majority* of EP memb's, or
– not adopt a joint text ⇒ LAW fails *(not pre-Amsterdam)*.

THIRD READING (CO-DECISION only)

COUNCIL

within 6 weeks, must – adopt the JT by QMV (pre-Amsterdam, reconfirm CP by QMV if no JT), or
– LAW fails

PARLIAMENT

within 6 weeks, must – adopt the JT by absolute majority, and LAW is passed, or
– LAW fails (or pre-Amsterdam, reject reconfirmed CP by absolute majority and LAW fails)

majority, otherwise the legislation falls. However, under the pre-Amsterdam co-decision procedure, if the conciliation committee had failed to produce a JT, at this stage the Council could choose by QMV to reaffirm its Common Position. And, following such a move, the CP becomes law unless the EP votes by an absolute majority to reject the reaffirmed CP.

Table 3.8 gives an indication of the use of these procedures between 1988 and 1997. Until 1997, a majority of all legislative proceedings were under the consultation procedure, but after the introduction of the co-decision procedure the various readings under that procedure have taken up an increasing proportion of the EP's legislative timetable: 20 per cent of proceedings in 1994, 22 per cent in 1995, 25 per cent in 1996, and 25 per cent in 1997. Furthermore, the Amsterdam Treaty passed most of the policy competencies covered by the cooperation procedure to the new co-decision procedure, and, consequently, the EP expects that close to 50 per cent of its legislative timetable will be consumed with co-decision procedure readings.

Theoretical models of EU bicameralism: Tsebelis and his critics

The above description sounds complex, but fortunately theoretical models allow us to reduce this picture to some simple propositions. The best-known model was proposed by George Tsebelis (1994) in respect of the cooperation procedure, which he has subsequently developed with Geoff Garrett to consider the (pre-Amsterdam) co-decision procedure (Tsebelis, 1995b, 1996; Garrett, 1996; Tsebelis and Garrett, 1997a, 1997b). Figure 3.6 shows a simplification of the Tsebelis–Garrett model, which starts with a series of assumptions about the spatial orientation of the actors in the legislative process:

- To represent QMV, the Council is deemed to have seven members, where a winning qualified majority is five out of seven (an approximation of 62 votes out of 87).
- There is a single dimension of legislative bargaining, between 'more' and 'less' European integration (equivalent to our pro-/anti-Europe dimension, above).
- The actors have 'ideal policy preferences' on this dimension and 'Euclidean preferences' – actors want outcomes that are as close as possible to their ideal policy, regardless of whether this is on the 'more' or 'less' integrationist side of their ideal policy, and they are 'indifferent' between proposals that are equally as far from their ideal position.
- The member states are aligned at different points along this single dimension (at positions 1, 2, 3, 4, 5, 6 and 7 in Figure 3.6).

Table 3.8 Volume of legislative proceedings in the EP, 1988–97

	1988	1989	1990	1991	1992	1993	1994	1995	1996	1997
Consultation	131	128	159	209	243	199	168	164	164	154
(amended or rejected by EP)	(66)	(76)	(105)	(152)	(148)	(120)	(118)	(92)	(90)	(70)
Cooperation, 1st reading	45	55	70	62	70	50	33	26	31	19
(amended or rejected by EP)	(41)	(45)	(52)	(52)	(43)	(45)	(30)	(24)	(26)	(17)
Cooperation, 2nd reading	45	71	49	37	66	46	21	12	34	15
(amended or rejected by EP)	(18)	(48)	(28)	(21)	(35)	(24)	(9)	(11)	(29)	(12)
Co-decision, 1st reading	–	–	–	–	–	5	18	35	34	3
(amended or rejected by EP)						(2)	(16)	(30)	(26)	(28)
Co-decision, 2nd reading	–	–	–	–	–	–	34	19	37	27
(amended or rejected by EP)							(22)	(15)	(22)	(18)
Co-decision, 3rd reading	–	–	–	–	–	–	8	7	9	21
(rejected by EP)							(1)	(1)	(0)	(0)
Assent	14	3	2	3	11	8	11	17	8	15
(assent refused by EP)	(0)	(0)	(0)	(0)	(3)	(1)	(0)	(0)	(0)	(0)
Total legislative proceedings	235	257	280	311	390	308	293	280	317	325
(amended/rejected by EP)	(125)	(169)	(185)	(225)	(229)	(192)	(196)	(173)	(193)	(145)

Source: General Reports on the Activities of the European Communities/European Union.

- The Commission and the EP are more pro-integration than any member state.
- The status quo (SQ) (if legislation is not adopted) is less integrationist than any member state.

These simple assumptions predict rather different legislative outcomes under the different EU procedures.

First, under the *consultation procedure* the final decision is by the Council, but the Commission and the EP will want to propose legislation that is as close to their 'ideal policy positions' as possible. However, with unanimity in the Council, the least integrationist member state is likely to veto any proposal that is not closer to its ideal point (at position 1) than the SQ. As a result, the most likely outcome is legislation that is more integrationist than 1, but closer to 1 than the SQ, for example at the position of member state 2 in the figure (cf. Steunenberg, 1994, Crombez, 1996).

Second, under the *cooperation procedure* the final decision is again with the Council, in the second reading. This time, however, the Council decides whether to accept EP amendments by QMV or reject them (and adopt their own proposals) by unanimity. From the analysis of the consultation procedure, for the Council to agree to a policy by unanimity the legislation must be supported by the least integrationist member state (at position 1), but from the EP's perspective it simply has to gain the

Figure 3.6   *Tsebelis–Garrett model of EP–Council legislative bargaining*

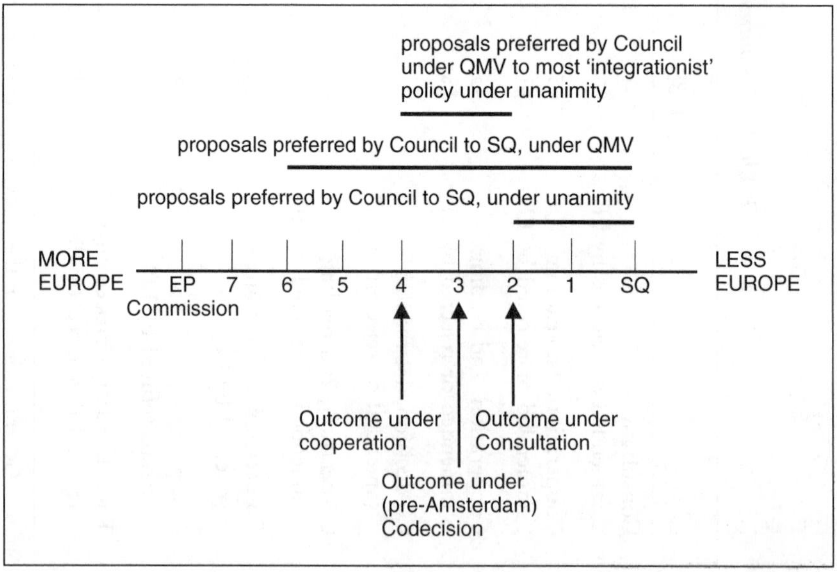

support of member state 3 for the Council to support its proposal by QMV, as member state 3 is 'pivotal' in creating a winning coalition (of states 7, 6, 5, 4 and 3). Member state 3 prefers any policy proposal in the range 6–SQ to SQ. However, if the EP makes a proposal at point 6, the Council will be able to agree at point 2 by unanimity (which member state 3 will support as it is closer to its ideal point than position 6), and consequently reject the EP's proposal. Nevertheless, the EP can make a proposal at position 4, which member state 3 will support, as it is indifferent between positions 4 and 2 (they are equally as far from 3's ideal policy). Hence, Tsebelis (1994) argues that under the cooperation procedure, the EP is 'the conditional agenda-setter': the EP can make proposals that the Council is more likely to support than reject, and hence produce legislation that is more integrationist than under the consultation procedure.

Third, under the *co-decision procedure* as established by the Maastricht Treaty, the EP has the last word instead of the Council, in the third reading. At face value this gives the EP more power than under the cooperation procedure, but the Tsebelis–Garrett model predicts that agenda-setting power under the co-decision procedure lies with the Council rather than the EP. In fact, the Council has an incentive to facilitate a break-down of the Conciliation Committee, so that it can reaffirm its original CP (common position). In this situation the EP only has an 'unconditional veto': it must either accept the Council CP or reject the CP and accept the status quo. As Figure 3.6 shows, however, because the EP is more integrationist than any member state, it will prefer any proposal by the Council to the SQ. Because the Council can adopt the CP by QMV, the CP is likely to be located at position 3: the pivotal actor under this decision rule. The Council can make this 'take-it-or-leave-it' proposal to the EP, which the EP will invariably accept (cf. Crombez, 1997). The likely outcome under co-decision is thus less integrationist than under cooperation (Garrett, 1995b), and Tsebelis (1995b, 1996) consequently argues that by introducing the co-decision procedure, the Maastricht Treaty actually reduced rather than strengthened the power of the EP.

However, this model has been much criticised. For example, the model of the cooperation procedure downplays the role of the Commission since the EP cannot submit something to the Council without the Commission accepting the proposal first (see for example Steunenberg, 1994; Crombez, 1996; Moser, 1996). And Tsebelis' provocative claims relating to the co-decision procedure have been particularly attacked; for example, both Moser (1997) and Scully (1997b, 1997c, 1997d) argue that the EP has more power under co-decision than the Tsebelis model predicts. For example, if conciliation breaks down, the Council is unlikely to go back to its CP from the first reading (which the model assumes) but is instead more likely to return to the position it held immediately prior to conciliation, when it accepted some but not all of the EP amendments made in the second reading. This would have been the legislative outcome had the cooperation procedure been used. Hence, they argue that in the worst case, the EP would be able to secure the same policy that it could have achieved under the cooperation procedure.

Furthermore, if a Joint Text is not agreed in conciliation the Council can still adopt EP amendments in the third reading before submitting a final text to the EP and at this stage the Council can adopt EP amendments that were rejected by the Commission. In the second reading, the Council needs unanimity to adopt EP amendments not supported by the Commission, whereas in the third reading it only requires QMV. Consequently, in the conciliation committee, the EP can focus its bargaining on those amendments that were not supported by the Council unanimity under the second reading, but might command a QMV in the Council in the third reading. As a result, Moser and Scully agree that in making a final offer to the EP, the Council really faces a choice between a position that would have been achieved under cooperation and something that is even closer to the ideal position of the EP.

Defending their model, Tsebelis and Garrett (1997a, 1997b) point out that because of 'backward induction' (taking account of the final round of negotiations at an earlier stage in the process), the Council is unlikely to make the same proposal in the second reading under the co-decision procedure as it would have done under the co-operation procedure. Whereas in the cooperation procedure, the second reading is the final round, under co-decision there are two further rounds of bargaining: in the conciliation committee and the third reading. Consequently, instead of giving way to the EP in the second reading, the Council will stick to its original CP (from the first reading), knowing that this will be the basis for negotiations in the final stages of the co-decision procedure.

However, the Amsterdam Treaty reforms have strengthened the role of the EP within the co-decision procedure. The key change is the inability of the Council to return to its CP in the third reading. The Council is no longer able to make a 'take-it-or-leave-it' proposal to the EP: it can only adopt the Joint Text, reject the text or refuse to act. This effectively makes the conciliation committee the final stage of the bicameral-game, rather than the third reading in the EP. The impact of this change is that the policy outcome is likely to be somewhere between the EP's ideal position and the Council CP from the first reading. Nonetheless, the outcome will still be closer to the Council CP, as the EP will prefer this to the SQ: which is the result if a Joint Text is not adopted by the conciliation committee (Steunenberg, 1997).

Figure 3.7   *EP–Council legislative bargaining on a left–right dimension*

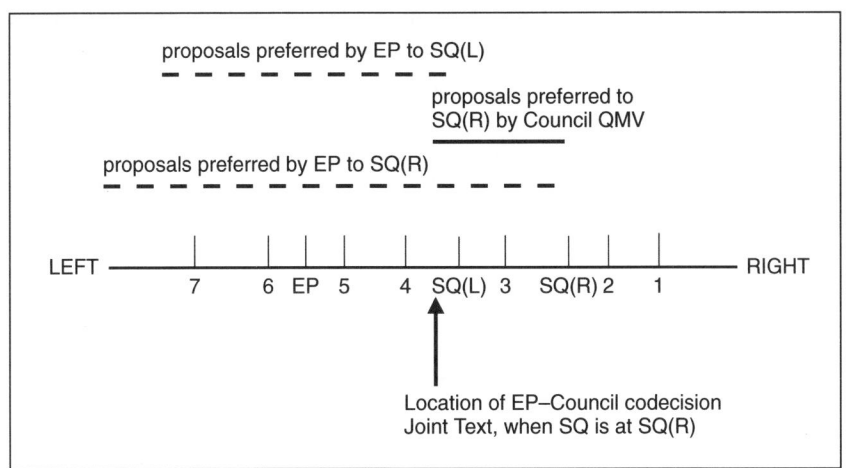

Furthermore, the legislative game between the Council and the EP is completely different if the dimension of competition is the left–right rather than more/less integration. For example, this is the case where legislation is reforming an existing piece of EU legislation instead of creating a new body of EU law. On the left–right dimension, the EP will not always prefer 'something-to-nothing'. A centre–left majority in the EP, as represented by the PES–EPP coalition or the PES as the most powerful party group under absolute-majority voting, will prefer the status quo to a Council proposal if the Council proposal is to the right of the status quo. This situation is shown in Figure 3.7, where the Council cannot construct a qualified majority that the EP prefers to SQ(L) (a hypothetical status quo that is to the left of the pivotal member of the Council under QMV). In this situation, under the pre-Amsterdam co-decision procedure the EP will veto the final submission from the Council, and under the post-Amsterdam co-decision procedure will prefer to see the conciliation committee break down.

But the game is different if the status quo is to the right of the pivotal member of the Council under QMV, as at SQ(R) in Figure 3.7. In this situation, the EP prefers any Council position to the left of SQ(R), and member state 3 prefers any position closer to its ideal point than SQ(R). As a result, in the conciliation committee the EP and the Council are likely to settle on a Joint Text somewhere between member state 4 and member state 3, which would move the EU policy regime slightly leftwards.

Finally, as a result of the introduction of the co-decision, the EP introduced a new rule in its rules of procedure (Rule 78), in a conscious effort to undermine the ability of the Council to reaffirm its CP in the third reading. This rule states that following the breakdown of the conciliation committee the EP will ask the Commission to withdraw the legislation, and if the Commission refuses and the Council decides to reaffirm its CP, the EP leadership will automatically propose a 'motion to reject the Council text' at the next EP plenary session. This rule consequently suggests that faced with a take-it-or-leave-it proposal from the Council, the EP leadership prefers to veto the legislation as a matter of principle, even if the Council proposal is closer to the EP's policy position than the status quo. This is a 'credible threat', as the EP leadership can argue to its members that the EP is involved in a long-term institutional game (to secure a further reform of the co-decision procedure) rather than a short-term policy bargain. The subsequent veto of a reaffirmed CP gave extra force to this threat (see below). And, since the adoption of Rule 78, the Council has not forced the EP vote on a single reaffirmed common position. As a result, the addition of Rule 78 implies that from the EP's point of view, the co-decision procedure as set out in the Maastricht Treaty stops with the conciliation committee.

Empirical evidence of EP power

The real test of these theoretical models is empirical. After the introduction of the cooperation procedure the EP had a significant influence on a number of important pieces of legislation (cf. Earnshaw and Judge, 1997). For example, in the area of health and safety at work, the Council accepted several significant EP amendments to the machine directive (89/392/EEC) and the display screen equipment directive (90/270/EEC) that would probably not have been accepted by the Council under the consultation procedure (Tsebelis, 1995a). Also, in the area of environmental policy, the EP secured significant amendments to the regulation establishing the European Environment Agency (1210/90/EEC), the directive on genetically-modified micro-organisms (90/219/EEC), the directive on the deliberate release of genetically-modified organisms (90/220/EEC), and the directive on car emissions (91/441/EEC) (Judge, Earnshaw and Cowan, 1994; Hubschmid and Moser, 1997). On all these issues, several member states were adamantly opposed to the EP proposals, which generally strengthened EU regulation against national regimes. Nevertheless, as the Tsebelis–Garrett model predicts, in these policy area there is a qualified majority in the Council that prefers to accept the EP proposals than see no EU legislation passed. Also, under the cooperation procedure the EP tried to reject several directives, but these were overturned in the second reading by the Council.

In addition, the EP has had an impact under the co-decision procedure. In July 1994 the EP exercised its third reading veto for the first time. On the draft directive on open network provision in voice telephony (ONP), the Council and the EP were unable to agree a Joint Text in the conciliation committee, and the Council subsequently reaffirmed its CP which was then rejected by an absolute majority in the EP. Also, in March 1995 the EP exercised a third-reading veto on the draft directive on biotechnology inventions. However, this time the situation was different, as in the conciliation committee the EP leadership had agreed to a Joint Text with the Council. But, following a lobbying campaign by the environmental movement, the rank-and-file MEPs (particularly in the PES group) rejected the EP leadership recommendation and voted against the Joint Text in the EP third reading.

On other occasions, the EP leadership would have liked to threaten a rejection of a Council CP, but the EP leadership has not been sure that it could guarantee an absolute majority vote in the third reading (Jacobs, 1997). Indeed, the veto of the ONP Directive was a special case, as the vote was held in the first session of the new EP following the June 1994 EP elections when there was a very high attendance of MEPs (Earnshaw and Judge, 1995). As a result, Miller (1995) estimates that of the first 26 Joint Texts agreed in conciliation committees, 12 (46 per cent) were effectively the same as the Council's CP, 6 (23 per cent) were closer to the EP's second reading position, and 8 (31 per cent) were genuine 'joint' texts. These figures seem to confirm Tsebelis and Garrett's scepticism.

When looking at individual EP amendments, however, the EP is convinced that it is more successful under the co-decision procedure than under the cooperation procedure. According to the EP's figures, as shown in Table 3.9, in the 400 cooperation procedures completed between 1987 and 1997 and the 82 co-decision procedures completed between 1993 and 1997, approximately the same proportion of EP amendments were accepted in the first reading under both procedures. However, the EP was much more successful in the second reading under the co-decision procedure than under the cooperation procedure, and was even able to get several amendments accepted in the third reading.

Consequently, the theoretical arguments and the empirical evidence help explain why in the Amsterdam Treaty negotiations the EP proposed replacing the cooperation procedure with the co-decision procedure and a reform of the co-decision procedure, and why the member states accepted this proposal (European Parliament, 1995a). From the point of view of the EP, it is more able to secure amendments under the co-decision procedure than under the cooperation procedure, and the removal of the third reading of the co-decision procedure strengthens the EP's power to

Table 3.9   *Proportion of EP amendments accepted, up to August 1997*

		400 Cooperation procedures completed between 1 July 1987 and 1 August 1997	82 Co-decision procedures completed between 1 November 1993 and 1 August 1997
Proportion of EP amendments accepted at first reading	By Commission:	54%	53%
	By Council:	41%	43%
Proportion of EP amendments accepted at second	By Commission:	43%	61%
	By Council:	21%	47%
Proportion of EP amendments accepted in conciliation committee	By Council:	—	13%

Source: European Parliament (1997), cf. Kreppel (1997).

bargain with the Council. From the member states' point of view, there was little risk in making these changes. First, the transfer of competences from cooperation to co-decision would reduce the agenda-setting powers of the EP. Second, as a result of the EP's Rule 78, the *de facto* operation of the old co-decision procedure was without the third reading. In this situation, the member states were indifferent between the old co-decision procedure and the proposal to delete the third reading, and so accepted the EP proposal.

Conclusion: complex but familiar politics

The EU has developed a sophisticated and effective legislative system. The Council and the EP are able to cope with the highly technical task of regulating a single market of over 350 million consumers, as well as appease the various national, sectoral and societal interests that are threatened by the process of harmonizing the member states' markets. To meet these challenges, the Council and the EP have evolved into highly organized and decentralized legislative chambers, and have tended to rule through consensus instead of by competition and division.

But, this is functionalist logic: legislative complexity and a plurality of interests produces legislative specialization and consensus. Contemporary theories of legislative behaviour see the internal organization of the Council and the EP and the processes of bargaining and coalition formation as products of the rational self-interests of the EU legislators: the governments in the Council, and the MEPs and party groups in the EP. The governments set up the Council presidency and the MEPs established the EP leadership structures to promote agenda-setting. Similarly, sectoral Councils and EP committees enable EU legislators with similar interests and/or informational requirements to monopolize the legislative agenda in their area, and the party groups enable MEPs and national delegations with similar preferences to reduce the transactions costs of coalition-formation and information-gathering.

Likewise, consensus and oversized majorities in coalition-formation in the Council and EP are less in response to diverse social interests than a result of institutional rules and policy preferences of the actors. On most legislative issues, the EP is required to act by an absolute majority, but with a low attendance at plenary sessions this forces an informal PES–EPP 'grand coalition'. However, this coalition is also fostered by the policy positions of the PES and EPP on the key policy dimension in Council–EP interaction: on the pro-/anti-Europe dimension, these two groups are both moderately pro-European. Similarly, in the Council, the requirement of unanimity on many legislative issues enforces consensus. And, on pro-/anti-Europe issues in the Council, the French and German governments are close to the pivotal member of the Council under qualified-majority voting, which enables them to make proposals that are likely to be accepted by the Council. But, if an issue polarizes the Council along left–right lines, the left-wing governments in France and Germany are too far from the pivotal member of the Council to control the agenda.

Finally, the underlying structure of contestation and conflict, driven by institutional interests and policy preferences, is revealed in bicameral interaction between the Council and the EP. Since the EP has been directly elected, it has tried to maximize its influence in the legislative process: by threatening to delay legislation under the consultation procedure, presenting the Council with take-it-leave-it proposals under the cooperation procedure, and trying to exercise its veto when Council has flaunted EP opinion under the co-decision procedure. The EP has not always won, but compared to many national parliaments in Europe, the EP has been quite successful in inserting amendments into EU legislation that the Council would not have adopted otherwise. As a result, in a relatively short space of time legislative politics in the EU has evolved into something that would be familiar to observers of two-chamber parliaments in other democratic political systems. As with all legislators, EU governments and MEPs seek legislation that satisfies their voters and support groups, furthers their personal careers, or promotes their ideological goals. And to achieve these goals EU legislators organize their institutions and compete/coalesce with each other in similar ways to other legislative systems.

Chapter 4

Judicial Politics

Political theories of constitutions and courts
The EU legal system and the European Court of Justice
'Constitutionalization' of the European Union
Penetration of the EU constitution into rational legal systems
Explanations of the development of the EU constitution
Conclusion: 'unknown destination' or emerging equilibrium?

The EU does not have a 'constitution' in the traditional sense of the word: a set of basic principles and rules in a single codified document. Nevertheless, the EU has gradually become 'constitutionalized' as a result of the interaction between the institutional choices of the national governments, the establishment of constitutional doctrines by the European Court of Justice (ECJ), and the incorporation of these doctrines into domestic constitutions by national courts. To help explain how this 'judicial politics' works, and why it has resulted in a quasi-constitutional framework for the EU, we can look at some theories in political science of constitutional establishment and the power and discretion of courts.

Political theories of constitutions and courts

A common argument in political science is that constitutions are created to resolve 'collective action problems' (Buchanan and Tullock, 1962; Taylor, 1976; Ostrom, 1990). A simply way of illustrating why collective action is often problematic is the so-called 'prisoners' dilemma game' (Luce and Raiffa, 1957; Hardin, 1971), and a version of this game using the example of the EU is shown in Figure 4.1 (cf. Ordeshook, 1992, p. 166).

In this hypothetical example, the EU has adopted the single market programme, which aims to open domestic markets to goods and services from other member states. However, without a constitution the member states are free to decide whether or not to implement the programme, and in making this decision each government calculates the costs and benefits of their available options. Suppose the cost for each government of implementing the single market is $10 million, and that if one member state opens its markets each state will benefit $7 million from the extra trade. Hence, if both member states implement the single market, each will

Figure 4.1   *A collective action problem in the establishment of the single market*

		Member State B	
		Don't implement single market ('defect')	Implement single market ('cooperate')
Member State A	Don't implement single market ('defect')	**Cell I** A = $0 B = $0	**Cell II** A = +$7 B = −$3m
	Implement single market ('cooperate')	**Cell III** A = −$3m B = +$7m	**Cell IV** A = +$4m B = +$4m

benefit $4 million: $(7 × 2) − 10 million. This would be the best ('optimal') collective solution, as it would produce the greatest total benefit: $8 million (cell IV).

However, this outcome is unlikely. Instead, each government will see that their 'best strategy' is to not implement the single market. For example, if member state A chooses not to implement the single market, either member state B will implement the programme, in which case member state A will gain $7 million (cell II), or member state B will not implement the programme, in which case member state A will lose nothing (cell I). Conversely, if member state A implements the single market, member state B can simply choose not to implement the programme, gaining $7 million while member state A loses $3 million. To minimize the risk of losing, and to prevent the other state 'free riding', the only option for member state A is to not implement the single market. Consequently, if each government pursues their best strategy, neither state will implement the programme. But, this is a 'sub-optimal' outcome as the EU as a whole then will miss the collective benefits of cooperation (cell IV). As a result, the prisoners' dilemma illustrates that in a constitution-free world, it may be in the collective interest to cooperate, but it is often in individuals' interests to 'defect'.

However, this collective action problem can be overcome if the parties can set up a 'rule of law'. By establishing that agreements are binding on participants, and by creating a set of mechanisms (courts) for punishing defection, cooperation can be enforced. In our example, if an EU constitution exists, a member state not implementing the single market programme can be challenged before the ECJ. In this situation, both member states have incentives to cooperate, which produces the optimal outcome.

This solution requires that enforcers of law (the courts) are independent from the legislative majority. If a legislative majority is able to determine whether or not there has been a breach of the law, the incentive to co-operate is reduced (Moe, 1990), and, hence, for the rule of law to be credible it must be supported by a 'separation of powers' between the judiciary and the legislative majority (see for example Dicey, 1939 [1885]). As Madison, Hamilton and Jay (1987 [1788], pp. 438–9) extol:

> If it be said that the legislative body are themselves the constitutional judges of their own powers . . . the Constitution could . . . enable the representatives of the people to substitute their *will* to that of their constituents. It is far more rational to suppose that the courts were designed to be an intermediate body between the people and the legislature in order . . . to keep the latter within the limits assigned to their authority.

This separation of powers consequently works because judges are neutral political actors: they exercise 'judgement' instead of 'will' (*ibid.*, p. 440). Or, put another way, the rule of law requires that judges simply follow the formula: 'Rules × Facts = Decisions' (Frank, 1973).

But judges do have 'wills', and constitutions are sufficiently flexible documents to enable them to exercise these wills. As the judicial review of legislative acts has evolved, and as societies have become more litigious, judges have become increasingly involved in making choices between different ideological positions. Consequently, 'judicial preferences', and the court judgements that result from these preferences, are crucial determinants of the final political outcome of the policy process (for example Cohen, 1992). This realization has spawned a growing literature on the comparative study of 'judicial politics' and 'judicial policy-making', of which the role of the European Court of Justice is part (for example Shapiro, 1981; Stone, 1992; Shapiro and Stone, 1994; Volcansek, 1993b).

To explain judicial policy-making, political scientists have begun to develop models of the interaction between governments/legislatures and courts (see for example Miller and Hammond, 1989; McCubbins, Noll and Weingast, 1990; Eskridge, 1991; Gely and Spillar, 1992; Vanberg, 1998). One such model, based on the United States' system of government, is illustrated in Figure 4.2 (cf. Weingast, 1996, pp. 172–4). The model assumes that the legislature, the executive and the court are unitary actors in a unidimensional political space, with ideal policy positions at points L, E and C, respectively (see Chapters 2 and 3 for more explanations of

Figure 4.2   *Court discretion in a separation of powers system*

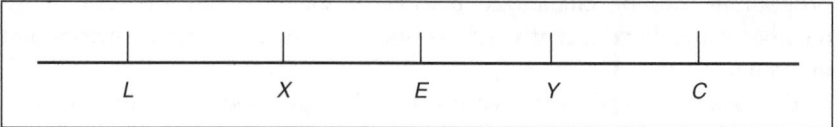

Note: L = position of the legislature; E = position of the executive; C = position of the court; X = position of a policy agreement between L and E; and X–E = E–Y (i.e. the executive is 'indifferent' between X and Y).

spatial analysis). Legislation X is the result of an agreement between the legislature and the executive. However, if the court is free to interpret the legislation when cases are brought before it, it will try to move the political outcome towards C. But politics is an on-going bargaining process, where the legislature and the executive can react to a court's interpretation by passing new legislation to overturn a court's judgement. With this in mind, though, the court can still move the policy outcome to point Y. This is equally as close to the ideal point of the executive as position X. As a result, the executive is 'indifferent' between X and Y, and so has no incentive to introduce new legislation to overturn the court's ruling.

An implication of this type of analysis, however, is that a court's discretion varies inversely with the probability that new legislation can be introduced to repeal its decisions (Ferejohn and Weingast, 1992; Cooter and Ginsburg, 1997). As the ease of adoption of new legislation goes up, the discretion of the court goes down, and as a consequence courts have most freedom in political systems where there are many legislative actors and multiple political preferences. With multiple political parties in a legislature, or where legislation must be approved by two legislative chambers or by an executive and a legislature, there are several 'veto players' that can block changes from the status quo (Tsebelis, 1995c). Hence, in separation-of-powers systems (such as the US and the EU), and where legislation must be adopted by oversized and multiple legislative majorities (as in Germany and the EU), a court can reasonably assume that at least one actor will prefer the court's interpretation to the original legislative intention, and hence block a repeal of the court's decision.

Conversely, the discretion of courts is more restricted under constitutional arrangements where there is a fusion of judicial and legislative powers. For example, in Britain there is no codified constitution and the doctrine of 'parliamentary sovereignty' asserts that no legislative majority can introduce rules or laws that bind a future majority: as a result, parliaments are free to overturn court rulings. Similarly, in France the Constitutional Council is composed of ex-politicians who are highly partisan, and it is consequently more like a 'third chamber of parliament' than an independent 'supreme court' (Stone, 1993, p. 30). Nevertheless, even in these systems the ability of judges to make policy has developed as the practice of judicial review has restrained the legislative authorities (see for example Stone, 1992; Drewry, 1993).

In sum, at the heart of judicial politics is a paradox. On the one hand, constitutions, backed by the rule of law and independent courts and judiciaries, are adopted by free citizens to enforce collective agreements. On the other hand, constitutions enable judges to 'make' law rather than simply 'apply' law. Legislative majorities could design constitutions to limit the power of judges or introduce new legislation to repeal court decisions, but this would undermine the ability of the legal system to preserve property rights and contracts.

The EU legal system and the European Court of Justice

EU law constitutes a separate legal system which is distinct but closely integrated with international law and the legal systems of the EU member states, and which derives from three main sources (cf. Hartley, 1994, pp. 95–189; Shaw, 1996, pp. 179–206).

First, there are the *'primary' acts between the governments of the EU member states*. These include the Treaty of Paris, the Treaty of Rome, the Merger Treaty (establishing a single set of institutions), the Single European Act, the Treaty on European Union (the Maastricht Treaty), the Treaty reforming the European Union Treaty (the Amsterdam Treaty), the four Accession Treaties, the two Budgetary Treaties and the various other Conventions reforming the basic institutional structure of the EU.

Second, there are the *'secondary' legislative and executive acts of the European Parliament, the Council, and the Commission*, that derive from the articles in these Treaties. Article 249 [ex 189] of the EU Treaty sets out five different kinds of secondary acts:

1. *Regulations*, which have general application, and which are binding at both the EU and the national level and are directly applicable in the member states;
2. *Directives*, which are addressed to any number of member states, and which are binding in terms of the result to be achieved but must be transposed into law by national authorities;
3. *Decisions*, which are addressed to member states or private citizens (or legal entities, such as firms), and which are binding in their entirety;
4. *Recommendations* and
5. *Opinions*, which can both be addressed to any member state or citizen, and which are not binding.

However, the description is somewhat misleading, particularly in the distinction between regulations and directives. Directives are often so detailed that they leave little room for manoeuvre in the transposition of the legislation by the member states. Also, through a series of judgements, the ECJ has made directives much closer to regulations, in terms of their ability to confer rights directly on private citizens.

In addition to these formal, written sources of law, a further source of EU law are *general principles of law*. As in all legal systems, primary and secondary sources of law are unable to resolve all legal issues. However, article 220 [ex 164] of the EU Treaty instructs the ECJ to ensure that 'the law is observed', which the ECJ has interpreted to mean that when applying the primary and secondary acts, it can apply general legal principles derived from the EU's basic principles (as expressed in other articles in the Treaty, such as the preamble) and from the constitutions of the member states. There are four main types of these principles:

- *Principles of administrative and legislative legality*, which are drawn from various member states' legal traditions, such as 'legal certainty' (laws cannot apply retroactively, and litigants can have legitimate expectations about EU actions), 'proportionality' (the means to achieve an end should be appropriate), and 'procedural fairness' (such as the right to a hearing and the right of legal professional privilege).
- *Economic freedoms*, which are drawn from the EU Treaty, and include the 'four freedoms' (the freedom of movement of goods, services, capital and persons), the freedom to trade, and the freedom of competition.
- *Fundamental human rights*, which are not defined in the EU Treaty, but are set out in most member states' constitutions and in the European Convention on Human Rights (of the Council of Europe).
- *Political rights*, which have been introduced in 'Declarations' by the member states and are referred to in the EU Treaties, such as 'transparency' (access to information) and 'subsidiarity' (the EU can only act in policy areas not included in the Treaties if the policy aims cannot sufficiently be achieved at the national level).

Composition and operation of the European Court of Justice

To apply these sources of law, the member states created the European Court of Justice, in Luxembourg (not to be confused with the European Court of Human Rights, in Strasbourg, which is the Court of the Council of Europe). The Court has 15 judges, one from each member state, and nine advocates-general. Article 223 [ex 167] of the Treaty sets out how they are appointed:

The Judges and Advocates-General shall be chosen from persons whose independence is beyond doubt and who possess the qualifications required for appointment to the highest judicial offices in their respective countries . . . they shall be appointed by common accord of the governments of the Member States for a term of six years. Every three years there shall be a partial replacement of the Judges.

The staggered terms of office of the judges ensures continuity. However, the other elements of the article are somewhat misleading. In practice, 'by common accord of the member states' means that each member state proposes a judge, who is then ratified by the other member states. Also, by convention, the five large member states each appoint one advocate-general, with the remaining four places rotating between the smaller member states. In addition, the independence and qualifications of the judges is sometimes compromised. There is little evidence of explicitly 'political' appointments to the ECJ, unlike the US Supreme Court, although several member states have tended to appoint 'academic lawyers' instead of recruiting judges from the senior ranks of their judiciary.

When a case comes before the ECJ, the court follows a carefully defined procedure:

- An advocate-general and a judge-*rapporteur* are appointed to gather the information relating to the case and to hold the necessary preparatory oral and written enquiries.
- A public hearing is then held at which the lawyers of the parties' involved present their views orally, and at which the judges and advocates-general question the lawyers.
- The advocate-general appointed to the case submits a report to the judge-*rapporteur*, outlining how the case fits with existing EU law and suggesting a judgement.
- On the basis of the advocate-general's report, the judge-*rapporteur* presents a draft decision to the Court.
- Each judge expresses an opinion on the decision, and the final decision is then taken by a simple majority vote (an odd number of judges has always been ensured, so an extra judge was appointed when there were only 12 member states).

There is a specific order of voting, where the most junior judge (in terms of their order of precedence) votes first and the most senior last. Unlike the US Supreme Court, there are no provisions for judges in the minority to register dissenting opinions, in fact the judges on the ECJ swear an oath to preserve the secrecy of the vote.

The workload of the ECJ has increased dramatically. The number of cases brought before the ECJ was 79 in 1970, 279 in 1980, 384 in 1990 and

354 in 1994. To cope with this increase, the Court of First Instance (CFI) was created in 1989, but the CFI soon became as back-logged as the ECJ. The ECJ also established procedures to allow cases to be handled in a 'chamber' of the court instead of the full plenary – the Court has four chambers of three judges and two chambers of seven judges. The ECJ has also introduced the US practice of 'docket control', whereby it can refuse to hear a case which it thinks should be resolved by a national court. Nevertheless, justice via the ECJ is a long and drawn-out process, with the average length of proceedings in 1994 at 21 months for direct actions, and 18 months for references for preliminary rulings. Various suggestions have been made to speed up this process, such as the creation of 'circuit courts' modelled on the US federal legal system (cf. Weiler, 1993). However, any fundamental reform would require amendment of the EU Treaty.

Jurisdiction of the European Court of Justice

As defined in the EU Treaty, the ECJ has jurisdiction in three main areas (cf. Weatherill and Beaumont, 1995). First, the ECJ can hear *actions brought against member states* to ensure that they comply with their obligations under the EU Treaties and under EU legislation. These actions, known as 'infringement proceedings', can either be brought by the Commission under article 226 [ex 169], by another member state under article 227 [ex 170], or in the area of state aids by either the Commission or a member state under article 88 [ex 93]. Article 228 [ex 171] also asserts that the member state concerned 'shall be required to take the necessary measures to comply with the judgement of the ECJ'. The ability of the ECJ to enforce rulings against the member states is limited. Until the Maastricht Treaty, the Commission was only able to introduce new infringement proceedings against a state in an effort to embarrass it into submission. Nevertheless, the Maastricht Treaty enabled the ECJ to impose financial sanctions on a member state if the Commission brings an additional action for failing to comply with the ECJ's original infringement judgement.

Second, like many national constitutional courts, the ECJ has the power of *'judicial review' of EU legislative and executive acts*. Under article 230 [ex 173], the ECJ can review the legality of acts (other than recommendations and opinions) adopted by the Council, the EP, the Commission and the European Central Bank, and acts of the EP intended to produce legal effects on third parties. Under this article, any member state, the Council or the Commission can bring an action to the ECJ under this article either on the grounds of lack of competence, or because of an infringement of the Treaty or procedural requirement. In contrast, the EP, the Court of Auditors and the European Central Bank can only bring actions to protect their own prerogatives. Finally, private citizens can bring actions against a decision by the EU institutions which is of direct concern to them. A further aspect of the ECJ's power of judicial review is the ability to hear actions against the EU institutions for failing to act when they have been called upon by the EU Treaty or a piece of secondary legislation (such as the delegation of powers to the Commission), under article 232 [ex 175]. These actions can be brought by any member state or EU institution.

Third, under article 234 [ex 177], the ECJ has jurisdiction to give *preliminary rulings on references by national courts*. Under this procedure, national courts can ask for the ECJ to make a judgement on any case brought before them that relates to any aspect of EU law, and the ECJ ruling is then used by the national courts in their own judgement on the case in hand. At face value this suggests that it is the national courts that give the final ruling on many cases of EU law, which was probably the intention of the drafters of the Treaty of Rome. In practice, however, the jurisdiction of the ECJ under this article has been far more significant for the development of EU law and the constitutionalization of the EU system than the ECJ's jurisdiction in any other area. Article 234 judgements constitute the majority of all ECJ judgements. On the one hand, this reveals a high penetration of EU law into the national legal systems (see below); on the other hand, by enabling national courts to enforce ECJ judgements, the preliminary references procedure has the effect of making national courts the lower tier of an integrated EU court system, and the ECJ the quasi-supreme court at its pinnacle.

The ECJ has jurisdiction in a number of other miscellaneous areas under which a small number of cases are heard each year. These include: actions for damages against the EU institutions by either a member state or a private individual, under article 235 [ex 178]; and employment disputes between the EU and the staff of the various EU institutions, under article 236 [ex 179]. These 'staff disputes' general account for about 8 per cent of all cases before the ECJ.

In sum, the Treaty of Rome created a new legal system and a powerful supranational court to enforce this system. Nevertheless, when signing the Treaties the 'founding fathers' probably did not realize the potential long-term implications of their actions: the gradual 'constitutionalization' of the EU through the operation of the legal system and the judgements of the ECJ.

'Constitutionalization' of the European Union

In a now renowned statement, in a judgement in 1986, the ECJ described the founding Treaties as a 'constitutional charter' (case 294/83 *Parti*

Ecologiste 'Les Verts' v. *European Parliament* [1986] ECR 1339). This was the first time the Court had used the term 'constitution' to describe the Treaties, although academic lawyers had been pointing to the constitutional status of the Treaties for some time (see for example Green, 1969). Nevertheless, the EU constitution lies less in the founding Treaties than in the gradual 'constitutionalization' of the EU legal system (Stein, 1981; Hartley, 1986; Mancini, 1989; Shapiro, 1992; Weiler, 1991, 1997a). The two central principles of this constitution are the *direct effect* and the *supremacy* of EU law, which are classic doctrines in 'federal' legal systems.

Direct-effect: EU law as 'the law of the land' for national citizens

The direct effect of EU law means that *individual citizens have rights under EU law that must be upheld by national courts*, and this makes EU law 'the law of the land' in the EU member states (Weiler, 1991, p. 2413). The ECJ first asserted the direct effect of EU law in a landmark judgement in 1963 (case 26/62 *Van Gend en Loos* v. *Nederlandse Administratie der Belastingen* [1963] ECR 1). In this case, a private firm sought to invoke EC law against the Dutch customs authority in a Dutch court, and the Dutch court made a reference to the ECJ for a preliminary ruling on whether EC law applied. The ECJ ruled that the individual did have the right to invoke EC law because 'the Community constitutes a new legal order . . . the subjects of which comprise not only member states but also their nationals'. This was accepted by the Dutch court. This ruling meant that direct effect applies to primary Treaty articles (in this case article 25 [ex 12]), and in subsequent judgements, the ECJ has expanded the doctrine to all categories of legal acts of the EU. However, direct effect works differently for regulations and directives. Regulations have 'vertical' and 'horizontal' direct effect: enabling citizens to defend their rights against both the state (vertical) and other individuals or legal entities (horizontal). In contrast, the ECJ has taken the view (against the opinion of several advocates-generals and academic commentators) that directives only have vertical direct effect, because they must be transposed into national law by the EU member states (case 152/84 *Marshall I* [1986] ECR 723; case C-91/92 *Faccini Dori* [1994] ECR I-3325).

However, to compensate for this lack of the horizontal direct effect of directives, the ECJ has developed the doctrine of 'states' liability'. This implies that the state is liable for all infringements of EU directives. For example, when an Italian firm became insolvent and did not make redundancy payments to its employees, the ECJ found that the Italian state should foot the bill because it had not transposed directive 80/987 properly, which required the establishment of guarantee funds for redundancy compensation (cases C-6,9/90 *Francovich I* [1991] ECR I-5357).

The central implication of direct effect is that EU law is more like domestic law than international law. The subjects of international law are states: if a state fails to abide by its obligations under an international convention, individuals cannot invoke the convention in their national courts unless the convention has been incorporated into domestic law. In contrast to international law, the subjects of domestic law are private citizens who can invoke their rights in domestic courts.

Unsurprisingly, the establishment of the doctrine of direct effect led to a dramatic increase in the number of cases brought by individuals in their national courts to defend their rights under EU law. The effect, as Weiler (1991, p. 2414) argues, was that:

> individuals . . . became the 'guardians' of the legal integrity of Community law within Europe similar to the way that individuals in the United States have been the principal actors in ensuring the vindication of the Bill of Rights and other federal law.

Supremacy: EU law as 'the higher Law of the Land'

Unlike the US Constitution, the EU Treaties do not contain a 'supremacy clause' stating that when there is a conflict between national and EU law, EU law is supreme. However, shortly after the establishment of direct effect, the ECJ asserted the supremacy of EU law, and like direct effect this doctrine was confirmed and reinforced in a series of subsequent cases.

The landmark judgement on this doctrine was in the case of *Costa* v. *ENEL* in 1964 (case 6/64 [1964] ECR 585). An Italian court asked the ECJ to give a preliminary ruling on a case where there was a clear contradiction between Italian and EC law, and the ECJ duly argued that:

> By creating a Community of unlimited duration, having its own institutions, its own personality, [and] its own legal capacity . . . the member states have limited their sovereign rights, albeit within limited fields, and have thus created a body of law which binds both their nationals and themselves. The integration into the laws of each member state of provisions which derive from the Community . . . make it impossible for the states, as a corollary, to accord precedence to a unilateral and subsequent measure over a legal system accepted by them on a basis of reciprocity.

In other words, the logic of the Court was that the doctrine of supremacy was implicit in the transfer of competences to the EU level and the direct effect of EU law.

However, EU law is superior over national law only in those areas where there is EU law. Nevertheless, as the competences of the EU have expanded into almost all areas of public policy, the application of supremacy no longer applies to the 'limited fields' to which the ECJ referred in 1964. And, through successive judgements, the ECJ has established that supremacy applies to all EU norms, whether an article of the EU Treaties, a secondary act of the EU institutions (no matter how minor, such as administrative regulations of the Commission), and even a 'general principle of EU law' as defined by the ECJ.

As a result, the supremacy doctrine further distanced the EU legal system from international law. Direct effect was insufficient by itself to establish the EU legal system as a system of domestic law. Where international conventions are incorporated into domestic law, individuals can invoke them in domestic courts, but if a domestic legislature subsequently adopts a national law that contravenes the international convention the provisions of the international law no longer apply. With the supremacy of EU law, in contrast, national legislative majorities are permanently bound by the provisions of EU law. As Weiler thus concludes: 'parallels of this kind of constitutional order . . . may be found only in the internal constitutional order of federal states' (Weiler, 1991, p. 2415). By establishing the dual doctrines of the direct effect and supremacy of EU law, the ECJ had transformed the EU from an international organization to a quasi-federal political system.

'Integration through law' and 'economic constitutionalism'

The application of these basic doctrines enabled the Court to play a central role in the economic and political integration of the EU system (cf. Weatherill and Beaumont, 1995, pp. 383–880). For example, in the area of economic freedoms, article 28 [ex 30] states simply that 'quantitative restrictions on imports and all measures having equivalent effect shall be prohibited between the member states'. This article seems pretty innocuous. However, through a series of judgements the ECJ has transformed the EU's economic system (see for example Alter and Meunier-Aitsahalia, 1994).

In 1974, in the *Dassonville* decision (case 8/74 [1974] ECR 837), the ECJ declared illegal any national rule that is 'capable of hindering, actually or potentially, directly or indirectly, intra-Community trade'. These hindrances not only cover quotas and other restrictions on imports, but also internal rules affecting the competitive position of imported goods. The implication of this interpretation became clear with the *Cassis de Dijon* judgement in 1979 (case 120/78 [1979] ECR 837). In this decision, the Court ruled that a German law that specified that a 'liquor' must have an alcohol content of at least 25 per cent cannot prevent the marketing of the French drink *Cassis de Dijon* in Germany as a liquor, which has an alcohol content of less than 20 per cent. This is known as the principle of 'mutual recognition': that any product that can be legally sold in one member state can be legally sold anywhere in the EU. Mutual recognition subsequently became one of the basic principles in the establishment of the single market (see Chapter 8).

This interpretation of article 30 is inherently 'deregulatory'. It obliges member states to delete numerous social and economic rules that in many cases were established as expressions of particular social and ideological preferences. The effect is a specific type of 'economic constitution' of the EU: where there is competition between different national regulatory regimes, which has the potential of facilitating a 'race to the bottom' (cf. Chalmers, 1995; Joerges, 1994; Streit and Mussler, 1995; Ehlermann and Hancher, 1995; Maduro, 1997) (see Chapter 8).

State-like properties: external sovereignty and internal coercion

As we discussed in Chapter 1, the EU is not a state. In particular, the EU does not have external sovereignty in the international legal system to act independently and above the interests of the member states, neither does the EU have the legitimate monopoly on the use of coercion to enforce its decisions. Nevertheless, the ECJ has been instrumental in developing 'state-like' properties for the EU in both these areas.

First, on the external side, the EU has the formal power to make treaties with third parties under article 133 [ex 113] (common commercial policy) and article 310 [ex 238] (association agreements). However, even in these limited fields most member states originally felt that these articles merely provided for the Commission to negotiate agreements on behalf of the member states, and that sovereignty remained with the member states. Nevertheless, in 1971 the ECJ established the principle that in making agreements with third countries, the EU is sovereign over any existing or future acts between the individual member states and the third countries involved (case 22/70 *ERTA* [1971] ECR 263). In the same judgement, the Court argued that the jurisdiction of the EU in the international sphere covers *all* areas of EU competence, not just those covered by articles 133 and 310. In other words, in one stroke the ECJ conferred new treaty-making powers to the EU and deprived the member states of their own independent powers relating to EU competences.

The ECJ's interpretation of the legal sovereignty of the EU in the international sphere was further expressed in two Opinions on the proposed 'European Economic Area' between the EU and the European Free Trade Area (EFTA) (opinion 1/91 *EEA I* [1991] ECR I-6079; opinion 1/92 *EEA II* [1992] ECR I-2821). The original proposal for the EEA, which was approved by the EU and EFTA states, provided for the establishment of the EEA as a new type of legal order, partially merged with the EU, but no longer under the sole judicial authority of the ECJ. However, the ECJ rejected this idea out of hand. The Court again argued that the EU Treaty is a 'constitutional charter of a Community based on the rule of law', and consequently that the proposed EEA arrangement would compromise the independence and sovereignty of the EU. The ECJ approved a revised version of the EEA agreement after it gave jurisdiction over the EEA exclusively to the ECJ (even over the national courts of the EFTA states). What was remarkable about this episode was that the supposedly sovereign nation-states of the EU accepted the ECJ's assertions and duly revised the international Treaty.

Second, on the internal side, article 10 [ex 5] of the EC section of the EU Treaty instructs the member states to 'take all appropriate measures . . . to ensure the fulfilment of their obligations arising out of the Treaty'. Most member states originally assumed that this article took effect only in relation to the other Treaty articles and to EU law. However, the ECJ has used this article as a substitute for the lack of direct enforcement powers of the EU system (cf. Shaw, 1996, pp. 208–13; Weatherill and Beaumont, 1995, pp. 192–218). For example, the ECJ has ruled that member states must adapt all relevant national rules to the requirements of EU law (cases 205–215/82 *Deutsche Milchkontor GmbH* v. *Germany* [1983] ECR 2633), and that article 10 applies to all state organs at all levels of government (Case C-8/88 *Germany* v. *Commission* [1990] ECR I-2321).

Furthermore, the ECJ has broadened the definition of the types of actions a member state must use to enforce EU law. For example, in 1997 the ECJ found that the French government should have used the state security forces more effectively to ensure the free movement of goods in the internal market (case C-265/95 *Commission* v. *France* [1997]). The Court recognized that member states 'retain exclusive competence as regards the maintenance of public order and the safeguarding of internal security', but the ECJ argued that:

> it falls to the Court . . . to verify . . . whether the member state concerned has adopted appropriate measures for ensuring the free movement of goods. . . . [In the present case] the French police were

either not present or did not intervene . . . the actions in question were not always rapid . . . [and] only a very small number of persons has been identified and prosecuted.

In other words, the EU does not need a police force of its own to have access to coercive powers. The EU simply obliges the member states to take all measures that are reasonable to enforce EU law, including the use of security forces.

The EU constitution is not codified like the constitutions of most member states. Ironically the member states, not 'the people', remain the sovereign 'masters' of the Treaties.

Nevertheless, the EU constitution exists in a 'formal-legal' sense: in terms of the rules governing the operation and powers of the EU institutions; and the quasi-federal rights the EU grants to individuals and member states (cf. Grimm, 1995; Habermas, 1995). And, the EU constitution exists in a 'social' sense, in terms of the acceptance of the EU system and the doctrines established by the Court of Justice by national legal and constitutional authorities.

Penetration of the EU constitution into national legal systems

The penetration of EU law into national legal systems has developed both quantitatively and qualitatively. On the quantitative side there has been a substantial increase in the use of the article 234 [ex 177] procedure for requesting preliminary rulings from the ECJ by national courts, and on the qualitative side national courts have gradually accepted the existence and supremacy of the EU legal system over national law and constitutions.

Quantitative: national courts' use of ECJ preliminary rulings

Figure 4.3 shows the absolute number of article 234 [ex 177] references by all national courts to the ECJ in each year, from the date of the first reference in 1961 to 1994. In this period, whereas the EU grew from six member states to 12, the number of references to the ECJ from the higher and lower national courts of these states grow from 1 to 2 per year to approximately 180 to 190 per year. The period of rapid growth in the 1970s immediately followed the establishment of the doctrines of direct effect and supremacy, which encouraged national courts to use the references procedure to strengthen their position in the domestic political systems, and encouraged private litigants to use the procedure to invoke their rights in the domestic courts (see below).

Figure 4.3   *Growth of Article 234 [ex 177] references*

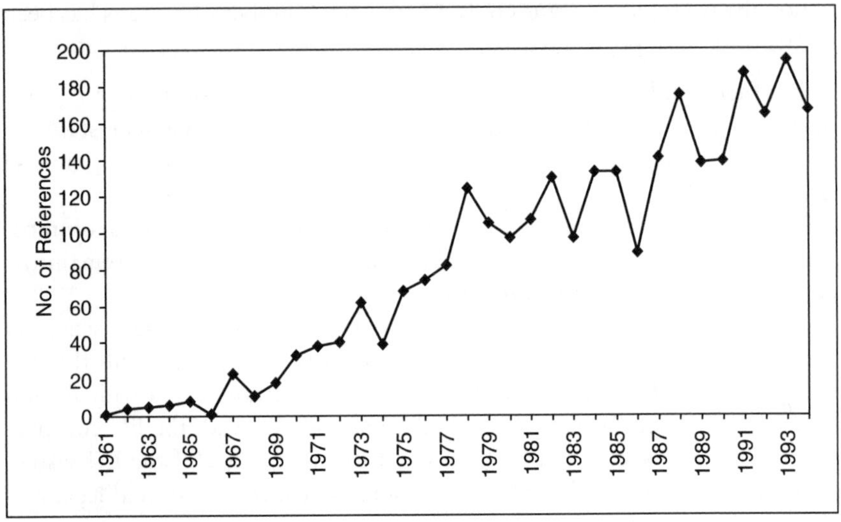

Source: Stone Sweet and Brunell (1998a, 1998b).

However, not all national courts use the references system to the same extent. As Table 4.1 shows, the number of references from each member state has risen over time, and the figures suggest a 'learning curve', with the original member states making more references in each period than the member states that joined later. Nevertheless, there are several other factors cross-cutting this trend. First, within each wave of EU members, the larger states made more references than the smaller states: Germany, France and Italy made more references than The Netherlands, Belgium and Luxembourg; the United Kingdom made more than Denmark and Ireland; and Spain made more than Portugal (cf. Stone Sweet and Brunell, 1998a, p. 79). Second, despite the learning curve, British courts made less references in the early 1990s than Dutch or Belgian courts, which perhaps reflects the sceptical attitudes towards the EU of the public and elite in Britain (Golub, 1996a). However, in Ireland, Portugal and Luxembourg, where the publics and elites are strongly pro-European, the courts also made few references to the ECJ.

Finally, the subject matter of the references to the ECJ from national courts has changed significantly. As Table 4.2 shows, in the whole period between 1971 and 1995 most references related to the Common Agricultural Policy. However, by the mid-1990s, issues relating to the operation of the internal market – such as the free movement of goods, social security and the free movement of workers, taxes, freedom of establishment, and the approximation of national laws – comprised almost half of all

Table 4.1 *Number of Article 234 [ex 177] references by member state*

| Member state | Average annual references in each period | | | |
	1961–73	1974–80	1981–87	1988–94
Germany	9.8	28.7	34.4	46.4
France	1.5	12.3	29.1	25.9
Italy	1.5	12.4	9.6	23.6
Netherlands	3.6	14.3	17.9	19.7
Belgium	2.2	10.3	12.7	19.7
United Kingdom	–	3.9	7.0	15.4
Greece	–	–	2.7	1.7
Spain	–	–	0.3	5.3
Denmark	–	1.1	2.4	3.6
Ireland	–	1.3	1.6	1.4
Portugal	–	–	0.0	1.6
Luxembourg	0.4	0.3	2.0	1.7

Source: Stone Sweet and Brunell (1998a, 1998b).

references to the ECJ. This consequently reflects the fact that the majority of laws governing the regulation of the market are set at the European rather than the national level (see Chapter 8).

Qualitative: national courts' acceptance of the EU legal system

Despite the above, not all national courts capitulated to the emerging constitutionalization of the EU at the same time (Mattli and Slaughter, 1998a, 1998b). The Benelux states accepted the direct effect and supremacy of EU law almost immediately upon the establishment of these doctrines: since the 1920s, Belgian courts have accepted that international law is inherently part of Belgian law, and saw their role *vis-à-vis* the EU and the ECJ as a logical extension of this practice (Bribosia, 1998). Dutch courts applied a similar norm, and the 1983 reform of the Dutch constitution introduced provisions explicitly referring to the application of EU law over Dutch law (Claes and de Witte, 1998).

Like the Benelux courts, the German Constitutional Court (*Bundesverssungsgericht*) originally acknowledged the ECJ's proclamation that the EU system constituted 'an autonomous legal order' (Kokott, 1998), and also accepted the supremacy of EU law, but in the narrow form of 'priority in application' rather than the more general 'priority of validity'. Nevertheless, the German Constitutional Court retreated from this position

Table 4.2   *Proportion of Article 234 [ex 177] references by subject matter*

| Subject matter | Percentage of total references in each period | | | | |
	1971–75	1976–80	1981–85	1986–90	1991–95
Agriculture	30.9	25.1	20.3	19.6	12.5
Free movement of goods	19.6	17.1	19.8	18.5	14.9
Social security	12.5	10.3	8.4	9.1	10.0
Taxes	2.0	4.6	4.8	8.0	8.5
Competition	6.3	3.6	4.5	5.0	8.2
Social provisions	0.3	1.1	3.7	4.2	8.8
Freedom of establishment	2.6	2.3	2.7	5.6	6.6
Approximation of laws	0.3	1.9	4.9	3.8	5.1
Free movement of workers	4.3	2.0	4.1	5.0	3.2
External economic relations	3.4	3.0	3.3	1.7	3.2
Transport	6.0	1.4	1.3	1.5	2.9
Environment	0.0	0.4	1.6	0.9	2.0
Total references in each period	352	702	754	816	1084
Per cent of all references in 1971–95	9.5	18.9	20.3	22.0	29.2

Source: Stone Sweet and Brunell (1998a, 1998b).

when in 1974 it ruled that where there is a conflict between national and EU law, the German Court can decide the limits on the supremacy of EU law. The implication of this ruling became clear with the landmark (*Brunner*) judgement of the German Constitutional Court in 1993 on the constitutionality of the Maastricht Treaty.

In the *Brunner* judgement, the German Court ruled that the German Basic Law limits the transfer of powers to the EU, and the Court argued that the EU is a *sui generis* organization which is not a 'state' based on democratic norms. It argued that because the German Constitutional Court is commanded under the German constitution to defend the basic rights and principles of democracy as set out in the German Basic Law, the German Court has the jurisdiction to declare acts of the EU *ultra vires* if they breach the German Basic Law (but it will seek to cooperate with the

ECJ if faced with such a prospect). Having said this, the German Court declared that the Maastricht Treaty can be ratified in Germany because the German parliament maintains the right to transfer (or withdraw) German government competences to the EU. The Court warned, however, that the EU can only legitimately become a 'state' if it is fully democratic: with the institutions of parliamentary democracy, and a single *demos* (Weiler, 1995).

The initial acceptance of the direct effect and supremacy doctrines by the Italian courts was more problematic (Catabia, 1998; Laderchi, 1998). Direct effect was accepted in 1973, but the highest Italian court refused to accept the supremacy of EU law and did not make a preliminary reference to the ECJ for four years following the *Costa* v. *ENEL* judgement. The Italian Court maintained this position by arguing that Italian and EU law are separate and parallel legal orders. Nevertheless, highly conscious of its almost complete isolation amongst EU courts, in 1984 the Italian Constitutional Court ruled that the EU does not have the power to repeal Italian law, but where EU law and national law apply in the same area, Italian judges should choose to apply EU law. In other words, this was a conditional acceptance of supremacy. Laderchi (*ibid.*, p. 166) hence points out that: 'The Court was cheating when it said that the results of its new doctrines coincided with the requirements set by the ECJ'.

In the United Kingdom, British courts accepted direct effect immediately upon accession to the EU in 1973. However, it was more difficult to accept the supremacy of EU law, as this doctrine inherently conflicts with the central concept of the British constitution, of 'parliamentary sovereignty' – that acts of parliament immediately override all existing law or legislation (Craig, 1998). Nevertheless, in 1990 the House of Lords found a way to reconcile parliamentary sovereignty and supremacy. On a reference from the House of Lords, the ECJ ruled that a 1988 act of the British parliament was in breach of EU law, and the House of Lords accepted this judgement on the grounds that in passing the 1972 act of accession to the EU, the British parliament had voluntarily accepted the EU legal system of which the supremacy of EU law is a central part. The House of Lords also argued that this does not compromise parliamentary sovereignty, as a future British parliament could repeal this act of accession.

In France there was a marked difference in how and when the EU legal system was accepted by the Cour de Cassation (the highest civil court) and the Conseil d'Etat (the highest administrative court) (Plötner, 1998). The French constitution combines a monist approach to international law, but a philosophy of parliamentary sovereignty. Initially, the French courts interpreted this combination to mean that EU law is supreme over acts of parliament prior to the Treaty of Rome, but that the French Courts are free to determine whether subsequent acts are in breach of EU law.

However, in 1975 the Cour de Cassation accepted that in all cases EU law is superior to French national law. The Conseil d'Etat, on the other hand, did not reach the same conclusion until 1990 and, in so doing, the Conseil d'Etat argued that EU legal supremacy only applies because *all* international Treaties ratified by the French parliament are sovereign over French law. In other words, the EU constitution was justified through the lens of national rather than European constitutional norms.

In sum, EU law is accepted as an integral part of national legal systems and is sovereign over national law. Nevertheless, in several states the highest national courts maintain that this is conditional on national constitutional norms: for example that parliaments remain sovereign to revoke the supremacy of EU law by withdrawing the transfer of sovereignty to the EU (as in Germany, Britain and France). One could argue that this solution is driven primarily by the desire of national courts not to renounce their previous positions towards the EU, or to declare basic constitutional principles null and void (such as parliamentary sovereignty in the British case). Only in Germany has a constitutional court withdrawn from a previously unconditional acceptance of supremacy.

Explanations of the development of the EU constitution

Why did the ECJ develop the doctrines of direct effect and supremacy, and why was this process accepted by the member state governments and the national courts? Scholars of the EU have come up with five different answers: (1) the structural and cultural formalism of law; (2) the interests and behaviour of the European Court of Justice; (3) the interests and behaviour of national courts; (4) the interests and behaviour of transnational litigants and the transnational legal community; and (5) the interests and behaviour of national governments.

Legal formalism and legal cultures

Legal scholars of the EU have traditionally emphasised the internal logic of law and the legal process. As Weiler (1994, p. 525) points out: 'The formalistic claim is that judicial process rests above or outside politics, a neutral arena in which courts scientifically interpret the meaning of policy decided by others'. In other words, the ECJ simply applies EU law as set out in the EU Treaties and in secondary legislation, without any conscious desire to promote its own power or institutional interests. Nevertheless, the EU constitution develops because the EU legal system has its own internal 'integrationist' logic. The ECJ promotes the integration of the EU legal system, for example by establishing direct effect and supremacy, simply as a logical extension of the basic EU Treaty goal of 'ever closer union'. Also, there is an *effect utile* in the legal workings of the EU, which compels the ECJ to promote legal integration to prevent the EU political system from becoming ineffective and unworkable (Cappelletti, Seccombe and Weiler, 1986).

In the same vein, legal formalist explanations posit that national courts were eager to find ways to reconcile their previous jurisprudence with the emerging EU legal system, and through the preliminary references system the ECJ provided national courts with the appropriate argumentation and rationale for them to accept the new doctrines in the national legal systems (cf. Wincott, 1995). Also, in the legal-formalism approach, variations in the use of the preliminary references system and the dates of acceptance of the ECJ doctrines result from variations in national legal 'cultures' and 'doctrines' (Chalmers, 1997; de Witte, 1998; Mattli and Slaughter, 1998a, 1998b; Maher, 1998; Stone Sweet, 1998). On the cultural side, different systems of training judges, different promotion systems, and different career paths produce different patterns of behaviour and reasoning by judges – such as formal versus pragmatic, deductive versus inductive, and abstract versus consensual. Also, each system has a different relationship between administrative, constitutional and common law courts, and different rules, traditions and powers of judicial review. On the doctrinal side, whether a state has a monist or dualist tradition in relation to international law, the place of fundamental rights in domestic constitutions, and how the concept of 'sovereignty' is defined, all affect the relationship between national legal norms and the EU constitution.

Nevertheless, legal-formalist approaches have some important shortcomings. At an empirical level, the doctrines of supremacy and direct effect are not simply logical extensions of the EU Treaty: if the federalization of the EU had been intended from the outset, the EU Treaty would have contained a 'supremacy clause' like other federal constitutions. Also, many national courts were not immediately convinced of the ECJ's justification of direct effect and supremacy (cf. Alter, 1998a, pp. 230–4). From the general study of courts and judicial politics, as we discussed, we know that the institutional interests of courts and the personal policy preferences of judges also drive judges' actions. In a sense, the structural and cultural logic of the law are simply another set of constraints within which courts and judges secure these aims. Consequently, at a theoretical level, explanations of the emergence of the EU constitution must also take account of the institutional and policy incentives of European and national judges, and the strategic motivations of other actors in the systems.

'Activism' by the European Court of Justice

In direct contrast to the legal-formalism approach, an alternative explanation sees the ECJ as an explicitly 'political' actor (for example Rasmussen, 1986; Mancini, 1989; Volcansek, 1993a; Weiler, 1981, 1991). The pioneering author from this perspective was Eric Stein (1981, p. 1), who opened his ground-breaking article with an oft-repeated quote:

> Tucked away in the fairyland Duchy of Luxembourg and blessed, until recently, with benign neglect by the powers that be and the mass media, the Court of Justice of the European Communities has fashioned a constitutional framework for a federal-type structure in Europe.

In this explanation the ECJ is a strategic actor, with specific *institutional interests* and *policy preferences* that it has promoted and protected. In terms of institutional interests, the ECJ wants to strengthen its position *vis-à-vis* the other EU institutions, and, hence, the Court has consciously sought to develop its powers of judicial review of Commission and Council actions. The Court has also used preliminary references by national courts to develop a 'policy-making' role in areas where the Treaty is vague or legislation is absent or incomplete, and has sought to establish a jurisdiction for itself in determining the division of competences between the national and EU systems.

In terms of its policy preferences, the ECJ has promoted European integration at every opportunity. The pursuit of this goal stems from the assumption that further economic and political integration will eventually turn the ECJ into an all-powerful supreme court – perhaps like the US Supreme Court. To this end, the Court has asserted the 'autonomy' of EU law from the very beginning, implying that the EU legal order is fundamentally different from international law. Also, the doctrines of direct effect and supremacy smack of an explicit federalist plan, and similarly, in establishing the principle of 'mutual recognition' the Court knew that the doctrine would be a powerful motor of economic integration (Alter and Meunier-Aitsahalia, 1994).

Nevertheless, this approach also has its limitations. At an empirical level, the 'activism' of the ECJ has not been linear (Chalmer, 1997). The ECJ has responded to the pace of the integration process, and has been sensitive to anti-Court feelings amongst certain national governments, but why did it take so long to establish the principle of mutual recognition? The strategic behaviour of the ECJ must be analysed in terms of the opportunities and constraints the court faces: from the institutional and cultural factors of the EU system, and in the face of the competing interests and preferences of the member state governments, national courts and private litigants.

Strategic national courts: judicial empowerment, national political contexts and inter-court competition

Related to this approach are explanations that see the constitutional development of the EU as a product of the strategic behaviour of national courts (see for example Burley and Mattli, 1993; Weiler, 1993; 1994; Alter, 1996, 1998b; Golub, 1996a; Mattli and Slaughter, 1998a, 1998b; Stone Sweet and Brunell, 1998a, 1998b). For both the ECJ and national courts, EU law is a 'mask' for the promotion of political goals (Burley and Mattli, 1993, pp. 72–3). Unlike the ECJ, however, national courts are not interested in the emergence of an EU constitution to promote the policy goal of European integration. Instead, national courts seek to use the EU legal system to secure their interests and policy preferences within their own national legal and political contexts. There are three different variants of this 'national courts approach'.

First, several scholars argue that national courts have been 'empowered' by the emergence of the EU constitution (for example Weiler, 1991, 1994; Burley and Mattli, 1993). In many domestic European political systems the powers of judicial review are weak, parliaments are sovereign, and governments have substantial administrative and political resources at their disposal. Consequently, national courts welcome the direct effect and supremacy of EU law and actively use the preliminary references system to strengthen their hand in the national policy process. At one extreme of this argument, the ECJ and its rulings are instruments of national courts in promoting the rule of law, judicial review and the protection of individual rights against the domestic state. For example, the ECJ has often been asked by national courts to make preliminary rulings on issues that are parochial national court obsessions (Volcansek, 1986). Alternatively, national courts are in cahoots with the ECJ to strengthen the judicial system against national governments at both the European and national levels of the EU political system. In the other words, the ECJ consciously seeks to appeal to national courts' self-interest (Weiler, 1994; Mancini, 1989).

Second, a more subtle variant of this explanation suggests that courts in different national settings face different political constraints on their behaviour (Golub, 1996a; Mattli and Slaughter, 1998a, 1998b). As Table 4.3 shows, in each member state there are different levels of public support for European integration, levels of awareness of the ECJ, levels of satisfaction with the ECJ, and general satisfaction with courts and judges (Caldeira and Gibson, 1995; Gibson and Caldeira, 1995, 1998). These different patterns of opinion constitute different policy preferences amongst national electorates and politicians. If courts ignore these preferences they risk provoking parliamentary challenges to their judicial autonomy and undermining the public acceptance of courts and the

Table 4.3 *National political contexts facing the ECJ*

Member state	General support for the EU		Level of satisfaction with courts	
	Support for EU membership	Aware of the European Court of Justice	Satisfied with the European Court of Justice	Satisfied with the National High Court
Belgium	64	31	39	47
Denmark	61	28	53	77
France	56	18	24	40
Germany (West)	59	38	41	73
Germany (East)	59	39	19	33
Greece	68	10	26	50
Ireland	75	26	61	58
Italy	71	8	32	42
Luxembourg	76	48	56	58
The Netherlands	80	16	54	79
Portugal	64	15	30	39
Spain	56	13	29	45
United Kingdom	48	12	60	65

Note: The responses for the first two questions are from the *Eurobarometer* 33 survey, in Spring 1993. The questions were as follows: *Support for EU membership*, 'Generally speaking do you think that (your country's) membership of the European Union is a good thing, a bad thing or neither good nor bad?' (the table shows the per cent of responses of 'a good thing'); and *Awareness of the European Court of Justice*, 'Which institutions of the European Union have you heard of? Please give me the names you remember' (the table shows the per cent of respondents who named the European Court of Justice). The responses to the *Level of Satisfaction with Courts* questions are from the *Eurobarometer* 32 survey, in Autumn 1992, and the *Eurobarometer* 34 survey, in Autumn 1993. The questions read as follows: 'Returning to the European Court of Justice for a moment, in general would you say that you are very satisfied, somewhat satisfied, not very satisfied or not satisfied at all with the way the Court of Justice has been working?' and 'Now, returning to the [highest court of your country], in general would you say that you are very satisfied, somewhat satisfied or not satisfied at all with the way the [highest court of your country] has been working?' (the table shows the per cent of responses of 'very satisfied' or 'somewhat satisfied'.

Source: Gibson and Caldeira (1998); *Eurobarometer*, 32 (Autumn 1992), 33 (Spring 1993) and 34 (Autumn 1994).

judicial systems. As a result, because courts are strategic in the pursuit of their interests and preferences they moderate their relationship with EU law. This consequently explains why some national courts used the preliminary references procedure more than others (Golub, 1996a), and why some national courts accepted ECJ doctrines before others (Craig, 1998). Direct effect and supremacy were accepted by the Netherlands, Germany and Belgium, followed by Italy, France and Great Britain, in that order. As Mattli and Slaughter (1998a, p. 268) point out:

> an observer ignorant of EC law and national legal doctrine but knowledgeable about relative public support for the EC in these various countries is likely to have predicted a similar sequence.

Third, within each national legal system, lower and higher courts have different institutional incentives *vis-à-vis* the EU legal system (Alter, 1996, 1998b). Alter (1996) contends that lower judges and courts have particular incentives to use EU law: to increase their prestige and power *vis-à-vis* higher courts. Through the preliminary references procedure, lower courts are able to 'play higher courts and the ECJ off against each other to influence legal developments in the direction their prefer' (Alter, 1998a, p. 242). In all member states except Luxembourg, either lower or intermediate level courts made more use of the preliminary references procedure than higher courts, and in seven member states both lower and intermediate level courts made more references than the higher courts (Stone Sweet and Brunell (1998b). In other words, EU legal integration is an 'inadvertent' product of this inter-court competition in the national arena.

At a theoretical level, these explanations develop sophisticated conceptions of the interaction between courts' preferences and their domestic institutional and political environments. However, at an empirical level they have some important shortcomings. For example, different levels of power of national courts *vis-à-vis* national governments (such as whether or not judicial review exists) do not explain why certain national courts accepted EU doctrines before others. There is also a low correlation between the use of preliminary references and support for the EU (Stone Sweet and Brunell, 1998a, p. 79), and, as Table 4.3 shows, the political context of court action is more complex than might be expected: the relationship between support for the EU and support for the ECJ does not appear to be very strong (for example, the British public is anti-European integration but highly satisfied with the ECJ). Finally, analysing their data on the use of preliminary references, Stone Sweet and Brunell (1998b, p. 90) dispute the inter-court competition argument:

> over the entire life of the Community, appellate courts have been more active than lower courts . . . [and] if we consider the fact that there are more lower than appellate courts, and that lower courts process the vast bulk of national litigation, this discrepancy is all the more striking.

Transnational litigants and lawyers: the other 'interlocutors' of the ECJ

In addition to national courts there are a number of other 'interlocutors' of the ECJ who have actively promoted the integration of the EU legal system (Weiler, 1993, 1994). Primary amongst these are private litigants. As noted, the doctrine of direct effect enables individual citizens to invoke EU law in national courts, and this gave private citizens a 'stake' in the EU legal system early in the integration process (Burley & Mattli, 1993, pp. 60–1). Nevertheless, certain social groups have more interest in promoting the application of EU law than others. For example, firms involved in the export and import of goods to other member states have a particular incentive to secure the effective application of the free movement of goods and other economic rights and freedoms; and these groups tend to have sufficient resources available to take actions 'all the way to the European Court', and to actively encourage national courts to seek preliminary references from the ECJ.

Stone Sweet and Brunell (1998a, 1998b) test this exact argument. They collected all the data on the average number of preliminary references by each member state's courts between 1961 and 1994 (cf. Golub, 1996d), and then correlated this data with the average annual volume of intra-EU trade in the same period – which they use as a proxy for the level of transnational economic interests in each member state. The results are impressive: the higher the volume of intra-EU trade, the more likely a state is to use the preliminary references procedure; and the relationship is strong ($R^2 = 0.91$), with only a small variation between member states from the trend. Furthermore, using pooled cross-sectional time-series analysis, they find a high correlation ($R^2 = 0.73$) between the annual number of references from each member state and the annual changes in the volume of intra-EU imports and exports. Finally, they find a significant relationship between the volume of inter-EU trade and preliminary references on issues relating to the operation and regulation of the internal market (Stone Sweet and Brunell, 1998a, p. 75). On this point they assume that transnational economic litigants are more interested in market regulation than agricultural issues, which are the other main source of preliminary references (as was shown in Table 4.2 above).

Another set of transnational interests with a vested interest in the development of the EU legal system is the 'legal community' outside the ECJ (Weiler, 1994). The process of European integration is primarily elite-driven, and this is as true in the legal field as in the political and social fields. Also, the legal community in Europe is already highly integrated at both economic and social levels, and so has a vested interest in promoting further legal and political integration of Europe to support their activities.

As a result, Stein (1981) argues that the list of actors that have played an active role in the promotion of EU law should include: the Legal Service of the Commission, the Legal Counsel of the Council, lawyers in national ministries, attorneys appearing before national courts, legal scholars and writers, and the 'legal establishment' in political positions. Weiler (1994) also points out that academic lawyers, particularly in continental Europe, are often 'custodians of *La Doctrine*'. In several states, this has enabled the law professorate to play a crucial role in the acceptance of EU legal norms, by supplying ideas and arguments to national courts to enable them to reconcile EU and national constitutional doctrines.

In other words, this explanation is a logical extension of general theories of European integration that place emphasis on the role of transnational economic and social activities in promoting integration: such as neo-functionalism (see Chapter 1) (for example Stone Sweet and Sandholtz, 1997). However, this explanation suffers from some of the same weaknesses as these more general approaches. In particular, it overemphasises the autonomy of supranational institutions and transnational interests in the promotion of EU legal integration. These scholars argue that once transnational activities and supranational institutions have been un-leashed, there is little national governments can do to stop them (see for example Pierson, 1996). However, national governments are the signatories of the Treaties, and if provoked they can restrict the powers of the ECJ and redefine the nature of the EU constitution. In other words, as with the ECJ and national courts, there are strategic constraints on the actions of transnational interests.

Strategic member-state governments

Finally, several scholars have argued that the development of the EU constitution has been a deliberate strategy of national governments (for example Garrett, 1992, 1995a; Garrett and Weingast, 1993; Cooter and Drexl, 1994; Garrett, Kelemen and Schulz, 1998). This explanation argues that governments have consciously allowed the ECJ, national courts and transnational litigants to promote legal integration in the EU, because it has been in the governments' political or economic interests. The flip-side of this interpretation is that if the ECJ or a national court took an action that is contrary to a governments' interest, the government will retaliate. Cases of high-profile clashes between the national governments and the ECJ or national courts over EU legal issues are rare, but this does not mean that governments are powerless in the face of court activism. It simply suggests one of two things: either (1) Courts are careful not to make decisions that threaten government interests; or (2) governments accept decisions that appear to be against them, because they are in fact in their long-term interests.

On the first issue, Garrett and Weingast (1993, pp. 201–2) explain why courts exercise restraint:

> Embedding a legal system in a broader political structure places direct constraints on the discretion of a court, even one with as much constitutional independence as the United States Supreme Court . . . The reason is that political actors have a range of avenues through which they may alter or limit the role of courts. . . . the *possibility of such a reaction drives a court that wishes to preserve its independence and legitimacy to remain in the arena of acceptable latitude.*

If courts are strategic actors, then they are constrained by the possibility of government threats, such as reform of the EU Treaty or passing new legislation. For example, faced with potential opposition from several national governments, the ECJ has refused to establish that directives have horizontal direct effect, despite the opinions of several advocates-general and numerous academic lawyers.

On the second issue, Garrett (1995a) proposes a simple model, shown in Figure 4.4, to explain why governments often accept ECJ rulings against them. The model posits that governments take two main factors into account: the domestic political clout of the industry that is harmed by the ECJ decision; and the potential gains to the whole national economy as a result of the decision. Consequently, if the industry is domestically weak and the general economic gains are large, the government will 'accept' the ECJ ruling (and put up with complaints from the domestic industry). For

Figure 4.4   *Garrett's model of government responses to ECJ decisions*

| | | Market share and political clout of industry potentially harmed by court decision | |
		Don't implement single market ('defect')	Implement single market ('cooperate')
Benefit to national economy of trade liberalization	**High**	Justify evasion	Accept
	Low	Overt evasion	Conceal evasion

Source: Garrett (1995a).

example, in the *Cassis de Dijon* judgement, Garrett argues that the German government accepted a ruling that would damage its spirits industry because the German economy stood to benefit from the trade liberalization that resulted from the principle of 'mutual recognition'. Faced with the contrary pressures, where the subject industry is domestically powerful and the general economic gains are small, the government will pursue 'overt evasion' of the Court's decision. However, following the Garrett/Weingast logic, this situation rarely occurs because the ECJ is careful to avoid such a show-down. The implication is that in the *Cassis de Dijon* case, the ECJ waited for the right case to come along to establish the principle of mutual recognition.

Nevertheless, by focusing on the centrality of national governments in the EU system, and conceptualizing their actions as highly rational, these explanations have some of the same limitations as the intergovernmentalist explanations of European integration (see Chapter 1). At an empirical level there is substantial evidence that the ECJ and national courts have often taken decisions that governments have opposed, and which have had negative effects on the competitiveness of national economies in the single market (Mattli and Slaughter, 1995). At a theoretical level this can be explained by the fact that governments do not have perfect information about the likely outcome of delegating adjudication to the ECJ and national courts (cf. Pierson, 1996). For example, when the EU Treaty was signed few governments realised that the EU could establish the doctrines of direct effect and supremacy, or the potential impact of the article 234 [ex 177] procedure (Alter, 1998b).

Conclusion: 'unknown destination' or emerging equilibrium?

The EU has a legal-constitutional framework that contains two of the basic doctrines of a federal legal system: the direct effect of EU law on individual citizens throughout the Union, and the supremacy of EU law over domestic law and constitutions. Also, in the European Court of Justice the EU has a powerful constitutional and administrative court overseeing the implementation of EU law and keeping the EU institutions in check.

How this came about is a matter of contention. The truth probably lies somewhere between the explanations we have discussed. On the one hand, political actors – national governments, the ECJ, national courts and transnational litigants – have particular interests and policy goals. However, these actors are constrained by their cultural, institutional, political and informational contexts (environmental constraints), and by the interests of other actors in the system (strategic constraints). In special 'windows of opportunity', nevertheless, actors can shape their environmental surroundings, for example by reforming institutional structures, establishing institutional norms or modifying national legal cultures.

Furthermore, as we saw in the discussion of general theories of judicial politics, courts have more discretion under certain institutional designs than others. Applying this logic to the EU, the ECJ has a relatively high room for manoeuvre because there is only a small probability that the EU Treaty will be reformed to reduce the ECJ's powers, or that new legislation will be passed to overturn one of its decisions. Because there are many 'veto players' in the EU system, at least one member state, the Commission, the European Parliament, or a group of powerful transnational economic actors is likely to bloc a reduction of the ECJ's powers or the overturning of one of its decisions.

But, the ECJ has imperfect information about how other actors will react to its decisions. For example, governments have shorter time horizons than courts because they have to be reelected every few years. This means that governments are less interested in the long-term implications of delegating powers to the ECJ than the immediate political salience of a decision. But, as new governments are elected, new political issues can be placed on the electoral agenda, and as a result the ECJ is uncertain about whether its decisions will become politically salient. However, even if the Court makes a miscalculation, the governments opposed to a particular decision must find a decision-making procedure that prevents actors sympathetic to the Court from vetoing an overturning of the ECJ decision. For example, because of a lack of information, the ECJ was surprised at the political salience of the *Barber* judgement (on the question of equal pension rights for men and women). But, the right institutional mechanisms needed to exist for the governments to alter the Court's decision, and the governments consequently used the Intergovernmental Conferences negotiating the Maastricht Treaty to add a protocol to the EU Treaty that prevented the retroactive application of the judgement. Following the protocol, the ECJ moderated its activism in this area.

This judicial politics game has produced an incomplete constitution. For example, the EU does not have a bill of rights and who has *Kompetenz-Kompetenz* is unclear. Weiler (1993) consequently argues that the EU has an 'unknown destination' (cf. Shonfield, 1973). But, our theoretical conclusions suggest that the current constitutional set-up is an equilibrium: a balance between the discretion of the ECJ/national courts on the one hand, and the conscious decision by national governments to construct a rule of law to enable economic integration on the other.

Nevertheless, this equilibrium could be upset by changes in the political context – such as public opinion, party competition and ideology, and interest group politics – which could push the EU towards a full-blooded federal constitutional arrangement, or even result in a constitutional step backwards (as happened with the German Constitutional Court ruling on the Maastricht Treaty). Consequently, it is to the political context of institutional politics that we turn in Part II of this book.

PART II

POLITICS

Chapter 5

Public Opinion and Political Cleavages

Theories of the social bases of politics
Mass support for the European Union
More or less integration: 'Europe – right or wrong?'
What the EU should do: 'Europe – right or left?'
The electoral connection: strategic dilemmas for Euro-elites
Conclusion: a politicized plural society

This chapter looks at what EU citizens think about the EU. The structure of social divisions within and between the EU member states provides a strategic environment, in which politicians at the national and European levels compete for electoral support and political legitimacy. Understanding public opinion towards European integration is hence essential to understand the constraints on the further institutional integration of the political system as well as the nature of political competition in the EU policy-making process.

Theories of the social bases of politics

Each individual has a set of beliefs, opinions, values and interests relating to the political process. These 'political preferences' often derive from deep historical or cultural identities such as nationality, religion or language. In many instances, however, political preferences stem from economic interests, such as whether a policy will increase a person's income. Inevitably, different individuals and social groups have different preferences, which produces competition in the political process. But how can we explain the structure of political preferences in the EU?

The 'cleavage-model' of politics posits that political divisions derive from 'critical junctures' in the development of a political system (Lipset and Rokkan, 1967). For example, in the domestic political systems in Europe, the 'democratic revolution' in the eighteenth and early nineteenth centuries produced a conflict between church and state (between liberals and conservatives), and the 'industrial revolution' of the nineteenth century divided workers against owners of capital (between socialists and liberals/conservatives). Using the Lipset–Rokkan model to conceptualize the social bases of EU politics, there are two main cleavages in the EU: *national/territorial* and *transnational/socio-economic*. First, the combination of a common territory, historical myths, a mass culture, legal rights and duties, and a national economy constitutes a powerful force for individual attachment to the nation-state (Smith, 1991, p. 14). As a result, the society of the EU is 'segmented' along national lines: between the EU member states, within which the bulk of individual social interactions and experiences take place and interests and identifications are formed (cf. Lijphart, 1977). This national/territorial cleavage becomes 'manifest' in EU politics when an issue on the political agenda puts individuals from different nations on different sides of the debate: for example, where one national group appears to gain at the expense of another.

Second, cross-cutting these national segments are 'latent' transnational divisions. On certain issues on the EU agenda, a group of citizens in one nation-state will share more in common with a similar group in another nation-state than with the rest of society in their own nation-state. For example, French and German farmers have collective interests to defend the Common Agricultural Policy, against the interests of French and German consumers. This transnational cleavage can be mobilized around traditional social divisions, such as class, but can also emerge around newer 'issue-divisions', such as post-materialism, age, education and information. These transnational divisions tend to be less salient in EU politics than the national–territorial cleavage, but they become increasingly important as the EU agenda shifts to questions of economic redistribution between functional rather than territorial groups (such as EU social policy) and questions of social and political values (such as EU environmental policy).

In this chapter I shall first discuss the general pattern of support for European integration and the difference between 'affective' and 'utilitarian' support for a political system. The chapter will then contrast different explanations of support for the EU: the question of 'Europe – right or wrong?'. The chapter then turns to the issue of how the socio-economic structure of European society shapes citizens' attitudes towards the direction of the EU policy agenda: the question of 'Europe – right or left? When the answers to these questions are combined, a two-dimensional map of EU politics emerges, within which political elites must compete for public support for their policies towards and within the EU.

Mass support for the European Union

End of the 'permissive consensus'?

In the 1950s and 1960s, following the Treaties of Paris and Rome, Lindberg and Scheingold (1970) argued that there was a 'permissive consensus' amongst Europe's publics in favour of European integration. This term came from V.O. Key (1961), who used it to describe support by the American public for certain government actions, particularly in foreign affairs. The same phenomenon was apparent amongst the publics of the founding members of the European Communities. As Inglehart explained:

> There was a favourable prevailing attitude toward the subject, but it was of low salience as a political issue – leaving national decision-makers free to take steps favourable to integration if they wished but also leaving them a wide liberty of choice. (Inglehart, 1970b, p. 773)

In other words, a large majority of European citizens in all member states were either not interested in European integration, and so had no opinion about their governments' actions on the issue, or generally supported their government's efforts to promote further integration.

However, these claims could not be tested without survey data. Since 1973 the European Commission has undertaken European-wide opinion polls every six months, conducted by private polling agencies in each member state through interviews of a sample of approximately 1000 people in each country. These *'Eurobarometer'* surveys consequently provide a large data-set for the study of citizens' attitudes towards European integration. As with national governments and national opinion polls, the European Commission, the European Parliament, the EU Council and even the European Court of Justice watch these polls carefully, to gauge the level of support or opposition towards further EU integration or specific EU policies.

For example, two questions that have been asked in most *Eurobarometers* since 1973 are:

> *Unification*: In general, are you for or against efforts being made to unify Western Europe? Response: 'very much for', 'to some extent for', 'don't know', 'to some extent against', 'very much against'.
> *Membership*: Generally speaking, do you think [your country's] membership of the Common Market/European Community/European Union is a 'good thing', a 'bad thing', or 'neither good nor bad'?

Figure 5.1 shows the percentage of EU citizens across all the member states who answered 'very much for' or 'to some extent for' to the first question (the upper graph), and those who answered 'good thing' for the second question (the lower graph). As the figure shows, in the early 1970s just over 50 per cent of the EU public was in favour of their country's membership of the EU, and slightly more were in favour of European unification: the gap between the two figures presumably accounts for those who are in favour of European integration but not through the EU

Figure 5.1   *Public support for European integration*

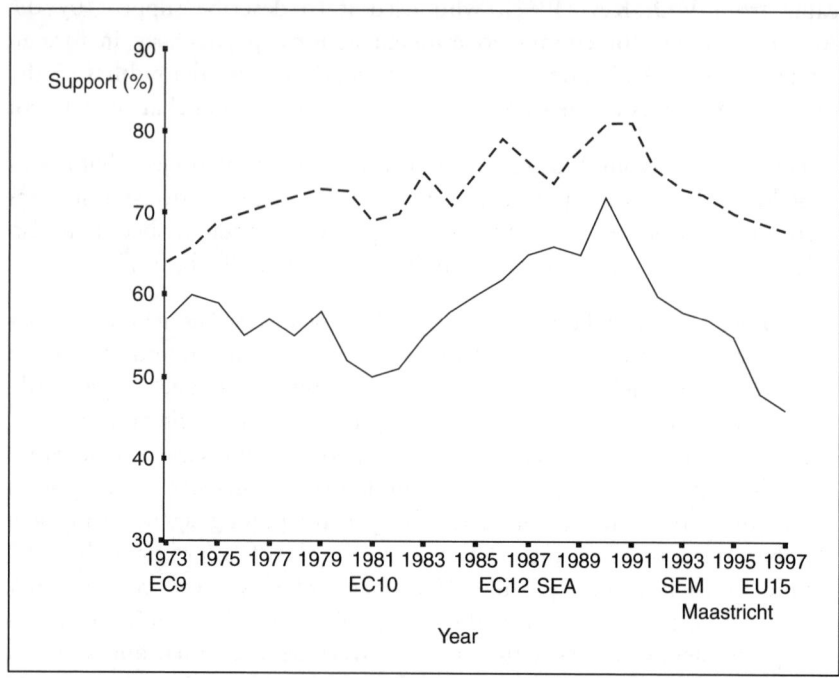

Note: Upper graph: answers of 'very much for' plus 'to some extent for' to unification question. Lower graph: answers of 'good thing' to membership question. EC9, EC10, EC12, EU15 = enlargements of the EU to 9, 10, 12 and 15 member states. SEA = Single European Act. SEM = Single European Market. Maastricht = Treaty on European Union.

institutions as currently designed. Throughout the 1980s support for European integration rose steadily, and a factor contributing to this rise in support was the popularity of the '1992 programme', the project of completing the single market by the end of 1992 (Inglehart and Reif, 1991) (see Chapter 8).

However, support peaked around 1990–91, with a high of 72 per cent in favour of their country's membership of the EU and 82 per cent in favour of European unification. By 1997, these had fallen considerably. Widespread opposition to the EU first emerged in the process of ratifying the Maastricht Treaty, in 1992 and 1993: in the referendums in France, Denmark and Ireland, the series of votes in the House of Commons in Britain, and the constitutional court challenge in Germany. This opposition continued in votes for anti-European parties in the 1994 European elections, in the 1994 referendums on EU enlargement in Austria, Finland, Sweden and Norway, in the European elections in 1995 and 1996 in

Austria, Sweden and Finland, and in opinion polls in 1996 and 1997 on EMU. Clearly, if a permissive consensus had existed in the first few decades of Europe integration, it no longer existed in the 1990s (cf. Niedermayer, 1995a). As Franklin, Marsh and McLaren (1994) elegantly put it: the anti-Europe 'bottle' had finally been 'uncorked'.

Nevertheless, this collapse in public support for the EU masks numerous subtleties. First, in 1997, there was still a majority in favour of European unification and, similarly, those in favour of their country's membership of the EU were still a 'plurality'. Furthermore, when EU citizens are asked to judge the performance of the EU institutions in comparison to their national institutions their response is fairly positive. For example, in the same *Eurobarometer* survey in January 1997 that revealed only 46 per cent in favour of membership of the EU, citizens were asked the following question:

> Many important decisions are made by the European Union. They might be in the interests of people like yourself, or they might not. To what extent do you feel you can rely on each of the following institutions to make sure that the decisions taken by this institution are in the interests of people like yourself?

As Figure 5.2 shows, more people feel they 'can rely on' their national institutions than the EU institutions, but more people feel they 'cannot rely' on their national institutions than feel they 'can rely' on them. And, the only institution at either level of government for which more people feel they 'can rely' than 'cannot rely' is the European Parliament. This is in line with the findings of other studies of public attitudes towards the EP, which show that although there is little understanding of what the EP does, it has widespread legitimacy in the eyes of Europe's citizens because it is a 'parliament' (see for example Niedermayer, 1991, Niedermayer and Sinnott, 1995).

In other words, in the late 1990s, when asked about general attitudes towards European integration, the amount of citizens in favour is considerably less than at the beginning of the 1990s. This suggests that governments are no longer able to assume that their publics will support their initiatives at the European level. However, less European citizens trust their national institutions than the EU institutions, which suggests the opposite: public support for a particular role for the EU institutions, and especially for increased powers for the EP. So, how can the process of decline in general support for integration be explained? And, how can falling general support be reconciled with the widespread belief that the EU institutions protect citizens' interests at least as well as national institutions?

Figure 5.2   *Public support for European and national institutions*

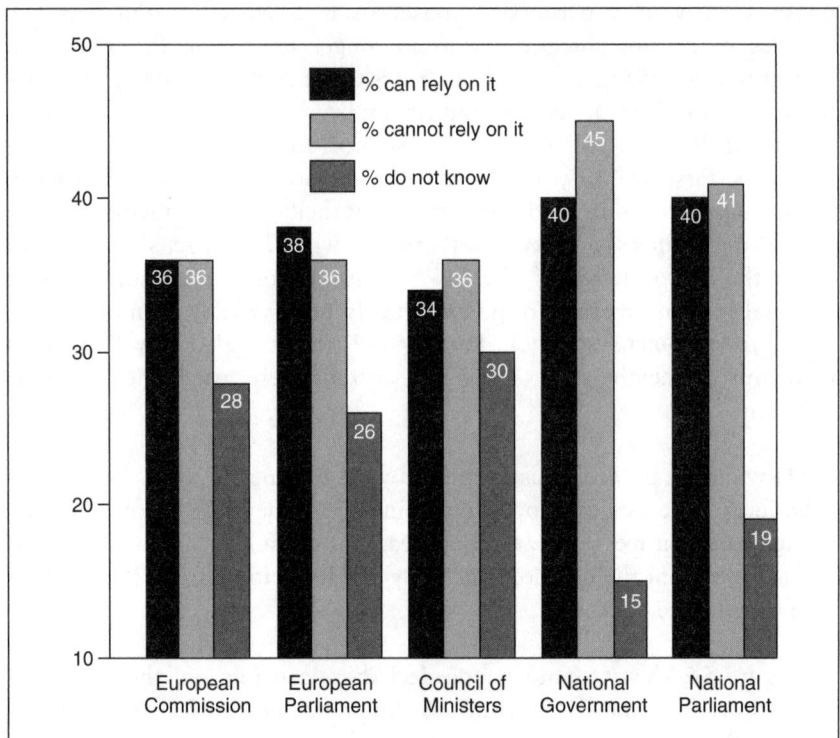

Easton's theory of affective and utilitarian support

Part of the answer lies in Easton's (1965, 1975) theory of the difference between 'affective' and 'utilitarian' support for political institutions. 'Affective' support is an ideological or non-material belief in the value of the political system; while 'utilitarian' support, in contrast, is the belief that the system promotes an individual's economic or political interests. Applying these notions to the EU, some people support European integration because they believe in the goal of a united Europe, regardless of whether they think they will benefit (affective), whereas others support European integration because it will make them personally better off (utilitarian) (Gabel, 1998a).

The problem is that a question about whether an individual supports 'European unification' does not allow us to differentiate between these two types of support: an individual can be in favour either because they 'love Europe' (affective) or because they think it will make them better off (utilitarian). Fortunately, though, the *Eurobarometer* polls do contain questions that are directly related to these two types of support:

> *Identity (affective)*: Do you ever think of yourself not only as a [nationality] citizen but also as a citizen of Europe? Response: 'often', 'sometimes', 'never'.
> *Benefit (utilitarian)*: Taking everything into consideration, would you say that [your country] has on balance benefited or not from being a member of the European Union? Response: 'benefited', 'don't know', 'not benefited'.

Figure 5.3 illustrates that the two aspects of support are not necessarily related. In the late 1980s, when Europe focused on completing the single market, utilitarian support for the EU increased but affective identification with 'Europe' reduced. Nevertheless, in the early 1990s, as the permissive consensus collapsed, both utilitarian and affective allegiance fell. This

Figure 5.3   *Affective and utilitarian support for European integration*

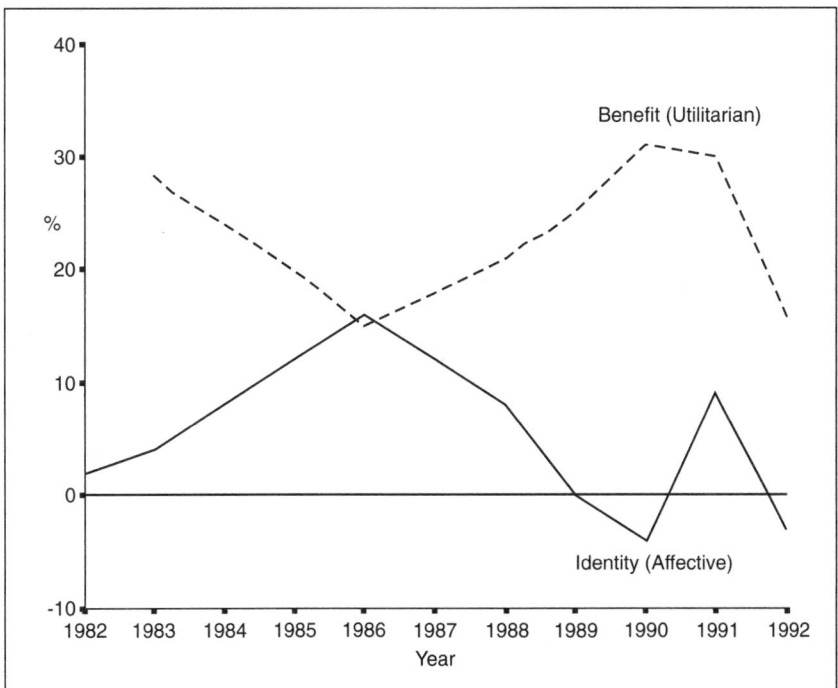

Note: Benefit (utilitarian) = proportion of 'benefit' minus proportion of 'not benefit'; Identity (affective) = proportion of 'often' and 'sometimes' minus proportion of 'never'. *Sources: Eurobarometer*, nos 17, 19, 24, 26, 30, 31, 33, 35 and 37.

pattern can be explained as follows: citizens with a strong affective European identity provide stable support for the EU, but this is only a small proportion of the total EU population. On the other hand, citizens with low affective European identity can be strong supporters of integration if they perceive a high utilitarian benefit of the EU. Consequently, in late 1990s with stable levels of affective support and growing awareness of the costs and benefits of European integration, utilitarian support matters more in explaining changing levels of support. As Gabel (1998a, p. 30) explains, 'as affective attachments decrease, utilitarian evaluations of integration have a stronger relationship with support for integration'. As a result, the public can be moderately sceptical of European integration yet still hope that the EU can protect their personal interests.

In other words, citizens' political preferences matter for the future of the EU. With the end of unquestioning or passive support for European integration in the early 1990s, the continued development of the EU depends as never before on the ability of Europe's leaders to promote the interests of large majorities of the EU public through their actions at the European level. To understand the shape of the strategic environment in which Europe's political leaders now operate, we consequently need to understand the structure of preferences amongst Europe's citizens, which is the subject of the next two sections.

More or less integration: 'Europe – right or wrong?'

As in the development of many political systems at the national level, European integration creates a 'centre–periphery' conflict: between groups whose interests are threatened by integration, and groups whose interests are promoted by integration (Rokkan, 1973). In the EU, this conflict emerges primarily between *national* interests as a result of the national/ territorial cleavage, but this conflict can also mobilize *transnational* socioeconomic divisions, such as the class cleavage and new social and value divisions. We shall first look at national interests and identities, before turning to economic interests, and finally new social and value divisions.

National cultures, interests and politics: the national cleavage

In addition to the territorial boundaries between the nation-states, there are numerous interests and traditions that divide Europe's nations. For example:

- Cultural differences – such as Latin vs Germanic, Catholic vs Protestant, North vs South, East vs West, high-trust vs low-trust societies, homogeneous vs multi-ethnic societies (see for example Almond and Verba, 1963; Rokkan, 1973; Inglehart, 1997).
- Economic differences – rich vs poor, urban/industrial vs rural/agricultural, service-based vs manufacturing-based, centre vs periphery, high vs low unemployment, large vs small income inequalities, oil/gas producers vs oil/gas consumers (for example Gourevitch, 1989; Krugman, 1991; Cole and Cole, 1997).
- Political differences – large vs small populations, long vs short democratic traditions, social democratic vs conservative governing traditions, majoritarian vs consensual, corporatist vs pluralist, Anglo-Saxon vs socialist/Christian Democratic welfare states (for example Lijphart, 1984; Esping-Anderson, 1990; Lange and Meadwell, 1991).

These produce a complex pattern of individual attitudes towards European integration.

Table 5.1 shows the results of the so-called 'mega-Eurobarometer' poll of February/March 1996, when over 65 000 interviews were conducted. As the table shows, in the late 1990s the publics of Italy, Ireland, Luxembourg and the Netherlands are the most consistently pro-European across the various indicators used, while at the other end of the scale are Austria, Denmark, the United Kingdom, Finland and Sweden, all of whom have large 'Euro-sceptic' sections of society. Interestingly, the German public seems to be the most sceptical of the founding member-states. So, how can this pattern be explained through these different cultural, economic and political experiences?

Beginning with *cultural* factors, a key factor is the length of a country's membership of the EU. The publics of the original member states were neither clearly pro- nor anti-European in the 1950s, but due to a variety of cultural factors there was a high level of 'trust' between these societies and a sense of 'community' (Inglehart, 1991; Niedermayer, 1995b). These values allowed the national elites to begin the process of integration. Building on this, the process of integration had a socializing effect – as the publics became used to the idea of integration, they were more willing to accept its consequences – and this led to generally increasing support for European integration across time (Anderson and Kalthenthaler, 1996; cf. Gabel, 1998b). Consequently, the publics of the nations that joined first – Germany, France, Italy, Belgium, the Netherlands and Luxembourg – are on average more in favour of integration than those that joined later – Ireland, Denmark, the United Kingdom (in 1973), Greece (in 1981), Spain and Portugal (in 1987). And the nations that joined in 1995 – Austria, Finland and Sweden – are the least supportive.

Table 5.1 *Nationality and European integration*

	Unification ('for')		Membership ('good thing')		Benefit ('benefited')		Identity ('European')		Average
	%	rank	%	rank	%	rank	%	rank	rank
Ireland	80.0	3	75.9	2	83.2	1	16.3	3	1
Luxembourg	81.6	2	71.6	3	66.2	3	20.6	2	2
Italy	84.7	1	68.3	4	48.6	5	30.3	1	3
Netherlands	77.7	4	77.3	1	64.6	6	15.8	5	4
Greece	70.3	5	59.0	5	65.1	4	10.3	=10	5
Portugal	75.9	6	54.2	6	67.9	2	9.8	12	6
France	71.0	8	53.7	8	41.2	8	16.2	4	7
Belgium	67.9	9	53.4	9	41.0	9	13.3	7	8
Spain	74.6	7	53.9	7	39.1	10	10.3	=10	9
Denmark	63.7	10	52.6	10	60.2	7	7.1	13	10
Germany	60.1	11	44.7	11	37.7	11	12.3	8	11
United Kingdom	54.5	15	41.0	13	34.7	13	14.2	6	12
Austria	55.0	14	33.8	14	36.4	12	11.2	9	13
Finland	57.6	13	42.6	12	34.6	14	3.8	15	14
Sweden	59.5	12	33.4	15	19.7	15	5.5	14	15

Note: *Unification:* 'In general, are you for or against efforts being made to unify Europe?' Response: 'very much for', 'to some extent for', 'to some extent against', 'very much against' (table shows per cent of 'very much for' plus 'to some extent for' responses). 'don't know', (table shows per cent of 'very much for' plus 'to some extent for' responses).
Membership: 'Generally speaking, do you think [your contry's] membership of the European Union is a "good thing", a "bad thing", or "neither good nor bad"?' (table shows per cent of 'a good thing' responses).
Benefit: 'Taking everything into consideration, would you say that [your country] has on balance benefited or not from being a member of the European Union?' Response: 'benefited', 'don't know', 'not benefited' (table shows per cent of 'benefited' responses).
Identity: 'In the near future do you see yourself above all as a citizen of the "European Union", a citizen of "[your country]" or a citizen of your "region"?' (table shows per cent of 'European Union' responses).
Source: *Eurobarometer* no. 44.2bis, 1996 (*n* = 65 178). Format adapted from Anderson (1995).

However, several economic and political factors cut across these cultural determinants. On the *economic* side, as the public learnt more about the EU they also become aware of how much their national economy stands to gain or lose from European integration. One factor is whether a country gains or loses under the EU budget, such as in the structural funds and the CAP (Bosch and Newton, 1995; Carrubba, 1997; Whitten, Gabel and Palmer, 1998) (see Chapter 9). Another issue is whether a national economy gains or loses from trade liberalization through the EU single market (Eichenberg and Dalton, 1993; Gabel and Palmer, 1995; Anderson and Reichert, 1996) (see Chapter 8).

Put together, these economic factors help explain much of the variation in levels of utilitarian support for European integration within the original member nations and between the nations that joined later (Gabel and Whitten, 1997; Gabel, 1998a). For example, the German economy benefits from the single market, but the Germany public has became increasingly aware that they are the major contributors to the EU budget and potentially stand to lose the most from monetary union. As a result, in 1997, the German public had a higher level of affective support (the 'identity' question) than utilitarian support (the 'benefit' question). Conversely, the publics of Ireland, Greece, Portugal and Spain, whose national economies benefit from EU cohesion policies and are highly dependent on the single market, have a high level of utilitarian support (the 'benefit' question). And, in Greece, Portugal and Ireland, who benefit most as a per cent of GDP from EU cohesion policies, more people see a benefit from EU membership than are in favour of EU membership.

Finally, different national *political* traditions shape attitudes towards European integration. Across the EU, citizens are generally uninformed about the EU: in 1996, only 16 per cent felt that they were well-informed about it and only 32 per cent were able to answer correctly to a series of basic questions about the EU. This 'information deficit' ensures that citizens tend to use the context of domestic politics to form opinions about European integration. Nevertheless, Anderson (1998) found that different domestic political factors matter in different nations. For example, in Denmark the level of support for the EU is determined by the popularity of the government rather than the party the person supports. In contrast, in France, government popularity is irrelevant but the position of the party the person supports is crucial. Furthermore, Martinotti and Stefanizzi (1995) show that in some countries, support for the EU increases as support for national political institutions increases (as in Britain and the Netherlands), whereas in others, support for the EU increases as support for national institutions decreases (as in Italy and Greece).

Also, the potential political benefits from European integration affect nation-states differently. For instance, the human and physical devastation in the Second World War was higher amongst the founding member states than those that joined later, so these nations had more to gain politically from a potential peace dividend resulting from economic and political integration in Europe (Gabel, 1998a). Similarly, if a nation-state does not have a stable tradition of democratic capitalism, voters who are in favour of this political end tend to be more in favour of European integration as a means to promote this. In contrast, voters in states with stable democratic histories have no such incentive to support European integration. These factors consequently help explain the different levels of support for integration in Italy, Spain, Portugal and Greece compared to Britain, Denmark and Sweden, if economic benefits and length of membership are taken as constant (*ibid.*).

Transnational economic interests: the class cleavage

The process of economic integration in Europe has differential effects on economic interests across Europe (see for example Eichengreen and Frieden, 1994). In *Interests and Integration*, Matthew Gabel (1998a) presents a theoretical framework to understand how this works (cf. Anderson and Reichert, 1996).

- First, the *free movement of goods in the single market* presents opportunities for citizens employed in export-oriented manufacturing or service industries in the private sector. The single market presents new opportunities to entrepreneurs, business owners and company directors to market their products elsewhere in the EU, and reap economies of scale from higher turnover. But, trade liberalization leads to new competition for sectors that are non-tradeable (such as the public sector), cater to national markets (such as small businesses in the retail sector), or compete with imported goods (such as local manufacturing). Moreover, EU competition and state aid policies present new challenges to jobs in industries that rely on government subsidies or protectionist trade policies (cf. Frieden, 1991; Smith and Wanke, 1993).
- Second, the *free movement of capital and a single currency* creates new investment opportunities for citizens with capital: in other words, with high personal incomes. Capital liberalization also leads to cross-border competition for investment, but whereas skilled workers attract investment by offering higher skills, manual workers attract investment by offering lower wages. Consequently, capital liberalization increases the opportunity of low-wage manual workers to attract investment, but threatens manual-workers in high-wage regions who might lose-out from capital flight. Also, the convergence criteria for EMU force

governments to restrict their public expenditure, consequently threatening welfare programmes that support low-income citizens and the unemployed.

- Third, the *free movement of services and persons* creates more competition for jobs in all sectors of the economy. But, citizens with high 'human capital', such as a high level of education and employment in professional or management positions, are likely to see this as a chance to use these resources to improve their status. Low-skilled manual workers, on the other hand, are likely to see this as more competition for their jobs.

- Fourth, *the Common Agricultural Policy* (CAP) is the only clearly distributive policy of the EU (see Chapter 9). The benefits of CAP subsidies are concentrated on one specific economic group (farmers), whereas the costs are spread amongst EU taxpayers and consumers. Nevertheless, some farmers benefit from the CAP more than others: generally, farmers with high incomes are likely to perceive that the CAP helps them secure markets for their products and subsidize their production, whereas farmers with low incomes are likely to perceive that the CAP does not benefit them.

This theoretical framework goes some way towards explaining the structure of socioeconomic attitudes towards European integration. Table 5.2 presents descriptive data on class support for the EU, using the same data-set as was used for national support (Gabel uses pooled cross-sectional time-series data from all the *Eurobarometer* polls between 1975 and 1992). First, the data shows that individuals in higher occupational categories are much more favourable towards European integration than those in lower categories. Professionals (such as doctors, lawyers and accountants), with highly mobile skills in the single market, are the most supportive of integration; and company owners and managing directors, with new profit opportunities, are also highly favourable.

White collar employees (over 15 per cent of EU voters) are generally less supportive, but more favourable than small business owners, who are predominantly in non-tradeable sectors. Farmers, surprisingly, are relatively sceptical, although this relative position hides a high variation between farmers' low levels of affective support for the EU (in response to the 'identity' question) and higher levels of utilitarian support (in response to the 'benefit' question). This suggests that although farmers are not cosmopolitans, they recognize the economic benefits of the EU, presumably as a result of the CAP.

Skilled workers (also over 15 per cent of EU voters) are much more favourable towards European integration than manual workers. And, of

Table 5.2 Social class and European integration

	N	Unification ('for')		Membership ('good thing')		Benefit ('benefited')		Identity ('European')		Average
		%	rank	%	rank	%	rank	%	rank	rank
Professionals	1798	81.6	1	68.7	1	59.7	1	22.9	1	1
Employers/directors	1880	74.7	4	62.2	3	54.1	=2	19.6	2	3
White collar employees	10205	75.5	3	60.4	4	51.8	4	16.9	4	4
Small business owners	2760	72.2	5	55.3	5	49.4	5	16.3	5	5
Farmers	2966	62.6	10	49.7	7	49.2	6	8.9	12	7
Skilled workers	10204	65.4	7	48.1	9	43.3	9	11.5	8	6
Manual workers	3008	60.0	11	43.1	11	40.7	10	11.0	=9	11
Students	6836	78.8	2	63.0	2	54.1	=2	18.8	3	2
Unemployed	4529	62.9	9	46.7	10	39.4	12	13.4	7	=8
Retired	12791	63.7	8	48.8	8	39.7	11	10.8	11	=8
Housepersons	8065	65.9	6	49.9	6	43.6	8	11.0	=9	10

Note: See the note to Table 5.1 for the wording of the questions.
Source: Eurobarometer no. 44.2bis, 1996.

the social groups that are not active in the labour market, students are highly supportive of integration and the unemployed are highly sceptical. In addition to immediate opportunities for subsidized educational exchange elsewhere in the EU, through such programmes as *Erasmus* and *Socrates*, students are likely to enter the professions or senior management positions, and hence show attitudes similar to these groups. At the other end of the social spectrum, the unemployed show high affective identification with Europe, but see low utilitarian benefits: they may have lost their jobs as a result of competitive pressures in the single market or government cut-backs to meet the convergence criteria for EMU.

To test the framework further, however, we need to discover whether the varying level of economic resources, human capital and comparative advantage alters the levels of support for the EU within these social groups. A good indicator of these variables is the level of an individual's income, where a higher income suggests:

- for employers/directors, more capital to invest;
- for professionals and skilled workers, more marketable skills in the single market;
- for white-collar employees, a greater likelihood of employment in the private rather than the public sector;
- for farmers, greater benefits from CAP; but
- for manual workers, better wage protection, as a result of trade union organization and collective bargaining or minimum wage and other social legislation, and hence a comparative *dis*advantage in the competition to attract cross-border investment.

As a result, we should expect that *as incomes rise, support for the EU should rise, for all social groups except manual workers.*

Using the same data, Figure 5.4 shows the impact of income on support for EU membership amongst the major social groups (these are linear regression lines). As incomes rise, support for the EU amongst professionals, employers/directors, white-collar employees, and skilled workers also rises. Farmers, in fact, show the fastest rate of increase. Moreover, this trend is clearly reversed for manual workers, where higher incomes reflect high levels of wage protection rather than skills, and are hence threatened in the single market by the ability of firms to transfer production to less-protected and lower-wage manual workforces.

Overall, therefore, transnational social class positions also shape attitudes towards European integration. This suggests that there are incentives for individuals from the same social class in different member states to mobilize to promote their interests in the EU policy process, and consciously compete with the structure of representation of 'national' interests in the Council. For example, organizations representing the professions,

Figure 5.4   *Influence of class and income on support for EU*

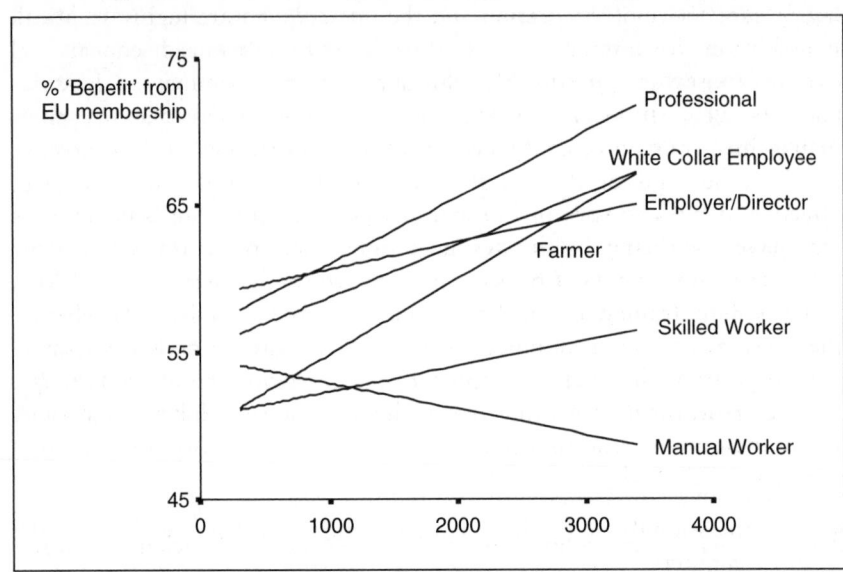

Note: The figure shows the per cent of 'benefit' responses to the 'Benefit' question. See note to Table 5.1 for the wording of the question.
Source: Eurobarometer 44.2bis, 1996. Idea from Gabel (1998a).

groups representing directors of large companies, and farmers lobbies all have incentives to protect their gains already made by the single market (see Chapter 7). However, the worker class is divided: whereas skilled workers and low-wage manual workers benefit from economic integration, high-wage manual workers are threatened by economic integration.

'New' transnational divisions: generation, education, knowledge, region

Nevertheless, since the 1960s class has declined as an indicator of general political attitudes in European politics. For example, 'class voting', where working classes vote for socialist parties and middle classes vote for liberal, Christian or conservative parties, has declined across Europe (Dalton, 1988; Franklin, 1992). Class identity has eroded as different production, consumption and educational life-experiences have produced cross-cutting socio-economic attitudes, interests and values (Dahrendorf, 1959; Bell, 1960; Giddens, 1973; Dunleavy, 1979). For example, Ronald Inglehart (1977a) argued that a *'Silent Revolution'* had taken place as a result of economic prosperity and peace: class-based 'materialist' values of economic and political security were being replaced through generational-change by 'post-material' values, such as environmentalism, women's and minorities' rights, democratic participation and nuclear disarmament.

However, other types of transnational social divisions shape attitudes towards European integration. For example, applying his theory of post-materialism to the issue of European integration, Inglehart argued that:

> ... we would expect post-materialists to have a significantly less parochial and more cosmopolitan outlook than materialists . . . First, the post-materialists are less pre-occupied with immediate concrete needs than are materialists; other things being equal they should have more psychic energy to invest in relatively remote abstractions such as the European Community. Moreover . . . the relative priority accorded to national security has fallen . . . [hence] one of the key symbols of nationalism has lost much of its potency – especially among post-materialists. (Inglehart, 1977b, p. 151)

Because younger age cohorts are more post-material, Inglehart proposed that support for European integration should be higher in younger groups (Inglehart, 1970b; 1977b; also Wessels, 1995a). Inglehart also developed several other hypotheses about non-class-based attitudes towards Europe. For example, he argued that individuals with greater 'cognitive skills' are more able to understand the abstract process of European integration (Inglehart, 1970a; Inglehart and Rabier, 1978; also Janssen, 1991), which suggests that individuals with higher levels of education are more likely to support European integration, and that individuals who are well-informed about the EU are also more likely to be favourable. These arguments are not self-evident, as one could argue the opposite: that more understanding and information about the EU would lead to greater awareness of its failings and limitations (such as the lack of democratic accountability, the secrecy of decision-making, or the corruption in the EU budget).

Using the same mega-Eurobarometer data as before, Table 5.3 shows how these propositions performed in 1996. First, all the variables are strong indicators of support for integration: with younger/more educated/better-informed respondents showing higher levels of affective ('identity') and utilitarian ('benefit') support for the EU than respondents with the opposite characteristics. Second, however, the amount of information a person has about the EU appears to be a stronger indicator of support for integration than either age or education. The variation between the level of support of individuals who are well-informed compared to uninformed is much greater than between groups with different education levels or different ages.

Table 5.3 Other transnational social divisions and European integration

	N	Unification ('for')		Membership ('good thing')		Benefit ('benefited')		Identity ('European')		Average
		%	rank	%	rank	%	rank	%	rank	rank
Age										
15–24	11 109	73.8	1	57.8	1	50.5	1	15.6	1	1
25–39	19 136	69.9	2	54.1	2	47.9	2	14.4	3	2
40–54	15 656	68.3	3	53.5	3	46.4	3	14.6	2	3
55+	19 238	64.2	4	49.2	4	41.1	4	11.0	4	4
Education (completed)										
Still studying	6 836	78.3	1	63.0	1	54.1	1	18.8	1	1
20+	14 531	75.9	2	62.8	2	54.9	2	17.8	3	2
16–19	24 187	66.8	3	51.1	3	44.1	3	13.2	2	3
Up to 15	19 585	61.7	4	44.2	4	38.9	4	9.8	4	4
Informed about EU										
Very well	1 881	81.8	1	69.7	1	73.2	1	29.3	1	1
Quite well	18 554	78.1	2	58.7	2	65.6	2	18.5	2	2
Not very well	29 194	68.9	3	43.7	3	51.1	3	12.2	3	3
Not at all well	13 542	53.8	4	32.3	4	38.6	4	8.5	4	4

Note: See the note to Table 5.1 for the wording of the questions.
Source: Eurobarometer no. 44.2bis, 1996, except for the 'Elite' responses, which are taken from the 'Top Decision-Makers Survey', of February–May 1996.

Inglehart (1977b) consequently concluded that his theory bodes well for European integration. Through successive generational change, higher levels of education in society, and growing awareness and understanding of the EU, the levels of support for European integration should increase. In other words, this theoretical framework was able to explain the growth in support for integration until the early 1990s. However, this argument cannot explain the collapse in support since 1992 (cf. Gabel, 1998b), because generational change cuts across the effects of utilitarian interests, such as class or national interest. And, as we discussed, utilitarian interests became stronger determinants of support for integration in the 1990s, perhaps because of the onset of recession and the concomitant decline in post-material values.

Finally, an additional 'new' social division is the emergence of regional identities and interests below the nation-state. It is often argued that regional decentralization goes hand in hand with European integration: as the nation-state is challenged from above, it unleashes pressures from below (see for example Jones and Keating, 1995; Hooghe, 1996b). Also, the effects of the single market, in terms of the relative competitiveness of sectors of the economy, are felt more intensively at the regional level where ancillary and subsidiary industries are concentrated, and the Commission has played an active role in fostering regional mobilization through the involvement of regions in the making and implementation of EU regional policies (see Chapters 7 and 9). Consequently, one would expect citizens in different regions of the EU to think differently about European integration, independently of their national affiliation.

The mega-Eurobarometer study of 1996 was the first European-wide survey with enough interviews in every region to allow regional-level analysis of public attitudes towards the EU. Consequently, Table 5.4 shows the aggregate figures for the 15 most pro-European and the 15 most anti-European regions. The data illustrate that national levels of support are also strong indicators of regional levels of support: for example, there are several Italian and Irish regions in the top 15, and several Swedish and Finnish regions in the bottom 15.

Nevertheless, there are some interesting variations within and between nations. Within each member state, regions have different levels of income, different centre–periphery relations, different economic and sectoral structures, and receive different levels of funds from the EU budget (cf. Whitten, Gabel and Palmer, 1998). A full-scale analysis of the relative strengths of these factors is beyond the scope of this chapter, and has not as yet been done using the 1996 mega-Eurobarometer data. Nevertheless, from this cursory look at descriptive data there is evidence that these factors undermine monolithic national interests. For example, although Germany has a moderate level of support, three of the less economically

Table 5.4 Regions and support for European integration

	N	Unification ('for')		Membership ('good thing')		Benefit ('benefited')		Identity ('European')		Average
		%	rank	%	rank	%	rank	%	rank	rank
Most pro-European regions										
Connaught/Ulster (Ireland)	550	87.8	3	82.5	1	89.6	1	16.7	20	1
Molise/Abruzzi (Italy)	181	77.9	=22	69.1	13	46.4	33	27.6	10	2
Lazio (Italy)	547	85.0	5	74.5	8	53.2	25	35.6	2	3
Leinster (Ireland)	688	83.2	9	78.5	4	88.1	2	15.7	=25	4
Emilia Romagna (Italy)	428	92.7	1	73.4	10	49.8	=29	36.6	1	5
Bruxelles-Brussel (Belgium)	351	80.9	13	68.1	17	57.3	21	31.6	4	6
Luxembourg (Luxembourg)	1034	82.4	12	72.6	11	65.2	=13	25.1	12	7
Noord (Netherlands)	378	79.9	=16	81.7	2	63.8	15	17.5	16	8
Campania (Italy)	610	84.7	6	69.3	12	54.4	23	28.4	9	9
Munster (Ireland)	863	75.2	=30	75.9	6	82.0	4	22.5	15	10
Lombardia (Italy)	971	88.5	2	69.0	14	45.6	35	31.3	5	11
Calabria/Puglia/Basilicata (Italy)	720	84.5	7	68.5	16	52.1	26	26.5	11	12
Oost (Netherlands)	788	77.5	25	80.1	3	67.1	9	16.0	24	=13
Trento/Veneto/Fruili (Italy)	729	86.3	4	66.4	=19	49.8	=29	29.5	8	=13
Piedmont/Liguria/D'Aosta (Italy)	682	82.5	11	66.4	=19	50.3	28	34.9	3	15

Most anti-European regions

Brandenburg (Germany)	551	56.2	=73	39.8	71	34.9	67	6.3	78	79
South West (UK)	482	52.1	=83	36.2	80	31.9	76	11.4	=53	80
Etelä-Suomi (Finland)	1210	55.7	=75	41.4	67	33.0	70	3.4	89	81
East Mid's/East Anglia (UK)	674	51.9	=85	34.2	82	30.8	82	11.4	=53	=82
Oberösterreich (Austria)	515	49.3	88	30.1	89	31.1	79	12.2	49	=82
Ostra Mellansverige (Sweden)	534	63.7	56	32.4	85	19.9	90	4.7	86	84
Mecklenburg (Germany)	429	52.7	81	37.4	75	32.4	74	4.2	=87	85
Sachsen (Germany)	1088	51.1	87	38.9	73	30.7	83	6.2	79	86
Västsverige (Sweden)	634	59.1	65	32.3	86	19.1	91	5.4	83	87
Småland Med Öarna (Sweden)	282	55.7	=75	31.2	87	20.9	89	5.3	=84	88
Itä-Suomi (Finland)	501	47.8	90	34.5	81	30.9	81	4.2	=87	89
Pohjois-Suomi (Finland)	374	52.1	83	32.6	84	29.7	84	1.6	93	90
Väli-Suomi (Finland)	463	47.5	91	33.3	83	29.2	85	2.6	92	91
Norra Mellansverige (Sweden)	339	49.3	89	23.6	92	13.0	92	2.9	91	92
Mellersta Noorland (Sweden)	331	46.8	92	18.1	93	8.8	93	3.0	90	93

Note: See the note to Table 5.1 for the wording of the questions.
Source: Eurobarometer no. 44.2bis, 1996; GDP/head taken from Cole and Cole (1997), for 1992.

developed new eastern *Länder* appear in the bottom 15; within the Swedish and Finnish regions, the peripheries are more anti-European than the centre; and within Britain the northern regions and Scotland and Wales, who benefit from EU regional funds, are more favourable towards the EU.

Overall, therefore, the nation cleavage, the old class cleavage and new social and value divisions produce a complex mix of responses to the question of 'Europe – right or wrong?' The most pro-European individual appears to be someone from Ireland, Italy or the Benelux who is a professional or employer, has high income, is highly educated, is well-informed about the EU, is relatively young, and lives in a region that benefits from the single market. As the EU is politicized, through growing realization of 'winners' and 'losers' as a result of EU policies, a pro- and anti-European cleavage becomes manifest in EU politics. This cleavage produces transnational/socioeconomic alliances on either side of the debate.

What the EU should do: 'Europe – right or left?'

If the issue of more or less European integration is about how far and how fast the EU political system should be built, this issue does not capture conflicts of interest and ideology over what the EU should do once it is set up. These questions are associated with a more traditional dimension of politics, relating to how far public institutions should constrain individual social, political and economic choices for a greater public good. At the domestic level in Europe these issues are collapsed into a single dimension of politics, the ubiquitous left–right, and consequently, as these questions are tackled at the European level, actors take up positions on these issues in the basis of their location on the left–right spectrum.

The demise of the left–right as the main dimension of politics has been reported since the 1950s (see for example Bell, 1960; Giddens, 1994). However, 'left' and 'right' remain the dominant categories for political differentiation, voter orientation and party competition throughout Europe (Bartolini and Mair, 1990; Franklin, Mackie and Valen, 1992; Laver and Budge, 1992; Huber and Inglehart, 1995). On a cognitive level, left–right enables individuals to differentiate themselves from each other in both a categorical (dichotomous) and a relative (continuous) sense. As a result, left and right are flexible concepts which have adapted over time as new issues are put on the political agenda. For example, in the early eighteenth century, left and right represented differences over the degree of individual *political and social freedom* from state power: with the left supporting 'liberty' and the right supporting state 'authority'. But, following the onset of industrial society, left and right came to represent differences of the degree of individual *economic freedom* from state power: with the left supporting state 'intervention' and the right supporting the 'free market'.

In the 1990s, following the social changes since the 1960s, both these aspects of the left–right are salient: liberty–authority issues, such as environmentalism and the demand for greater democratic accountability; and intervention – free market, such as welfare policies, unemployment and inflation (cf. Lijphart, 1981; Flanagan, 1987). As a result, the contemporary left and right are summary positions in a two-dimensional political space (Laver and Hunt, 1992). Left denotes equality: 'intervention' to promote equitable outcomes in the market, but 'liberty' to promote social and political equality before the law. Right, on the other hand, denotes inequality: allowing the inequalities inherent in the 'free market' and the privileges protected by 'authority' and tradition (Bobbio, 1995). This does not preclude intermediate positions: intervention/authority (the traditional stance of Christian Democrats), and *laissez-faire*/liberty (such as liberals). However, it does explain why these positions are less common in the 1990s than the oft-observed 'left-libertarianism' (such as greens and social democrats) and 'right-authoritarianism' (such as conservatives and contemporary Christian Democrats) (cf. Finer, 1987; Dunleavy and O'Leary, 1987; Kitschelt, 1994, 1995).

In EU politics, therefore, we should expect individuals on the *left* to favour the EU tackling:

- *economic 'intervention' issues*, such as an EU social policy, an EU tax system, an EU unemployment policy, EU aid for poorer regions, and EU aid for the Third World; and
- *sociopolitical 'liberty' issues*, such as an EU environmental policy, more democratic accountability, citizenship rights, human rights, consumer rights, and sexual equality.

Conversely, we should expect individuals on the *right* to favour the EU tackling:

- *economic 'free market' issues*, such as the single market and a single currency; and
- *sociopolitical 'authority' issues*, such as fighting drug trafficking, and tackling organised crime, and an EU immigration policy.

Using the mega-Eurobarometer data, Table 5.5 shows what European citizens at different locations on the left–right axis think should be on the EU agenda. The descriptive data illustrate that citizens on both left and right think that environmental policy and international organized crime should be the top priority of the EU. This accords with the logic of 'subsidiarity': that issues should only be tackled at the European level that

Table 5.5 Left–right location and EU policy preferences

Self-placement = N =	Far-left 4566 %	rank	Centre-left 13212 %	rank	Centre 22766 %	rank	Centre-right 10389 %	rank	Far-right 3071 %	rank
To make progress, the EU needs . . .										
A European environmental policy	77.7	1	83.1	1	80.1	1	80.8	1	73.0	1
A common agricultural policy	61.7	3	65.7	3	64.7	2	65.3	3	54.0	4
A single market	60.5	4	65.2	4	64.6	3	68.0	2	64.0	2
A European social policy	66.6	2	67.2	2	62.5	4	58.8	4	59.1	3
One foreign policy	54.6	6	57.3	5	58.2	5	54.9	5	47.7	7
One European currency	55.3	5	51.9	7	53.1	6	54.5	6	46.6	8
An elected European government	53.2	7	52.5	6	50.1	7	48.6	8	50.6	5
A European citizenship	50.5	8	48.1	9	49.1	8	48.7	7	39.6	9
One tax system	49.8	9	48.3	8	47.2	9	46.3	9	49.0	6
Key priority of the EU?										
Fighting organized crime	85.9	2	87.6	1	89.9	1	90.4	1	87.7	2
Fighting drug trafficking	84.2	4	85.8	3	89.3	2	89.6	2	87.9	1
Programmes to fight unemployment	86.0	1	86.6	2	85.1	3	81.6	3	81.1	3
Promoting human rights	85.3	3	85.3	4	82.6	4	81.3	4	77.6	4
Dealing with immigration	73.2	8	72.6	5	73.5	5	74.3	5	73.9	5
Protecting consumers	74.2	7	70.1	9	71.2	6	69.2	6	72.9	6
Equality between men and women	75.1	6	72.4	=6	69.8	7	63.7	8	65.4	8
Supporting poorer regions	72.7	9	72.4	=6	68.6	8	65.2	7	65.5	7
Equality for minorities	75.4	5	71.3	8	66.8	9	60.9	9	63.4	9
Aid to the Third World	66.9	10	63.0	10	58.0	10	51.2	10	56.5	10

Note to Table 5.5:
First Question: 'Do you think that, to make further progress in building Europe, it is necessary or not to have . . . ?' Response: 'yes, necessary'; 'no, not necessary'; 'don't know' (table shows per cent of 'yes, necesssary' responses).
Second Question: 'Some people expect the EU to become (even) more active than now in certain areas. For each of the following, please tell me if you consider it a key priority or not'. Response: 'key priority', 'not key-priority', 'don't know' (table shows per cent of 'key priority' responses).
Left–right: 'In political matters people talk of "the left" and "the right". How would you place your views on this scale?' (Show Card: 1 = Left, 2, 3, 4, 5, 6, 7, 8, 9, 10 = Right). The responses were then recoded as follows: 1, 2 = Left, 3, 4 = Centre-left, 5, 6 = Centre, 7, 8 = Centre-right, 9, 10 = Right.
Source: Eurobarometer no. 44.2bis, 1996.

---

cannot be tackled by national governments, since environmental destruction and international organized crime are immune to national borders (cf. Sinnott, 1995).

But, on the question of the relative importance of issues on the EU agenda, the left and right disagree. The variation in the rank ordering of the importance of issues by the left and right is as expected. EU social policy, an elected European government, a single tax system, programmes to fight unemployment, equality between men and women, and between minorities, and support for poorer regions are higher priorities for the centre-left than the centre-right. Conversely, a single market, a single currency, EU citizenship, fighting drug trafficking, and consumer protection are higher priorities for the centre-right than the centre-left. Nevertheless, in addition to the environment and organized crime, the centre-left and centre-right place equal priority on the common agricultural policy, common foreign policy, dealing with immigration, and aid to the Third World (bottom of both lists).

Furthermore, the variation on individual issues is broadly as expected. For example, the centre-left is more in favour than the centre-right of EU environmental policy, EU social policy, an elected EU government, a single tax system, programmes to fight unemployment, human rights, consumer protection, equality for men and women, support for poorer regions, equality for minorities, and aid to the Third World. Conversely, the centre-right is more in favour than the centre-left of the single market, a single currency, fighting organized crime, fighting drug trafficking, and dealing with immigration.

In addition, there is a clear pattern of variation between centre-left and far-left, and between the centre-right and far-right. On the citizenship question, for example, the far-left is more favourable than either the centre-left or centre-right. This issue is one of several issues on which the far-left is more favourable than the centre-left – the others include a single currency, an elected European government, and a single tax system. However, this portfolio of issues represents a coherent position: of a European state, with the institutional, fiscal and legal means to undertake European-wide redistribution. At the other end of the spectrum, the far-right prefers several issues to the centre-right – such as an EU social policy, an elected European government, and a single tax system – which imply support for a state-like system with genuine redistributive powers. These positions consequently accord with the expectation that both far-left and far-right support more radical social and economic transformation than the centre-left and centre-right, and hence advocate equipping the EU with the institutional and policy tools to achieve this.

In sum, independent of pro- and anti-European positions, EU citizens are divided over what the EU should do. As we showed in the previous section, social groups with shared interests might lobby for an EU competence in a particular area: for example, highly paid white-collar employees and highly skilled workers are likely to ally with employers/directors and professionals to promote economic integration. But, once this has occurred, this pro-European alliance will divide into left and right positions: with the left supporting social and environmental regulation of the single market, and the right supporting deregulatory policies (cf. Rhodes and van Apeldoorn, 1997; Hooghe and Marks, 1998; Hix, 1999) (see Chapter 8).

The 'electoral connection': strategic dilemmas for Euro-elites

Put together, these two dimensions – pro-/anti-Europe and left–right – produce a strategic environment within which Europe's political elites must compete for electoral support. One problem, however, is that Europe's elites are more pro-European than their citizens (cf. Slater, 1982). In February/May 1996, the Commission undertook the first survey of elite attitudes towards integration – the so-called 'Top Decision-Makers Survey'. In every member state, the survey interviewed between 200 and 500 senior elected politicians, senior civil servants, business and trade union leaders, leading media owners and editors, influential academics, and leading cultural and religious figures. Some of the results of this survey are presented in Table 5.6, in comparison with the mass attitudes revealed in the general *Eurobarometer* survey of October/November 1996.

The data illustrates three things. First, in all member states the elite is more in favour of European integration than the mass public. For example, 94 per cent of all elites see EU membership as a good thing, compared with

Table 5.6   *Comparison of elite and mass support for European integration*

| | Membership ('good thing') | | Benefit ('benefited') | | EMU ('in favour') | | Average Elite – Mass difference |
	Elite (%)	Mass (%)	Elite (%)	Mass (%)	Elite (%)	Mass (%)	(%)
Germany	98	39	98	33	90	39	58
Belgium	96	45	95	40	98	55	50
Austria	86	31	73	34	78	35	46
Sweden	84	27	63	18	65	32	45
France	93	46	91	44	90	56	43
Finland	88	39	70	37	69	29	43
United Kingdom	86	36	84	34	60	31	43
Spain	97	51	83	37	95	65	41
Denmark	84	44	91	55	76	33	40
Greece	92	57	92	66	92	63	30
Italy	97	68	91	51	88	73	28
Luxembourg	93	73	97	64	93	66	27
Portugal	91	54	94	69	77	57	27
Netherlands	96	74	97	69	91	69	24
Ireland	95	76	98	86	89	64	19
EU15	94	48	90	42	85	51	43
Range	14	49	35	68	38	44	—
Standard deviation	4.8	15.4	9.9	17.9	11.4	15.5	—

Note: See the note to Table 5.1 for the wording of the 'Membership' and 'Benefit' questions. The 'EMU' question read as follows: 'Are you for or against the European Union having one European currency in all Member States, including [your country]? That is, replacing the [name of national currency] by the European currency, that is the Euro?' Response: 'very much for', 'somewhat for', 'somewhat against', 'very much against' (table shows per cent of 'very much for' plus 'somewhat for' responses).
Source: Eurobarometer no. 44.2bis, 1996.

only 48 per cent of the general public. Second, despite this there is considerable variation in the elite–mass gap in different member states. For example, the elite–mass gap is much larger in Germany, Belgium, Austria and Sweden than in Ireland, the Netherlands, Portugal, Luxembourg and Italy. Third, there is a higher level of cohesion amongst elites from different nations than amongst the mass publics – as indicated by the lower ranges and standard deviations for the elite scores. For example, in every member state, a majority of every national elite supports the single currency.

This might suggest that European integration is conducted by a 'cartel of elites', which has emerged to overcome and control the deep divisions between the national mass public (Dahrendorf, 1959). However, elites cannot simply do as they please, in the face of public opposition: political elites, for example, must compete in national and European elections. If a party competes in these elections on a strongly pro-European platform and the median voter in their country is anti-European, they are likely to lose the election. This 'electoral connection' consequently presents a powerful incentive for political elites to behave 'as if' they share the opinions of the general public, even when in reality they are more pro-European. Testing this argument, Carrubba (1998) and Wessels (1995) find that party manifesto promises about Europe are very close to the attitudes of their supporters.

Consequently, despite an elite–mass gap, political leaders *are* forced to compete in the new strategic environment. Figure 5.5 shows the approximate location of the electorate in the EU issue space, where the 'X's mark the mean positions of the occupational groups in response to two questions: (1) where they place themselves on the left–right; and (2) whether they think their country benefits from EU membership. The positions of the occupational groups illustrate that the EU political market is fragmented: intra-class alliances such as manual workers and skilled workers, white-collar workers and professionals, or employers and small business owners, may hold together on left–right issues (such as the level of social regulation of the single market), but if the pro-/anti-Europe dimension is salient these alliances are likely to break down.

This, consequently, presents problems for political parties. For example, as the traditional constituency (manual workers) of social democratic parties has declined, these parties have built alliances with groups that are close on the left–right dimension (such as white-collar employees, students and the liberal professions) (Kitschelt, 1994). However, because of the differing attitudes of these groups towards European integration, this cross-class alliance cannot hold together on the pro-/anti-Europe dimension. On the other side, conservative parties and Christian Democrats have traditionally attracted the support of farmers, employers, professionals, and small businessmen – who are logically adjacent on the left–right dimension – but these interests are far apart on the question of more or less Europe.

As a result, parties are forced to pursue one of two strategies to ensure that there is no party competition on this dimension of EU politics (Hix, 1999):

1. Parties can refuse to differentiate themselves from each other on this dimension, by taking up identical (usually moderately pro-Europe) positions.

Figure 5.5 *Location of classes in the two-dimensional EU political space*

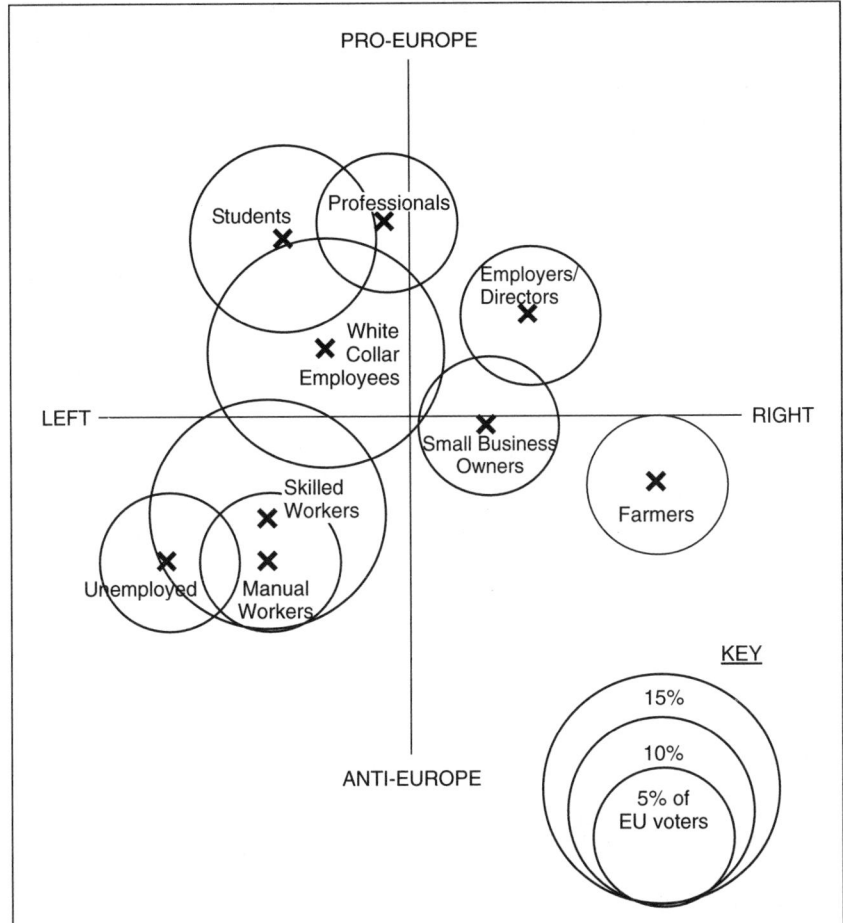

Note: The Xs represent the mean responses of each occupational group to the 'Benefit' and 'Left–Right' questions (see the note to Tables 5.1 and 5.5 respectively for the wording of these questions). The origin represents a result of 1.40 (where 'benefit' scores '1' and 'not benefit' scores '2') on the benefit question and 3.0 ('Centre') on the left–right question. The scales of the axes are proportional, such that the average standard deviation from the mean on both questions (for all occupational groups) is the same cartesian distance on each dimension in the figure. The ovals represent the range of preferences of approximately 15 per cent of each occupational group, as a proportion of the standard deviation of each question. The size of the ovals is consequently proportional to the size of each occupation group as a proportion of the total EU population.

Source: Calculated from data in *Eurobarometer*, 44.2bis, 1996.

2. Parties can play down the differences between them on this dimension, by refusing to address the question of European integration in domestic electoral contests.

Either strategy reduces the saliency of the pro-/anti-Europe cleavage.

Figure 5.6 in fact shows how electorates see the relationship between the left–right and pro-/anti-European dimensions in each member state, and suggests that three different patterns of political competition in the EU issue space have emerged. First, in Ireland, Portugal, France, Belgium and Germany, the centre-left and centre-right are pro-European, whereas the far-left and far-right are anti-European. In these systems, parties on the moderate left and right can pursue the first strategy to minimize interparty competition: of convergence on the question of Europe, and allowing extremist movements to advocate anti-European positions. This has been the case particularly in France and Germany.

Second, in Greece, Luxembourg, Sweden, Denmark and Finland, the right is more pro-European than the left. In Scandinavia, for example, European integration is seen as a threat to national welfare states. Third, in Italy, Spain, the Netherlands, Germany, the United Kingdom and Austria, the left is more pro-European than the right. For example, in Italy, Spain and the United Kingdom, European integration is seen as a progressive democratizing force and in Austria and the Netherlands as a liberal-cosmopolitan project.

In both the second and third models, the question of Europe has the potential of becoming a cleavage in the domestic party system. In these systems, party leaders face a dilemma: pressure for interparty competition on the question of Europe, but the difficulty of building a cross-class alliance that could sustain a coherent pro- or anti-European stance. In this situation, the likely outcome is the second strategy: attempts to play down the significance of Europe in domestic party competition. The result, however, is likely to be internal party fragmentation, between party leaders and rank-and-file members. This has happened in the United Kingdom, Denmark, Austria, Sweden, Finland and Greece.

Overall, political elites from different nations share similar pro-European attitudes, but the ability to build a cross-party pro-European alliance at the electoral level is increasingly difficult in the face of an electorate that is fragmented on the old left–right divide. Similarly, the establishment of transnational centre-left or centre-right alliances either for or against Europe is equally difficult, as natural class allies have different interests and attitudes towards European integration. In other words, the emergence of elite competition in the EU political space is unlikely without a fragmentation of the existing structure of partisan competition, which was 'frozen' to the left–right dimension of conflict by the establishment of electoral democracy prior to the process of European integration (Lipset and Rokkan, 1967).

Figure 5.6   *Three models of political competition in the EU issue space*

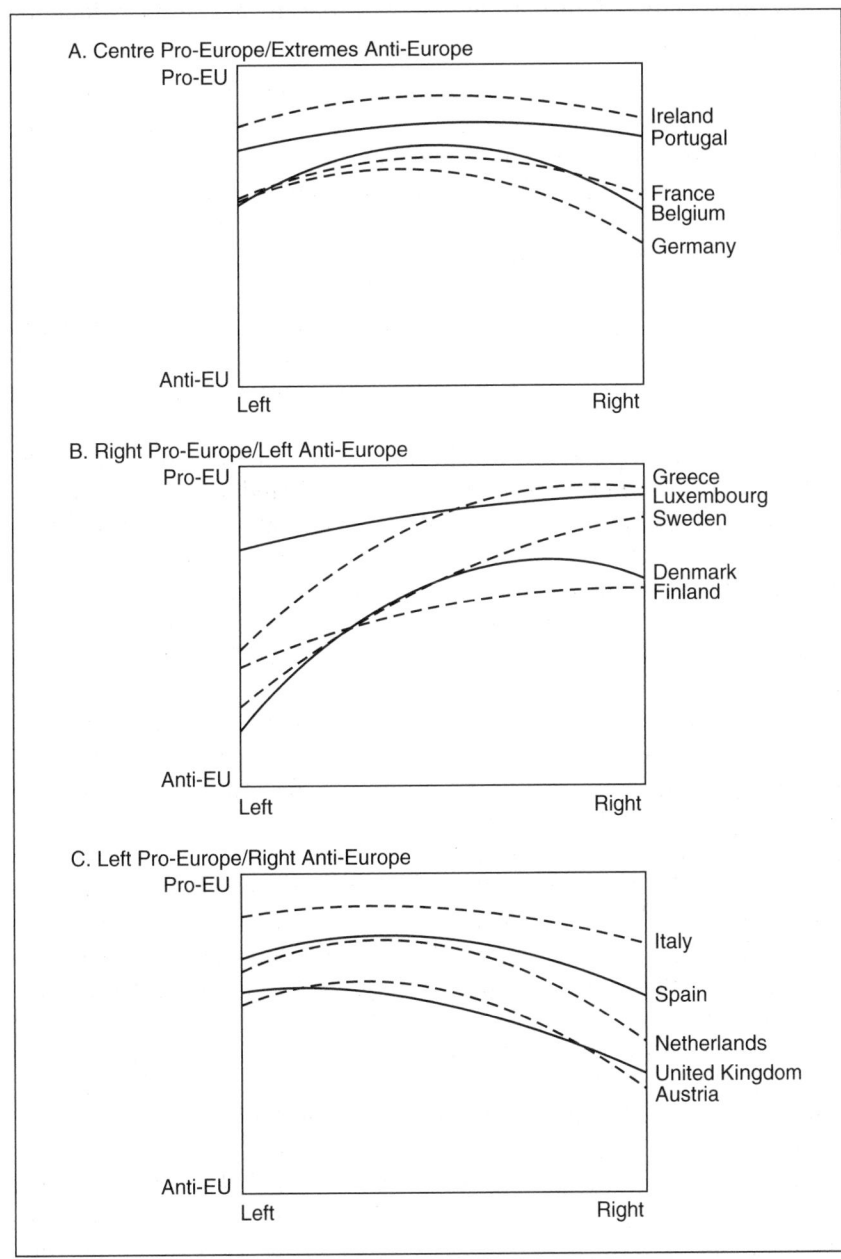

Note: The graphs are quadratic regression models, where responses to the left–right placement question is the independent variable and responses the 'benefit' question is the dependent variable.

Source: Calculated from data in *Eurobarometer*, no. 44.2bis, 1996.

Conclusion: a politicized plural society

> Social homogeneity and political consensus are regarded as prerequisites for, or factors strongly conducive to, stable democracy . . . but it is not *impossible* to achieve and maintain stable democratic government in a plural society. In a consociational democracy, the centrifugal tendencies inherent in a plural society are counteracted by the co-operative attitudes and behaviour of the leaders of the different segments of the population. (Lijphart, 1977, p. 1).

The EU is a 'plural society' divided between the nation-states of Europe. Until the 1990s, however, the EU was a stable system of governance. This was essentially because of a pattern of elite behaviour prescribed in Lijphart's theory: where national elites had shared interests in promoting European integration yet preventing the erosion of national interests that provided their own legitimacy (cf. Taylor, 1991; Chryssochoou, 1994). The result was the so-called 'permissive consensus', whereby Europe's publics were content to delegate responsibility to their leaders to tackle the European integration project.

However, the permissive consensus has collapsed, and the result is a more complex pattern of social and political interaction. At the societal level, European integration no longer commands widespread support and, new transnational socioeconomic and value-based divisions are shaping people's attitudes towards the EU. In different nation-states, members of the same social class share the same interests in the single market, and consequently share the same attitudes towards the EU. Similarly, in different nation-states individuals from the same generation or educational group share similar political values that also produce similar attitudes towards European integration.

But, EU politics is not simply about how far and how fast the process of integration should proceed. For example, should the EU promote the free market or protect the welfare state? Should the EU promote civil rights and freedoms or protect European social and cultural traditions? On these questions, the attitudes of EU citizens are determined less by national affiliation than by their positions on the traditional left–right dimension of politics.

Consequently, in this post-consensus environment, Europe's elites are faced with a dilemma. They can continue the pattern of consensus politics, but this strategy risks provoking public opposition to the EU. Alternatively, elites could abandon consensus politics and compete on the question of European integration *between* nations: with different national elites taking up different pro- and anti-European positions. However, this would inevitable result in the breakdown of the EU system. Or, elites could compete on issues on the EU agenda in the same way they do in the domestic arena: with left and right parties advocating different EU policy agendas. However, this would provoke a breakdown of existing class-party alliances, as different groups within both the working class and the middle classes have different interests in the single market.

In short, the structure of public opinion relating to the EU presents a new strategic environment for Europe's leaders. In the short term, elites will be forced to react to these constraints by changing their own patterns of competition and coalition formation both at the domestic and European levels. Nevertheless, in the longer term, political leaders could seek to change these constraints by shaping the formation of public opinion to alleviate their own strategic dilemmas.

Chapter 6

Parties, Elections and EU Democracy

Theory of elections: choosing parties, leaders and policies
The European Union party system
Party organization at the European level
European Parliament elections: second-order national contests
Alternative mechanisms: direct democracy and presidentialism
Conclusion: towards representational government?

This chapter looks at how the two central processes of representative democracy operate in the EU: party competition and elections. At the domestic level in Europe, parties and elections operate hand-in-hand in the 'competitive party government' model. There is an emerging 'party system' at the European level: European-wide elections are held every five years, and party organizations exist in the EP (the party groups) and between the national party leaders (the transnational party federations). But, competitive party democracy at the European level remains some way off.

Theory of elections: choosing parties, leaders and policies

Elections are the central mechanism of representative democracy, and operate in two interlinked ways (King, 1981). On the one hand, elections allow voters to choose between rival agendas for public policy. These are presented by political parties or leaders, and the winning 'team' implements their agenda by taking control of the levers of public policy. On the other hand, elections allow voters to choose between rival office-holders: voters choose between rival candidates for public office, as much on their personality as on their policy platform or party affiliation, and the winning candidate becomes the head of the executive branch of government. Either way, elections allow voters to 'throw the scoundrels out' if they flaunt their electoral promises, prove incompetent, or less popular than a rival group of elites. In other words, the essence of democracy is choice, which requires competition between rival agendas and/or candidates (Schumpeter, 1943).

In most democratic systems, these two processes are combined in a single model of 'competitive party government' (ibid., Weber, 1946 [1919];

Schattschneider, 1942). In this model, the leader of the party that wins the election becomes the head of the executive (that is, the prime minister), and the party acts cohesively in the legislative arena to implement the policy agenda presented in the electoral 'manifesto'. In the competitive-party-government model, therefore, voters exercise an indirect choice about office-holders and the policy agenda, via the vehicle of the cohesive party organization. As a result, the party leader or the policy agenda can be changed by the winning party without necessarily requiring the consent of the voters in another election.

Although this is the predominant model in western democracies, alternative models allow voters to exercise a direct choice over office-holders and/or the policy agenda. First, in a presidential model voters directly elect the head of the executive. Parties will tend to propose a single candidate. However, the election campaign is invariably about the policies and personality of the individual candidates, rather than the overall policy platform and leadership team of the political parties. Moreover, the winner of the presidential election is directly accountable to the voters, over the head of his/her political party.

Second, through referendums voters can exercise a direct choice over the policy agenda. Again, parties will tend to advocate one or other side in a referendum, and the (un)popularity of the parties on each side of the debate (particularly those in government) will have a significant impact on the way citizens vote in a referendum. Nevertheless, if a referendum outcome is binding, the result is a direct impact on public policy, in that parties will not be able to amend the choice of the voters in subsequent legislative action. Consequently, the basic difference to the competitive-party-government model holds for both presidential elections and referendums: where cohesive political parties are not required, or do not interfere, in the translation of voters' choices into executive or legislative action.

So, which model for the EU? Following the logic of the competitive-party-government model, most commentators on the EU democratic deficit argued, first, that the EP should be directly elected and, second, it should be given greater powers in the EU legislative process and in the selection of the EU executive (that is, the Commission). As a result, direct elections to the EP were introduced in 1979 and have been held at five-year intervals ever since, and in a series of institutional reforms the EP has been given a greater power in the EU legislative process vis-à-vis the Council and in the selection of the president of the Commission. At face value, then, the democratic deficit has been closed. However, a genuine system of competitive party democracy will not come about simply because the right rules are in place; the model also requires that actors behave in a certain way within these rules. In other words:

- political parties should compete in EP elections over issues on the EU policy agenda and/or for EU political office;
- voters should make a choice in EP elections on the basis of these rival policy platforms or candidates; and
- the winning electoral choices should be translated into legislative and executive action at the European level via cohesive political parties.

If this pattern of behaviour does not exist, the democratic deficit will still exist. Nevertheless, further institutional mechanisms may be able to facilitate genuine competitive party democracy in the EU, or alternative (direct) forms of democracy may be introduced such as European-wide referendums or an election of the Commission president.

The European Union party system

Political parties are the main aggregate political organizations in European politics. This may not seem immediately obvious when observing the EU. However, on closer inspection, party organizations, affiliations, alignments, ideologies and interests take centrestage. All politicians in Europe are party politicians, including those in the Council, the Commission and the EP. As the main organs in election campaigns, parties are the key actors in domestic elections and in EP elections, and as the main organs connecting governments to parliaments and parliaments to voters, parties are central to the relations between the EU institutions and between the national and EU levels. To understand how EU politics work, therefore, we must also understand how parties work.

Parties as organizations pursue two types of political goals. On the one hand they pursue political office (Downs, 1957), and in the EU the key political office is national government. Despite the growing role of the EU in many areas of public policy, national governmental office still gives party leaders control of the key levers of public policy: especially in the large areas of public expenditure such as education, health and housing. Moreover, national governmental office also gives party leaders a central role in EU-level decision-making in the Council. On the other hand, parties pursue policy: the outputs of the political process (Strom, 1990). In the EU system, these policies are promised in election manifestos and party programmes and secured through outputs from the national and EU decision-making processes.

The operation of democracy in the EU consequently depends on how parties secure these goals. On the one hand this is determined by the rules of the game, such as whether the EP has significant power in the EU legislative process. However, it also depends on the shape of the 'strategic environment' in which parties operate: the number of issue dimensions in the EU party system, the levels of electoral support for the different political parties, and the locations of the different political parties on these issue dimensions.

In terms of the dimensionality of the EU party system, we can build on the findings of the previous chapter. As discussed, divisions (cleavages) in society produce issue dimensions, around which political elites can mobilize. At the domestic level in Europe, most social divisions are summarized in the single ubiquitous left–right dimension. At the European level, until recently, the dominant dimension of political competition has been between actors favouring further integration and those that favour the status quo or less integration: an integration–sovereignty cleavage (see for example Garrett 1992). Nevertheless, as EU policy-making starts to encroach into traditional areas of domestic political competition, the left–right dimension can be expected to emerge at the European level.

Within this two-dimensional space, the position of the party families are as shown in Figure 6.1: where the 'X's represent the mean position of the party families and the ovals illustrate the range of the locations of the individual parties in each party family along the two dimensions (Hix and Lord 1997, pp. 49–53). The figure illustrates several key features of the EU party system. First, the shape of the ellipses, and the different degrees of overlap on the two dimensions, reveals that most party families are more coherent on the left–right dimension than on the pro-/anti-Europe dimension. This is because the core party families – Socialists, Christian Democrats, Liberals and Conservatives – differentiate themselves from each other on the left–right dimension of politics in the domestic arena, and not on the question of European integration. In contrast, the Regionalists and Anti-Europeans, who define themselves, respectively, 'against' and 'for' the existing structure of the nation-state in Europe, occupy a more coherent space on the European-integration-issue dimension, but not on the left-right dimension.

Second, these party locations suggest that the core EU party families prefer to compete on left–right rather than integration–sovereignty issues. When questions relating to more or less European integration emerge, it is difficult for party families to remain internally cohesive, as divisions will emerge within each party family (between parties from different member states) rather than between each party family. As a result, parties would rather couch the issue of 'Europe' in left–right terms, which explains why the mean positions of the main party families are close together on the pro-/anti-Europe dimension in the figure, and far apart on the left–right dimension. In the 1990s, the main party families refuse to compete on the question of European integration, all preferring to advocate moderately pro-integration positions. This is a very different structure to party

Figure 6.1   *Positions of the party families in the EU party system*

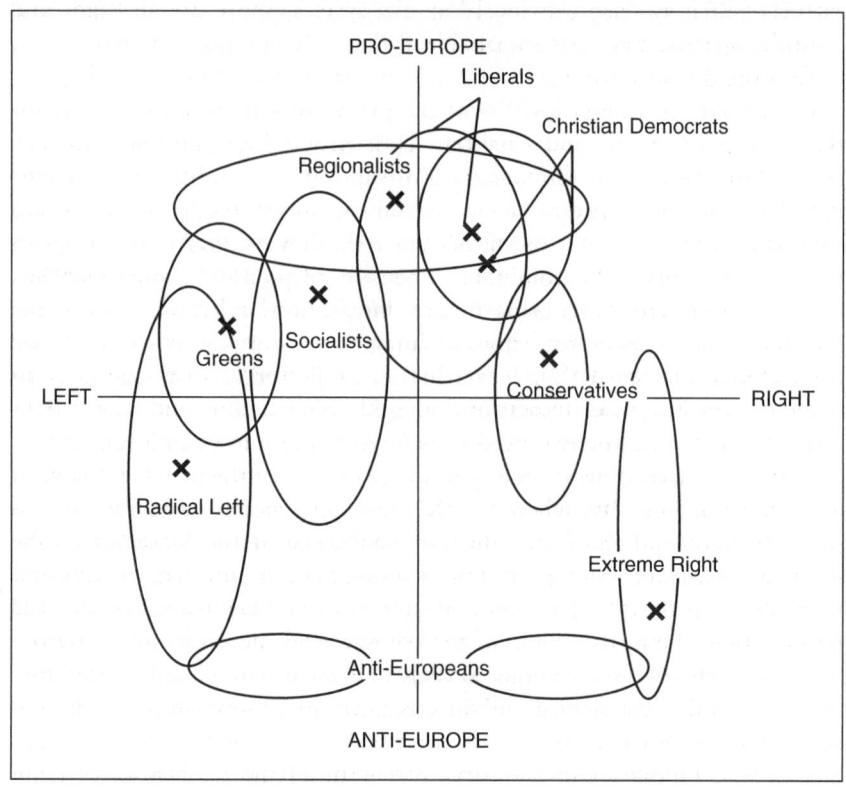

Source: Hix and Lord (1997, p. 50).

competition in the 1970s and early 1980s, when most Socialist parties were sceptical of European integration. To avoid internal divisions on the question of Europe within the Socialist family, and between elites and party members within many parties, the only strategy was to advocate the same position as the main families on the right of the party system (cf. Hix 1998b).

In addition, the locations of the families in the policy space, and the overlaps between them, suggest that there are several different combinations of likely alliances in the EU party system. The clearest natural allies are the Christian Democrats and Liberals, both of whom are moderately centre-right and pro-European. The Socialists, in contrast, are faced with a choice: a potential alliance with these two parties on a common pro-European platform, which could also include the Regionalists, or an alliance with the Greens and Radical Left in a common left-wing bloc. However, this later alliance would be divided on the question of more or less European integration. Similarly, an opposing centre-right coalition including the Conservatives would be divided on European questions. By virtue of their isolation in the EU party system, the Extreme Right and Anti-Europeans are 'un-coalitionable'.

As a result, there are two main types of coalition politics in the EU party system. First, there is a large centrist 'pro-European bloc', of Socialists, Regionalists, Liberals and Christian Democrats. An opposing 'anti-European bloc', based on the Greens, Radical Left, Conservatives, Extreme Right and Anti-Europeans, would be almost impossible to construct and maintain because there are large differences between these party families on left–right issues. Second, there is a 'left bloc', led by the Socialists, which is opposed by a 'centre-right bloc', of the Liberals, Christian Democrats and Conservatives. However, this second type of coalition politics can only exist if left–right issues predominate over questions of more or less European integration as both the left bloc and centre-right bloc are internally divided on European integration issues. Consequently, the ability of coalitions to be constructed in a European electoral contest and held together through common action in the European institutions depends on the nature of the issues confronting the EU. For example, if the EU is preoccupied with institutional questions, as in an Intergovernmental Conference, competition between left and centre-right blocs would be hard to maintain. Conversely, on issues like the level of social and environmental protection in the single market or how to combat EU unemployment, a single pro-European alliance is likely to dissolve into the left and centre-right camps.

Finally, in terms of the electoral strengths of the various parties and political blocs, as Table 6.1 shows, in national and European elections between 1990 and 1994 the left and centre-right were evenly balanced, with around 40 per cent of the votes across the EU. However, whereas the Socialists are the largest party in the left bloc in every member state, no single party family predominates on the right in EU politics: with the Christian Democrats, Liberals and Conservatives evenly balanced, and with different party families large in some member states and small or even non-existent in others. The figures also suggest that a potential Socialist–Liberal, centre-left coalition would have the same numerical strength as a left-bloc. However, in EU politics, given the location and overlap between the Liberals and Christian Democrats, the Socialists may as well construct a broader pro-European alliance, and because of the balance between left, centre-left and centre-right, this broad pro-European alliance is the only one with any real chance of gaining majority support amongst the European voters: with about 60 per cent of the vote between 1990 and 1994.

We can draw several conclusions from this analysis. First, politics in the EU is dominated by political parties, who seek political office at the national level and policy outputs from national and EU decision-making.

Table 6.1 *Electoral strengths of the party families and political blocs*

| | LEFT | | | PRO-EUROPE | | | | | |
| | Rad. Left | Green | Soc. | Reg. | CENTRE-RIGHT | | | Extr. Right | Anti-Euro. |
					Lib.	C.Dem	Con.		
Austria	0.2	4.6	**31.4**		3.0	**39.8**		16.7	
Belgium		10.8	**24.0**	6.0	17.0	**24.4**	9.3		
Denmark	9.0	0.4	**26.6**	5.5	**26.4**	1.7	16.9	4.7	22.2
Finland	10.1	6.8	**22.1**	0.3	**30.8**	3.1	19.3		
France	7.9	6.6	**17.4**		8.0	5.0	**28.0**	10.7	6.2
Germany	3.8	7.9	**33.2**		7.1	**40.3**		3.4	
Greece	12.1	0.5	**41.0**		2.8		**42.5**	0.7	
Ireland	3.2	4.7	**15.2**		**42.7**	24.4			
Italy	6.0	3.1	**26.8**	8.4	4.6	18.8	**19.2**	10.4	
Luxembourg	2.6	9.8	**24.8**		18.8	**31.5**		0.3	
Netherlands	1.2	4.9	**23.5**		**32.5**	26.5		1.1	7.2
Portugal	9.0	1.0	**32.0**		**42.2**	8.5		0.4	
Spain	11.6	0.8	**34.9**	11.1	1.0		**37.7**	0.1	
Sweden	4.5	3.3	**37.6**	17.6	7.1		**21.9**	6.7	
U.Kingdom	0.1	2.4	**39.3**	6.4	17.1		**34.4**	0.1	
Average	5.2	4.6	**30.1**	3.8	11.0	15.9	**18.9**	5.0	1.6
		39.9%				45.8%			
				60.8%					

Note: The percentages refer to the average strengths of the party families in national and European elections between 1990 and 1994. For Denmark, however, the figure for the anti-European movement is for the European elections of 1989 and 1994. The numbers in bold are the strongest parties in the centre-right and left blocs in each member state.
Source: Hix and Lord (1997: 52)

Second, the policies pursued by parties in the EU arena are derived from the positions of the historical party families, but these families are defined on left–right issues and are internally divided on questions of European integration. Third, left and centre-right blocs could be constructed in the European arena, but this structure of competition requires a predominance of left–right issues on the EU agenda, and neither of these blocs are likely to be able to construct majority support. Overall, political parties may wish to influence policy outcomes from the EU institutions, but the strategic environment of EU politics makes it very difficult to construct coherent, cohesive and majority-winning coalitions in pursuit of this goal.

Party organization at the European level

We can test these arguments by looking at how parties behave at the European level: within and between the EU institutions. There are two different party organizational structures at this level. First, the party groups in the EP were first formed between national parties from the same party families in the old Assembly of the European Coal and Steel Community in 1953 – the precursor of the modern EP (Oudenhave, 1965). In the more than 40-year period since this development, the EP party groups have evolved into highly developed organizations with their own budgets, leadership structures, administrative support stuff, rules of procedure, offices, committees and working groups. The party groups seek to structure the working agenda of the Parliament, organize the behaviour of their MEPs, and secure the placement of their MEPs into the positions in the EP – such as the president of the EP, the Committee chairpersons, and the *rapporteurs* on key pieces of EU legislation. In other words, the EP party groups are as development and operate in the same way as the party 'factions' within the national parliaments of the EU member states.

The second element of party organization at the European level are the so-called 'transnational party federations'. These are organizations of national parties in the EC member states that were formed in the build-up to the first direct elections in the mid-1970s, in the expectation that elections could be fought on European-wide electoral programmes. The Confederation of Socialists Parties of the EC was the first to be established, in April 1974, soon followed by the Federation of Liberal and Democratic Parties of the EC, in March 1976, and the European People's Party (EPP), of Christian Democratic parties, in April 1976. Despite their names, these were very loose organizations which had no real coherent organization at the European level, and no coherent policy orientation despite bi-annual European party conferences.

At the instigation of the secretaries-general of the three party federations, however, the Maastricht Treaty introduced a new 'party article' (article 191 [ex 138a]) which states that:

> Political parties at the European level are important as a factor for integration within the Union. They contribute to forming a European awareness and to expressing the will of the citizens of the Union.

Following this article, the Socialist, Liberal and Christian Democrat party federations established new and more coherent organizations. The Party of European Socialists (PES) was launched in November 1992, the EPP adopted a set of new statutes in November 1992, a new European Federation of Green Parties (EFGP) was launched in June 1993, and the European Liberal, Democratic and Reform Party (ELDR) was established in December 1993. Moreover, each of these organizations reinforced their links to the party groups in the EP, and to the representatives of these parties in the Commission, Council and European Council. Instead of simply transnational umbrella organizations for fighting the EP elections, these new 'Euro-parties' were beginning to develop as 'extra-parliamentary' party organizations at the European level: like the extra-parliamentary central offices and central committees of parties in the domestic arena (Hix, 1995a).

As Table 6.2 shows, between 1990 and 1994, politicians from parties in the party organizations of the centre-right dominated the EU institutions. In the Parliament, the two blocs were fairly evenly balanced: with 35 per cent of MEPs from the PES party federation the major group on the left; and on the centre-right, 20 per cent from the parties of the EPP party federation, 10 per cent from parties of the ELDR party federation, and 15 per cent from Conservative parties that were not members of the EPP party federation, such as the British Conservatives. In the Commission and Council, however, the centre-right were in a clear majority: with 67 per cent of the commissioners and 76 per cent of all national government ministries (that is, those who sit in the EU Council).

In the 1995 to 1999 period the picture is somewhat different. The left and centre-right remained balanced in the Parliament, but 9 out of 20 commissioners were Socialist, and Socialist parties controlled 46 per cent of all national government ministries. This change was partly as a result of EU enlargement on 1 January 1995 to include Austria, Finland and Sweden: two of whom nominated Socialist commissioners and all of whom had Socialists in government, either ruling alone or as a major party in a coalition government. Nevertheless, this shift was also due to Socialist party victories in Italy, Portugal, the Netherlands, Britain, France and Germany in this period.

If the model of competitive party government works in the EU, this change should produce a concomitant shift in the policy agenda of the EU away from market deregulation and towards social protection and social expenditure. However, as discussed above, this translation from party strengths to policy outputs requires party actors from the same party family to cooperate, and winning coalitions to be constructed between different party families. Consequently, this depends on the cohesive behaviour of, and coalition-building between, the party organizations at the European level: the party groups in the EP and the transnational party federations within and between the other EU institutions.

Table 6.2 Strengths of political parties in the EU institutions

Party federation/family	Parliament 1990–94	Parliament 1995–99	Commission 1990–94	Commission 1995–99	Council 1990–94	Council 1995–99	All 1990–94	All 1995–99
PES (Socialists)	35	34	33	45	24	46	31	42
EFGP (Greens)	6	5				2	2	2
Radical Left	9	5				1	3	2
Total Left	**50**	**44**	**33**	**45**	**24**	**49**	**36**	**46**
EPP (Chr.Dems and Cons)	20	22	31	20	28	29	26	24
Non-EPP Conservatives	15	13	18	20	30	13	21	15
ELDR (Liberals)	10	9	18	15	18	8	15	11
Total Centre-Right	**45**	**44**	**67**	**55**	**76**	**50**	**62**	**50**
Regionalists	3	3					1	1
Total Pro-Europe	**65**	**68**	**82**	**80**	**70**	**83**	**72**	**77**
Extreme Right	1	5				1	1	2
Anti-Europeans	1	3					1	1

Note: Party Federations: PES = Party of European Socialists, EFGP = European Federation of Green Parties, EPP = European People's Party, ELDR = European Liberal, Democrat and Reform Party. As in Table 6.1, the 'pro-Europe' bloc is the PES, EPP, ELDR and the Regionalists. The figures for the Council refer to the per cent of all national government ministries controlled by each party family.
Source: Calculated from data in Corbett *et al.* (1994), Edwards and Spence (1997), Hix and Lord (1997).

Party behaviour and cohesion in the European Parliament

The EP party groups have been relatively successful in organizing the behaviour of MEPs. The ability of MEPs to be reselected is controlled by national political parties (see Chapter 3), and once in the Parliament the party groups possess certain resources to encourage MEPs to abide by their party groups' wishes. For example, the party groups control the nomination of the key offices of the Parliament, such as the EP president, the appointment of committee chairpersons, internal offices within the groups, and the *rapporteur*ships on the different pieces of EU legislation (Raunio, 1996a, pp. 44–86). As MEPs have learned that their ability to play an influential role in the EP is increasingly dependent upon the party groups, there has been a growing 'cohesion' of the groups in the legislative workings of the parliament (Attinà, 1990; Quanjel and Wolters, 1993). This structure also provides incentives for the smaller groups that tend to be created after each set of EP elections to join the larger groups by the end of the Parliament term (Bardi, 1996).

The simplest way of measuring the cohesion of parliamentary parties is to look at the frequency with which their members vote as a block. An 'Index of Agreement' is used to measure this level of cohesion in 'roll-call votes': where 100 means that all the members of the group voted the same way in every such vote; and 0 means that the group was divided against itself (in other words 50 per cent vs 50 per cent) in every vote. As Table 6.3 shows, the index of agreement for the EP groups is relatively high, especially if compared to similar measures of the performance of the Democrats and Republicans in the US Congress (Brzinski, 1995). Moreover, cohesion of the main party groups has risen over time; for example, the Socialists improved their performance from 62.2 in the 1984–89 parliament to 78.6 in the 1989–94 parliament. The party groups have also become increasingly cohesive despite the fact that the number of national delegations in the major parties has increased; for example, between the 1984–89 and 1989–94 parliaments, the Italian Socialists joined the PES, and the Spanish, British and French Conservatives joined the EPP.

Furthermore, the party groups have been able to organize a coherent structure of inter-party competition and coalition-formation in the parliament. Table 6.4 shows the percentage of times the majority of each party group voted with the majority of another party group in a series of votes at the beginning of the 1994–99 parliament, and these results illustrate several key elements of interparty competition in the parliament. First, the main dimension of competition is the left–right – the percentage of times a party group votes with another decreases as the group is further away on the left–right spectrum. The only case where this rule does not hold is for the Europe of Nations group. But this fits into the two-dimensional picture of

Table 6.3 *Party group cohesion in the European Parliament*

Party group (left to right)	1984–89	1989–94
Left Unity (Orthodox Communists)	—	93.8
European Unitarian Left (Radical Left)	71.2	92.3
Greens (Greens and Allies)	—	87.5
Party of European Socialists (Socialists)	62.2	78.6
Rainbow Group (Regionalists and Greens)	67.8	69.5
Liberal, Democratic and Reform Party (Liberals)	69.5	85.7
European People's Party (Christian Democrats and Conservatives)	84.1	88.2
European Democratic Alliance (French, Irish and Portuguese Conservatives)	75.7	64.5
European Democratic Group (British Conservatives)	82.9	92.2
European Right (Exteme Right)	96.1	99.9
Average	76.2	84.1

Note: The scores are 'Indices of Agreement' (IA) (Attinà, 1990). An IA is a measure of the relationship between the three modalities of votes cast by the members of a party group ('in favour', 'against', and 'abstain'), in relation to the total number of votes cast by the members of the group. Formally:

$$IA = \frac{\text{highest modality} - \text{sum of the other two modalities}}{\text{total number of votes cast by the party group}} \times 100$$

In other words, the index is equal to 100 if all the members of the group vote the same way, and is equal to 0 if exactly half the members of a group vote one way and the rest vote another way.
Source: Calculated from data in Attinà (1990), Raunio (1996).

EU politics as this group is aligned on the pro-/anti-Europe dimension of EU politics rather than the left–right dimension, and hence votes more with the European Unitarian Left (at the other end of the left–right) than the parties on the centre-right (who are pro-European).

Second, however, the figures demonstrate that the most common coalition in the Parliament is a grand-coalition between the three main party groups/party federations – the EPP, the ELDR and the PES. There are two main reasons for this coalition. First, in most legislative votes an 'absolute majority' of all MEPs is required, which in practice means at least 65 per cent of all those MEPs showing up to vote. Second, in most EP votes the EP sees itself as a united institution, in some cases this is against the Commission, but more often than not it is against the member states in the Council. As a result, despite the existence of a left–right alignment, there is no real sense of a 'governing' vs 'opposing' blocs in the parliament.

Table 6.4 *Party-political alignments and coalitions in the European Parliament*

	Europe of Nations	European Democratic Alliance	Forza Europa	European People's Party	Liberal, Democratic and Reform Party	Party of European Socialists	European Radical Alliance	Greens	European Unitarian Left
Greens									67.8
European Radical Alliance								64.5	56.0
Party of European Socialists							76.3	61.0	57.6
Liberal, Democratic and Reform Party						81.4	69.5	57.6	54.2
European People's Party					74.9	74.6	64.4	44.1	45.8
Forza Europa				64.4	49.2	52.5	35.6	37.3	37.3
European Democratic Alliance			49.2	50.9	44.1	45.8	33.9	30.5	30.5
Europe of Nations		33.9	47.5	32.2	32.2	33.9	18.6	25.4	35.6

Note: The data is based on a sample of 59 randomly selected plenary votes between June 1994 and July 1995. The figures are the percentage of occasions when the majority of one party group voted the same way as the majority of another party group in these votes. The figures in bold show the frequency of the EPP–ELDR–PES alliance.
Source: Hix and Lord (1997: 139).

In other words, evidence from the behaviour of the EP groups leads to contradictory conclusions about the possibility of these groups being able to translate voters' choices into policy action. On the one hand the EP groups are increasingly cohesive, and there is a left–right divide. On the other hand the dominant coalition in the parliament spans the left and centre-ight blocs. Hence, if the strengths of the two blocs changes, due to changing voter preferences, this will not change the policy direction of the EP.

Party leaders' summits and the European Council

The transnational party federations have also undergone substantial evolution since their establishment in the 1970s. One of the most important changes has been the institutionalization of the 'party leaders' summits'. These were initially informal meetings of the national party leaders, but in the late 1980s they became the central decision-making organs within each of the party federations. More significantly for the operation of the EU, these party leaders' meetings began to be organized around the agenda and dates, and often in the same venue as, the six-monthly European Council. For the first time in the history of the EU, national party leaders from the

Table 6.5 *Development of the party leaders' summits*

	Average no. of party leaders' meetings per year		Percentage of leaders' meetings close to a European Council		Average turnout of party leaders (%)	
	1985–89	*1990–94*	*1985–89*	*1990–94*	*1985–89*	*1990–94*
PES	1.6	3.4	25.0	70.6	67.4	73.3
ELDR	1.8	1.8	11.1	77.8	59.5	55.8
EPP	1.8	3.0	11.1	66.7	72.1	84.9
All parties	1.7	2.7	15.4	70.7	66.5	72.9

Source: Calculated from data in Hix (1995a).

same party family now had an incentive to come together to try to agree common platforms before the key meeting of EU heads of government that sets the medium- and long-term agenda of the Union.

As Table 6.5 shows, all the party federations increased the proportion of leaders' summits held immediately before or after ('close') to a European Council meeting between the 1985–89 and 1990–94 periods. However, this strategy was only really successful for the PES and EPP, for which the average number of party leaders' meetings increased from less than two per year in the 1985–89 period to more than three per year in the 1990–94 period. And, the percentage of party leaders that actually attended these meetings, as opposed to sending a lesser party official (such as the international secretary of the party) increased from less than 70 per cent to almost 80 per cent in the same period. The strategy was probably not so effective for the ELDR because they actually had very few participants in the European Council meetings in this period.

This does not suggest that the party federations were able to have a great influence on decisions in the European Council – although there were instances when this was the case (Hix and Lord, 1997, p. 188–95). But, it does demonstrate that for the first time these extra-parliamentary party organizations at the European level had a high-level forum for coordinating their policies, behaviour and strategies. For example, in this format, party leaders' summits could become vehicles for organizing the selection of candidates for the Commission president.

In sum, party organization at the European level is relatively underdeveloped compared to national party systems. However, the EP party groups do behave like national parliamentary parties. And, given the right institutional setting – such as the requirement for simple parliamentary majorities – a more partisan structure of coalition behaviour may evolve, based around the left–right divide. Also, the party federations – especially the PES and the EPP – are nascent extra-parliamentary organizations. They are beginning to provide the essential interinstitutional links between the key party actors (the national party leaders) in the national and European arenas. A further question for EU democracy, however, is whether EU voters are able to choose between these Euro-parties in European electoral competition.

European Parliament elections: second-order national contests

Direct and universal elections to the European Parliament (EP) were first held in the member states of the then European Community in June 1979; and have been held every five years since, in June 1984, 1989 and 1994. In the build-up to the first elections, many scholars argued (hoped) that elections to the EP would provide a new legitimacy not only for this institution but also for the whole EU project (see for example Fitzmaurice, 1978; Marquand, 1978; Pridham and Pridham, 1979). As Walter Hallstein (1972, p. 74), the former President of the European Commission, stated:

> Such a campaign would force those entitled to vote to look at and examine the questions and the various options on which the European Parliament would have to decide in the months and years ahead. It would give candidates who emerged victorious from such a campaign a truly European mandate from their electors; and it would encourage the emergence of truly European political parties.

However, evidence from all the European elections has shown that this view could not have been further from the truth.

This is because EP elections are fought not as 'European elections' but as 'second order national contests'. As Reif and Schmitt (1980) first pointed out, European elections are in fact about national political issues, national political parties, and the fight for national government office. As discussed above, the main goal of political parties in the EU is to win national government office, and elections that decide who holds national executive office are consequently 'first order' contests. Political parties cannot resist the opportunity to use all other elections – such as European elections, regional and local elections, second-chamber elections or elections to choose a ceremonial head of state – as 'beauty contests' on the performance of the party/ies that won the last 'first-order' election. These other contests are hence 'second-order'.

As a result of this second-order phenomenon, Reif and Schmitt developed several arguments about European elections. First, because second-order contests are less important than first-order elections, there is likely to be a lower turnout in European than national elections. Second, because the elections are really about the performance of national governments, the people who do vote will vote differently than if a national election were held at the same time. People will either vote sincerely instead of strategically ('vote with the heart'), or they will try to punish governing parties ('put the boot in') (Oppenhuis, van der Eijk and Franklin, 1996). Either way, the likely result is that governing parties and large opposition parties will lose votes, and small parties and protest parties will gain votes.

These hypotheses seemed to be confirmed in the aggregate results of the 1979 and 1984 European elections (Reif, 1984). However, to test these arguments at an individual level, a team of researchers surveyed 36 000 people immediately after the 1989 elections and 13 500 immediately after the 1994 elections. They asked them a series of questions such as, did they vote, why did they vote, which party did they vote for, and how they would have voted if it were a national election? (van der Eijk and Franklin, 1996). If people did vote differently in the European election than in a hypothetical national election, they were said to have 'quasi-switched' their vote. Some of the results of these 'European elections studies' are summarized in Table 6.6.

The outcomes in 1989 and 1994 confirm that European elections are second-order national elections at the individual level, in terms of individual voter behaviour, as well as at the aggregate level, in terms of the total votes for each party. First, in terms of electoral turnout there are significantly lower levels of turnout in the EU member states where national elections were not held concurrently or where voting is not compulsory. Moreover, the average turnout-difference between national and European elections increased from − 25.3 per cent in 1989 to − 27.8 per cent in 1994. And, from individual surveys the key determining factor of people staying away from the polls was the perceived lack of political importance of the elections. By 'political importance', voters were not apathetic because of the lack of impact of the elections on European politics (for example because of the weakness of the EP), they are more concerned about the inability of the elections to change national politics (Franklin, van der Eijk and Oppenhuis, 1995).

Second, individual voters clearly behave differently in European elections compared with national elections. Approximately 20 per cent of voters in all member states vote in European elections for parties they would not have voted for if it were a contest for national government office. And, as Oppenhuis, van der Eijk and Franklin (1995) illustrate,

Table 6.6   *The second-order European election phenomenon*

Member state	Turnout – level of voter turnout in European elections compared to previous national election (%)		Quasi-switching – number of voters in European elections who would have voted for a different party if it were a national election (%)	
	1989	1994	1989	1994
Belgium[a]	− 2.7	− 3.3	12.6	18.5
Denmark	− 38.3	− 36.2	35.4	42.9
France	− 17.4	− 25.3	27.2	40.8
Germany	− 22.0	− 17.8	11.8	14.2
Greece[a]	− 3.8	− 8.8	8.1	12.4
Ireland	− 0.2[b]	− 24.2	28.7[b]	23.8
Italy	− 10.1	− 11.3	19.7	20.7
Luxembourg[a]	− 2.6[b]	+ 0.2[b]	15.0[b]	14.3[b]
The Netherlands	− 38.3	− 43.1	12.4	19.6
Portugal	− 21.5	− 33.4	9.7	12.7
Spain	− 15.9	− 17.6	22.2	12.5
United Kingdom	− 38.8	− 41.3	13.0	16.0
Average, all member states	− 17.6	− 21.8	18.0	20.7
Average, excluding cases of concurrent national elections and compulsory voting	− 25.3	− 27.8	—	—

Note:
[a] = member states where voting is compulsory.
[b] = cases were national elections and European elections were held concurrently.
Source: Calculated from data in Mackie and Rose (1991), Koole and Mair (1995), van der Eijk and Franklin (1996) and Lodge (1996).

these votes go away from governing parties and towards opposition, small and protest parties. For example, this explains the success of Green parties in many member states in the 1989 European elections. This individual-level analysis consequently confirms that the aggregate losses of government parties in European elections is not simply explained by a fall in turnout, where government supporters actually do not bother to vote; what actually happens is that voters do change their votes in European elections. Moreover, the individual surveys revealed that voters did not change their votes because of parties' policies on the question of

European integration (van der Eijk, Franklin and Oppenhuis 1996). The partial exceptions to this rule were Denmark in 1989 and 1994 and France in 1994, where the party systems in European elections were different to those in national elections; for example, with large anti-European movements. However, even in these cases there was evidence that voters acted strategically to influence the national (rather than European) political process; either to punish governing parties, or to reward opposition parties, or to support parties that they might consider would be a wasted vote in a more important election.

These results have several consequences for the ability of elections to the EP to reduce the democratic deficit in the EU. First, and foremost, European elections are patently not about Europe. Despite the increased powers of the EP in both the legislative arena (vis-à-vis the Council) and the executive arena (vis-à-vis selection and accountability of the Commission), EP elections are still fought by national parties. In 1994 there was a possibility of connecting the EP elections to the process of selecting the Commission president as a result of the Maastricht Treaty, which gave the EP the power to vote on the candidate for Commission president immediately following the European elections. However, even if different candidates for Commission president had been put forward in the 1994 elections, the contest would still have been second-order. As Reif (1997, p. 221) explains: the national arena would still be the 'first-order political arena' and the European arena as a collective 'sub-system' of the primary arena. Consequently, regardless of the ability of the EP elections to influence the make-up of the EU executive, EP elections will never allow Europe's voters to 'throw the scoundrels out' while national parties have an incentive to use the elections in their wider pursuit of national government office.

Nevertheless, there is some hope. As van der Eijk, Franklin and Oppenhuis (1996, p. 365) explain:

> The lack of European content in European elections [is] not attributed to inherent limitations of European voters. . . When it comes to voting choice only differences in political context are at issue. If such differences were removed, this would also remove the differences we observe in the manner in which party choices are made. Voters in different countries have not been socialized into country-specific modes of expressing at the ballot box their interests, hopes and fears. The answer to the question 'one electorate or many?' when interpreted in these terms is unequivocally in the singular.

In other words, given a genuine 'European' contest, fought between rival European-wide movements instead of national parties, and about who holds European executive office or about the direction of the European legislative agenda, voters will behave towards such a contest in the same way in every member state. The challenge, therefore, is to design an electoral contest that would meet these criteria, and prevent national parties and issues from interfering. One option would be to introduce a uniform electoral procedure for EP elections, where candidates are chosen by local, regional and European parties rather than by national party organizations. However, the evidence from previous EP elections suggests that even this would be insufficient to guarantee a European contest, as national parties would still be able to couch the elections as referendums on the performance of the governing parties. EP elections under a uniform procedure would still be second-order national contests. However, there are other options, to which we shall now turn.

Alternative mechanisms: direct democracy and presidentialism

Given the structural inability of EP elections to enable Europe's voters to choose between rival visions for European action, two alternative types of mechanisms, that exist in many political systems in the world, have been proposed as potential solutions: European-wide referendums; and the direct election of the Commission president.

Euro-referendums?

Philippe Schmitter (1996) and Joseph Weiler (1997b) *inter alia* have proposed European-wide referendums for reducing the EU democratic deficit. The underlying reasoning behind these arguments is that because the EU does not have a 'government . . . to throw out', there should be more opportunity for direct democracy. This is exactly the same logic as in the Swiss system, where referendums are used to overrule decisions by the Swiss federal government, which is a fixed-member organization that in practice cannot be overturned in parliamentary elections. Various different schemes have been proposed, with the most common being the opportunity of citizens to vote on a series of 'legislative initiatives' at the same time as the EP elections. These initiatives would be allowed onto the ballot paper with the support of a certain number of signatures in every EU member state.

However, evidence from research on referendums in many member states has shown that referendums are also not always fought on the issues on the ballot paper. Instead, and like second-order EP or regional elections, how people vote in referendums is often strongly influenced by their support or opposition for the government, and which side of the issue the government supports (Butler and Ranney 1994). For example, a key factor in the referendums on the Maastricht Treaty in France, on EU membership in Norway and on the European Economic Area agreement in Switzerland was the unpopularity of the governing parties (Franklin, van der Eijk and Marsh, 1995; Schneider and Weitsman, 1996). Therefore, in addition to the problem of voter apathy towards everything European, proposals for EU-wide referendums must provide evidence that they can be fought as 'European' rather than 'national' contests.

Election of the Commission president?

The Maastricht Treaty allowed the EP to vote on the governments' nominee for the Commission president: in other words, establishing a classic element of the parliamentary model of executive selection (cf. Corbett, Jacobs and Shackleton, 1995, p. 249). However, if EP elections cannot be fought on the rival candidates for the presidency, because they remain second-order national contests, the other key element of the link between voters and executive power in a 'parliamentary' model of executive selection is still missing (Hix, 1997). Hence, the logical conclusion would be to opt not for a parliamentary model, but for a presidential model of executive selection through the direct election of the Commission president (cf. Bogdanor, 1986). For example, candidates could be selected by a certain number of MPs and MEPs in a certain number of member states, and then put to the voters in a two-round contest, as in the French presidential election (Laver *et al.*, 1995). Or, if candidates require the backing of a political party in every member state, this would guarantee that one section of the elite in every member state would be responsible to the voters for the performance of the winning candidate (Hix, 1997).

Alternatively, the Commission president could be chosen by an 'electoral college', on the United States' model (Hix, 1998). For example, an electoral college could be composed of all the MPs and MEPs in every EU member state, where each parliamentarian has a certain number of votes, in proportion to the total number of MPs and MEPs from their country and the size of the national electorate they represent. These votes could then be allocated en bloc for one or other candidate for the Commission president. Such a system would overcome the problem of a European electorate that is not yet prepared (interested!) to vote in a contest for the Commission president. If the electorate comprises national and European parliamentarians, national parties would not be able to argue to the electorate that the election is a trial-run of the next national general election, as they do in EP elections. Moreover, there would be a high turnout, alignments could be organized along European rather than national party lines (that is, a centre-left versus a centre-right candidate), and the winner would have the support of a section of parliamentarians in every member state.

However, this too has problems. A directly elected Commission president would be inherently more powerful than he is today, with a new legitimacy and a new mandate to speak for all of Europe. This would consequently reduce the ability of the Commission to act as an impartial broker in the EU legislative and regulatory processes (see for example Dehousse, 1995). Moreover, this would be a giant step towards a more integrated Europe, which Europe's voters may neither support nor be prepared for. Also, because it would reduce their relative power in the EU system, Europe's governments would resist it tooth and nail.

Conclusion: towards representative government?

The EU is not a representative democracy. We elect our governments, who negotiate on our behalf in Brussels, and decide who forms the EU executive: the Commission. However, national governments are the product of national electoral contests, about national issues, fought by national parties, and over the control of national governmental office. EP elections, moreover, are sub-products of this process. Because the main goal in the EU political system that national parties want to win is national governmental office, EP elections are fought as second-order national contests and not about the policy agenda or executive office-holders at the European level. In no sense, therefore, are Europe's voters able to choose between rival programmes for Europe or 'throw out' those who exercise political power at the European level.

However, all is not lost. Given the opportunity, Europe's voters and the nascent European-level party organizations are up to the task of representative democracy in the EU. First, in EP elections the same factors explain the behaviour of EU voters in every election: there are no inherent cultural differences that would prevent EU citizens behaving as a single electorate. Second, an EU party system is beginning to emerge: party alliances in this system are along the left–right rather than pro- and anti-EU dimension, and between parties from the same ideological party families. And, these alliances are organized into cohesive party groups in the EP and in an emerging extra-parliamentary framework for bringing together the key partisan actors in each party family from the national and European levels (the party federation leaders' summits).

The task, therefore, would be to design institutional mechanisms for competitive party government to function. First, an electoral contest would need to operate such that European-wide party organizations fight the campaign on European issues, or as a way of placing their candidates in key EU political office. Second, the winning coalition in such a contest should be able to translate its victory into legislative and executive action at the European level. This may mean reforming the existing system of EP elections by reducing the ability of national parties to control the process and the selection of candidates, in parallel to allowing the EP a greater say in the EU legislative process and in the selection of the Commission president. Alternatively, this may mean adopting elements of direct democracy, either via EU-wide referendums, or some form of direct or indirect election of the Commission president.

As discussed in the previous chapter, a European demos may not exist at present. Nevertheless, as in other political systems, a common European democratic identity may emerge through genuine European-wide democratic praxis (Habermas, 1995). Until the EU is as democratic as national political systems, where voters are able to shape their own political destiny, it is rational for Europe's citizens to be sceptical of the European integration process.

Interest Representation

This chapter looks at the representation of societal interests at the European level. Interest groups play a central role in the policy-making process in all democratic political systems, where private organizations represent 'civil society' against the interests of the state. Civil society at the European level is highly developed. Brussels in this sense is like Washington. But, does EU policy-making suffer some of the problems of American government – such as those who spend most on lobbying reap the biggest rewards? Or, is the EU more like most national European systems, where the relationship between interests and the state is more 'consensual'?

Theories of interest intermediation

How private and public interests are represented in the policy process varies considerably across political systems. There are three main models of interest intermediation, each of which exists to some extent in the EU: pluralism, corporatism and consociationalism. The main differences between these models are summarized in Table 7.1.

Pluralism is the classic model of interest group politics in democratic systems. The central idea is that the organization of competing social interests creates societal 'checks and balances' against powerful state officials and/or special interest groups. The assumption is that for every group pressing on one side of a debate, another group will present the opposing view. If there are cross-cutting (rather than reinforcing) social divisions, there will be 'multiple oppositions', and no single interest will ever be able to monopolize the political process (Lipset, 1959). In other words, there is always 'countervailing power', which will lead to 'social equilibrium' (Bentley, 1967). A central requirement of the pluralist model, therefore, is that opposing interests have equal access to the political

Table 7.1   *Types of interest intermediation*

	Pluralism	*Corporatism*	*Consociationalism*
Social divisions	Cross-cutting	Class	Cultural
Interests	Private vs. Public	Capital vs. Labour	French vs. German vs. British etc.
Style	Competitive	Consensual	Consensual
Policy network	Open	Closed	Closed
Role of the state	Neutral	Proactive	Neutral

process. For example, environmentalist groups should have equal influence on government officials as the industrial lobby. If this is the case, governmental officials need only act as 'referees' of the interest group game, weighing up the arguments of both sides of the debate and determining the course of action most in the 'public interest' (see for example Truman, 1951).

The problem, however, is that perfect pluralism never really exists. First, in most societies one type of social division tends to dominate all others, so that the side of the divide which is numerically, economically or political most powerful will dominate the political process; such as the capitalist elite where class is the dominant social conflict, or the largest linguistic or religious group where cultural divisions are dominant. Second, even where there are cross-cutting social divisions, opposing groups rarely have equal access to power (Galbraith, 1953; Schattschneider, 1960). This is a product of the so-called 'logic of collective action': where there are incentives to join a group that seek benefits for only those members of the group ('private interests'), and no incentive to join a group that seeks benefits for all of society ('public interests') (Olson, 1965). With public interests, people can simply 'free ride': reap the benefits of higher environmental protection, for example, without helping an environmentalist group lobby government. As a result, private interests, such as individual firms and industrial lobbies, are more able to organize than 'diffuse interests', like labour unions, consumer groups, environmentalists or civil rights movements (cf. Aspinwall and Greenwood, 1998). The result is unequal access to political power, the capture of state officials by groups with the most resources, and outputs that benefit special interests at the expense of society.

Nevertheless, a possible solution is for state officials to cease to be neutral arbiters. Instead, bureaucrats could deliberately seek out, subsidize and give privileged access to underrepresented public interests (see for example Lindblom, 1977). This activist role of the state within the general model of private organization and open access to the policy process has been described as *neo-pluralism* (Dunleavy and O'Leary, 1987; Petracca, 1994).

Corporatism, on the other hand, is a model of interest intermediation that is diametrically opposed to pluralism. Rather than society divided into multiple social divisions, the corporatist model assumes that class is the dominant social cleavage, and that society is divided into two opposing sets of interests: capitalists/business and workers/labour. Corporatism assumes that if pluralism prevails, business interests will inevitably dominate. The solution is for the state to recognize, license and grant representational monopolies to both sides of the class divide: the 'social partners'. Instead of open 'policy networks', the leaders of the business community and the trade union movement participate in closed 'tripartite' meetings with state officials. If agreement can be brokered in these meetings, the assumption is that policy outcomes will reflect a broader social consensus (Schmitter 1974; Schmitter and Lehmbruch, 1979).

The problem, however, is that postindustrial society is no longer simply divided between capital and labour. First, class has declined as the major determinant of individuals' political, economic and social interests and values (see for example Inglehart, 1977a). And, excluded from corporatist arrangements, individuals with 'postmaterial' value orientations have tended to join 'new social movements', such as the civil rights movement, the ecology movement, antinuclear and peace protests, the women's movement, the gay and lesbian movement, consumer lobbies, road protests and pensioners' alliances (Dalton, Kuechler and Bürklin, 1990). As a result, social consensus in postindustrial society cannot be guaranteed by simply allowing industry and labour to participate in the policy process. Second, if the consent of both sides of industry is required for all major policies of the state, corporatism can prevent policy innovation, even when it is badly needed. As in the pluralist model, capital and labour interests look after their own short-term interests first, and long-term interests of the rest of society later. The result can be an impenetrable political process and policy stagnation.

Consociationalism is similar to corporatism in that one particular set of social groups is granted privileged and equal status in the policy process as a means to prevent the inevitable dominance of a particular group. However, whereas corporatism privileges the class cleavage (business vs labour), consociationalism is a system of interest intermediation in societies that are deeply divided ('segmented') around cultural divisions such as language, ethnicity, religion or nationality (Lijphart, 1977). Also, instead of state officials bargaining with private interests, the political process is governed by a set of institutional rules to guarantee political consensus. The majority of policy competencies are decentralized within each segment; only the elites of the segments participate in central decision-making; each group is proportionally represented in the state bureaucracy and in the decision-making process, and has proportional access to public finances (the *proporzprincip*); and each elite can veto any policy that threatens the vital interests or identity of its segment (Lehmbruch, 1967; Lijphart, 1968). For example, this is the dominant model of interest articulation in the Netherlands, Belgium and Switzerland.

Also like corporatism, however, consociationalism breeds inertia. If the consent of every group is required to move forward, outcomes are inevitably 'lowest-common-denominator'. Put another way, the existence of multiple 'veto players', leads to policy *immobilisme* and sub-optimal solutions (Scharpf, 1988; Tsebelis, 1995c). In addition, consociationalism is inherently undemocratic. Like corporatism, it relies on a closed 'cartel of elites', the exclusion of rank-and-file members of the main social groups, and the conscious effort to undermine the emergence of social interests and loyalties that cross-cut the privileged cleavage. If cross-cutting interests emerge, such as class or postmaterial values, the legitimacy of consociational arrangements is undermined.

Consequently, there are two underlying issues for scholars of interest groups in the EU. First, which model of interest intermediation dominates EU policy-making? Second, from what we know about the strengths and weaknesses of these models, what are the implications of this finding for the operation and legitimacy of the EU?

Lobbying Europe: interest groups and EU policy-making

The volume of private individuals and groups seeking to influence the EU policy process increased dramatically towards the end of the 1980s (Greenwood, Grote and Ronit, 1992; Mazey and Richardson, 1993; Pedlar and Van Schendelen, 1994; Greenwood and Aspinwall, 1998). Until the mid-1980s, it was possible to identify between 400 and 500 interest groups with offices in Brussels (see for example Butt Philip, 1985), and this number trebled by the mid-1990s. Table 7.2 shows the number of different types of private groups with offices in Brussels, as recorded in the 1995 issue of the *European Public Affairs Directory*, which is a leading source of

Table 7.2   *Types of interest groups in Brussels, 1995*

Type of interest	Number
Individual companies	561
European interest associations	314
Private lobbyists (e.g. political consultants, public affairs and law firms)	302
Miscellaneous interest groups (mostly public interest)	147
International organizations and non-EU state bodies	101
National interest associations	93
Regions	80
Chambers of commerce	47
Individual trade unions	21
Think-tanks	12
Total	1678

Source: Calculated from data in Wessels (1997b).

information for individuals and firms wishing to get their voice heard in the EU policy process.

As the table shows, by far the largest type of interest represented at the European level are individual companies, many of whom have their 'European public affairs' divisions in Brussels. The second largest type of representation are European interest associations: such as European federations of business, trade unions, sectoral industries, or professions. There are also over 300 private 'lobbyist' firms in Brussels – political consultants, public affairs companies, public relations firms, and specialist EC law firms – who monitor and approach the EU on behalf of their 'clients'. Business interests are also represented in Brussels by the numerous national, European and sectoral chambers of commerce.

In contrast, there are less offices of individual trade unions and national public interests groups in Brussels. Representation in the EU decision-process for these diffuse interests is more through national and European interest associations: such as the European association of national consumer groups. Some of these groups employ private consultants, although private companies tend to be the only organizations that can afford consultants' fees. Finally, numerous European regions (such as the German *Länder* governments), various state bodies from non-EU countries (such as the US states), and international organizations (such as the International Labour Organization) have their own offices in Brussels for the specific purpose of influencing the EU.

Business interests: 'the large firm as a political actor'

Lobbying of the political process by private firms only really took off at the national level in Europe in the 1970s and 1980s, as governments began to set standards for the marketplace through new forms of economic and social regulation. However, with the European single market these standards are now set at the European level, and business interests are thus naturally drawn to the new political centre.

Business interests have not only responded to the emergence of regulatory competencies in Brussels, they have actively promoted this development. Even if certain European industries have been opposed to global free trade, most sectors of the European economy have been in favour of removing barriers to the free movement of goods, services and capital between European countries. This observation was at the heart of neo-functionalist theories of European integration in the 1950s: where business interests were the first to transfer their loyalties to the European level, and to promote new European competences in sectors that were originally excluded (Haas, 1958, pp. 162–213). The situation was similar with the European single market, where European multinationals urged national governments and the Commission to pursue further market integration to help Europe recover from the recession of the 1970s (see for example Sandholtz and Zysman, 1989).

A survey of over 200 business groups in Brussels in 1996 revealed that the majority of these groups employ less than five people, yet have a turnover of over €100 000 (Greenwood, 1997, pp. 102–3). Many of these are national associations, offices of individual firms, or sector-specific European associations such as the Committee of Agricultural Organization in the EC (COPA), of national farmers associations. However, there are also several powerful cross-sectoral European-level associations: most notably the Union of Industrial and Employers' Confederations (UNICE), the peak association of national business associations; the Association of Chambers of Commerce and Industry (EUROCHAMBRES); the European Round Table of Industrialists (ERT), comprising the chief executives of some of the largest European firms; the EU Committee of the American Chamber of Commerce (AMCHAM-EU), of American firms in Europe; and the European Association of Craft, Small and Medium-sized Enterprises (UEAPME).

UNICE, for example, is a confederation of 32 national federations of business from 22 European countries – hence, EU as well as non-EU – that was established in 1958. The UNICE office in Brussels has a permanent staff of 30, but the bulk of its work is in a network of committees and working groups which involve over 1000 officials from the member organizations. UNICE plays a high-profile role in EU policy-making, and its officials meet on a daily basis with Commission staff. It also regularly makes formal submissions to the EU institutions, such as Commission and Council working groups, and EP committees, but these formal submissions are usually only statements of business interests designed to alienate as few member organizations as possible. A problem for UNICE is that member businesses and national associations have several exit options through their own private channels of representation if they think UNICE is not representing their interests effectively enough.

One of these exit options was the establishment of ERT in 1983, by a select group of chief executive officers of some of the largest firms in Europe. Its membership is by invitation only, and in 1996 it comprised 46 firms in a wide variety of sectors, with a collective turnover of over €550 billion and over 3 million employees. The primary focus of ERT was the single market project: on the one hand to promote the removal of technical barriers to trade in Europe, and on the other to prevent the introduction of high social and environmental standards that would impose high costs to business (Cowles, 1995). As a result of a more specific membership ERT tends to be more focused than UNICE but, together with AMCHAM-EU, UNICE and ERT constitute the 'big business troika' at the heart of the Brussels lobbying system. Moreover, this troika is held together by regular meetings of the private consultants of the leading European and American companies who try to coordinate campaigns through the largely informal European Enterprise Group (Cowles, 1997, 1998).

However, this monolithic picture of business interests campaigning together to drive the EU policy process masks the reality that it is individual firms in pursuit of their own private interests that is at the heart of the Brussels lobbying system. Individual firms, whether national, multinational, or non-European, will only participate in these umbrella organizations if they perceive benefits greater than the costs of participating. The growth in membership of these cross-sectoral organizations may suggest that these bodies are able to guarantee results: in other words, policy outputs from the EU system in individual firms' interests. Nonetheless, in the post-single market era, individual firms have developed much more sophisticated lobbying strategies, beyond simply paying dues to national and European peak associations.

Table 7.3, for example, shows the results of a survey of 300 firms on how they allocate resources to influence the EU policy process (Coen, 1997). As the table illustrates, by the mid-1990s firms were allocating approximately equal resources to European and national associations. More significantly, however, individual firms have dramatically increased private contacts with the Commission, either in addition to or deliberately bypassing the European-level associations. Moreover, when asked to determine which of these strategies produced the highest pay-offs,

Table 7.3 *Where firms go to influence the EU policy-process*

Channel	1984	1994
European Commission	16%	23%
National association	33%	23%
European association	15%	20%
National government	17%	13%
Regional government	5%	4%
Private lobbyist	3%	4%
European MEP	2%	4%
European Parliament	2%	4%
National MP	5%	3%
Other	2%	3%

Source: Calculated from data in Coen (1997).

approaching the Commission directly was the clear winner (*ibid.*, p. 103). Surprisingly, the employment of specialist lobbyists in Brussels did not seem to be a rewarding strategy. Rather, private consultants tend to be used to provide specialist information and monitoring services as a supplement rather than a substitute for direct political action by individual firms.

In other words, the interests of business and the owners of capital are powerfully represented in the EU policy process. The regulation of the market at the European level is a strong incentive for firms to spend valuable resources to ensure that policy outcomes do not harm their interests. Moreover, individual firms have become increasingly sophisticated in their lobbying strategies, pursuing multiple channels and diversifying their public affairs expenditure. The open access of these interests to the Commission, and the multiplicity of actors involved, suggests a pluralist model of intermediation of business interests, but for pluralism to work, groups with opposing interests to the business community need to be equally well organized.

Trade unions, public interests and social movements

Groups with interests often diametrically opposed to the owners of business were not well represented in Brussels until the early 1990s. Representatives of a variety of societal interests have been formally represented in the Economic and Social Committee since its establishment following the Treaty of Rome, as an early attempt to inject an element of corporatism into the EU policy process. However, its status is purely consultative. Nevertheless, a wide variety of social interests, such as trade unions, environmentalists and consumer groups, became interested in the Brussels process as a result the new EU competences in such areas as health and safety at work, environmental policy, consumer protection and social policy, in the wake of the Single European Act and Maastricht Treaty. But, it was not until the 1990s that these groups really began to compete on a more equal basis with business groups.

The European Trade Union Confederation (ETUC) was founded in 1972. Like UNICE, ETUC is an umbrella organization, whose members are national trade union federations in 22 EU and non-EU states. These national federations together comprise over 45 million individual trade union members, approximately one-fifth of whom are members of the British or German trade union federations (Greenwood, 1997, p. 164). Also like UNICE, the size and diversity of the members of ETUC undermine any really coherent European-level trade union strategy (Visser and Ebbinghaus, 1992). Unlike UNICE, ETUC is not linked into a network of like-minded public interest groups. But, the members of ETUC have limited resources and opportunities to pursue alternative lobbying strategies.

However, ETUC has increasingly been able to gain a place at the bargaining table as the legitimate 'social partner' of UNICE and the European Centre of Public Enterprises (CEEP), who represent the nationalized industries. In 1984, Commission President Jacques Delors announced that no new social policy initiatives would be forthcoming without the prior approval of both sides of industry, as represented by UNICE and ETUC. In the early years of this 'social dialogue', little progress was made since UNICE insisted that its members would not be bound by any agreement it reached with ETUC. However, persistent Commission sympathy for the ETUC cause ensured that the social dialogue did not dissolve. Delors launched the Commission's strategy for a European social policy at an ETUC meeting in May 1988, and the Commission supported the ETUC proposal for a European Social Charter, which was signed in 1989 by all the member states except Britain. And, as a result of further Commission pressure, in 1990 the social dialogue produced three joint proposals which the Commission duly proposed as legislation (Story, 1996).

A boost for the ETUC came with the Maastricht Treaty, which institutionalized the social dialogue in the area of social policy. The Maastricht 'Social Agreement' extended the competences of the EU in the social policy field for all member states except Britain. Under the rules of the Social Agreement, the Commission is statutorily obliged to consult both business and labour before submitting proposals for social policy legislation. In addition, a member state may request that business and labour seek to reach an agreement on the implementation of directives adopted under the Social Agreement. And, most significantly, if business and labour reach a collective agreement on a particular policy issue, this can serve as a direct substitute for European legislation. In other words, this is the adoption of a classic model of corporatism in a central area of EU socioeconomic policy (Obradovic, 1996; Falkner, 1997).

A similar development has occurred with other diffuse interests, such as environmental and consumer groups. Few public interest groups had a voice in Brussels before the late 1980s, but by the 1990s public interests played a central role in many EU policy debates. As with the labour movement, the key change was the activist role of the Commission. For example, the main European-level consumer association, the European Office of Consumer Unions (BEUC) receives €750 000 a year from the Commission (Greenwood, 1997, p. 195). Also, the Commission has breathed new life into the institutional mechanism for incorporating consumer interests in the EU policy process. The Consumers Contact Committee (CCC) was set up in 1961, but was plagued by a lack of commitment on the side of the Commission and the rival interests of the various European-level consumer associations. However, in 1995 the Commission transformed its own Consumer Policy Service into a proper directorate-general, and reorganized the CCC into the Consumers' Committee (CC). The CC has a much more streamlined structure, with a small number of representatives (one from each of the five European-level consumer associations), and is chaired by a Commission official. The result is a system that will increase the effectiveness of consumer representation in Brussels, and improve the speed and quality of information about consumer interests supplied to the Commission (Young, 1997, 1998).

Similarly, the Commission is the main core funder of environmental groups (Webster, 1998). For example, the main European-level environment association, the European Environment Bureau (EEB), received over €400 000 from DGXI (environment) in 1995. The EEB also has privileged access to the director-general of DGXI, has been an observer in several meetings of the Environment Council, and was even a member of the Commission's delegation to the 1992 Earth Summit in Rio de Janeiro. The same story can be told of numerous public interest groups. For example, Migrants Forum, representing EU citizens who live in other member states and third-country nationals who are resident in the EU, was established by a grant from the European Parliament. The Commission also spent a total of €7 million on the funding of public interest groups in 1994 (Greenwood, 1997, p. 186). In other words, whereas the Commission was instrumental in the establishment of a corporatist model of interest intermediation in the social policy field, the Commission is pursuing a neo-pluralist strategy in many other policy areas.

Nevertheless, a consequence of corporatism and neo-pluralism is the cooptation of the participant public interest groups. The process whereby state officials proactively choose partners creates a distinction between 'insider' and 'outsider' groups. ETUC, BEUC, EEB and Migrants Forum are clearly insiders in the EU policy processes: numerous other social interests remain excluded. Nevertheless, this has provoked 'the mobilisation of domestic groups and resources against policies emanating from Brussels by using tools of contentious collective action' (Tarrow, 1995, p. 230). This is particularly the case were the same groups in different member states feel their interests are not represented by the formal structures either of national representation, via the governments in the Council, or of transnational representation, via the European Parliament or European associations' links to the Commission.

For example, farmers from several member states have often taken to the streets of Brussels to protest against the reform of the Common Agricultural Policy or other farming issues, often against the explicit mandate of COPA, their European association. And numerous other groups have protested in recent years on the streets of Brussels or outside the European Parliament, from bikers protesting against limits on motorbike engine sizes to animal rights campaigners protesting against the live transport of animals. However, the Europeanization of social conflicts through non-formal channels of representation is dependent upon the level of pan-European politicization of an issue as well as the resources of the groups concerned. As a result, compared to the growing involvement of insider groups, such as the ETUC, the record and ability of outsider groups to mobilize in Brussels is highly variable (Marks and McAdam, 1996).

Territorial interests: at the heart of 'multi-level governance'

Another set of non-business interests that has established an important role in the EU policy process are subnational regions. Table 7.4 shows the numbers of offices of substate authorities in Brussels. These include office of state governments of the German, Belgian and Austria federal systems; regional councils and other official organs of the decentralized unitary states of Italy, France and Spain; local government bodies of the unitary states of Britain, Ireland, Denmark, the Netherlands, Sweden, Greece, Portugal and Finland; and various intermediary associations of local authorities, communities, municipalities, towns, cities, regions and subnational units.

Some of these subnational groups have been represented in Brussels since the start of the 1970s, but the majority only began to mobilize in the late 1980s following the reform of EU regional policies. The 1988 reform of

Table 7.4 *Regions and localities with offices in Brussels, 1996*

Member state	No. of substate offices in Brussels
United Kingdom	29
France	20
Germany	18
Belgium	13
Spain	12
Austria	11
Denmark	9
Italy	9
Sweden	6
Netherlands	4
Finland	3
Ireland	2
Portugal	1

Source: Calculated from data in Greenwood (1997).

the structural funds led to the conscious 'outflanking' of national governments by the Commission and the regions (Pollack, 1995b). On the one hand, the Commission consciously sought the involvement of regional interests in the initiation, adoption and implementation of regional policy. On the other hand, regional interests made the most of their opportunity to bypass national governments, many of whom were governed by parties of opposing political hues or were cutting back on national regional spending. 'Partnership' between the Commission and the regional level of government became the central guiding principle in this policy area. Regional bodies were now invited to submit funding proposals directly to the Commission and funds were then given directly to regional authorities without passing through central government treasuries. In addition, regional bodies were responsible for implementing their specific 'framework programmes', monitored by Commission officials.

The formal role of regions in EU policy-making was further institutionalized by the creation of the Committee of the Regions (CoR) by the Maastricht Treaty (Hooghe, 1995). The CoR replaced the Consultative Council of Regional and Local Authorities (CCLRA) that was set up by the Commission in 1988 as part of the new regional policy regime. The members of the CCLRA were appointed by two European-wide subnational associations: the Assembly of European Regions (AER) and the

Council for European Municipalities and Regions (CEMR). In the new CoR, in contrast, these transnational associations were replaced with direct representatives of regional and local governments of all the EU member states. Some of these were nominated by central governments, as in Britain, but in most cases they were independently nominated by the subnational bodies such as the French regional assemblies and the German states. Furthermore, the Maastricht Treaty specified that the CoR had the right to be consulted not only in the adoption and implementation of EU regional policies but also in all policy areas that have implications for European 'economic and social cohesion'. This includes all EU policies that effect the level of economic and social disparities in Europe, such as the Common Agricultural Policy and the Common Transport Policy.

Nevertheless, the existence of EU competencies in the area of regional policy, and the deliberate funding and promotion of regional representation by the Commission, are not the only explanations of the different levels of regional mobilization. Another important factor is whether the member state of which a region is part has a tradition of private/pluralist or state-funded/corporatist interest representation. Nevertheless, as Marks, Nielsen, Ray and Salk (1996, p. 61) explain: 'The greater the overlap between the competencies of subnational and supranational government, the more likely that a subnational government will be represented in Brussels'. In other words, regions tend to establish offices in Brussels not because of the competencies of the EU, but rather because of their own competencies *vis-à-vis* national governments. As a result, the subnational governments with the broadest range of policy competencies, such as the German and Belgian states, all have offices in Brussels. Furthermore, backed by constitutional statutes, the German and Belgian states have forced their national governments to formally include them in the German and Belgian delegations in the Council when the agenda touches on subnational competencies.

The result, so many claim, is a system of 'multi-level governance', where policies are made through interaction between regional, national and European-level authorities. Because of the role of regional authorities in the operation of the structural funds, the multilevel governance approach was developed in the study of regional policy (Marks, 1993). However, as regional interests have been incorporated into other EU policies, and as European policy deliberation and implementation has involved a growing number of participants at the regional and local levels, the multilevel governance conception has gradual evolved into a general model of EU decision-making (Hooghe and Marks, 1996). There are, however, inherent shortcomings in the extrapolation of a general theory of the EU from the structure of interest intermediation in a single policy area. For example, regions play a minor role compared to the ETUC in the social policy area.

In response, leading proponents of multilevel governance argue that the conception refers to the emergence of multiple levels of bargaining outside the dominance of the national governments, and not to the simplistic conception that the EU is a three-level system (see for example Marks, Hooghe and Blank, 1996; Kohler-Koch, 1996).

In sum, from the single market project on, Brussels has become more like Washington than most national European capitals in terms of the volume and intensity of private lobbying of the political process. The bulk of this activity is by individual firms and national and European associations representing business interests. However, fostered by the EU institutions, public interests, old and new social movements, and subnational governmental bodies have begun to fight back. The result is a sophisticated and complex system which has elements of pluralism, neo-pluralism and corporatism.

National interests and the consociational cartel

The informal and quasi-formal systems of *transnational* interest representation compete in the EU policy process with a highly institutionalized system of *national* interest representation. The EU is a multinational political system, and the structure of the policy process is deliberately designed to accommodate as many, if not all, national preferences, cultures, styles and traditions. This is not only in the adoption of EU law, where national governments are the formal participants in the central legislative and executive organs (the Council and European Council), but is also in the initiation/agenda-setting and policy implementation/adjudication stages of the EU policy process.

At the agenda-setting stage, the Commission has a formal monopoly on legislative initiative in most areas of social and economic policy. However, in practice the Commission develops policy proposals in cooperation with representatives from national administrations. At a formal level this operates through a network of working groups comprised of national civil servants and chaired by a Commission official. At an informal level the Commission is highly understaffed and relies on national officials and representatives from national constituencies – such as national peak associations of business or professional groups – to supply knowledge and information about existing national policy regimes and interests. Furthermore, the Commission itself is a multinational bureaucracy, with senior officials linked to specific national constituencies and national interest groups. The result is an ongoing bargaining process between the Commission and the representatives of state and non-state national interests. At this stage, the Commission aims to discover policy ideas that accommodate as many national preferences as possible in the hope that excluded interests can be incorporated at a later stage, in the formal legislative bargaining stage in the Committee of Permanent Representatives and the Council.

This system of articulation and accommodation between national interests at the agenda-setting stage, coordinated by central officials, is similar to the Swiss system of statutory 'pre-parliamentary hearings' (*Vernehmlassungen*) of all major pieces of legislation. In these hearings, representatives from the different ethnic and religious societal groups – from political parties, interest groups and/or cantonal administrations – negotiate with central government officials to set the boundaries of the central political agenda. Only after broad agreement has been reached with the representatives of the main cultural divisions in Swiss society can the Swiss federal government formally submit a proposal to the Swiss legislature (Lehner and Homann, 1987).

The same process of national incorporation exists at the implementation and adjudication stage. European directives need to be transposed into law through national instruments, which gives a specific role to national administrations to implement EU law. In terms of the incorporation of interests, moreover, this specifically allows different national legal and administrative traditions to be reconciled with EU action. Furthermore, the implementation process is overseen by a network of supervisory and regulatory Committees, the 'comitology' system, and these committees are composed of national civil servants, chaired by Commission officials. Again, the aim is the widest possible accommodation of national interests in the pursuit of common EU goals. No single national group can be seen to be the 'winner' of EU policies, at the expense of other national groups. Such arrangements for the joint administration of policies by central and subsystem representatives are widely used in culturally-segmented political systems, especially in policy areas that undermine the identity of the cultural group, such as education policy (Lijphart, 1977).

In other words, the EU policy process possesses all the classic aspects of the consociational model of interest intermediation (cf. Taylor, 1991; Chryssochoou, 1994; Gabel, 1998c). As we discussed in the previous chapter, the society of the EU is primarily divided along cultural rather than socioeconomic lines: into the different nation-states of western Europe. The elites of these national 'segments' – national governments, national public administrations, and representatives from national interest groups – are the main participants in the EU policy process. In this sense, the national administrations in the EU, who incorporate the views of national interest groups before coming to the EU bargaining table, are the functional equivalent of the ethnic, linguistic and religious political parties in the Dutch, Belgian and Swiss consociational systems.

These elites are able to present and defend their perceived 'national interests' above all other types of political conflict at the European level. This facilitates the calculation of winners and losers of policy proposals along national rather than transnational/socioeconomic lines. The need to secure cross-class support in national elections ensures that national governments defend the interests of all their constituents over interests in other member states that may be closer ideologically. For example, a French Socialist government would defend French business interests against the interests of the working class in another member state. The result is an EU policy process with the primary intention of accommodating all national interests rather than all transnational ones.

This consociational model of nationally-segmented interest intermediation is different to the classic inter-state bargaining in international organizations. In international organizations, national governments negotiate as if outcomes are zero-sum (about dividing-the-pie), and can always exit the organization if the costs of defeat are too great. In the EU, in contrast, there is a high level of mutual interest amongst the elites of the national groups, who consequently perceive the policy process as a positive-sum exercise (about increasing the size of the EU pie). Moreover, exit from the consensual pattern of decision-making has a high price for all national groups, as they would be unable to maintain the same level of social and economic development outside the EU system. The result is a 'symbiotic' relationship where the national groups have an interest in promoting the role of the EU, and the EU has an interest in preserving the existence and autonomy of the national groups (Taylor, 1996, p. 91).

Finally, the role of national executives in the EU policy process is similar to the role of substate executives in a 'cooperative federal' system: where substate executives participate directly in the adoption of central government legislation, and are responsible for the implementation of central government policies (see for example Scharpf, 1988). Nevertheless, there are some subtle differences between 'national' consociationalism and co-operative federalism. In cooperative federal systems, substate executives are represented because they are the formal organs of the state at the lower level; they do not claim a specific legitimacy for this role as representatives of cultural interests. In the EU, in contrast, national governments are not only the substate executives of the EU system; as representatives of the collective interests of their constituents, governments are also the 'peak associations' of the European nation-states. And it is for this latter reason that national administrations play such a central role at every level of the EU policy process: a means of legitimizing the EU system. In this way, consociationalism has the same logic as corporatism: if all sides of the dominant social division can be incorporated in collective decision-making, the outcome will be accepted by all.

Explaining the pattern of interest representation

This complex system of European-level interest articulation and inter-mediation has evolved through an interaction between the growing *demand* for participation by non-state actors in the EU decision process, and the *supply* of formal and informal channels of representation by supranational governmental officials. The goals of these actors have remained stable: for interest groups, policy outcomes close to their interests; and for EU governmental actors, more power in the EU decision-making process. However, the strategies of the actors have evolved in response to the changing 'structure of opportunities' in Europe in the last two decades.

Demand for representation: globalization and Europeanization

On the demand side, public and private interests in Europe have faced a transformation in economic and political institutions since the 1960s. First, the globalization of the economy – through the expansion of cross-border trade and capital movements – has challenged the traditional patterns of capital–labour relations in Europe. The removal of tariff barriers, and the resultant globalization of product markets, has forced individual firms who compete in international markets to pursue new competitive strategies. Freed from restraints on capital mobility, these strategies have included cross-border relocation, merger, joint ventures, specialization and diversification. As a result, companies have had to become multi-national to survive.

This has produced new relationships between economic and governmental actors. Multinational firms are less interested in securing 'national' defence of their products and markets than transnational policies that allow them greater freedom to increase productivity. Instead of lobbying politicians for 'national protection', therefore, companies are increasingly interested in lobbying politicians and regulators to secure neo-liberal and deregulatory policies. From an individual firm's point of view, the rewards from national corporatist bargaining with governmental and labour actors, and even membership of 'national' peak associations of business, have receded as the benefits of private action have increased. As we showed above, in the last ten years individual companies in Europe have become less interested in national policy processes and national business associations, and more interested in approaching market regulators privately and directly, whether at the regional, national, European or international levels and even in other national systems.

This consequently undermines the ability of national state officials to incorporate business actors in consensual models of interest intermediation in the national system (Streeck and Schmitter, 1991; Crouch and Menon, 1997). Also, as business interests exit there is little incentive for governments to start talking to the other side. Moreover, whereas individual companies possess the resources to organize at new levels of politics, labour and other public interests need collective organizations to secure substantial resources. But transnational collective organizations cannot be created without genuine transnational solidaristic bonds, which are far from apparent as was illustrated in the previous chapter.

Second, the opportunity structure for social and economic interests in Europe has also transformed through the accumulation and concentration of market regulation functions at the European level: most notably in the Commission. Firms are not interested in the large public spending priorities, such as health, education and welfare, which are still controlled by national governments. What they are interested in, and why they began to be interested in politics at the domestic level in Europe in the first few decades of the postwar period, are rules governing the production, distribution and exchange of goods, products and services in the marketplace. Multinational corporations were quick to realise that centralization of market regulation in the EU institutions would significantly reduce transactions costs for business in Europe. Individual companies were consequently some of the most vocal proponents of the single market, and since the establishment of the single market the position of Brussels at the centre of multinational lobbying strategies has been confirmed.

However, with a single political centre regulating the European market, the cost of mobilization of non-business interests has also reduced. Instead of trying to prevent industry-wide cost-cutting in several European states by a coordinated transnational plan of action, public interests can go straight to Brussels to campaign for their causes. For example, against the deregulatory policies of the British Conservative governments in the 1980s, the British trade union movement became one of the strongest financial sponsors and political backers of the activities of the ETUC. Similarly, it is much cheaper for environmental and consumer groups to defend their interests in Brussels than in every national capital.

As a result, similar factors explain the desire of private and public interests to want to be organized at the European level (cf. Jordan, 1998). Driven by economic globalization, private companies have abandoned national interest intermediation in favour of direct action at the European level to promote market liberalization. Driven by political Europeanization, diffuse interests have discovered Brussels as a new political centre in the pursuit of European-wide social interests, as an adjunct and sometimes substitute for national structures of interest intermediation.

Supply of accommodation: policy expertise and legislative bargaining

However, without corresponding interest from European decision-makers, these new interest group strategies would have been ineffectual and short-lived. The fact that all forms of EU lobbying have increased suggests that the demand for representation was met with a concomitant supply of access to the policy process by political actors in the EU institutions (Pollack, 1997b; Cram, 1998).

As discussed throughout, the key institution in the supply of access for non-state interests is the Commission, which grants private interest groups access in exchange for specific information and expertise. Given the size and complexity of the task of regulating a single market of over 300 million people across 15 existing national regulatory systems, the Commission is an extremely small bureaucracy. 'Not surprisingly, officials often lack the necessary detailed expertise and knowledge of sectoral practices and problems' (Mazey and Richardson, 1997, p. 198). The Commission has even sought to formalize this process. As a guide to Commission staff, the Commission has drawn up directories listing all known national and European-level interests groups by policy area, as part of a 'procedural ambition' to maximize Commission consultation with European civil society. In addition, where the Commission identifies that a European-level group is missing, it attempts to create and sustain one. The Commission has also adopted the British practice of publishing 'Green Papers' – preliminary legislative proposals – as a means of opening up the debate about EU policy to a wider audience. The Commission refers to this overall strategy as an 'open and structured dialogue with special interest groups' (European Commission, 1992; McLaughlin and Greenwood, 1995).

The European Parliament has pursued a similar strategy to the Commission. Although not responsible for policy initiation, the Parliament requires detailed policy expertise to be able to scrutinize the behaviour of the Commission and compete with the Council in the legislative process. Whereas the Council has national public administrations to supply information, individual MEPs have limited research budgets. Consequently, in the process of writing reports and proposals for EP resolutions, *rapporteurs* seek out key interest groups to canvass their views. Indeed, some EP reports have even been written by representatives from European interest associations. Not surprisingly, then, in a recent survey of MEPs relations with interest groups, Kohler-Koch (1997) found that MEPs value 'gaining expert knowledge' as the primary purpose for meeting a lobbyist, rather than 'nationality', 'relating to constituency', 'personal acquaintance' or 'political allegiance'. The result is a myriad of lobbyists lining the corridors of the *Palais de Europe* during EP plenary sessions in Strasbourg and the *Espace Leopold* during EP committees meetings in Brussels.

Nevertheless, the primary motivation behind the supply of representation on the part of the Commission and the Parliament is the ongoing power game in the EU legislative process (cf. Cram, 1998). In other words, information and expertise matter, but only as a way of increasing the chances of securing what Commission officials and MEPs want from the EU legislative process. Interest groups possess what Greenwood (1997, pp. 18–23) calls a set of 'bargaining chips', that they offer actors in the EU political process. In addition to information and expertise, these include the ability to influence the national member organizations of a European association and the ability to help in the implementation of policy. Both these can be used by the Commission and the Parliament to undermine opposition to a proposal in the Council. For example, the German government would be reluctant to oppose a legislative initiative if the Commission or Parliament can demonstrate that the key German interest groups support the initiative, and are willing to facilitate the transposition of the policy into national practice.

Whereas the mobilization of national loyalties and interests strengthens the position of national governments in the Council, the mobilization and incorporation of transnational interests strengthens the hand of the supranational institutions. As a result, the institutional structure of the EU system provides an incentive for the Commission and the Parliament to supply negotiating space and resources to groups that represent transnational socioeconomic constituencies, which includes the labour movement, environmentalists and consumers as well as individual companies and business organizations.

Conclusion: a mix of representational styles

The system of interest representation at the European level is complex and opaque. Business interests, with greater immediate incentives and substantially more financial and political resources than public interests, are particularly capable of navigating this complex system. The practical result may hence be little different to primitive pluralism, where there is little countervailing power to block manipulation of the political process by the owners of capital. Without cohesive European political parties to promote their interests through formal channels of representation, public interests will always struggle to compete with the more highly organized and resourced business lobby. This vision of Europe dominated by an alliance of big-business and right-wing governments against the people of Europe was a common criticism by left-wing parties and Marxist scholars in the 1970s and early 1980s (for example Holland, 1980).

However, national interests are also privileged as a result of the institutionalization of consociational practices: such as committees of national experts, and bargaining in the Council. Policies are never adopted without the consent of a large majority of national groups. Consequently, where these national constituencies are closer to labour or public interests, business groups cannot monopolize the policy process. For example, viewed from Britain, where business interests dominated the 1980s, the EU policy process appears to replicate the continental corporatist model; whereas from Denmark, where public interests have managed to secure high levels of labour, environmental and consumer protection, the EU appears to favour Anglo-Saxon pluralism.

A further brake on pluralism is the increasing organization and participation of public interests at the European level. On the one hand, the centralization of market regulation policy competencies in Brussels provides a centre for social movements at the European level. On the other hand, the process of institutional competition provides an incentive for the Commission and Parliament to formalize neo-pluralist and corporatist practices. Promotion of transnational alliances spanning both sides of a policy debate strengthens the credibility of these supranational actors against the Council in the day-to-day legislative process. Also, by fostering the emergence of socioeconomic allegiances that cross-cut national divisions in Europe, these strategies promote medium- and long-term support bases for the Commission and the Parliament.

Nevertheless, this incorporation of multiple actors in the EU policy process may lead to policy *immobilisme*. The constant interaction between consociational accommodation of national interests and pluralist, neo-pluralist and corporatist intermediation of transnational socioeconomic interests is slow, opaque and unpredictable. Without a dominant executive actor, such as a president or governing political party, who is the ultimate arbiter, any well-connected group of interests can block a policy initiative. Nevertheless, the EU has been able to incorporate a wide variety of interests in the policy process and still produce significant policy outputs (see Chapters 7, 8 and 9 especially).

At the national level, interest representation exists side by side with the formal channels of representative government, via party competition and elections. As the previous chapter has shown, the EU does not have a real system of 'competitive party government'. However, interest groups may provide a way of bringing the EU 'closer to the citizen'. Schmitter (1996) consequently proposes a way of doing this, where EU citizens are able to choose which interest groups should receive funds from the EU budget to represent them in the policy process. But, if EU citizens were ready for such a scheme, they would also be ready for European-wide competitive party democracy.

PART III

POLICY-MAKING

Chapter 8

Regulation of the Single Market

Theories of regulation
Deregulatory policies: negative integration
Reregulatory policies: positive integration
Explaining EU regulatory policies
Conclusion: neo-liberalism meets the social market

Modern studies of public policy differentiate between three basic types of economic policies: (1) market regulation; (2) budgetary allocation and redistribution; and (3) macroeconomic stabilization (see for example Musgrave, 1959; Lowi, 1964). The EU supplies all three of these policy types: this chapter deals with market regulation, Chapter 9 tackles redistribution, and Chapter 10 looks at the macroeconomic issues involved in economic and monetary union.

Approximately 80 per cent of all social, economic and environmental regulation applicable in the member states is adopted through the EU policy process. This chapter analyses these policy outputs, and seeks to explain how the EU policy process works in the adoption of regulation policies. To help in this task, we shall first look at some general political science explanations of regulation and regulatory policy-making.

Theories of regulation

Economic policies have two possible effects: redistribution and efficiency. The difference between these is illustrated in Figure 8.1. In this hypothetical society there are two citizens, A and B, and the current government policy, X, produces benefits of AX and BX for the citizens. The government considers two possible policy changes: Y and Z. A move to policy Y would have a redistributive outcome: making citizen A better off (by $AY - AX$) but citizen B worse-off (by $BY - BX$). In fact, any policy change along the line that goes through X and Y would mean a redistribution of benefits from one citizen to the other. In contrast, a move to policy Z would benefit both citizens (by $AZ - AX$ and $BZ - BX$, respectively). In fact, any policy change from X to somewhere in the shaded area would make one citizen better off without making the other worse off. This is known as a 'pareto-efficient' outcome (after the Italian sociologist Vilfredo Pareto).

Figure 8.1 *Difference between redistributive and efficient policies*

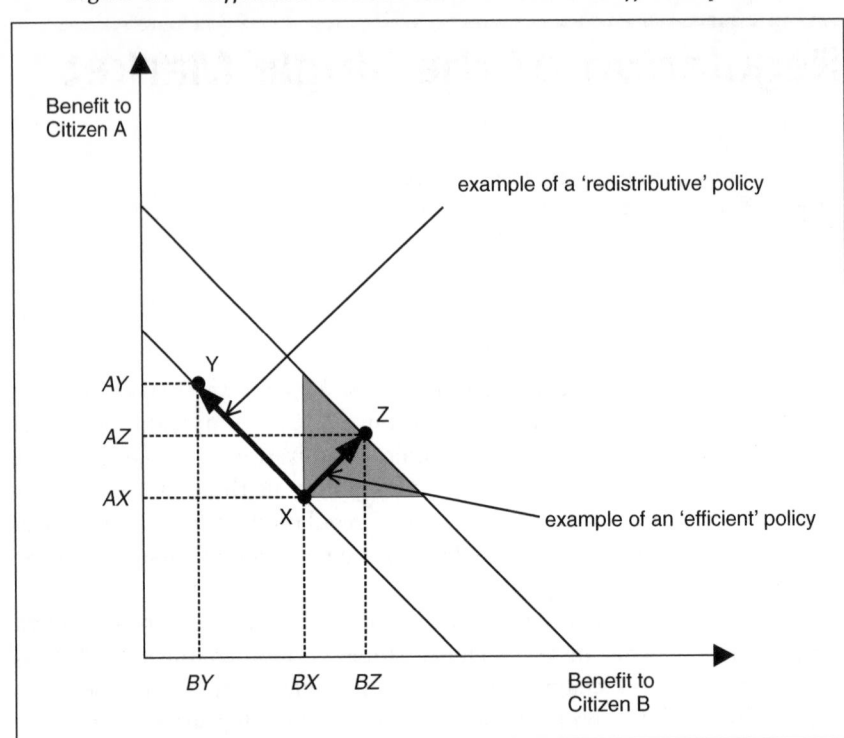

Producing outcomes that are in the interests of everyone (the 'public interest') is the traditional aim of regulatory policies (Mitnick, 1980; Sunstein, 1990). In neo-classical economic theory, free markets are naturally pareto-efficient, but in the real world there are numerous 'market failures'. But, 'regulation' can be used to correct these markets; for example:

- *Technical standards* and *consumer protection standards* enable consumers to gain information about the quality of products which would otherwise not be available.
- *Health and safety standards* and *environmental standards* reduce the adverse effects ('externalities') of market transactions on individuals not participating in the transactions.
- *Competition policies* prevent monopolistic markets from emerging, market distortions (through state subsidies), and anti-competitive practices (such as price collusion).
- *Industry regulators*, through such instruments as price controls, ensure that 'natural monopolies' operate according to market practices.

However, if economic policies are made by 'majoritarian' institutions, such as parliaments or governments, they will tend to be redistributive rather than efficient. These institutions are controlled by political parties, who will try to achieve policy outputs that benefit their supporters (see Chapter 6). Electoral majorities do not include the losers of the electoral contest. Unrestrained parliamentary majorities consequently tend to produce policies that redistribute resources from the losing minority to the winning majority (Lijphart, 1994; Majone, 1998). Madison hence argued that the 'tyranny of the majority' must be constrained if the public interest is to be protected.

Consequently, if regulation is to produce pareto-efficient outcomes, it should be made by 'non-majoritarian', or 'independent', institutions. As early as the 1880s, the US government established independent agencies to regulate the US market (Skowronek, 1982), and European governments began to take similar steps in the 1980s (Majone, 1994). At the domestic level, independent agencies have been set up to regulate industries that were previously publicly owned, and at the EU level the Commission has been delegated the responsibility for regulating the single market. However, this traditional 'public interest' justification of regulation is essentially 'normative' (Joskow and Noll, 1981). Contemporary political science also analyses policy outputs using 'positive' theories. The first (and most enduring) positive approach was Stigler's (1971) so-called 'economic theory of regulation', in which regulation is 'demanded' by private interests and 'supplied' by politicians.

On the demand side, applying Olson's (1965) theory of interest-group organization, certain interests groups are more able to mobilize to influence regulators than others (see Chapter 7). For example, the cost to a monopolistic firm of a price control is large (selective), whereas the benefit to an individual consumer or taxpayer is small (diffuse). Consequently, producer groups (business interests) are more able to exert influence on regulators than diffuse 'public' interests, such as consumers, taxpayers, environmentalists or employees. On the supply side, using Downs's (1957) theory of electoral politics, Stigler assumed that politicians primarily seek reelection. Politicians recognise that regulations impose costs on some voters and benefits for others, and that groups that are the subject of regulation tend to have more resources available to finance politicians' campaigns. The general voter tends to be 'rationally ignorant' about the details of specific regulatory policy proposals, and, as a result, politicians have an incentive to supply regulatory policies to producers. Stigler (1971, p. 94) consequently concludes that 'as a rule, regulation is acquired by the industry and is designed and operated primarily for its benefit'.

This positive theory consequently leads to directly opposing conclusions about how regulation should be organized to the traditional normative analyses. However, the reality tends to be somewhere between these perspectives (Peltzman, 1989). In practice, no single producer, industry or profession is ever able to capture a regulatory agency completely, and regulations are invariably supplied that provide at least some benefits to consumers and other diffuse interests (see for example Stigler and Friedland, 1962; Jordan, 1972). In fact, as the losses to consumers increase, their incentive to mobilize to prevent regulatory capture also increases (Peltzman, 1976; Becker, 1983).

In addition, these perspectives tend to ignore the role of institutions in shaping the way regulators behave. Regulation is made in a complex institutional environment, involving legislatures, courts, executives and multiple regulatory agencies on multiple levels of government. For example, in multilevel political systems, like the US and the EU, regulation can be pursued at several levels of government. Given a choice, producers would prefer to have market regulation done at the highest level of government. First, because it is more expense to organize at a higher level, it will be harder for diffuse interests to mobilize against producers at a higher political level (cf. Cawson and Saunders, 1983; Dunleavy, 1997). For example, at the national level in Europe, corporatist patterns of interest intermediation enable trade unions and other public interest groups to participate alongside firms in the policy-making process (see Chapter 7). Second, at the higher level, there can be 'competition' between different local regulatory regimes which will enable foot-loose capital to 'choose' the least regulated regions and force governments to introduce deregulatory policies to attract capital (see for example Scharpf, 1997a).

However, the discretion of regulatory agencies can be limited through institutional controls (as we saw in Chapter 2): a legislature can use a variety of institutional mechanisms to ensure that a regulator does not supply policies that are solely for the benefit of the subject producer. For example, a parliament can specify the public interest criteria in a regulator's contract, choose a new head of the agency every few years, and require the regulator to consult diffuse interests, and report to a parliamentary committee and the media (cf. Fiorina, 1982; Weingast and Moran, 1983; Moe, 1987; Horn, 1995). Nevertheless, if a regulatory agency is tightly controlled by a legislative majority, we are back to where we started: with a parliamentary majority using regulation as a means to redistribute benefits to a particular electoral majority rather than in the interests of all of society.

Consequently, regulatory policy-making is a struggle. Normative analysis tells us that if regulatory policies are to be efficient (in their attempts to overcome 'market failures'), they should be delegated to non-majoritarian institutions (such as the European Commission). However, once this has been achieved, the subjects of regulation (producer groups) are more likely to be able to influence regulators than public interest groups. In addition, business interests will tend to demand institutional configurations that allow them to 'capture' the regulator, such as regulatory agencies at the highest political level. Faced with this situation, politicians can introduce mechanisms to limit regulatory discretion. However, politicians like to provide policies that cater to supporters' interests, and as a result they might wish to allow regulatory capture by a particular sector of the economy (such as the French agricultural sector or the British financial services sector), if this sector is a powerful supporter of their party or government. Alternatively, politicians could simply capture the regulatory authority themselves: by reconnecting the regulator to a parliamentary majority and dictating its policy outputs (for example, by limiting the independence of the Commission).

Deregulatory policies: negative integration

The EU produces two different sorts of regulatory policies: *negative integration* policies, through the removal of barriers to international trade and competition; and *positive integration* policies, though the establishment of new EU-wide regulations (Tinbergen, 1965; Scharpf, 1996). Negative integration policies include the establishment of the *single market* and *competition policies*. Because these policies involve the abolition of national rules (and because neo-liberals are generally in favour of these policies), they are often seen as 'deregulatory' rather than regulatory (see for example Grahl and Teague, 1990).

The single market: the '1992 programme' and beyond

At the Milan European Council in June 1985, the EU heads of government adopted the Single European Act (SEA) and the Commission's White Paper on *Completing the Internal Market* (European Commission, 1985). The SEA established the deadline of 31 December 1992 for the implementation of the Commission's proposals, and introduced a new institutional mechanism for achieving this goal: through qualified-majority voting in the Council and (in most areas) the cooperation procedure with the European Parliament (see Chapter 3). The Commission White Paper set out approximately 280 pieces of legislation that would be necessary to complete the single market. This legislation covered three main areas: physical barriers, technical barriers and fiscal barriers (cf. Pelkmans and Winters, 1988).

First, on *physical barriers*, the Commission proposed lifting controls on the movement of goods and persons. By the end of 1991 the Council agreed to abolish customs formalities, paperwork and inspections at borders between the member states (amounting to approximately 60 million documents a year). In October 1992, the Commission issued the Common Customs Code, and customs barriers were then finally abolished on 31 December 1992. Eighty-one measures were also adopted by the end of 1992 on issues relating to the movement of agricultural produce and the compensation of farmers at borders under the Common Agricultural Policy. However, less progress was made on barriers to the movement of persons: Britain, Ireland and Denmark refused to accept the abolition of passport controls and the introduction of common visa requirements. However, the other member states signed the Schengen Accord, and the EU gained new institutional mechanisms and legal instruments to take action in this area with the justice and home affairs pillar of the Maastricht Treaty and the subsequent reforms to this pillar in the Amsterdam Treaty (see Chapter 11).

Second, the Commission used the heading of *technical barriers* as a catch-all category. On product standards, in 1979 the European Court of Justice had ruled that any product meeting the standards of one member state could be legally sold in another (in the *Cassis de Dijon* judgement – see Chapter 4). Building on this principle of 'mutual recognition', the Commission proposed a 'new approach to technical harmonization' (Pelkmans, 1990). This involved establishing mutual recognition as a basic principle in the single market; restricting harmonization to minimum technical and health and safety standards; contracting with pan-European standard organizations – such as CEN (European Standardization Committee) and CENELEC (European Electrotechnical Standardization Committee) – to develop voluntary European standards; and introducing the 'CE mark' for products that met the essential European standards.

On public procurement, governments were prevented from favouring home companies in government contracts. On the free movement of labour and the professions, residency rights were extended to non-workers (such as students and retirees); non-nationals gained access to state subsidies and social benefits; and rules were established for comparing education and professional qualifications. In the area of services, a host of directives were passed on the liberalization of financial services, air, water and road transport, and the opening-up of national telecommunications and television markets. On the movement of capital, controls on the free flow of capital between the member states were abolished. Finally, on company law, various rules governing cross-border company activity were harmonized (although a European Company Statute was not adopted), and common rules on the protection of intellectual property were agreed.

Third, to remove *fiscal barriers* the Commission proposed the harmonization of value added tax (VAT) ('sales tax') and excise duties (on goods like alcohol and tobacco). After protracted negotiations, the Council adopted a framework for harmonizing VAT in October 1992 which involved a standard minimum rate of 15 per cent in each member state, the abolition of luxury rates (and lower rates on special items for a transition period), and rules on where VAT should be paid (on cross-border trade, for example, VAT is paid in the country of destination). Also in October 1992, the Council agreed a harmonized structure for excise duties: with the elimination of restrictions on cross-border purchases of goods like alcoholic drinks and tobacco (for personal use), and the eventual abolition of duty-free on planes and boats (in 1999).

However, the single market programme did not stop at the end of 1992. The implementation and transposition of the legislative programme was not completed on time, and many pieces of single market legislation needed reforming and updating. In March 1992 the Commission consequently set up the High Level Group on the Operation of the Internal Market, chaired by Peter Sutherland (a former commissioner). The report of the group, the so-called Sutherland Report, proposed more consultation with the actors affected by single market regulation, greater access to the EU decision-making process, and better cooperation between the Commission and national administrations to ensure that the uneven implementation of legislation does not create barriers to trade (Sutherland *et al.*, 1992). Acting on these recommendations, the Commission drafted an action plan for the Single Market, which was adopted at the Amsterdam European Council in June 1997. The Action Plan promised progress on two levels: a rolling programme of simplification of single market legislation (the SLIM programme – simpler legislation in the single market); and co-ordinated efforts between the Commission and member states to secure the implementation of existing legislation. To embarrass the member states into action, in November 1997 the Commission launched a 'Single Market Scoreboard'. This is a record of the member states' efforts to implement single market legislation and the frequency of single market infringements by each member state. As Table 8.1 shows, in May 1998, despite a high level of transposition in each individual member state, almost 20 per cent of single market legislation remained to be transposed in all the member states, and between 1997 and 1998 several member states were consistently in breach of single market rules.

Competition policies

Article 3(g) of the EC Treaty states that the EU shall include 'a system ensuring that competition in the internal market is not distorted'. To

Table 8.1   *The single market scoreboard, May 1998*

Rank	Member state	Per cent of single market legislation not transposed into national law	Infringement proceedings for breaches of single market rules, May 1997–May 1998	
			Letters of formal notice	Rulings of the ECJ
1.	Finland	1.2	14	0
2.	Sweden	2.0	17	0
3.	Denmark	2.2	8	0
4.	Netherlands	2.2	17	1
5.	Spain	3.3	45	3
6.	United Kingdom	3.8	17	1
7.	Austria	5.2	22	0
8.	Ireland	5.4	9	1
9.	Germany	5.4	45	7
10.	Greece	5.5	24	4
11.	Luxembourg	5.6	7	0
12.	France	5.6	70	9
13.	Portugal	5.9	25	0
14.	Italy	6.4	50	9
15.	Belgium	7.1	22	6
	EU total	18.2*	392	41

Note: * = per cent of single market legislation not transposed in all member states.
Source: European Commission (1998d).

achieve this goal, the Treaty includes a chapter on 'rules applying to competition'. These articles endow the Commission with powerful policy tools to prevent anti-competitive practices from undermining free trade and competition in the single market, including the ability to impose fines (the highest was €75 million in a case in 1992). These primary laws have been supplemented with a series of secondary regulations, and the result is three main strands of EU competition policy:

● *Anti-trust regulations* – article 81 [ex 85] outlaws collusion between companies to fix prices or control production to the detriment of trade between the member states (except where it is in the public interest), Article 82 [ex 86] outlaws unfair and predatory pricing, exclusive sales agreements and discrimination on the grounds of nationality by large firms with a 'dominant position' in a national market, and Article 86 [ex 90] requires member states to ensure that publicly-owned industries abide by EU competition rules.

- *Merger control* – in December 1989, the Council adopted the merger regulation, which gave the Commission the power to scrutinize and block mergers where the aggregate worldwide turnover of the companies involved exceeds €5 billion, and the EU-wide turnover of at least two of the companies exceeds €250 million (unless both companies derive more than two-thirds of their EU-wide turnover within one member state).
- *Regulation of state aids* – Articles 87 to 89 [ex 92 to 94] outlaw public subsidies to industry that threaten competition and trade between the member states (unless the aid promotes the interests of the Union or specific sectoral or regional objectives).

Table 8.2 shows the procedures for decision-making in each of these areas. Each year, the Commission undertakes approximately 450 new anti-trust proceedings, 100 new merger proceedings (of which only 3–4 are refused or 'approved with conditions'), and 600 new state-aid proceedings (of which only 5–10 result in negative final decisions) (cf. European Commission, 1998e). This competition policy is very much based on the US model of 'anti-trust' regulation; in fact US competition lawyers helped draft the competition articles in the Treaty of Rome, and were eager to prevent European cartels that would be protected in competition with US companies. However, unlike US competition policy, which is concerned with preventing anti-competitive practices in the private sector, EU competition policy also deals with anti-competitive practices by government-owned and government-subsidized businesses.

Nevertheless, for a variety of reasons, directorate-general IV has not always pursued a policy of 'perfect competition', particularly in the regulation of public sector industries. First, DGIV is constrained by the lack of political power of the Commission against certain member states, especially in the face of potentially high economic and sectoral costs of competition policy decisions. Second, until the mid-1980s, most commissioners responsible for competition policy where ideologically in favour of promoting 'Euro-champions'. However, the Commission's status in competition policy was enhanced as a result of the political commitment behind the single market programme. In the wake of the Single European Act, a series of commissioners responsible for competition policy – Peter Sutherland (1985–89), Leon Brittan (1989–93) and Karel Van Miert (1993–99) – eagerly sought opportunities to confront member states and multi-nationals. This enabled them to raise the status of DGIV within the Commission and further there own political careers. Responding to the rise in cross-border mergers in anticipation of the single market and to heavy lobbying by multinational firms (in the European Round-Table of Industrialists), the member states finally adopted the merger regulation in 1989,

Table 8.2 *Decision procedures under EU competition policies*

	Anti-trust	Mergers	State aids
Notification to Commission	1. notification by firms concerned 2. own-initiative of Commission 3. complaint by third party	Mandatory notification within 1 week of proposed merger, if: ecu 5bn worldwide turnover & ecu 250m EU-wide turnover	Mandatory notification of new state aids or changes to existing aids before implementation.
First stage	*Commission:* • case dropped or • 'comfort/discomfort letter' or • move to second stage.	*Commission* (within 1 month): • outside scope of regulation or • approval or • move to second stage.	*Commission* (within 2 months): • approval/no investigation or • initiate proceedings.
Second stage (Initiation of proceedings)	*Commission:* • case dropped (if firms have responded to letter) or • move to next stages (Third stage): Written reply from firms Hearings with firms/third parties (Fourth stage): Consultation with member states Advisory Committee Opinion	Detailed appraisal Advisory Committee Opinion	Third parties invited to comment
Final decision	*Commission:* • approval or • exemption or • prohibition (and possible fines).	*Commission* (within 4 months): • approval or • conditional approval or • prohibition.	*Commission* (within 6 months): • approval or • refusal.
Follow-up	Appeal to the ECJ	Appeal to the ECJ (within 2 months)	Appeal to the ECJ

Source: Procedures specified in regulations 17/62 (EEC), 99/63 (EEC) and 4064/89 (EEC).

after over 15 years of negotiations. The regulation established a 'one-stop-shop' system at the EU level, which would be run by the new merger task force in DGIV.

Nevertheless, questions are continually raised over the 'neutrality' of DGIV's competition decisions. The replacement as competition commissioner of Brittan, a Conservative neo-liberal, with Van Miert, a Belgian Socialist, caused particular concern to several multinationals and national competition agencies. Van Miert has since established himself as an arch-defender of the consumer against uncompetitive practices by governments and multinationals; but DGIV occasionally bows to political pressures, and the competition commissioner can always be out-voted by his fellow commissioners if the issue is highly politicized. For example, in 1998, the ECJ ruled that the French government's aid package to Air France, which had been approved by DGIV, contravened EU competition rules, but, against the arguments of certain commissioners (such as Brittan), the Commission supported Van Miert's proposal that Air France would not have to return the funds. Consequently, a number of commentators and national regulators argue that to prevent the political use of competition policy, DGIV should be removed from the Commission bureaucracy and established as an independent European Cartel Office, along the lines of the German Cartel Office (Wilks and McGowan, 1995). This would allow an independent competition regulator to simply 'apply the rules', while leaving the definition of the rules to the political authorities in the Council, European Parliament and Commission.

Impact of the single market: liberalization and regulatory competition

The single market programme and EU competition policies have both a 'direct' and an 'indirect' impact on national sectors and industrial policies (Helm and Smith, 1989). On the direct side, having taken over the responsibility for regulating capital, goods and services from the member states, the EU has liberalized trade between the member states and liberalized competition within several national markets. On the indirect side, through competition policies and regulations and directives that supplement the operation of the single market, the EU has forced member states to reduce their interventions in the economy. On this latter point, under Article 86 [ex 90], DGIV has pursued a policy of 'contestable competition': that national markets do not have to be perfect, but firms (either domestically located or from other member states) must be free to enter and leave the market without significant costs.

The result has been a deregulation of a large number of industrial sectors (Kassim and Menon, 1996), for example:

- *Financial services* – the banking, securities and insurance markets have been opened to competition from other member states, which includes a 'single passport' for financial firms to operate anywhere in the EU and reciprocal access to the EU market for services from non-EU states.
- *Air transport* – liberalization 'packages' were adopted in 1987, 1990 and 1992 and domestic air markets were opened to any EU-based airline from April 1997, and through competition policy the Commission has prevented consolidation where it would have created monopolies on certain routes and forced governments to reduce state subsidies to their airlines.
- *Telecommunications* – open competition in telecoms equipment was agreed in 1988, competition in voice telephony and telex services was established from 1993, and open competition in the supply of infrastructure and the provision of all telecoms services in both fixed and mobile telephony ('open networks provision') began in January 1998.
- *Electricity supply* – a directive was adopted in 1996 to liberalize national electricity markets over a nine-year period, leading to vertical disintegration in the industry (a separation of production, transmission and distribution), which in most cases will mean privatization of electricity production and supply.

Furthermore, the application of mutual recognition of national standards introduces the potential of competition between national rules and regulators (Siebert, 1990; Neven, 1992; Hosli, 1995a). With open access to any national market in the single market, firms could choose to be registered in the member state with the lowest regulatory costs. The effect could be a 'race to the bottom' or 'social dumping': where member states are forced to reduce the regulatory burden on firms by lowering labour standards and tax rates to attract capital (see for example Joerges, 1997). In the US the notion that regulatory competition has a deregulatory effect is known as the 'Delaware effect', after the East Coast state that successfully used an absence of regulation to attract investment (Carey, 1974).

However, there has been little evidence of a Delaware effect in the EU (Woolcock, 1994; Sun and Pelkmans, 1995). For most companies the costs of regulation are marginal when making decisions about where to locate. Far more important are proximity to markets, labour quality and financial incentives from regional or central governments (Goodhart, 1998). In fact, economic integration and regulatory competition can push the level of regulation upwards. High standards can favour domestic producers in gaining access to foreign markets, resulting in a 'race to the top'. For example, California has been the leader in environmental standards both nationally and globally in the US (Vogel, 1995). The same is true in sectors were there is international cooperation between the EU and the USA such as in financial services, where higher standards became the norm (Genschel and Plümper, 1997).

It is too early to tell whether the 'Delaware' or 'California' effects are most prevalent in the EU. What is certain, though, is that economic and monetary union will facilitate further regulatory competition as a result of the reduction in transactions costs resulting from exchange-rate stability and greater price transparency in regulatory costs. Consequently, the single market combined with monetary union is likely to have a broad impact on national macroeconomic policies, forcing member states to hold-down tax rates on capital and non-wage labour costs (Krugman, 1987; Scharpf, 1997a).

In sum, the single market was set up with a 'pareto-efficient' policy aim: where every member state, industry, consumer and citizen will benefit from the economies of scale in a larger market and the efficiency effects of trade and market liberalization (Cecchini, 1988; Smith and Wanke, 1993). Also, the single market and EU competition policies were established to tackle market failures – where harmonized standards for goods and services reduce information asymmetries; and public procurement rules, state-aid regulations and merger controls address the problem of market power (Gatsios and Seabright, 1989; Pelkmans, 1990). Nevertheless, by tackling these issues at the European level, the ability of national administrations to use rules and goods and services to achieve value-allocative goals is reduced: such as protection of a particular industry, high labour and other process standards, or culturally-specific product standards. Hence, as Dehousse argues (1992, p. 399): 'It is difficult to avoid the conclusion that the combined effect of market integration and power fragmentation is to make government intervention more difficult'.

Reregulatory policies: positive integration

The EU has also developed a series of 'positive integration' policies as a conscious supplement to the single market programme: the most significant of which are *environmental policy* and *social policy*. Because these policies replace previous national rules with common EU rules, they can be seen as 're'-regulatory policies. However, these policies are not only regulatory, because they are not intended to secure purely pareto-efficient outcomes, they involve choosing values that are preferred by some citizens and not others. As Easton (1965, p. 50) explains:

An allocation may deprive a person of a valued thing already possessed, it may obstruct the attainment of values which would otherwise have been attained, or it main give some persons access to values and deny them to others.

As a result, EU environmental and social policies may not redistribute resources, but they do produce a reallocation of values in European society.

Environmental policy

Although not originally mentioned in the Treaty of Rome, in 1972 the heads of government agreed to launch a series of environmental action programmes. These culminated in the fifth action programme (on 'sustainable development'), covering the period 1992–2000. Environmental policy became a full competence of the EU with the Single European Act, and was strengthened and extended by the Maastricht Treaty with the introduction of majority voting in the Council on environmental legislation and the principle of sustainable development as a central aim of the EU. While allowing member states to apply higher environmental protection standards, the Treaty requires the EU to develop common environment policies which achieve 'a high level of protection', rectify environmental damage at source, pursue preventative action, and are based on the 'polluter pays' principle.

To this end, the main EU actions in the environment field have been as follows:

- *Air pollution* – since 1970 the EU has adopted ever-stricter directives on air pollution by vehicles, large combustion plants and power stations, the Commission has proposed measures to phase-out chloroflourocarbons and to introduce an 'energy tax' on carbon dioxide emissions, and there are EU rules on noise pollution by motor vehicles, aircraft, lawnmowers, household equipment and building-site machinery.
- *Waste disposal* – since 1975 a series of directives have established EU regulations on toxic and dangerous waste, the trans-frontier shipment of hazardous waste, and the disposal of specific types of waste.
- *Water pollution* – since 1976 a number of directives have established common standards for surface and underground water, bathing water, drinking water, fresh water, the discharge of toxic substances (now strictly controlled), and the EU has signed several international conventions to reduce pollution in international waterways.
- *Chemical products* – following the industrial disaster in Seveso in 1977, the EU adopted a series of directives regulating the use, storage, handling, packaging and labelling of a wide variety of dangerous

chemicals, and providing for a European inventory of all chemical substances on the market.

- *Nature protection* – between 1982 and 1992, the EU adopted directives implementing the international Convention on Trade in Endangered Species (CITES), which established EU rules on the conservation of wild birds, on the protection of natural habitats, and on scientific experiments on animals, and the EU offers financial support for projects to conserve natural habitats.
- *Environmental impact assessment* – in 1985 the Council adopted a directive, which has subsequently been extended, requiring environmental impact assessments in all public and private industrial or infrastructure projects above a certain size, and which require that the public be consulted in the process.
- *Eco-labelling and eco-audits* – in 1992 the Council adopted a regulation laying down rules for granting EU 'eco-labels' to environmentally-friendly products, and in 1993 the Council adopted a regulation establishing a voluntary environmental auditing scheme.
- *European Environment Agency* (EEA) – the EEA was set up in 1994 in Copenhagen, and is responsible for collecting data and supplying information for new environmental legislation, developing forecasting techniques to enable preventative measures to be taken, and ensuring that EU environmental data are incorporated into international environmental programmes.

As a result, the EU has been able to adopt common environmental standards on a wide variety of subjects. This fits the view that EU regulation addresses market failures inherent in the single market (Gatsios and Seabright, 1989; Eichener, 1997; Majone, 1996). First, environmental pollution is an unwanted side-effect (negative externalities) of almost all economic activity, affecting many persons not involved in the transactions that produced the pollution. Second, without environmental standards and environmental labelling, consumers lack the necessary information to make judgements about the quality and environmental-friendliness of the goods they buy. To limit these market failures, the EU has regulated environmental standards at all stages of the economic process: from production (such as chemical emissions), through distribution (such as eco-labelling) and consumption (such as vehicle emissions), to disposal (such as waste management).

However, there are several aspects of EU environmental policy that do not fit this regulatory justification (Weale, 1996; Lee, 1997; Marin, 1997). For example, EU environmental regulation covers far more than simply cross-border pollution. The EU sets standards at both the national and European levels, EU environmental regulations have almost universally been based on the 'high standards' of the most environmentally advanced member states such as Denmark, Germany and the Netherlands, rather than the 'low standards' of Britain, Ireland and southern Europe. The low standards, in most cases, would have been sufficient to protect against negative externalities and provided a degree of information to consumers.

Instead, environmental policy at the EU level is driven primarily by a desire to prevent a 'distortion of competition' in the single market – an ideological argument disguised as the need to address a market failure. The Commission and the member states with strong environmental movements and Green Parties have continually argued that the single market would force them to lower their environmental standards to remain competitive. These efforts have been supported by a highly developed environmental movement at the European level – through such organizations as the European Environmental Bureau and Greenpeace – whose lobbying activities are heavily subsidized from the EU budget (see Chapter 7). Hence, in this policy area, diffuse interests have equal access to regulators as private sectoral and industrial interests (Pollack, 1997b, Webster, 1998).

In addition, in most cases the member states with lower environmental standards have been willing to accept this argument. They are aware that their publics support environmental issues being tackled at the European level (see Chapter 5), and they are also aware that their industries will need to meet high environmental standards to gain access to markets in North America and Japan. The result, as Sbragia (1996, p. 253) points out is, 'rather than "environmental dumping", the Union's policy-making process has led to "up-market environmentalism"'. In other words, in the area of environmental regulation, particularly in the case of product standards (such as packaging and labelling rules), the EU has experienced a California effect rather than a Delaware effect (Vogel, 1997).

Social policy

The Treaty of Rome provided for an EU social policy in several ways:

- a general objective of promoting 'social progress and a high level of employment';
- a section in the main body of the Treaty allowing for closer cooperation (by unanimity in the Council) in the improvement of living and working conditions;
- a requirement that the member states secure equal pay for men and women;
- a European Social Fund to help occupational and geographic mobility; and
- the principle of free movement of workers, with rights to residence, social security and non-discrimination in employment.

Little progress was made on these issues in the 1970s and 1980s, except on the coordination of social security systems for migrant workers and equal pay for women.

However, EU social policy received a new impetus in the 1980s. Fearing that the single market would primarily benefit capital rather than labour, the French Socialists François Mitterrand (the French president) and Jacques Delors (the Commission president) argued for a 'social dimension' of European integration. As a result, the Single European Act provided for the harmonization of health and safety standards at work using qualified-majority voting in the Council and a 'social dialogue' between the two sides of industry in the preparation of legislation (as represented by the European labour, business and public employers associations) (see Chapter 7). In December 1989, 11 member states (excluding Britain) signed the Commission's proposed Charter on the Fundamental Rights of Workers (the 'Social Charter'), which listed 47 actions for the establishment of a social dimension of the single market programme, that the Commission then turned into legislative proposals in the subsequent Social Action Programme.

In negotiating the Maastricht Treaty in 1992, a majority of member states proposed incorporating the aims of the Social Charter into the EU Treaty, and qualified-majority voting in the Council on most social policy issues. However, the British Conservative government vetoed this proposal. The solution was a separate Agreement on Social Policy between the other 11 member states. This 'Social Protocol' provided for qualified-majority voting in areas such as working conditions and workers' consultation, unanimity-voting in more sensitive areas like social security, and greater consulting of the social partners in the drafting of social legislation, including the possibility of 'Euro-agreements' between the social partners taking the place of legislation. Nevertheless, in December 1997 the British Labour government agreed to the Amsterdam Treaty which incorporated the Social Protocol into a new Social Chapter of the EU Treaty. The Amsterdam Treaty also included provisions for cooperation between the member states to combat unemployment (article 125–130). The Treaty bases and decision-making procedures for passing EU social legislation following the reforms of the Amsterdam Treaty are shown in Table 8.3.

Despite the above, examples of EU social legislation have been few and far between in comparison to environmental legislation. The main recent developments in EU social policy have been as follows:

- *Free movement of workers* – residency rights have been extended to students, retirees, ex-employers and the self-employed, but there are repeated problems with the application of freedom of movement of persons, and migrant workers do not have fully equal social rights (see Chapter 11).

- *Health and safety at work* – directives have been passed establishing a general health and safety framework covering all the main sectors and specialized rules for particular industries and health and safety protection for part-time workers, and in 1995 the Commission proposed a Medium-Term Action Programme for Health and Safety at Work 1996–2000.

- *Working conditions* – directives on the protection of pregnant women at work and the provision of proof on an employment contract were adopted in 1991 and 1992 respectively, but the working time directive was delayed until 1993, the directive on parental leave was passed under the Maastricht Social Protocol in 1996 (without the UK), and the directive on equal rights for temporary workers was held up until 1996.

- *Worker consultation* – despite repeated proposals by the Commission since the 1970s on rights of workers' consultation and participation in company decisions, the works council directive was not adopted until 1994, and only then under the Maastricht Social Protocol (without the UK).

- *Equality between men and women* – little new legislation has been adopted on sexual equality since the mid-1980s, but the Commission proposed a fourth community action programme on equal opportunities for men and women (1996–2000), which includes a draft directive on the burden of proof in sexual discrimination at work and a series of draft recommendations relating to the involvement of women in the workforce.

- *Unemployment* – following the Commission's 1993 White Paper on *Growth, Competitiveness and Employment*, unemployment has been high on the EU agenda, but the member states disagree over how best to achieve this (through supply-side policies or labour market 'flexibility'), and the capacity in the EU in this field is restricted to agreeing non-binding targets and guidelines (in the new Employment chapter).

As this shows, social legislation at the EU level is far from the traditional 'social policy' of domestic 'welfare states': where the state takes on the responsibility of supplying social goods, such as social insurance, health care, welfare services, education and housing (for example, Titmus, 1974). These core redistributive powers remain firmly under the control of national administrations (although the EU does undertake certain direct redistributive policies in other areas, see Chapter 9). Social policy at the EU level is really 'social regulation': to address market failures rather than redistribute resources between employers and workers or between rich and poor (Majone, 1993a).

Table 8.3 *Treaty bases and decision procedures for EU social legislation*

Treaty article	Policy issue	Council voting	Role of EP
Social Policy chapter (Title XI – chapter 1)			
137(1) [ex 118]	Health and safety at work	QMV	Co-decision
	Working conditions		
	Information and consultation of workers		
	Integration of persons excluded from the labour market		
	Equal opportunities and treatment of men and women		
137(3) [ex 118]	Social security	Unanimity	Consultation
	Protection of workers where their contracts are terminated		
	Representation of workers, including codetermination		
	Conditions of employment for third-country nationals		
	Financial contributions for promoting employment		
139 [ex 118b]	Contractual agreements between management and labour		
	– issues under Article 137(1)	QMV	None
	– issues under Article 137(3)	Unanimity	None
141 [ex 119]	Equal pay, treatment and opportunities for men and women	QMV	Co-decision
Other provisions in the Treaty			
37 [ex 43]	Safeguard of employment and living standards of farmers	QMV	Consultation
40 [ex 49]	Free movement of workers	QMV	Co-decision
42 [ex 51]	Social security (necessary for freedom of movement)	Unanimity	Co-decision
44 [ex 54]	Freedom of establishment	QMV	Co-decision
47 [ex 57]	Mutual recognition of diplomas	QMV	Co-decision
71 [ex 75]	Transport safety	QMV	Co-decision
94 [ex 100]	Harmonization of laws in the single market	Unanimity	Consultation
95 [ex 100a]	Harmonization of laws in the single market	QMV	Co-decision
308 [ex 235]	New policy competences for the EU	Unanimity	Consultation

Note: QMV = qualified-majority voting (see Chapter 3). The operation of the consultation and co-decision procedures is analysed in Chapter 3.

As a result, the most developed areas of EU social policy are social security rights for migrant workers, health and safety standards and product safety standards (Eichener, 1992, 1997; Leibfried and Pierson, 1996). Social security for migrant workers increases the efficiency of the labour market as part of the general single market goal; health and safety and product standards reduce information costs to consumers and reduce the external effects of production processes on the health of workers. The costs of these standards are spread between all producers and consumers, and the benefits are collected by all consumers and industrial workers. Hence, both costs and benefits are diffuse.

The EU has been much less successful in adopting common rules relating to working conditions and industrial relations, and in pursuing labour market policies. On working conditions, few EU standards have been agreed: for example, on working time, rights of part-time and temporary employees and maternity leave. And, in contrast to health and safety standards, these rules have not tended to apply the general standards of the most advanced member states, but rather basic requirements with a high degree of flexibility of application (Streeck, 1995, 1996; Armstrong and Bulmer, 1998, pp. 226–54; Bastian, 1998). On industrial relations, there are no common rules on worker consultation and codetermination, and the works council directive only applies to large multinational firms and allows a high degree of flexibility in its application (Rhodes, 1995; Falkner, 1996; Streeck, 1997). Finally, despite the Employment chapter of the EU Treaty, the EU does not have the power to force member states to adopt common labour market policies.

Again, this fits the 'social regulation' theory of EU social policy: these policies are less about addressing market standards than applying particular ideological choices about the operation of European capitalism (Teague, 1994; Jackman, 1998). Hence, policies on these issues at the national level reflect the different levels of support for Socialist parties, the varying power of national trade union movements and the historical development of interparty and capital–labour compromises (see for example, Esping-Anderson, 1990).

The EU's reregulatory regime: between harmonization and voluntarism

The result of this mix of environmental and social policies is a particular EU reregulatory regime (cf. Scharpf, 1996; Kassim and Hine, 1998). First, in a number of areas, EU reregulatory policies have led to the harmonization of existing national regulations, or the establishment of regulations where no existing national rules existed, into a single 'integrated' European regulatory framework. This is particularly the case in the area of 'product standards', such as technical specifications, environmental protection and labelling and other consumer protection rules. However, a single European-wide regulatory framework also covers health and safety at work. Many of these areas fit the theory of regulation as the redress of market failures.

Second, in several other areas, EU reregulatory policies have led to the setting of common European norms and values which go well beyond the narrow market failure justification of regulation. For example, in environmental policy EU rules have established some of the highest standards in the world and in social policy the EU has begun to regulate 'process standards', such as workers' rights and industrial relations practices. Neverthless, on these issues the EU reregulatory regime is essentially 'voluntarist' (Streeck, 1995, 1996). As Streeck (1996, pp. 424–31) explains:

> Neovoluntarism stands for a type of social policy that tries to do with a minimum of compulsory modification of both market outcomes and national policy choices, presenting itself as an alternative to hard regulation as well as to no regulation at all. In particular, neovoluntarism allows countries to exit from common standards . . . Neovoluntarism would represent a break with the practice of European welfare states, which is to create hard, legally enforceable status rights and obligations for individual citizens and organised collectivities

Perhaps the only area of proactive EU social policy that does not fit this neovoluntarism argument is on the equal pay, treatment and opportunities for men and women: where EU rules and norms have been at the vanguard of developments in the member states (Ostner and Lewis, 1995; Mazey, 1998)

Nevertheless, reregulatory policies do have a powerful indirect redistributive impact, and are hence a form of 'welfare state' at the European level (Leibfreid, 1992; Leibfried and Pierson, 1995; Montanari, 1995; Gomà, 1996; Scharpf, 1997a). The EU does not have the direct redistributive capacity of national welfare states (see Chapter 9), but the emerging EU reregulatory regime reflects a particular welfare compromise at the European level that constrains existing welfare compromises and choices at the domestic level. This places 'downward' pressure on states with high labour market standards (such as Germany and Scandinavia), and 'upward' pressure on states with low labour market standards (such as Britain and southern Europe). Moreover, these constraints on domestic redistributive and value-allocative choices will be further reinforced as the EU attempts to harmonize national fiscal policies in economic and monetary union (see Chapter 10).

Explaining EU regulatory policies

There are two main developments in EU regulatory policies that need explaining:

- why has the EU been more able to adopt deregulatory ('negative integration') than reregulatory ('positive integration') policies; and
- within the area of reregulation, why has the EU been more able to adopt 'product standards' (such as environmental standards) than 'process standards' (such as labour market regulations)?

In answering these questions, scholars of the EU have focused on four different aspects of the EU policy-making process: (1) the 'demand' for EU deregulation and reregulation by national governments; (2) the 'demand' for EU deregulation and reregulation by private interests; (3) the 'supply' of regulatory policies and policy ideas by the Commission, and the different 'policy-styles' in Brussels; and (4) the institutional constraints on this demand and supply in the EU legislative process. Each of these will now be discussed.

Demand for regulation: intergovernmental bargaining

With the SEA, the member governments of the EU agreed by unanimity to the creation of the single market. This consensus for a deregulatory project at the European level arose from a new ideological compromise that emerged in the mid-1980s (Cameron, 1992; Garrett, 1992). On one side, the British Conservative government, led by Margaret Thatcher, saw the single market as a way of exporting the British deregulatory model to the Continent. On the other side, following the failure of Mitterrand's 'socialism in one country' experiment in the early 1980s, the French Socialist government saw the single market as a means of developing Europe's industrial competitiveness and capacity against the United States and Japan. For Mitterrand and the other Socialist governments, liberalization of intra-EU trade and deregulation of national markets was a necessary evil to reap the long-term benefits of lower transactions costs and higher economies of scale. In other words, once the single market project was perceived as pareto-efficient, the benefits of collective action outweighed the costs (cf. Moravcsik, 1991, 1993). The EU governments consequently agreed to delegate powers to the Commission to propose a plan to complete the single market.

However, parallel to the deregulatory project of the single market, the Socialist governments also argued for EU environmental and social policies, and attempted to include provisions in the SEA to secure these

Figure 8.2 *Intergovernmental bargaining on product and process regulations*

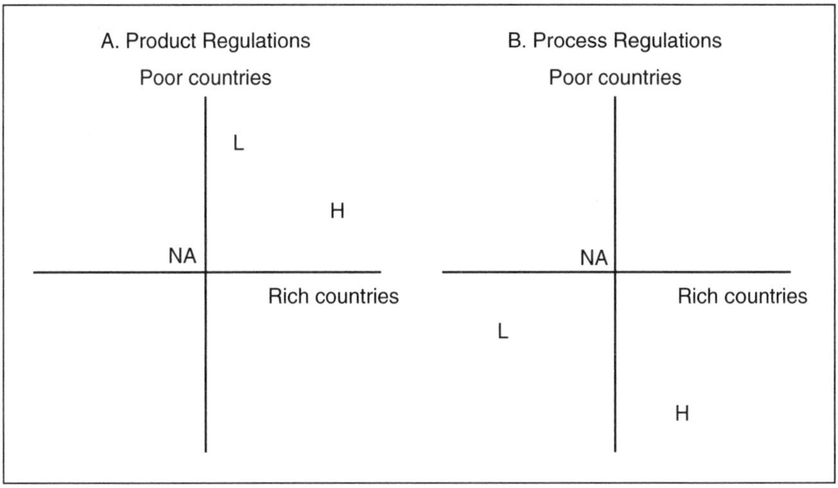

```
        A. Product Regulations              B. Process Regulations
           Poor countries                      Poor countries
                    |                                    |
              L     |                                    |
                    |                                    |
                    |     H                              |
                    |                                    |
         NA  _____|_____            NA  _____|_____
                    |     Rich countries                 |      Rich countries
                    |                          L          |
                    |                                     |
                    |                                     |       H
                    |                                     |
```

Note: NA = benefits of non-agreement; L = benefits of agreement on low standards; and H = benefits of agreements on high standards.
Source: Scharpf (1996).

ends. But, as Scharpf (1996) explains, consensus support is more easily achieved on 'product'-related regulations (such as environmental product standards, technical standards and product safety) than on 'process'-related standards (such as working conditions and industrial relations rules). As Figure 8.2 shows, on product regulations, rich countries prefer agreement on 'high standards' while poor countries prefer agreement on 'low standards'; but both states prefer either 'low' or 'high' standards (or some location between the two) to 'non-agreement'. On these issues, the continued existence of different national rules would lead to significant market failures in the single market (distortions of competition, negative externalities of cross-border pollution and information asymmetries) (Majone, 1993a, 1996). The same situation exists for a specific category of process standards – health and safety rules and certain environmental standards – where negative externalities are high (Scharpf, 1997b). Consequently, there is broad support for the reregulation of product standards (and certain specific process standards) at the EU level to a relatively high level. This enables the member governments to agree to delegate powers to the Commission to initiate policy ideas in this area and introduce majority voting in the Council to increase the efficiency of decision-making on these issues. As a result, on these issues the 'leaders' are able to drag the 'laggards' along (Héritier, 1994; Héritier, Knill and Mingers, 1996; Sbragia, 1996; Liefferink and Andersen, 1998).

On process regulations, in contrast, rich member states (and especially when Socialist parties are in power) fear that regulatory competition will force them to lower their standards – leading to 'social dumping'. Ideally, then, rich states want high process standards imposed at the EU level, but if this cannot be achieved rich countries prefer non-agreement to common low standards, as this will enable them to maintain their high standards and compete over productivity. On the other hand, poor countries favour non-agreement over either low or high standards, as this will enable them to offer cheaper production costs to footloose capital. Hence, the outcome on these issues is 'non-agreement': an acceptance of existing national 'regulatory diversity' on workers' rights (and process-related environmental standards that do not address market failures); and a resistance by several members states to qualified-majority voting in the Council on these issues (Lange, 1993; Golub, 1996b, 1996c; Héritier, 1996).

Demand for regulation: private interests and Euro-pluralism

In opposition to this 'intergovernmentalist' account, other scholars emphasise the role of private (non-state) interests in promoting European integration and influencing the EU policy process (Sandholtz and Stone Sweet, 1997). In this interpretation, variations in the development of EU regulatory policies stem from the different levels of influence of business interests and public interests in the EU policy process. As we saw in Chapter 7, business interests are more organized at the EU level than environmentalists, consumer groups and trade unions. There are three reasons for this. First, as a result of the 'logic of collection action' (see Chapter 7), business interests (who can reap specific benefits from the EU policy process) are more able to secure the resources from their members to lobby the EU than public interests (who can only obtain 'diffuse benefits' from the EU policy process). Second, as the general theories of regulation predict (see above), in multilevel political systems business interests have a particular incentive to promote regulatory policies at the higher level – they realise that they are more able to influence the policy process at a higher level than their 'opponents'. However, business interests would also like to promote regulatory competition between the different lower regimes, to facilitate downward pressure on domestic regulations (Dunleavy, 1997). Third, business interests have a particular incentive in the EU system to remove regulatory policy-making from the national level: where 'corporatism' is the prevalent style of regulatory policy-making (Streeck and Schmitter, 1991).

As a result, business interests, through the European Round-Table of Industrialists (ERT) and other transnational business associations, lobbied heavily for the single market programme to be promoted by the Commission and adopted by national governments (Sandholtz and Zysman, 1989; Cowles, 1995). Moreover, business interests were willing to tolerate the regulation of common product-standards at a high level, as these are less costly than process-standards, they reduce market distortions, and they enable European products to be sold in the North American and Japanese markets. In contrast, on process-standards, businesses in richer states would like to see their standards lowered to increase their competitiveness, and businesses in poorer states fear that EU rules in this area will impose new production costs. As a result, the ERT and the Union of Industrial and Employers Confederations of Europe (UNICE) have only been willing to allow voluntaristic process regulations, as in the working time and works councils directives.

Nevertheless, this Stiglerian 'capture' of the EU regulatory process by business interests is not complete. The Commission is a multiparty institution (see Chapter 6), and Socialist commissioners (particular in the social affairs and environment portfolios) have been eager to involve the trade union movement and environmental and consumer groups in the EU policy process, including funding their activities from the EU budget (see Chapter 7). Likewise, Socialist governments in the Council (particularly from states with high product standards) have continually supported the Commission's attempts to promote directives harmonizing product standards, as in the Social Charter. The result is the involvement of the European Trade Union Confederation in pre-legislative bargaining with UNICE under the Agreement on Social Policy (Rhodes, 1995). Without this element of neo-corporatism at the European level, it is unlikely that the Commission would have proposed and the member states would have agreed to the several key process-related directives in the post-Maastricht era: on parental leave, working time and works councils (Falkner, 1996, 1997; Pollack, 1997b).

Supply of regulation: policy entrepreneurship, ideas and decision-framing

Nevertheless, policy outcomes are not only the result of demands by governments and interest groups. Policy is also determined by variations in the 'supply' of policies – through the initiation of policy ideas by the Commission and the shaping of policy choices in the Brussels policy process. For a number of reasons the supply of policies does not always match the demand. First, the Commission's institutional interests are different from those of the governments. Like all bureaucracies, it has an incentive to increase its own power and prestige in the policy process, and once powers have been delegated to the Commission (for example for the initiation of regulatory policies), the Commission has a degree of discretion in how it exercises these powers (see Chapter 2). Second, how a policy issue is 'framed' can determine how actors order, up-date and act on their policy preferences (Tversky and Kahneman, 1981; Riker, 1986; Majone, 1989). And, by controlling the initiation of policy, the Commission is free to frame policy issues in the way it perceives is most likely to secure support in the legislative process. Putting these two together, the Commission is a 'policy entrepreneur' (Kingdon, 1984): selecting the policies that promote its interests; restricting the available choices for governments; continually pressing and negotiating until it gets what it wants; and involving other actors in the policy process to force reluctant governments to accept its proposals (cf. Peters, 1992, 1994; Richardson, 1996; Cram, 1997; Majone, 1996, pp. 74–8).

For example, in the White Paper on *Completing the Internal Market*, the Commission proposed the 'new approach to harmonization'. This was a particular 'cultural frame': with the new method of harmonization for rules of exchange (and rules of exchange concentrated in export-oriented industries); mutual recognition for the establishment of property rights (and applying to only a few industries, such as financial services and the professions); and enforcement of these rules by national administrations (Fligstein and Mara-Drita, 1996). Moreover, using the Cecchini Report on the *Cost of Non-Europe* (Cecchini *et al.*, 1988), the Commission made it clear that the proposals of the White Paper would be beneficial to all member states: hence, a pareto-efficient project. As a result, the Commission was able to overcome the deadlock in the Council over the achievement of one of the original goals of the Treaty of Rome (cf. Garrett and Weingast, 1993; Dehousse and Majone, 1994; Pierson, 1996). Moreover, in policing the operation of the single market the Commission has been highly activist in extending EU competition rules to cover a wide variety of public utilities (Schmidt, 1998).

A similar story can be told about advances in reregulatory policies, where intergovernmental bargaining or business interest lobbying would not have produced EU policies without the agenda-setting role and strategies of the Commission (cf. Cram, 1993). On environmental issues, the Commission proposed high standards and involved environmental interest groups in EU decision-making to increase its prestige amongst the 'green' member states and to gain the support of the majority in the European Parliament (cf. Eichener, 1997; Héritier, 1997; Lenschow, 1997; Pollack, 1997b). On workers' rights and worker consultation, the Commission proposed the 'social dialogue' as a conscious way of circumventing a lack of consensus in the Council (Rhodes, 1995; Falkner, 1996). Also, in the area of health and safety at work, the Commission deliberately promoted the use of 'scientific expertise' through the comitology system (see Chapter 2). This gave particular credibility to proposals that many member states and business interests would otherwise have been reluctant to accept (Eichener, 1997). All in all, by promoting innovative policy networks and mechanisms of interest accommodation, and by controlling the supply of expertise and information to national governments, the Commission has found ways of forcing the hand of a reluctant Council. Héritier (1997) consequently calls this 'policy-making by subterfuge'.

Institutional constraints: legislative rules and political structure

The demand for and supply of EU regulation policies does not go on in an institution-free environment. Contemporary 'new institutional' theories of political science explain policy outcomes by focusing on how institutions constrain, shape and channel political behaviour (cf. March and Olsen, 1989). These approaches tend to fall into two camps: 'institutional rational choice' (for example Shepsle, 1989; Tsebelis, 1994) and a 'historical institutionalism' (for example Thelen and Steinmo, 1992). However, these two camps share many assumptions about the interaction between institutions and actors' preferences and about institutional choice, and are hence much closer to each other than traditional rational choice and structural-functionalist theories (Hall and Taylor, 1996). Following the general political science vogue, a growing number of scholars of the EU use these two new institutional theories to explain EU policy outputs (cf. Pollack, 1996).

From an institutional rational choice perspective, the variations in the rules of the EU legislative process produce variations in policy outcomes (see Chapter 4). Where unanimity is required in the Council, as in the consultation procedure, any member state can veto a policy proposal it dislikes. But the agenda-setting power resides with the Commission, and even the least pro-integration member states are often willing to consider policy changes that are marginally more integrationist than the status quo (of no EU regulation). Consequently, if the Commission proposes a policy that the least pro-integration member states prefer to the status quo, unanimity voting rules will not lead to 'lowest-common-denominator' outcomes (Garrett, 1992, 1995b; Tsebelis and Garrett, 1996). Furthermore, under the cooperation procedure (and now the co-decision procedure), where there is qualified-majority voting in the Council and the EP has a powerful rule in the legislative process, the Commission or the EP can be 'conditional agenda-setters' (Tsebelis, 1994). As long as a majority in the Council prefers a Commission or EP proposal to the status quo, the minority will not be able to block it. This, then, goes some way towards explaining why the EU has been able to adopt reregulatory policies in health and safety and process-related environmental standards, which would not have been accepted under unanimity rules (cf. Golub, 1996b, 1996c; Weale, 1996; Gehring, 1997; Pollack, 1997a).

Historical institutionalists, on the other hand, tend to focus on the structural properties of the EU system, and the resulting 'path-dependency'. For example, in Pierson's (1996) account, because governments have to be reelected every few years they tend to have short 'time horizons'. The Commission, in contrast, can take the longview. Also, because different political parties win national elections, nationals governments in the Council do not have stable policy preferences, so that when designing decision-rules and delegating powers to the Commission, the Council does not tend to think about the long-term implications. This consequently explains why governments were unable to predict how the Commission and the EP were able to use qualified-majority voting rules to achieve outcomes that were not intended when the governments adopted the SEA. Using similar logic, Bulmer argues that different policy areas have different 'policy logics' (Bulmer 1994; Armstrong and Bulmer, 1998, pp. 43–64). For example, there are different normative programmes associated with different policy issues: the single market project is a 'collective good', and environmental standards should be as rigorous as possible (cf. Jachtenfuchs, 1995). Also, in an argument similar to the early neo-functionalist theory of policy 'spillover', once the EU has become responsible for regulation process-standards, it becomes a focus for societal expectations and lobbying for the expansion of regulation into product-standards.

Conclusion: neo-liberalism meets the social market

The single market has fundamentally changed the process of governance in Europe. Rules on the production, distribution and exchange of goods, services and capital are now predominantly set at the European level and this has produced a particular regulatory regime in Europe which combines 'neo-liberal' *deregulation* and 'social-market' *reregulation*.

The single market programme has had a powerful deregulatory impact. 'Mutual recognition' and the 'new approach to harmonization', combined with EU competition policies, have led to the removal of tariff barriers between EU member states and to the liberalization of most sectors of the European economy. National governments are no longer free to use trade barriers, state aids or special operating licences to protect their industries from competition from firms in other EU member states. As a result, for some on the left in Europe (particularly in Scandinavia, Britain and France), the single market programme is a victory of the 'neo-liberal project' (see for example Grahl and Teague, 1990).

Nevertheless, there are important 're'-regulatory elements of the single market regime. First, the harmonization of national *product standards* is meant to achieve *efficient* policy outcomes: in the European 'public interest'. Instead of reducing rules applying to goods and services, the EU has been particularly successful in establishing new EU-wide product standards (such as vehicle emissions), and in most cases these new EU standards are at higher levels than in most member states.

Second, the harmonization of *process standards* is meant to achieve *redistributive* policy outcomes. These regulations do not redistribute resources directly: by taking resources from one group (through taxation) and giving them to another (through public expenditure). Nevertheless, EU regulations on production processes have an *indirect* redistributional impact – by imposing costs on producers and protecting the values and interests of environmentalists, consumers, workers and other diffuse interests. The redistributional impact of these rules has meant that producer groups and centre-right political parties have mobilized to prevent their harmonization at the EU level. But, where qualified-majority voting has existed in the legislative process, and because the Commission has been supported by a centre-left majority in the European Parliament, these anti-regulation forces have been unable to block new 'redistributive coalitions' being reestablished at the European level. This has been the case in the area of health and safety at work and in numerous process-related environmental regulations.

In contrast, where unanimity is required in the Council, centre-right governments and business interests were able to block the adoption of EU-wide process-standards (as in the areas of workers' rights and industrial relations). However, the Commission has used entrepreneurial strategies – such as encouraging voluntary agreements between labour and business interests at the EU level – to unblock the legislative veto. The final legislation has had to be 'neo-voluntarist' (rather than strict harmonization) to pass the Council. Nonetheless, these rules have begun to define a regulatory regime at the EU level that is fundamentally different from neoliberalism. This regime establishes new rights and powers for diffuse interests, and imposes additional costs on (particularly multinational) European industries.

The forces of social democracy may have been in the doldrums in the mid to late 1980s. However, Social Democrats and the interests they represent remain a powerful force in Europe, and they are also increasingly institutionalized at the EU level (see Chapter 6). Against Stigler's theory, the Commission has supplied regulation for both producer groups and diffuse interests. Whereas some Commission directorate-generals are heavily linked to transnational business interests, others are 'captured' by EU-level environmental, consumer and trade union groups. Also, as the

European Parliament gains more power in the EU legislative process, these groups can expect to secure more benefits, particularly if the Socialist group remains the key agenda-setter within the EP. Finally, at the end of the 1990s, electorates across Europe voted for governments who promised to mediate the effects of trade liberalization on national welfare states.

The EU regulatory regime is a powerful constraint on domestic welfare coalitions. But, reports of the demise of the European 'social-market' model as a result of the new EU regulatory regime are grossly exaggerated.

Chapter 9

Redistributive Policies

Compared to national political systems, the capacity of the EU to redistribute resources between individuals and states through taxation and public spending is limited. The EU budget constitutes less than 2 per cent of total EU GDP. However, for individuals, farmers, regions, states and private organizations who receive money from the EU budget, the absolute sums involved are quite considerable, and someone, somewhere in the EU pays for these benefits. To help understand how EU expenditure policies are made, and 'who gets what and why', we shall first take a look at some general theories about public finances and redistribution.

Theories of public expenditure and redistribution

A common starting point for the analysis of public finances is Musgrave's (1959) famous three-fold typology of the goals of public expenditure:

- *Allocation (or 'efficiency')* – public expenditure is often used to address 'market failures' (also see Chapter 8), and in so doing is meant to promote the 'public interest' rather than to achieve 'winners' and 'losers' out of the public purse.
- *Redistribution* – in stark contrast to this first goal, much of government expenditure is for the specific purpose of redistributing resources from one group of citizens or localities to another, for example through 'progressive taxation', social security expenditure and subsidies to poor regions.
- *Stabilization* – public expenditure is also used to achieve macro economic goals, such as lower unemployment, lower inflation and higher productivity, either from the 'demand side' (by increasing welfare spending) or from the 'supply side' (by increasing spending on education, training, research and infrastructure).

241

Table 9.1   *Government expenditure in the EU and elsewhere*

State	GDP per head ($)	Government expenditure as % of national GDP		% of central government expenditure on social services
	(1995)	(1960)	(1995)	(1995)
Sweden	23 750	31.0	68.8	64.6
Denmark	29 890	24.8	63.9	56.9
Finland	20 580	26.6	58.7	63.5
Belgium	24 710	30.3	56.4	7.2
France	24 990	34.6	54.9	72.5
Netherlands	24 000	33.7	54.4	68.7
Italy	19 020	30.1	53.9	na
Luxembourg	41 210	30.5	52.7	na
Austria	26 890	35.7	51.5	77.8
Portugal	9 740	17.0	51.5	na
Germany	27 510	32.4	49.0	na
Greece	8 210	17.4	47.9	34.1
Spain	14 580	n.a.	45.6	54.0
Ireland	14 710	28.0	43.8	57.5
United Kingdom	18 700	32.2	42.9	54.5
EU-15 average	21 830	28.9	53.1	55.6
United States	26 980	27.0	33.5	55.0
Japan	39 640	17.5	35.8	59.2

Source: Calculated from data in El-Agraa (1998), OECD.

Table 9.1 illustrates that public expenditure constitutes a major part of GDP throughout the western world, and that there was a rapid growth in public expenditure between the 1960s and the 1990s, particularly in Europe. Nevertheless, richer states tend to spend a larger proportion of GDP in the public sector than poorer states. For example, in 1995 most EU states with a higher GDP per head than the EU average also had a higher level of government expenditure as a percentage of GDP than the EU average (cf. Scharpf, 1997a). Finally, a major proportion of public expenditure goes on 'social services', such as social security, health care, housing and education.

The traditional explanation for the development of the redistributive powers of the state, through the growth of public expenditure, is *normative*: to achieve greater equality (for example Marshall, 1950; Rawls, 1971). As Esping-Andersen (1990) famously observed, different normative projects have created three different 'worlds of welfare capitalism':

- a *liberal* regime, where 'means testing' is used to determine whether individuals qualify for benefits and entitlements are stigmatized (as in the United States);
- a *corporatist* (or Christian-democratic) regime, where the state provides social insurance, benefits are primarily geared towards the family, and the overall redistributive impact is small (as in Germany, France and Italy); and
- a *social-democratic* regime, where benefits are generally 'universal', the state replaces the market in many spheres, and the redistributive impact is large (as in Scandinavia).

In each of these models redistribution in justified on the grounds of reducing inequality (Wilensky, 1975; Heidenheimer, Heclo and Adams 1990). The difference between the models relates to the amount of equality that they aim to achieve.

From a completely different perspective, the growth of redistributive policies can be explained by *positive* theory (cf. Mueller, 1989, pp. 445–65). Majority decision-making in a democracy results in the transfer of resources from the minority to the majority. One might expect that because there are more citizens on low-incomes than on high-incomes, governments would pursue progressive taxation and welfare programmes for the poor (Meltzer and Richard, 1981). However, because the median-voter in most western societies tends to be middle-class (particularly in societies where voter-turnout is low), political parties will advocate expenditure programmes that disproportionately benefit the middle-class (see for example Stigler, 1970; Tullock, 1971).

In addition, when voting on budgetary packages it is easier for legislators to increase the size of government spending than to reduce it. If government spending remains stable, a change in the structure of public expenditure will mean some social groups gaining at the expense of others. However, if the budget can be increased, benefits can be distributed in such a way that everyone gains at least something (see Figure 8.1 in the previous chapter). For example, legislators from rural constituencies can vote for welfare programmes for the urban poor, in return for legislators from inner cities voting for welfare programmes for farmers. This 'vote-trading' consequently leads to an expansion of public expenditure, and an increase in public deficits (cf. Weingast, Shepsle and Johnson, 1981).

Nonetheless, budgetary expansion can be restricted by institutional mechanisms. For example, a balanced-budget rule (like the proposed 'balanced-budget amendment' in the United States) prevents expenditure from being expanded without also raising revenue. If the budget cannot be expanded, changes in the budget can only occur through removing expenditure from one programme (group of citizens) and giving it to another. In addition, if the budget has to be adopted by unanimity (as is the case with multi-annual budgetary packages in the EU), any decision-maker can veto a proposed change that redistributes resources away from their supporters. As a result of these constraints, each legislator will be able to demand that contributions by their supporters into the budget are exactly equal to the compensation they receive. This compensation can take two forms: *direct* benefits from expenditure programmes ('side-payments'); and *indirect* benefits from non-expenditure programmes.

However, according to Olson's (1965) theory of collective action (Chapter 7), different interest groups face different incentives to organize to secure benefits from government. The benefits of a welfare programme tend to be concentrated, whereas the costs are diffuse. For example, the benefits of agricultural subsidies to each individual farmer are much larger than the costs to each individual consumer or taxpayer. As a result, farmers are more likely to lobby governments and fund political campaigns to secure farm-subsidies than consumer groups are to try to prevent these subsidies. Also, some groups find it harder to organize than others. Because of a lack of resources and information, low-income citizens tend to be underrepresented in the policy process, whereas doctors and pensioners tend to be more powerful. Hence, public expenditure programmes tend to benefit highly organized or concentrated minorities at the expense of unorganized minorities and the diffuse majority.

In sum, public expenditure is a core responsibility of government, and is primarily used to redistribute resources from one group in society to another. At face value, redistributive policies aim to reduce inequalities in society, but the reality is often very different. Who gains from redistributive policies depends on the interests of political decision-makers, the political power of organized interests, and the institutional rules of budgetary decision-making.

The budget of the European Union

Since 1988, the Council has adopted the EU budget through multi-annual packages which fix the overall 'ceiling' of the budget relative to the gross national product (GNP) of the EU member states, the structure of revenues, and the relative size of the various expenditure categories. Within these multi-annual deals, the precise amounts of revenue and expenditure are agreed in an annual budgetary cycle. In both these processes, the EU operates a *balanced-budget* principle: every year, revenue must equal or exceed expenditure. Unlike national governments, the EU cannot go into debt.

Revenue and the own-resources system *

The EU budget is funded through the four 'own resources' of the EU:

1. *Agriculture levies* – which are charged on imports of agricultural products originating from non-EU countries, under the Common Agricultural Policy (CAP).
2. *Customs duties* – which are common customs tariff duties and other duties levied on imports from non-EU countries.
3. *Value added tax* (VAT) – which is a harmonized rate applied in all member states, and which by 1999 cannot exceed 1 per cent of the EU GNP.
4. *GNP-based own resource* – based on the GNP of the member states, to cover the difference between planned expenditure and the amount yielded from the other three resources.

As Figure 9.1 shows, the balance between these sources of income changed between 1980 and 1995. The Council established the first three resources in 1970 to replace the old system of financing the EU by direct contributions of the EU member states based on their relative GNP. The member states

Figure 9.1 *Relative composition of EU own resources*

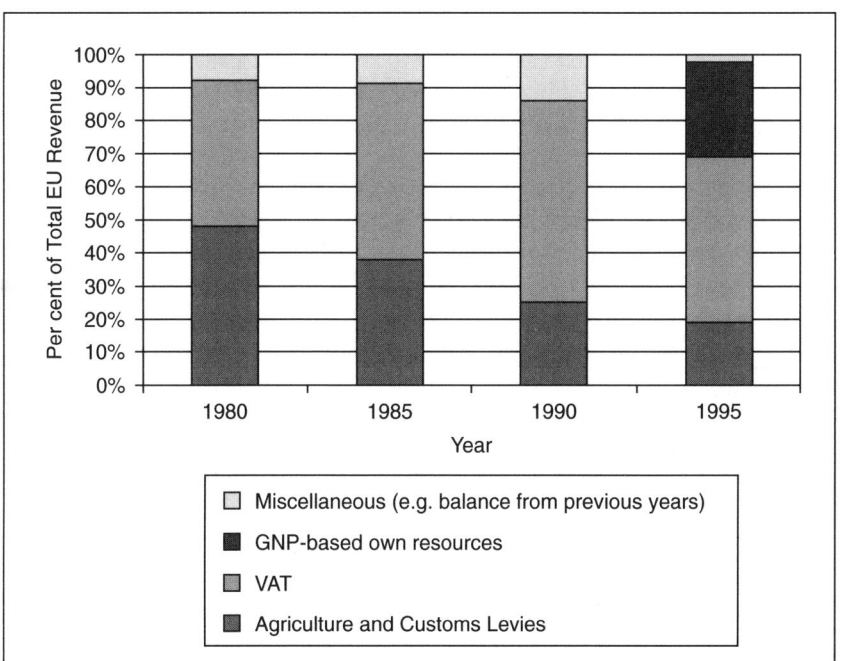

Source: Adapted from data in Laffan (1997).

expected that import levies and VAT would be sufficient to cover EU expenditure, but two factors meant that this was unsustainable. First, as the EU became a net exporter in the 1980s, revenues from agriculture and other import duties fell. Second, in the early 1990s the EU budget grew as a percentage of EU GNP (see below). Consequently, the Commission proposed the reintroduction of GNP-based contributions by national governments (a 'fourth own resource'). This is calculated on an annual basis, to cover the short-fall in revenues from import levies and the VAT levy.

Expenditure

The expenditure of the EU has grown as the policy competences of the EU have expanded. Following the plan for the single market and the new competences established by the Single European Act, a new budget package was adopted in February 1988 for the period 1988–92. This so-called 'Delors I' plan (after the Commission president) proposed to increase the EU budget between 1988 and 1992 by 7.6 per cent: from €27 500m to €29 600m (at 1988 prices). Following the Maastricht Treaty, the preparations for Economic and Monetary Union and the prospective enlargement of the EU to Austria, Finland, Sweden and Norway, a new budget package for the period 1993–99 was agreed in December 1992. This 'Delors II' plan proposed to increase the EU budget between 1993 and 1999 by 22 per cent: from €69 177m to €84 089m (at 1992 prices). The plan was revised, as shown in Table 9.2, following the membership of only Austria, Finland and Sweden in January 1995.

Table 9.2   *Delors II budget plan, adjusted for enlargement*
(m. €, 1995 prices)

Expenditure category	1995	1996	1997	1998	1999
Common Agricultural Policy	37 944	39 546	40 267	41 006	41 764
Cohesion Policy	26 329	27 710	29 375	31 164	32 956
Other internal policies	5 060	5 233	5 449	5 677	5 894
External policies	4 895	5 162	5 468	5 865	6 340
EU institution administration	4 022	4 110	4 232	4 295	4 359
Reserves	1 146	1 140	1 140	1 140	1 140
Compensations	1 547	701	212	99	0
Total	80 943	83 602	86 143	89 246	92 453
Expenditure as % of EU GNP	1.20	1.21	1.22	1.24	1.25
Own resources as % of EU GNP	1.21	1.22	1.24	1.26	1.27

Source: Calculated from data in Laffan (1997).

Figure 9.2 *Relative composition of EU expenditure*

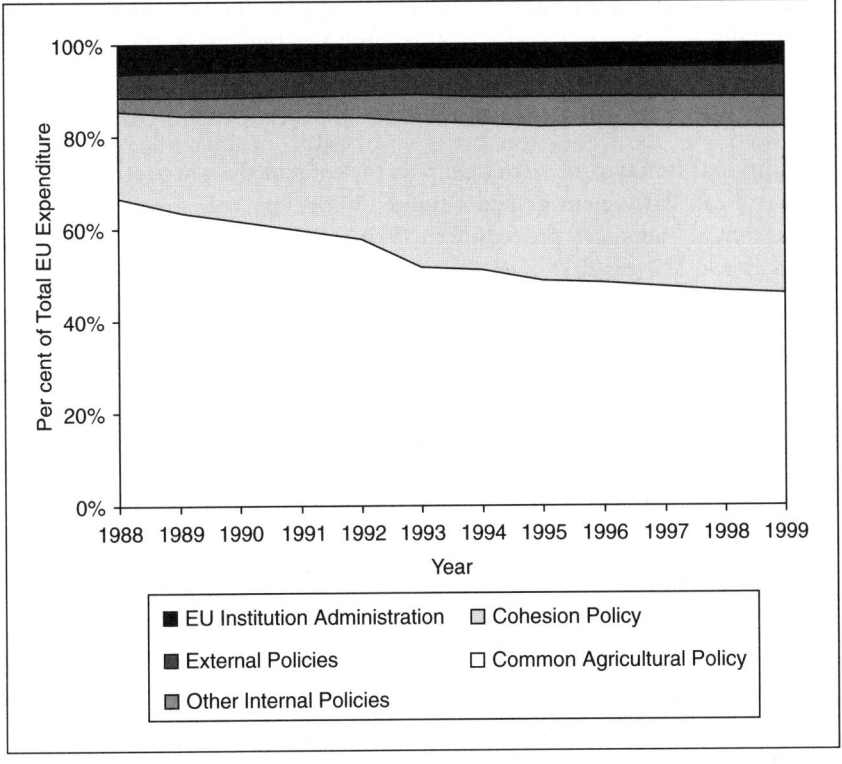

Source: Calculated from data in Laffan (1997).

The composition of EU expenditure between different budget categories also changed considerably in the 1980s and 1990s. The two main expenditure categories are the CAP and cohesion policy. The Delors I package proposed the doubling of expenditure on economic and social cohesion and a reform of the expenditure under the CAP, and the Delors II package continued this strategy with a new 'Cohesion Fund' as part of the social and economic cohesion budget and further scaling-down of expenditure on the CAP. As a result, as Figure 9.2 shows, expenditure under the CAP declined from almost 70 per cent of the EU budget in 1988 to 45 per cent in 1999. In contrast, in the same period, expenditure on cohesion policy increased from under 20 per cent of the EU budget to over 35 per cent.

Consequently, in 1999, expenditure on agriculture and cohesion policies consumed approximately 81 per cent of the EU budget. The remaining proportion is spent as follows: approximately 6 per cent on other internal policies (mostly on research and development); about 7 per cent on external policies (mostly on humanitarian and development aid); about 5 per cent on running the EU institutions (mostly on the Commission); and the remaining 1 per cent is placed into the EU's budgetary reserves.

The annual budget procedure: the 'power of the purse'

A traditional function of parliaments is to 'control the purse strings', and the European Parliament gained a limited budgetary role through reforms to the annual budgetary procedure in 1970 and 1975. This procedure is set out in article 272 [ex 203] of the Treaty. However, as Table 9.3 shows, the 1993 interinstitutional agreement between the Council, the EP and the Commission determines how the procedure operates in practice.

The Council has the final say on 'compulsory expenditure' – expenditure that is necessary from the treaties. This is mostly expenditure under the CAP and the small amount of expenditure arising from international agreements. The EP, on the other hand, has the final say on 'non-compulsory expenditure' which covers annual expenditure on economic and social cohesion and most expenditure on other internal policies (such as research and education programmes).

Also, in contrast to the requirement of unanimity in the Council for the multiannual package deals, the annual budget is adopted in the Council by only a qualified majority and by an absolute majority in the EP (see Chapter 3 for the voting rules in the EP and the Council). The budget is prepared by the budget directorate-general of the Commission (DGXIX), and is negotiated by the members of the EP's budget committee, the Budget Committee of the Committee of Permanent Representatives (COREPER), and the Budget Council (of junior ministers from the national Finance Ministries).

In this procedure, each institution has its own interests: the Commission to promote further European integration and defend its support groups; the Council to promote national interests and national constituencies; and the EP to promote integration and policies that increase its power in the EU system (see Chapter 2 and 3). Conflicts between these interests are resolved through the interinstitutional triologue and in an EP–Council conciliation procedure. Nevertheless, the EP has used its limited veto-powers to extract concessions from the Commission and the Council, for example by adding budget-lines as a substitute for a lack of legislative initiative power (see Chapter 3). For example, in the adoption of the 1995 budget, the EP forced the Council to accept increased expenditure on education and training, which the Council had cut in both the first and second readings (Laffan, 1997, pp. 80–1).

However, the EP is constrained by its absence from the multiannual package deals, its inability to alter compulsory expenditure, and the limited overall size of the EU budget relative to national expenditure.

Table 9.3 *The annual budget cycle*

Stage of budget procedure	1993 Interinstitutional Agreement timetable (of preceding year)	Article 272 Deadlines
EP–Council–Commission trialogue meeting on budget priorities	April	—
EP–Council conciliation meetings on compulsory expenditure	July	—
Commission submits a Preliminary Draft Budget to the Council	15 June	1 September
EP–Council conciliation meeting before Council 1st reading	June/July	—
Council 1st reading	July	31 July
Draft budget and Council position sent to EP	early September	5 October
EP 1st reading	end of October	19 November
EP–Council conciliation meeting before Council 2nd reading	early November	—
Council 2nd reading	end of November	4 December
EP 2nd reading	early December	within 15 days
EP President declares budget approved or rejected by EP	early December	—
Deadline for new budget	1 January (of budget year)	1 January (of budget year)

Source: Adapted from Laffan (1997).

Consequently, the EP's redistributive power is weak compared to national parliaments in Europe and the US Congress.

The Common Agricultural Policy

Agriculture may seem a minor issue compared to foreign affairs or the state of the economy. But the Common Agricultural Policy is the largest area of EU expenditure, it was the first genuinely supranational policy of the EU, several member states maintain a romantic attachment to rural society, and the EU public is increasingly concerned about food safety and animal rights. As a result, the political stakes are high when it comes to the making and reform of the CAP.

Objectives and operation of the CAP

The Treaty of Rome established the CAP as a central policy of the European Economic Community. Article 33 [ex 39] of the Treaty set out its objectives as follows:

(a) to increase agricultural productivity, by promoting technical progress and ensuring rational development of agricultural production and the optimum utilization of the factors of production, particularly labour;
(b) to ensure a fair standard of living for the agricultural community, in particular by increasing the individual earnings of persons engaged in agriculture;
(c) to stabilize markets;
(d) to ensure the availability of supply; and
(e) to ensure that supplies reach consumers at reasonable prices.

These goals encompass all three of Musgrave and Musgrave's policy types: (d) and (e) are about 'allocation', to ensure the supply of food at a price that the market could not achieve by itself in 1960s Europe; (b) is about 'redistribution', a 'welfare policy for farmers'; and (a) and (c) are about 'stabilization', to use demand-side and supply-side management to control inflation, secure agricultural employment and increase productivity in the agriculture sector.

The Commission brought forward proposals in June 1960 for how these goals could be achieved through three main 'guiding principles':

- *A single market* – a removal of barriers to the free movement of agricultural products between the member states.
- *Community preference* – priority should be given to produce from the EC member states.
- *Financial solidarity* – the cost of the policy should be borne by the Community as a whole rather than by the individual member states.

After protracted negotiations, in 1962 the member states agreed to turn these principles into practice through three mechanisms to protect the price of agricultural goods supplied by farmers in the member states:

1. *Protection against low internal prices* – through a system of buying surplus goods from farmers (paid out of the EAGGF) when goods fell below an agreed 'guarantee price' in the European market.
2. *Protection against low import prices* – through a system of import quotas and 'levies' (paid into the EAGGF) on imported agricultural goods when the world price falls below an agreed price.
3. *Subsidies to achieve a low export price* – through a system of 'refunds' (paid out of the EAGGF) for the export of agriculture goods when the world price falls below an agreed price.

The result is a system of indirect income support for farmers, paid for by European taxpayers (through the EU budget) and by European consumers (through the extra prices charged on imported agricultural goods).

Problems

When the CAP was set up, Europe was not self-sufficient in most agricultural goods. However, as agricultural production stabilized and Europe became a net exporter of agricultural goods, the CAP price-support mechanism created some intractable problems:

- guaranteed prices encouraged overproduction, and production grew faster than demand, resulting in 'wine lakes' and 'grain mountains';
- these surpluses had to be stored at additional costs to the CAP budget;
- environmental destruction resulted from overintensive land-use and over-use of herbicides, pesticides and artificial fertilisers;
- the bulk of revenues went to larger farmers (who earned more because they produced more), whereas smaller farmers were in need of most welfare support;
- import quotas and levies created numerous trade disputes and prevented the development of global free trade in agricultural goods; and
- export subsidies depressed world prices, distorted agriculture markets in the Third World, and hence contributed to global development problems.

The original goals had been fulfilled. However, the allocation function was no longer necessary as goods could be supplied by the open market at cheap prices, the redistribution of resources to farmers had made some farmers better off than others (and better off than many other sections of society), and markets no longer needed to be stabilized. Moreover, while the CAP consumed ever-greater resources, its utility to European taxpayers and small farmers fell, and its distortion of global agriculture markets increased. Consequently, by the end of the 1980s, the CAP was no longer sustainable in its original form. Consumer and environmental groups, several member state governments and a number of foreign governments demanded reform.

Reform of the CAP: towards a new type of (welfare) policy

In 1992, the EU member states agreed the first major reform of the CAP. These reforms were drafted and negotiated through the agriculture council by Ray MacSharry, the Irish Agriculture Commissioner. The MacSharry Plan made four main changes to the policy:

- *Price cuts in certain sectors* – guarantee prices for cereals and beef were reduced over a three-year period, by 29 per cent and 15 per cent respectively, to levels that were much closer to world market prices (price cuts were later introduced on fruit and vegetables).
- *Direct income support for farmers* – a system of direct payments to farmers was introduced (in addition to the price support schemes), to compensate for historical price reductions in particular farm sectors.
- *Set-aside scheme* – a system was introduced where farmers in certain sectors (particularly cereals) and in specific regions are paid to leave their land fallow ('set-aside'), instead of growing crops that would have to be bought by the EU.
- *Accompanying measures* – new aid programmes were introduced to promote rural development, environmentally-friendly agriculture, the replacement of agricultural land with forests, and early retirement of farmers.

In July 1997, agriculture commissioner, Franz Fischler, unveiled proposals for further CAP reform, as part of the Commission's 'Agenda 2000' budget package to prepare for EU enlargement to central and eastern Europe. On one level, the Fischler plan proposed to extend the MacSharry reforms: by extending price cuts in the cereals and beef sectors and introducing new price cuts in the milk, olive oil and wine sectors. However, on another level the Fischler plan proposed the transformation of the CAP from a policy of price support to one of income support. Also, Fischler proposed to strengthen the non-welfare objectives to the policy: environmental protection; food safety (following the mad-cow disease crisis); and animal welfare (following public protests about the transport of live animals).

As a result, on the basis of the MacSharry and Fischler plans prices for agricultural goods are increasingly set by the free market and consequently the CAP is no longer about allocation or market stabilization. Instead, the

CAP fulfils two other purposes. First, through a shift to direct income support the redistributive function will become paramount. In other words, the CAP is becoming a 'liberal' welfare state regime (in Esping-Andersen's typology): public programmes are funded via taxation instead of charging higher prices to consumers, and means-testing is used to establish who qualifies for welfare subsidies – in this case, low-income farmers.

Second, the 'new CAP' aims to redress market failures resulting from agricultural production (see Chapter 8). For example, environmental destruction and rural underdevelopment are 'negative externalities' of transactions in the agriculture market, and in the supply of agricultural goods there are 'information asymmetries' about food quality and safety – where the consumer has less information than the producer. Consequently, by addressing environmental protection, rural development and food safety the CAP aims to recreate the allocative efficiency of the market, in the general European 'public interest' rather than the narrow interest of farmers.

Nevertheless, as with the establishment of the CAP and the MacSharry reforms, further CAP reform will only be achieved if the necessary ideas, interests and circumstances coincide in the EU policy process in the agriculture sector.

Making agriculture policy: can the iron triangle be broken?

Agriculture policy is made by an 'iron triangle' of agriculture ministers, agriculture officials in the Commission, and European-level farming interests.

First, the Agriculture Council, which meets at least every month, is the central decision-making body – the role of the EP is limited as CAP legislation is passed under the consultation procedure. Agriculture ministers are often from political parties supported by farmers (such as the Irish Fianna Fail, the French Gaullists, the Italian Christian Democrats, and the Bavarian Christian Social Union) and/or represent rural regions (such as Bavaria, rural France and Spain, East Anglia in Britain and Danish Jutland). Moreover, the work of the Agriculture Council is supported by the Special Committee of Agriculture (SCA) rather than the usual Committee of Permanent Representatives (COREPER), and the SCA is staffed by officials from national agriculture ministries, whereas the members of COREPER tend to be career diplomats.

Finance ministers only intervene on major questions concerning the financing of the CAP, and the heads of government (in the European Council) are usually only called into play to negotiate the major reform packages. Also, there are often disputes between agriculture and finance ministers; for example, on several occasions in the 1980s the German agriculture minister (from the Bavarian Christian Social Union) opposed proposals by the German finance minister to scale down CAP subsidies.

Second, agriculture interests are protected by the way the CAP is managed by the Commission. The agriculture commissioner responsible for initiating reform proposals and changes to the CAP regime has always been from a farming state, and usually also from a political party with close links to farming interests. Franz Fischler, for example, is an Austrian Christian Democrat. The agriculture directorate-general (DGVI) is the largest DG in the Commission (see Chapter 2), is staffed predominantly by officials from the main farming member states – such as France and Germany – and, as a result, is rarely prepared to listen to the views of the consumer, environment and economic affairs DGs. Also, the day-to-day management of the CAP is undertaken through the network of agriculture, veterinary and food safety committees around the Commission, and these committees are staffed with 'national experts', most of whom are nominated by and answerable to national agriculture ministries.

Third, farming interests are powerfully represented at the national and European levels (Keeler, 1996). In most member states, the 'corporatist' relationship between national farmers' associations and agriculture ministries, ensures that farmers play a central role in making national agriculture policies. At the European level, the Confederation of Professional Agricultural Organizations (COPA) is the most well-resourced, well-staffed and highly-organized of all the supranational sectoral associations (see Chapter 7).

Each element of this triangle has a vested interest to defend the interests of the other: subsidies to farmers, the centrality of the CAP in the EU decision-making process for agriculture commissioners and DGVI, and the independence of the Agriculture Council and the protection of the domestic supporters of agriculture ministers. In contrast, there are few incentives for consumers to mobilize to attempt to break the iron triangle, as the costs of the CAP to each individual consumer or taxpayer are smaller than the cost of organizing an anti-CAP campaign (Nedergaard, 1995).

Nevertheless, the CAP iron triangle has been undermined by two developments. First, social, economic and political changes in Europe have reduced the power of agricultural interests. Table 9.4 shows that between the 1950s and the 1990s there was a dramatic change in the status of agriculture in the national economy – the share of agriculture as a percentage of the labour force of the member states declined from over 20 per cent to under 10 per cent, and as a percentage of national income of the member states it declined from over 10 per cent to under 3 per cent. Also,

Table 9.4 *Changing status of agriculture in the member states*

	Share of agriculture as % of labour force		Share of agriculture as % of national GDP		% of farms larger than 20 hectares	
	1955	1995	1955	1995	1960	1993
Austria	—	13.3	—	2.2	n.a.	n.a.
Belgium	9.3	2.5	8.1	1.6	7	32
Denmark	25.4	5.7	19.2	2.5	26	59
Finland	—	8.3	—	1.8	n.a.	n.a.
France	25.9	4.8	12.3	2.0	26	50
Germany	18.9	3.0	8.5	0.8	9	34
Greece	33.2[a]	20.8	19.0[b]	7.5	2[a]	3
Ireland	38.8	12.0	29.6	5.4	26	47
Italy	39.5	7.9	21.6	2.6	5	7
Luxembourg	25.0	2.8	9.0	0.9	24	57
Netherlands	13.7	4.0	12.0	3.2	12	32
Portugal	21.9[c]	11.6	7.3[b]	2.0	5[a]	5
Spain	16.1[c]	9.8	8.9[d]	2.7	14[a]	15
Sweden	—	3.7	—	1.0	n.a.	n.a.
United Kingdom	4.8	2.2	5.0	0.9	42	60
EU Average[e]	22.1	7.5	11.9	2.5	14	33

Note: a = 1973, *b* = 1975, *c* = 1986, *d* = 1970, *e* = EU averages are calculated only for the states that were EU members.
Source: Calculated from data in El-Agraa (1998), European Commission (1995).

the proportion of large farms, which are most likely to survive in a free agriculture market, increased from under 15 per cent to over 30 per cent of all farms. Moreover, these economic changes have facilitated a decline in rural populations and urbanization.

As a result, at the turn of the century, active farmers comprise approximately 4 per cent of the electorate in most member states. This has forced many agricultural parties, and parties with traditional support in rural areas – such as Christian Democrats – to appeal to urban middle-class voters who are the ones paying for the CAP. Voters with a 'strong agricultural attribute' – including farmers, retired farmers, spouses of farmers, voting-age children of farmers, and former farmers in other occupations – may still constitute as much as 17 per cent of the electorate in some member states (Keeler, 1996, p. 129). Also, placed between the middle class and the urban working class, this constituency can be 'pivotal' in determining electoral outcomes. But, in the 1990s, Socialist parties swept to power throughout the EU, and Socialists comprised 50 per cent of the Santer Commission. For the first time, then, non-rural parties occupied a large number of agriculture ministries, and with these parties in power, agricultural issues were relegated to secondary status behind combating industrial unemployment, and restraining public finances to qualify for economic and monetary union.

Second, external pressures have created new incentives for the CAP to be reformed. This began with the negotiations in the General Agreement on Tariffs and Trade (GATT) Uruguay Round multilateral trade negotiations in 1987 and 1988. Without a reform of subsidies to European agriculture, a ground-breaking agreement on global trade liberalization could not be achieved. The GATT agreement was finally signed, with the EU trade ministers and heads of state promising to reform the CAP as part of the deal (Patterson, 1997). The MacSharry reform plan was immediately proposed, with the highest level pressure on agriculture ministers to approve the reform package.

A similar situation exists at the end of the 1990s, with the prospective enlargement of the EU to central and eastern Europe. The result of the enlargement is an expected increase of 50 per cent of agricultural land in the EU, and a 100 per cent increase in agricultural labour. Without a reform away from price support, enlargement would bankrupt the EU budget.

As with the GATT agreement, agriculture ministers and COPA may prefer to delay enlargement in order to protect their interests, but this decision is out of their hands. Also, once international trade issues or enlargement become associated with reform of the CAP, an 'issue linkage' is established, which creates new specific incentives for non-agricultural industrial interests to lobby against the CAP. For many industrial sectors, the benefits of GATT and enlargement are greater than the costs of mobilizing to break the grip of the farm lobby at the national and European levels.

Cohesion policy

According to the EU Treaty, one of the central aims of the EU is to promote 'economic and social cohesion' – the reduction of disparities between different regions and social groups in the EU. This is the classic normative redistributive goal. To achieve this goal an ever-larger proportion of the EU budget has been transferred to less-developed regions. Nevertheless, how far cohesion policy is a genuine 'welfare policy' and how far it has been able to reduce social and economic disparities in Europe is open to question.

Operation of the policy

The EU has four *Structural Funds*:

- The European Regional Development Fund (ERDF), which was set up in 1975, is managed by DGXVI, and accounted for 49 per cent of the 1994–99 cohesion budget.
- The European Social Fund (ESF), which was set up in 1960, is managed by DGV, and accounted for 30 per cent of the 1994–99 cohesion budget.
- The Guidance Section of the European Agricultural Guidance and Guarantee Fund (EAGGF), which was set up as part of the CAP in 1962, is managed by DGVI, and accounted for 18 per cent of the 1994–99 cohesion budget.
- The Financial Instrument for Fisheries (FIFG), which was set up in 1994, is managed by DGXIV, and accounted for 3 per cent of the 1994–99 cohesion budget.

From 1988, these funds have been managed according to four key principles.

- *Additionality* – the member states cannot use EU resources to reduce national spending on regional development, so EU resources go directly to regions or managing authorities rather than through national treasuries.
- *Partnership* – the policy operates through close cooperation between the Commission, national governments and regional authorities (which in some states had to be created to meet this goal), from the preparation of projects to the implementation and monitoring of expenditure.
- *Programming* – expenditure is delivered through multi-annual development programmes (see below).
- *Concentration* – EU assistance measures are concentrated on a series of priority 'objectives'.

Since 1995, the structural funds have had six such objectives:

Ob.1. Promoting development and structural adjustment in *regions lagging behind*, defined as having GDP per head below 75 per cent of the EU average (funded by ERDF, ESF and EAGGF).

Ob.2. Aiding the conversion of *regions in industrial decline*, defined as having mainly industrial employment and higher unemployment than the EU average (funded by ERDF and ESF).

Ob.3. Combating long-term *unemployment*, youth employment and social exclusion, and promoting equal opportunities for men and women (funded by ESF).

Ob.4. Facilitating the adaptation of workers to *industrial change* (funded by ESF).

Ob.5.   Promoting *rural development* by:

  5a. aiding structural adjustment of agricultural and fisheries sectors (funded by EAGGF and FIFG), and

  5b. structural adjustment in rural areas, defined as having mainly agricultural employment and lower agricultural incomes than the EU average or a depopulation trend (funded by ESF and EAGGF).

Ob.6.   Promoting development and structural adjustment of *regions with low population density*, defined as having less than 8 inhabitants per square kilometre (funded by ERDF, ESF and EAGGF).

Whereas objectives 1, 2, 5b and 6 are regional-based, objectives 3, 4 and 5a and 'non-regional' – projects in any region of the EU can qualify for support if they meet the required goals.

In addition to the expenditure under these objectives, the Commission has set up separate 'Community Initiatives', which are also funded by the structural funds. In the 1994–99 period, Community initiatives covered the following areas:

- Planning and cooperation between border regions (*Interreg II*) – €3530m.
- Adapting labour markets to industrial change (*Adapt*), and employment opportunities for women (*Now*), the disabled (*Horizon*), young persons (*Youthstart*), and the socially-excluded (*Inclusion*) – €3479m.
- Structural change in regions dependent on coal-mining (*Recher II*), steel (*Resider II*), the defence industry (*Konver*), textiles (*Retex*), and fisheries (*Pesca*) – €2665m.
- Rural development (*Leader II*) – €1759m.
- Competitiveness of small and medium-sized enterprises (*SME*) – €1077m.
- Urban regeneration (*Urban*) – €819m.
- Integration of remote regions (*Regis II*) – €608m
- Promoting peace in Northern Ireland (*Peace*) – €300m.

In addition to the structural funds, a *Cohesion Fund* was established in 1994 as part of the implementation of the Maastricht Treaty, and linked to the specific goal of Economic and Monetary Union (EMU). Because qualification for EMU involved meeting strict budgetary and fiscal discipline as part of the convergence criteria (see Chapter 10), the cohesion fund was geared towards increasing the growth capacity of the four poorer member states: Greece, Ireland, Portugal and Spain. Two types of projects are supported by the fund: environmental protection, and transport and other infrastructure networks.

Table 9.5 shows how much each member state was set to receive under the 1994–99 budget for cohesion policy. The main beneficiaries of the policy are the four 'cohesion countries': Ireland, Portugal, Greece, and

Table 9.5 *Member state receipts from cohesion policy, 1994–99 (m. €, 1994 prices)*

	Structural Funds						Community initiatives	Cohesion Fund*	Total (m. €)	Total/head (€)
	Obj. 1	Obj. 2	Obj. 3&4	Obj. 5a	Obj. 5b	Obj. 6				
Ireland	5 620						483	1 350	7 453	2 070
Portugal	13 980						1 058	2 700	17 738	1 791
Greece	13 980						1 151	2 700	17 831	1 698
Spain	26 300	2 416	1 843	446	664		2 774	8 250	42 693	1 089
Italy	14 860	1 463	1 715	814	901		1 893		21 646	378
Finland		179	336	347	190	450	150		1 652	324
Germany	13 650	1 566	1 942	1 143	1 227		2 206		21 724	265
Luxembourg		15	23	40	6		20		104	260
France	2 190	3 774	3 203	1 933	2 238		1 601		14 938	257
United Kingdom	2 360	4 581	3 377	450	817		1 570		13 155	225
Belgium	730	342	465	195	77		287		2 096	207
Austria	162	99	387	380	403		143		1 574	194
Netherlands	150	650	1 079	165	150		421		2 615	169
Denmark		119	301	267	54		102		843	162
Sweden		157	509	204	135	247	125		1 377	156
EU Total	93 972	15 360	15 180	6 916	6 862	697	14 051	15 000	168 038	417

Note: For Austria, Finland and Sweden the figures are for 1995–99. * = Cohesion Fund amounts are estimates.
Source: http://europa.eu.int/en/comm/dg16/guide/guid34.htm

Spain. The other regions that benefit are Southern Italy, the new German *Länder*, Northern Ireland, Scotland and the North of England, the industrial North and the rural South of France, and the rural areas of Finland.

Finally, like the CAP, EU cohesion policy will be reformed as part of the Agenda 2000 budget reform. The prospective enlargement of the EU to central and eastern Europe will bring into the EU much poorer regions than any of the existing regions of the EU, and with specific structural problems. Also, as the last column of Table 9.5 shows, certain member states that were large recipients under the 1994–99 programme no longer have a low GDP per head (such as Ireland and Spain). Consequently, in the draft Agenda 2000 package, the Commission proposed that the existing EU population covered by the structural funds should be reduced to 35–40 per cent (rather than the current 51 per cent), that Objective 1 should be geared towards improving competitiveness, Objective 2 should be geared towards economic diversification, and spending under the ESF should be integrated with the EU's employment strategy.

Impact: A supply-side policy with uncertain convergence implications

The result is a policy that combines elements of redistribution and allocation. Through cohesion policy, there are significant fiscal transfers through the EU budget from taxpayers in the wealthier regions of the EU (in Belgium, the Netherlands, Luxembourg, Austria, northern Italy, the Paris basin, southern Germany, the south of England and southern Scandinavia) to the four 'cohesion states' (Ireland, Portugal, Greece and Spain) and the poorer regions in the wealthier states (particularly Southern Italy and Eastern Germany). For the main recipient regions, revenues from the structural funds and the cohesion fund amount to between 3 and 5 per cent of regional GDP. In other words, there is at least a certain amount of 'fiscal federalism' – where fiscal transfers are between territorial units through a central budget.

However, as Table 9.5 shows, not only the poor member states are recipients under the cohesion policies. In fact, as with the CAP, *every* EU member state receives resources from the cohesion policy budget. Over 50 per cent of the EU's population lives in regions covered by the regional-based objectives: 25 per cent in Objective 1 regions; 16 per cent in Objective 2 regions; 9 per cent in Objective 5b regions; 0.4 per cent in Objective 6 regions.

This is a product of the design of the EU cohesion policy. The policy is a *regional* policy, where transfers are made at the sub-state level, rather than pure *fiscal federalism*, where transfers would be made between EU member states. Also, the GDP/head and unemployment criteria are designed in such a way that every member state can claim to have a poor or backward region. When measured at the level of the member states, EU cohesion policy is as much about subsidies for the 'middle-income' member states as it is about increasing the living standards of 'low-income' member states (as is the case with many domestic welfare programmes).

In addition, EU cohesion policy is more about 'supply-side' macro-economic stabilization than 'demand-side' income support. If it were a classic (Keynesian) welfare policy, subsidies would be given directly to low-income regions, families or individuals, for them to spend how ever they see fit. Such a policy would increase the spending power of low income groups, and hence the demand for goods and services in the single market. In contrast, cohesion resources are primarily spent on 'infra-structure' projects, such as improving transport and telecommunications networks and education facilities. Such a policy increases the efficient supply of the factors of production (land, labour and capital) and, as a result, the competitiveness (and 'comparative advantage') of recipient regions in the single market (see for example Leonardi, 1993; Martin and Rogers, 1996). In other words, the basic aim of cohesion policy is the convergence between regional *economies* rather than between regional *incomes* (Anderson, 1995; Bufacchi and Garmise, 1995).

Furthermore, how far cohesion policy has reduced social and economic disparities in the EU is uncertain. At a theoretical level, there is a basic difference between 'convergence' and 'divergence' theories (Leonardi, 1993). On the one hand, a convergence in incomes and economies may occur naturally in a free market: as capital flows to where land and labour are cheapest (for example Krugman, 1991). On the other hand, economic integration in a free market could lead to divergence: as capital flows from the 'periphery', where infrastructure is weak and demand is low, to the 'core', where infrastructure is plentiful and there is a high return on investment (see for example Myrdal, 1957).

At an empirical level, as Table 9.6 shows, in terms of GDP per head the gap between the richest and poorest regions in the EU, relative to the EU average reduced by only 2 per cent between 1980 and 1992 (cf. Helgadottir, 1994). At this rate, the six poorer regions would reach the EU average in 300 years! (Cole and Cole, 1998, p. 296). Nevertheless, Leonardi (1993, 1995) finds that if convergence is measured as the average deviation from the mean for all regions, there was considerable convergence in terms of GDP/head between 1960 and 1992. Because Leonardi appears to accept the divergence theory, he concludes that this convergence must have come about because of EU cohesion policies. However, as discussed, cohesion is not purely about GDP/head, but about reducing 'economic' disparities. For example, some of the regions with the highest GDP/head, such as

Table 9.6   *GDP/head* in the richest and poorest regions, 1980 and 1992*

1980		1992	
Six richest regions		*Six richest regions*	
Groningen (Netherlands)	207	Hamburg (Germany)	196
Hamburg (Germany)	186	Brussels (Belgium)	174
Brussels (Belgium)	167	Darmstadt (Germany)	174
Ile de France (France)	161	Ile de France (France)	169
Bremen (Germany)	157	Oberbayern (Germany)	157
Darmstadt (Germany)	148	Luxembourg	156
Average	171	Average	171
Six poorest regions		*Six poorest regions*	
Anatoliki Macedonia (Greece)	49	Ionia Nisia (Greece)	53
Dytiki Ellada (Greece)	49	Dytiki Ellada (Greece)	52
Centro (Portugal)	47	Centro (Portugal)	48
Extramadura (Spain)	45	Ipeiros (Greece)	47
Ipeiros (Greece)	45	Voreio Aigaio (Greece)	45
Voreio Aigaio (Greece)	43	Alentejo (Portugal)	41
Average	46	Average	48

Note: *EU average = 100
Source: Eurostat (1995b).

Hamburg and Bremen, have considerable socioeconomic, infrastructural and unemployment problems (Keating, 1995). Steinle (1992) finds that the most competitive regions in the single market are those with 'intermediate' levels of economic development, and Fagerberg and Verspagen (1996) find that EU cohesion policy may actually have increased disparities in certain important economic variables, such as access to research and development resources.

Making cohesion policy: Commission, governments and regions

As with the CAP, EU cohesion policy is made through a triangular interaction between the main legislative body (the Council), the main executive actors in the Commission, and the subject private interests (the regional authorities). Nevertheless, unlike the CAP, these three actors do not have mutually-reinforcing interests. This produces two competing policy logics rather than a unified iron triangle: intergovernmental bargaining in the Council on the basis of national costs and benefits; and strategic behaviour by the Commission and the regions to undermine the autonomy of the national governments (Hooghe and Keating, 1994).

The volume of resources available through the structural funds, and the package deal determining which member states gain the most and which regions qualify for support, is decided by the national governments in the Council. Also, in the implementation of cohesion policy 90 per cent of expenditure is spent through 'national initiatives'. At the beginning of each programme period, each member state submits proposals to the Commission in the form of regional development plans or single programming documents, on the basis of which two to six-year regional development programmes are negotiated between the Commission and the member-state governments, with significant input from the regional authorities concerned. Implementation of the programmes is supervised by the monitoring committees which are made up of representatives of the regions, the member state governments and the Commission.

However, the member states are not in full control of the policy. The Commission came up with the idea of the four main 'principles' of the policy, each of which constrains the autonomy of national governments. For example, 'additionality' forced several member states to alter their accounting practices for managing the distribution of regional funds; and 'partnership' enabled the Commission to bypass national governments and negotiate directly with representatives from the regions on the preparation and implementation of projects, and encouraged several member states to set up new regional authorities. The Commission has also deliberately developed expenditure and programmes under the 'community initiatives' scheme, where projects are initiated by the Commission rather than the member states, with the specific objective of addressing European-wide concerns.

Linked to this principle, representatives from subnational authorities have sought to influence EU cohesion policies directly. There are over 200 offices of regions and local authorities in Brussels (see Chapter 7) many of which have established direct informal contacts in the Commission, particularly in DGXVI (regional policy) and DGXXII (coordination of the structural funds). Senior officials in these DGs tend to be from regions that receive substantial resources under the structural funds, such as the Spanish Basque and Scotland, and are consequently connected to networks of subnational elites (cf. Ansell, Parsons and Darden 1997). Moreover, the Maastricht Treaty established the Committee of the Regions (CoR), which provides representatives from subnational authorities and assemblies a formal 'consultation' role in the making and implementation of regional policy (much like that of the European Parliament under the consultation procedure), and has institutionalized transnational contacts between governmental authorities below the level of the state (Loughlin, 1996).

The access to and influence of regions in the EU policy process varies considerably between the member states. Generally, the regions from federal states, such as Germany and Belgium, and regions with strong identities, as in parts of Spain, Italy, France and the United Kingdom, tend to be most influential in Brussels (cf. Conzelmann, 1995; Marks, Nielsen, Ray and Salk, 1996). Nevertheless, several authors claim that the EU regional policies have contributed to the process of decentralization and devolution in states where no previous regional authorities existed, as in France, the United Kingdom, Portugal, Ireland and Greece (Jones and Keating, 1995; Balme and Jouve, 1996; Ioakimidis, 1996; Hooghe, 1996b; Nanetti, 1996).

The EU may be some way from a 'Europe of regions' – where regions have replaced nation-states as the main territorial unit of the EU political system (Anderson, 1990; Borras-Alomar, Christiansen and Rodriguez-Pose, 1994). But cohesion policies have pushed the EU towards a 'Europe *with* the regions'. Regions are active players in the EU policy-making process alongside national governments and the Commission, and the redistribution of resources directly to subnational territorial units is an integral part of the EU political system (Hooghe, 1996a; Marks, Hooghe and Blank, 1996).

Other internal policies

As discussed, approximately 6 per cent of the EU budget is spent on other internal policies, and Table 9.7 shows how this was broken down for the 1992–96 period. The largest proportion was spent on investment in science, research and development, with the remaining proportion evenly split between two areas: programmes to improve infrastructure and industrial competitiveness in the EU; and projects fostering a 'civil society' at the European level and 'social integration' in the EU.

Research and development

EU expenditure on research and development took off in the 1980s primarily as a result of concerns that Europe was falling behind the level of technological development in the United States and Japan. In 1982, the Commission and the 'big-twelve' European high-technology firms (such as Philips, Siemens, Thomson and Olivetti) persuaded the member states to agree to the *ESPRIT* programme (European Strategic Programme for Research and Development in Information Technologies) (cf. Sandholtz, 1992). The success of *ESPRIT* enabled the Commission to secure funding for a number of parallel programmes and the first multiannual 'Framework Programme' for 1984–87, with a budget of €3800m. This was

Table 9.7 *Expenditure on other internal policies, 1992–96*

Policy area	Amount (m. €)	% of other internal policies expenditure	% of total EU expenditure
Research and development	12 556	64.4	3.8
Infrastructure	3 258	16.7	1.0
Trans-European Networks	987	5.1	0.3
Internal Market	705	3.6	0.2
Other agricultural operations (non-EAGGF)	605	3.1	0.2
Industry	228	1.2	0.1
Energy	198	1.0	0.1
Fisheries	107	0.5	0.0
Other regional operations (non-ERDF)	235	1.2	0.0
Transport	76	0.4	0.0
Information Market	59	0.3	0.0
Nuclear Safety	58	0.3	0.0
Social Integration and Civil Society	3 207	16.4	1.0
Education, Vocational Training and Youth	1 510	7.7	0.5
Other social operations (non-ESF)	716	3.7	0.2
Culture and Audiovisual Media	480	2.5	0.1
Environment	427	2.2	0.1
Consumer Protection	74	0.4	0.0
Other Areas	481	2.5	0.2
Information (on the EU)	239	1.2	0.1
Statistical Information	183	0.9	0.1
Internal EU Disaster Aid	50	0.3	0.0
Justice and Home Affairs Cooperation	5	0.0	0.0
Measures to Combat Fraud	4	0.0	0.0
Total	19 502	100.0	6.0

Source: European Commission (1998a).

followed by the Second Framework Programme (1987–91), with a budget of €5400m, the Third Framework Programme (1990–94), with a budget of €5700m (a reduction in real terms), and the Fourth Framework Programme (1994–98), with a budget of €13 100m.

Expenditure under these research programmes is distributed through an agreed set of headings, for which academic and private researchers bid for funding. Under the Fourth Framework Programme, the main areas of expenditure were as follows:

- Information technology (25 per cent).
- Energy (18 per cent).
- Industrial technologies (16 per cent).
- Biotechnology and life sciences (13 per cent).
- Environmental technologies (9 per cent).
- Training and mobility of researchers (6 per cent).

There was also a limited amount of expenditure on social scientific research (about €18m in 1996), under the heading of 'targeted socio-economic research' and particularly focused on explaining and combating social exclusion.

The amount of resources spent on research, and the amount under each heading, is set by a Commission–Council–EP interaction. Since the Maastricht Treaty, the framework programmes are adopted through the codecision procedure between the Council and the EP. In the Council, the national governments seek to ensure funding on areas of research in which their own universities, public institutions and firms have particularly interests. For example, Britain and Germany, with the leading biotechnology firms in Europe, have consistently argued that investment in biotechnology research is essential for Europe to catchup with Japan and the United States. Nevertheless, the member states are also careful to restrain the EU budget in this area, and usually reduce the Commission's proposals. The European Parliament, in contrast, usually reinstates the level of funds originally proposed by the Commission, and in negotiating the Fourth Framework Programme, the European Parliament's centre-left majority pushed for industrial and environmental technologies.

Nevertheless, the Commission, in collaboration with the public and private-sector elite in the pan-European research community, controls the setting of the overall research policy agenda – for example by determining which types of research should be funded by the EU (see for example Cram, 1997). The Commission also dominates the implementation of research policy, in terms of deciding which actual projects receive funds. As Peterson (1995a, p. 408) argues:

Every five years, intergovernmental bargaining between the Council and the other institutions, eventually produces a budget and agreement on the broad institutional parameters of the Framework Programme. But the institutional framework for EU research policy does not change much or suddenly over time, thus empowering a technocrocy that is well-entrenched after ten years of the Framework Programme's existence . . . the Commission . . . can be counted on to remain the 'ringleader' of the EU research policy networks that correspond to individual EU initiatives.

Infrastructure

Several lines of the EU budget are devoted to investment in 'infrastructure', in the broadest meaning of the word. The largest of these is the Trans-European Networks programme (TENs), which was established in 1993 for upgrading infrastructure and fostering infrastructure links and compatibility between the member states in three areas:

- *information networks*, particularly telecommunications networks;
- *transport networks*, particularly high-speed train links; and
- *energy networks*, such as electricity supplies.

Other budget lines related to this include promoting information exchange between small firms (under 'internal market'), promoting the European 'information society' and the EU multimedia industry (under 'industry' and 'information market'), and promoting energy efficiency and renewable energy resources (under 'energy'). Also, many of the projects funded from this section of the EU budget are also supported by loans from the European Investment Bank.

On these issues, again the member states have the ultimate sanction. However, the amount of resources under each individual programme is small, and bargaining between the member states on budgetary issues tends to concentrate on the larger budget items: such as CAP, cohesion and research. As a result, the Commission has been relatively free to experiment with new infrastructure project ideas, and once a project is set up it has the habit of remaining a line in future budgets. Nevertheless, the member states did block a Commission proposal, linked to the TENs programme, for a new financial instrument (a 'Union bond') which would enable the EU to raise finances for infrastructure projects on the international capital markets. Most national governments felt that this would give the Commission access to funds that would not be subject to the same fiscal restraint as the rest of the EU budget, and that the Commission was trying to bypass the European Investment Bank.

Social integration and a European civil society

Since the 1970s, a portion of the EU budget has been devoted to promoting 'social integration' in Europe. For example, in 1996, almost €400m was spent on educational exchanges, cross-border vocational training schemes, and cooperation on youth policies. A major part of this funding is the *Erasmus* programme, which has enabled a significant proportion of university students (the future European intellectual and professional elite) to spend six-months or more studying in another member state. In addition, the EU runs the European City of Culture project and helps in the production and distribution of European-made television programmes and films throughout the EU in the *Media* programme (under 'culture and audiovisual policy'). And the EU funds cross-border collaborative projects promoting sustainable development in the *Nutura 2000* programme (under 'environment').

Finally, as Laffan (1997, pp. 129–30) points out:

> many obscure budgetary lines are used to create an embryonic civil society that is transnational in nature and to counteract the excessive representation of producer groups in the Union's governance structures.

For example, the EU funds the 'social dialogue' between European-level labour and employers' peak associations (under 'other social operations'), and the activities of the peak association representing consumers at the European level (under 'consumer protection').

Several member states have questioned this use of EU resources. But the Commission argues that these funds are essential to establish a 'neo-pluralist' policy community in Brussels, where public and private interests have equal access to decision-makers (see Chapter 7). And, the European Parliament has used its powers over 'non-compulsory expenditure' to secure funding for groups with close ideological or organizational links to the EP party groups or ties to individual MEPs. For example, Glynn Ford MEP proposed the establishment of the European Migrants Forum (representing minorities in the EU member states in Brussels), and was able to secure funding for the Forum through a special line in the EU budget.

In sum, the primary justification for EU expenditure on research and infrastructure is not a redistribution of resources from rich to poor. In Musgrave and Musgrave's terms, these policies are supply-side measures to foster macroeconomic stabilization in the EU (Sharp and Pavitt, 1993). On the one hand, they enable resources to be used more productively within the EU, and hence complement the macroeconomic goals of cohesion policy. On the other hand, they aim to increase EU competitiveness *vis-à-vis* the US and Japan. However, a byproduct of EU expenditure on research is the creation of a supranational technocracy around the

Commission. As a result, EU research policy is in fact redistributive: from EU taxpayers to the elite scientific community, and especially to the technocracy with links to the Commission. Similarly, expenditure on civil society measures and social integration is explicitly political: to take from EU taxpayers and supply services to the not-for-profit community in Brussels, and the pro-European cultural interests and social activities in the member states.

Explaining EU redistributive policies

There are three interrelated issues concerning EU redistributive policies that need explaining:

- Why does the EU tax and spend to the amount that it does – in other words, why is the EU budget so small?
- Why is the bulk of expenditure in two main areas – agriculture and cohesion policy – and what explains the decline of agriculture and the rise of cohesion spending?
- Why are some individuals, regions and member states net winners, while others are net losers?

In answering these questions, academic analyses have focused on four different aspects of the making of EU redistributive policies: (1) bargaining over national costs and benefits by the member state governments; (2) the power of particular interest groups; (3) strategic behaviour by the Commission to promote its own institutional interests; and (4) the institutional rules of the redistributive game (see Chapter 8).

Intergovernmental bargaining: 'national' cost–benefit calculations

The design of the EU budget is a product of a series of intergovernmental bargains between the national governments of the EU member states. The EU budget is an 'equilibrium' outcome of a bargaining game between the governments: where each government is willing to pay into/take out of the EU budget exactly how much they believe they are gaining/losing from the non-fiscal policies of the EU (such as the single market and monetary union) (Carrubba, 1997). As a result, changes in the redistributive policies of the EU, and particularly expansions of the budget and extension of spending on the main policy areas, occur because 'losers' from the process of economic integration and regulation demand fiscal compensation (Pollack, 1995b, pp. 363–73; cf. Moravcsik, 1993, 1998).

From this perspective, the CAP was set up to support French farmers in return for German access to French agricultural markets. Similarly, the ERDF was established as part of the package that secured British and Irish accession to the EU. In the Single European Act, the doubling of the structural funds was explicitly linked to the completion of the single market, which Spain, Ireland, Greece and Portugal argued would primarily benefit the core economies of Europe at the expense of the periphery. In the Maastricht Treaty, the cohesion fund was Spain's price for supporting a Germany-oriented design of Economic and Monetary Union. And, Objective 6 of the structural funds was an extra carrot for Swedish and Finnish accession to the EU, in the expectation that without such a provision they would be large net contributors to the EU budget.

The result, as Table 9.8 shows, is a redistributive bargain which is not based on a state's wealth (GDP/head), but rather on whether or not a state is likely to gain or lose from trade liberalization (cf. Frieden, 1991). On one side, the main net contributors are the export-based member states (such as Germany, the Netherlands, Sweden, the United Kingdom and Austria), whose industries will be able to secure new markets as a result of the single market and Economic and Monetary Union. On the other side, the main net recipients are the states where production is predominantly for the national market (the four 'cohesion states'), whose industries are likely to suffer under competitive pressure from importers as a result of trade liberalization in the EU.

However, there are two important subtleties within this general rule. First, Denmark appears to be an anomaly: a wealthy state with an export-based economy, but a net recipient under the EU budget (particularly from the CAP). But this can easily be explained in the intergovernmental logic (Carrubba, 1997). Governments in the member states are primarily concerned with reelection: for wealthy states whose publics support European integration, the median voter is willing to allow contributions into the budget in return for benefits to the national economy (of the single market, for example). However, in states where the public is anti-European (see Chapter 5), governments will demand more from the EU in return for their continued participation in EU integration. As a result, Denmark has been able to remain a net recipient. Using similar arguments, the UK government negotiated a budget rebate in the early 1980s when Thatcher demanded 'our money back'.

Second, as Table 9.8 shows, the benefits to individual net recipient states are higher (on average 6.3 per cent national government revenue for the four 'cohesion state' in 1995) than the costs to individual net contributor states (on average − 0.7 per cent of national government revenue). This leads to a particular type of bargaining situation once the redistributive bargain has been struck: where the benefits are 'concentrated' but the costs

Table 9.8 *Net fiscal transfers between the member states*

Member state (ranked by 1995 EU receipts as % of national govt. revenue)	GDP/head as % of EU average (1995, pps)	1995		1977 to 1990*	
		Net receipts from EU (m. €)	EU receipts as % of national government revenues	Average annual net receipts from EU (m. €)	Average EU receipts as % of national government revenues
Greece	60.0	3 489	8.8	1 284	7.1
Ireland	85.3	1 887	7.3	1 049	10.8
Portugal	67.9	2 381	5.4	393	2.2
Spain	76.1	7 218	3.7	741	0.2
Denmark	112.0	306	0.4	359	1.0
Italy	101.7	− 614	− 0.1	436	0.4
France	107.2	− 1 727	− 0.2	− 679	− 0.2
Belgium	110.4	− 311	− 0.2	− 456	− 0.7
Finland	92.5	− 165	− 0.3	—	—
Luxembourg	128.2	− 45	− 0.7	− 32	− 0.9
Austria	109.3	− 905	− 0.9	—	—
United Kingdom	98.2	− 4 720	− 0.9	− 1 717	− 0.7
Sweden	95.3	− 937	− 1.0	—	—
Netherlands	100.4	− 2 005	− 1.0	372	0.4
Germany	106.7	− 13 431	− 1.5	− 3 321	− 0.8

Note: * For Greece, Spain and Portugal, the data in the last two columns applies from the date of joining the EU until 1994.
Source: Calculated from data in *The Economist* (1996), Carrubba (1997), El-Agraa (1998).

are 'diffuse'. As a result, each recipient state has more at stake than each contributor state in negotiations over increases or decreases in the EU budget. As net contributions for individual states rise, the political costs of EU integration also rise. For example, in the negotiations on Agenda 2000, Germany (the largest net contributor in all definitions of the meaning) and the Netherlands (which has moved from a net recipient to a contributor) demanded British-style rebates from the EU budget (Laffan, 1997, pp. 47–60). However, because of the amounts involved, these states are more likely to continue paying in than Spain, Greece, Ireland and Portugal are to give up their significant EU hand-outs.

Private interests: farmers, regions, scientists and 'Euro-pork'

The benefits of EU redistributive policies are also felt at an individual level or by collectivities below the level of the EU member states. For example, a country's receipts from the CAP are felt by farmers and not by the country's consumers. Also, in the majority of member states there are regions whose citizens are net contributors to the EU budget while other regions are net recipients under cohesion policy; and, in research policy, money is targeted to specific scientific communities at the expense of EU taxpayers.

In this interpretation, the EU gives out 'pork' from the Euro-barrel to those individuals and groups that ask loud enough. As was discussed in the theoretical introduction, Olson's (1965) 'logic of collective action' tells us that groups who can secure concentrated and selective benefits (for only those members of their group) are more likely to be able to organize to influence the policy process than groups with diffuse interests. The benefits to each individual farmer under the CAP, to each individual recipient region under cohesion policy, and to each individual scientist under EU research policy, are far greater than the costs to each individual taxpayer in the EU. As a result, farmers are a powerful lobby in Brussels, through COPA, and have continued to campaign against the reform of the CAP (see for example Keeler, 1996). Similarly, a key determinant of whether a regional authority sets up an office in Brussels is whether it is an Objective 1, 2, 5b or 6 region (cf. Marks, Nielsen, Ray and Salk, 1996). For example, from Britain, the regions in Scotland and the North of England were the first to be present in Brussels (Keating and Jones, 1995, pp. 100–8). Non-European multinational firms have been able to secure participants in *ESPRIT* and the other research and development programmes through continued lobbying of the Commission and national governments (Wyatt-Walker, 1995). Also, private consultants and lobby firms in Brussels sell advice to numerous private and public interest groups about how to secure a 'grant' from the EU budget (Laffan, 1997, pp. 90–3).

In fact, Laffan (1997, p. 90) estimates that every day the Commission awards approximately three separate grants (usually in exchange for advice, research or representation).

In this explanation, the equilibrium level of redistribution is different to the intergovernmental approach. Taxpayers do not pay into the EU budget in relation to what they benefit from EU integration. Instead, redistribution occurs at the level at which diffuse costs to taxpayers are equal to the individual costs of mobilizing to reduce the tax burden: in other words, they are indifferent between paying into the EU budget and organizing to reform the CAP or cohesion policies (Becker, 1983). However, this equilibrium can be unsettled by issue-linkage: which creates selective incentives for particular interests that are net contributors to the EU budget. For example, when the success of the GATT negotiations was linked to a reform of the CAP, multinational firms began to have a vested interest to pressure the Commission, and national governments to agree a reform of the CAP. One can envisage a similar situation if enlargement to eastern and central Europe is linked to a reform of cohesion spending: where companies, regions and member states with large exports to central and eastern Europe seek to counterbalance the influence of recipient regions.

Commission entrepreneurship: promoting 'multilevel governance'

The redistributive game is not simply a battle between competing member states or rival interest groups. As the referee of this game, the Commission can use its agenda-setting powers to shape policy outcomes and promote its institutional interests (Peters, 1992, 1994; Tsebelis and Garrett, 1996; Cram, 1997; Pollack, 1997a). First, the Commission has an interest in promoting European integration in the expectation that further integration will lead to further delegation of executive power from the Council to the Commission, and greater Commission influence in a greater number of policy domains. Second, in the everyday bargaining process of EU politics to secure approval of its policy proposals by the Council and the European Parliament, the Commission has an incentive to support key member states and influential societal groups and private interests.

Consequently, DGVI obstructed CAP reform in the 1970s and 1980s to protect its position and the interests of its support-group (COPA). Similarly, and the College of Commissioners promoted reform in the 1990s to protect the policy credibility of the Commission in other areas, in particular trade negotiations (cf. Grant, 1997, pp. 147–60). In cohesion policies, the Commission introduction of the principles of additionality, partnership and concentration in the 1988 reform of the structural funds was a deliberate effort to bypass national governments in the implementation of policy and to promote decentralization and federalization within the member states (see Marks, 1992, 1993). And, in the 1993 reform of the structural funds the Commission successfully negotiated a more substantial package of funds for the regions than most member states desired at the beginning of the negotiations. The Commission achieved this by carefully securing bilateral commitments from each member state and enlisting the support of regional authorities against reluctant governments (Marks, 1996; Hooghe, 1996a). In research policy, the Commission has promoted projects that lead to transnational cooperation between national firms and the creation of 'Euro-champions', often against national government policies to protect 'national champions' (Peterson, 1991, 1995a; Pollack, 1995b).

According to this perspective, Commission activism has facilitated redistributive policies that do more to undermine national government interests than protect them. There is a high correlation between individual attitudes to European integration and whether or not the individual is a member of a group, region or member state that receives funds from the EU budget (Whitten, Gabel and Palmer, 1998). In a sense, by targeting funds to groups below the level of the state, the Commission can hope to 'divide and rule' the governments. Similarly, by providing financial support for public interest groups, such as non-governmental organizations and consumer groups, the Commission can weaken the influence of powerful private interests, such as farmers (Pollack, 1997b).

In other words, the Commission has attempted to use redistributive policies to promote the development of 'multilevel' rather than 'state-centric' governance (Marks, 1993; Jachtenfuchs, 1995; Marks, Hooghe and Blank, 1996; Kohler-Koch, 1996). First, the Commission promotes the participation of private interests and subnational authorities alongside national authorities. Second, the Commission manipulates this 'policy-centric' and 'non-hierarchical' structure of policy-making to maximize its influence over policy outcomes.

Institutional rules: unanimity, majority and agenda-setting

Nevertheless, the interaction between governments, private interests and the Commission is shaped by the institutional rules of the redistributive game. The multiannual budgetary bargains, which determine the overall size of the EU budget and the relative increases or reductions in the various redistributive policies, are decided by unanimity between national governments in the Council. These rules produce a particular type of policy outcome. If every member state has a veto, they can demand that their receipts from the EU budget are exactly equivalent to how much they can expect to gain from non-fiscal EU policies (such as the single market). Moreover, by 'exchanging' support for each other's projects, every member state can be accommodated in a budgetary bargain.

In other words, by using a unanimity rule the overall policy impact must be allocative rather than redistributive: everyone must win, otherwise an individual member would exercise a veto (Mueller, 1989, pp. 43–49). This is similar to the type of distributive bargain in a 'consociational' system, where the state supplies finances to each societal segment regardless of their specific welfare needs (Lijphart, 1968). However, once the budgetary ceiling and the relative weight of the redistributive policies is set in the multiannual budgetary deals, majority-voting is used to determine policy changes and implementation issues within the budgetary constraints; and, these decisions can have significant redistributive implications. For example, at this level of bargaining the EU decides issues like appropriations and expenditure in the annual budgetary cycle, which types of crops are supported under the CAP, which regions qualify for support under the cohesion policy, which projects are funded under research policy, and which interest groups receive funds to support their organization in Brussels.

The move from unanimity to majority voting has two implications. First, as discussed in the introduction section, majority voting enables a majority to redistribute resources from the minority. For example, the large recipients under the EU budget and the indifferent states can out-vote the large net contributors. Second, majority-voting gives agenda-setting power to the actor who is responsible for policy initiation. Under the EU's decision-making rules, the Council only requires a qualified majority to support a Commission proposal but needs unanimity to overrule the Commission (see Chapter 3). For example, in the redesign of the structural funds in 1993, the French and British governments were opposed to the Commission's plan, but were unable to block majority support for the reforms (Marks, 1996). Similarly, under the annual budgetary procedure the EP has used its agenda-setting power to force the Council to accept the funding of pet schemes and interest groups of the main EP party groups.

And once these redistributive bargains are struck, they are difficult to un-pick because of the return to unanimity when it comes to the larger bargains. For example, the CAP may originally have been an allocative pay-off, but as a result of the changes in the structure of agriculture, the influence of DGVI, the power of the agricultural lobby and the interests of farm ministers, the CAP has become a redistributive policy: from taxpayers and consumers to farmers. But, any major reform of the CAP will require a new budgetary package deal to be passed by unanimity in the Council. Under this rule, the farming states can veto the reform or demand some other kind of compensation.

Conclusion: a series of welfare bargains

The absolute volume of resources channelled through the EU budget is small relative to governments at the national level in Europe or the federal government in the United States. Nevertheless, EU fiscal policies aim to achieve all the classic goals of public finance: of allocation, stabilization and redistribution. For example, allocation was one of the original goals of the CAP and is a central dynamic of multiannual budgetary packages: to off-set losses by certain member states in non-fiscal policy areas. Also, stabilization, through supply-side measures, is a core goal of cohesion, science and infrastructure policies.

However, as in other political systems, the dominant objective of EU public expenditure policies is *redistribution*. First, this is an inevitable product of political bargaining in a democratic society. Certain groups, such as farmers, are more able to organize to secure and protect benefits than are contributors into the EU budget, namely EU taxpayers. The size of the EU budget may be small, but the resources received from the EU by individual farmers, regions, scientists or non-governmental organizations are substantial.

Second, redistribution has been a deliberate strategy of the Commission. The Commission has used its agenda-setting powers to foster 'winners' from the EU budget at the expense of European taxpayers and net contributor member states. Through this strategy, the Commission targets resources at non-state actors who will undermine the dominance of the national governments in the EU policy process. However, the Commission has also promoted redistribution to groups to 'buy' support for European integration, such as farmers, backward regions and anti-European member states.

Third, once redistributive outcomes have been achieved, they are notoriously difficult to reform. Redistribution creates entrenched interests who are willing to spend resources to protect their subsidies. CAP would be easier to reform if it were purely an allocative policy; and the same is true for cohesion policy, if it were purely a stabilization policy. The fact that these have become 'welfare policies' for farmers and regions, respectively, means that it is unlikely that the net contributor states and EU taxpayers will be able to secure a fundamental reform of these policies without a major external shock.

The result is a redistributive equilibrium: between the amount the Commission and recipient groups can gain, and how much contributor states and EU taxpayers are willing to lose. But two such external shocks are just round the corner: potential pressures for fiscal federalism in Economic and Monetary Union, and enlargement to eastern and central Europe. These developments are likely to unbalance the delicate equilibrium of EU expenditure policies, and provoke new redistributive bargains.

Chapter 10

Economic and Monetary Union

The theory of monetary union
Development of economic and monetary union in Europe
Explaining economic and monetary union
Making monetary and economic policy in EMU
Conclusion: political commitment and political flexibility

Economic and Monetary Union (EMU) was launched between 11 EU member states on 1 January 1999. This chapter seeks to answer two questions about this project. First, why did these governments decide to replace their national currencies with a single European currency (the Euro)? Second, how will EMU work? To help answer these questions we shall first look at some general theories of why monetary unions are formed.

The theory of monetary union

The discipline of economics has a theory to analyse whether or not independent nation-states should form a monetary union. Pioneered by Mundell (1961), the theory says that an 'optimal currency area' (OCA) exists if the economic benefits of joining or forming a monetary union exceed the costs (see also McKinnon, 1963; Kenen, 1969). In the OCA theory, the *cost of a monetary union* is the loss of a major macroeconomic policy tool: an independent exchange rate. In classical economic theory, this tool is used to protect economies from varying economic conditions between states – known as 'asymmetric shocks'. One of the basic laws of economics is the existence of 'economic cycles': where economic growth ('boom') is following by recession ('bust'), which is followed by growth, and so on. Consequently, asymmetric shocks occur if the economic cycles of two states are not synchronized: if there is growing demand in one state while there is falling demand in another.

When this occurs, governments can pursue different macroeconomic policies: such as a devaluation of the currency (for example, through low interest rates) during a recession to stimulate demand, and a revaluation of the currency (or high interest rates) in a period of growth to prevent 'overheating'. But, this is impossible in a monetary union, as exchange rates are fixed and there is a 'one-size-fits-all' interest rate policy.

Nevertheless, asymmetric shocks can be addressed through several other mechanisms:

- *Labour mobility* – the unemployed in the state where there is a recession could move to take up jobs in the state where there is high growth.
- *Wage flexibility/capital mobility* – the workers in the state where there is low demand could reduce their wages (increasing the supply of labour at a given price), and (assuming that capital is mobile) attract capital from the high demand state to the state in recession.
- *Fiscal transfers* – the growing state could increase taxes to reduce demand, and transfer these tax revenues to a state in recession, where they can be spent to increased demand (also called 'fiscal federalism').
- *Budget deficits* – the state in recession can run a budgetary surplus and spend the extra resources to increase demand.

However, economic theory suggests that fiscal transfers and the use of budgetary deficits are only temporary solutions to an asymmetric shock. If the demand shock is more permanent than simply a cyclical down-turn, governments will either run up significant public deficits, or will become reliant on fiscal transfers. Moreover, if fiscal transfers and budget deficits become a permanent feature, they can be a substitute for wage and price changes and labour movement.

Consequently, in his original formulation of the OCA theory, Mundell (1961) argued that states faced with asymmetric shocks should weigh up two possible strategies: (1) reduction of the exchange rate; and (2) stable exchange rates, but with wage reductions and labour mobility. If the economic and social costs of the second strategy are more painful than the first, then Mundell concluded that a state should not join a single currency.

However, there are three main problems with this argument. First, the OCA theory excludes the benefits of a single currency, which may out-weigh the costs of giving up floating exchange-rates. Second, more recent economic theory has raised doubts about the benefits of using exchange rate reductions as a macroeconomic tool. Third, the OCA theory ignores the influence of political calculations in the making of macroeconomic policy decisions.

Starting with the first of these issues, the main economic benefits of a single currency are (Eichengreen, 1990; De Grauwe, 1997):

- *Lower transactions costs* – by removing the cost of exchanging currencies, firms involved in trade between states do not have to pay exchange-rate commissions or insure themselves against currency fluctuations.

- *A more efficient market* – a common currency reduces the possibility for price discrimination, eliminates the information costs of consuming goods or locating businesses across borders, and hence promotes market integration and market efficiency.
- *Greater economic certainty* – exchange-rate stability increases certainty of prices and revenues, which improves the quality of production, investment and consumption decisions (which, in turn, increases collective welfare).
- *Lower interest rates* – greater economic certainty also reduces the 'risk premium' on interest rates, and so interest rates are likely to be lower in a larger economy and in an economy which is less exposed to trade in a foreign currency.
- *Higher economic growth* – 'new-growth' theorists argue that larger and more integrated economies with greater productivity, more capital accumulation, better information, more economies of scale and lower interest rates can produce permanently higher levels of economic growth.

Some of these benefits are open to dispute amongst economists. The potential for lower interest rates and higher growth rates tend to be overemphasised by supporters of monetary union in Europe. Indeed, one economic theory predicts that reducing uncertainty in exchange rates does not necessarily reduce systematic risk in the economy, as political decision-makers will tend to compensate the loss of exchange-rate manipulation with increased use of other macroeconomic tools, such as the money supply (Poole, 1970). Also, the empirical evidence for new-growth theory remains weak, both in Europe and the United States, and the theoretical arguments have come under increased attack (see for example Krugman, 1998). The market efficiency gains are unlikely to take effect in the short term, and even the transactions-cost benefits of the elimination of currency exchange must be weighed against the loss to the banking industry of revenues from service charges on currency exchange – which some estimate to be as high as 5 per cent of European banks' revenues.

Nevertheless, most commentators accept that even if the non-certain benefits are discounted, there will be certain direct transactions-cost benefits as a result of the removal of currency speculation and exchange for firms involved in cross-border trade in a currency union. For example, the European Commission estimates that these benefits by themselves could amount to savings worth between 0.25 and 0.5 per cent of EU GDP (European Commission, 1990).

Turning to the second of the problems in the OCA theory, there are important *limits on the use of the exchange rate as a shock absorber*. In the short term, devaluation will increase demand for exported goods by lowering their price in other markets. However, it also raises the price of imported goods, which raises the costs of production and provokes higher wage demands. Consequently, the long-term effect of this is usually higher prices and lower output. In other words, even if states have vastly different economic conditions, the exchange rate is a relatively ineffective way of adjusting to these differences. As a result, if the long-term benefits of floating exchange rates are lower than the OCA theory assumes, the costs of joining a single currency are smaller.

As for the third weakness of the OCA theory, *political considerations* often override economic calculations. Voters and elites have different preferences about inflation, unemployment, welfare protection and government debt. A large electoral majority (of the centre-left) may be in favour of maintaining a high level of employment and welfare protection, and be willing to finance these policies through high taxes or a large public debt. In this situation, a government is unlikely to be able to force wage reductions or labour market reforms to attract capital investment. As a result, a government in a low-growth state may decide that the *political* costs of structural adjustment inherent in a monetary union would be too high to pay, and hence decide to maintain a separate currency.

Alternatively, a public may support economic and political union for non-economic reasons. A public can have a high level of 'affective' support for political integration, even if they perceive that they may be economically worse off in the short term (see Chapter 5). This support may enable a government in a low-demand state to use the promise of economic and political integration to enforce structural adjustment programmes. Conversely, in a high-growth state, public support for currency union may enable a government to sanction fiscal transfers to other states to maintain the currency union.

Finally, there are two other political implications of currency union that must be placed alongside the potential economic costs and benefits:

- *A single voice in the global economy* – a single currency has external political implications; for example, in the case of the EU, the Euro may rival the US Dollar as the dominant global currency, which will give the EU political clout on global currency issues.
- *A step towards political union* – a single currency is likely to facilitate further political integration, either through pressures for fiscal federalism and tax harmonization, or through demands for a political 'government' over monetary policy, or through the emergence of new allegiances and identities towards the EU institutions.

For publics in favour of further political integration these are potential benefits of monetary union, but for publics opposed to further political integration these are clearly costs of monetary union. In other words, mass political preferences will influence elite calculations when deciding whether to establish or join a monetary union.

In sum, the main cost of monetary union is the inability to use a reduction of the exchange rate to absorb a demand shock. However, this cost must be weighed against the long-term ineffectiveness of exchange-rate policies and the potential economic benefits of a single currency, in particular the lower transactions costs. In addition, these economic calculations are often constrained by publics' and governments' political preferences concerning inflation, unemployment, wage levels, labour market policies, and the desirability of further political integration.

Development of economic and monetary union in Europe

The Maastricht Treaty set out the plan for EMU, but the idea of EMU had been discussed as far back as 1956 in the negotiations on the Treaty of Rome. Also, there were two major precursors to the Maastricht plan that were important for the eventual preparations for, and the design of, EMU (Dyson, 1994). The first of these was the Werner Report of 1971, which proposed a plan for EMU by 1980, but this plan was never achieved after Europe plunged into recession in the mid-1970s. The second precursor was the Economic and Monetary System (EMS), which was set up in 1979. The EMS had two main elements: a basket of currencies (the Ecu), weighted according to the strengths of the participating currencies; and an Exchange-Rate Mechanism (ERM), with a permissible band of fluctuation around the central ecu rate and a system of buying and selling currencies to ensure that they remained within this band. The initial band was set at ±2.25 per cent. This was sustainable until the international currency crises of 1992, when the Italian and British currencies were unceremoniously expelled from the EMS and a new ±15 per cent band was set up for the remaining members' currencies.

The Delors Report

The 1985 Single European Act proposed that EMU should be an eventual goal of the EU, but did not set out how this could be achieved. Consequently, at the 1988 Hanover European Council, the governments set up a committee chaired by Commission president Jacques Delors to prepare a report on the best way to launch EMU. The 'Delors Committee' was composed of two commissioners, the 12 central bank governors of the EU member states, and three independent experts. The final report of the committee – the 'Delors Report' – which was delivered to the European Council in June 1989, proposed a particular model of EMU (Committee for the Study of Economic and Monetary Union, 1989).

First, the report argued that monetary union should involve the irrevocable fixing of exchange rates (not necessarily with a single set of notes and coins), and the complete liberalization of capital transactions and integration of the banking and financial markets. Second, the report argued that economic union should involve a single market, competition policies to strengthen market mechanisms, common policies aimed at structural change and regional development (with the possibility of significant fiscal transfers), and macroeconomic policy coordination, with binding rules on budget deficits. Third, the report set out a three-stage plan:

- Stage I – the establishment of free capital movement and the start of macroeconomic coordination between the member state governments (by 1 July 1990).
- Stage II – reform of the Treaties, the establishment of European System of Central Banks, with a supervisory role for the European Parliament and the Council, and restrictive margins of fluctuation for national currencies.
- Stage III – the fixing of exchange rates and the establishment of an independent European Central Bank, with the single goal of maintaining 'price stability'.

From the experience of the Werner Report, the Delors Committee proposed a phased approach but was careful not to define it too precisely. And from the experience of the EMS, the Committee emphasised the importance of economic coordination and convergence as a precondition for monetary union. The plan also constituted a compromise. On one side, Delors aimed to design a project that was irreversible – 'the decision to enter upon the first stage should be a decision to embark on the entire process' (*ibid.*, p. 31). On the other side, the governor of the German Bundesbank, Karl Otto Pöhl, needed to be persuaded that the single currency would be as stable as the Deutschmark, and so argued for constraints on national deficits and a fully-independent European Central Bank.

The Delors Report made no comment on whether or not the project was desirable. But the Commission soon made it clear where it stood on this issue when in October 1990 it published a report entitled *One Market, One Money*, which argued that the full benefits of the single market could not be realised without a single currency (European Commission, 1990).

The Maastricht Treaty design

Meanwhile, in June 1990 the Dublin European Council decided to convene an Intergovernmental Conference (IGC) to prepare the necessary Treaty reforms to implement Delors' proposals. At the Rome European Council in October 1990, the heads of government agreed by a majority (with Margaret Thatcher against) that Stage II of EMU would begin in January 1994 and that the IGC would propose a fixed timetable for Stage III. The IGC was duly launched at a second Rome European Council in December 1990 and was completed at the Maastricht European Council in December 1991, with the agreement on the Treaty on European Union (the Maastricht Treaty).

The Maastricht Treaty provided the legal framework for the implementation of the Delors Report through four key provisions. First, the Treaty set out the *timetable*. Stage II was set for January 1994, when the European Monetary Institute was established to prepare the ground for Stage III. Stage III would then start in one of two ways: either by *choice*, in January 1997 if a majority of EU states met a set of required economic conditions; or *automatically*, on 1 January 1999, between the EU states that met the required criteria. As a result, the plan could not be cancelled or postponed without breach of the Treaty.

Second, the Treaty set out the four *convergence criteria* for qualifying for EMU:

1. *Price stability* – an average inflation rate not exceeding by more than 1.5 per cent that of the three best-performing member states.
2. *Interest rates* – an average nominal long-term interest rate not exceeding by more than 2 percent that of the three best-performing member states.
3. *Government budgetary position* – an annual current account deficit not exceeding 3 per cent of GDP, and a gross public debt ratio not exceeding 60 per cent of GDP.
4. *Currency stability* – membership of the narrow band of the ERM (with fluctuations of less than 2.5 per cent around the central rate) for at least two years, with no devaluations.

Third, the Treaty set out the *institutional structure* of the European Central Bank (ECB) and the European System of Central Banks (ESCB). The ECB would be comprised of an Executive Board and a Governing Council. The European Council would appoint the six members of the Executive Board for non-renewable eight-year terms, subject to approval by the European Parliament. The Governing Board would comprise the six Executive Board members together with the governors of the national banks in the ESCB (of the member states in EMU), who are appointed by national governments for renewable five-year terms.

Fourth, the Treaty set out how *monetary policy would operate in EMU*:

- *An independent Central Bank* – 'neither the ECB, nor a national central bank, nor any member of the decision-making bodies shall seek or take instructions from Community institutions or bodies, from any government of a member state or from any other body' (article 108 [ex 107]).
- *A main goal of price stability* – 'the primary objective of the ESCB shall be to maintain price stability. Without prejudice to the objective of price stability, the ESCB shall support the economic policies in the Community with a view to contributing to the achievement of the objectives of the Community' (article 105 [ex 105]) (the 'objectives of the Community' are set out in article 2 [ex B] of the Treaty, and include 'economic progress' and 'a high level of employment').
- *The role of the ECB in monetary policy* – the basic tasks of the ECB and ESCB are to

   - define and implement monetary policy,
   - conduct foreign exchange operations,
   - hold and manage the official reserves of the member states, and
   - promote the smooth operation of payments systems.

- *The role of the Council in monetary policy* – the Council of Economic and Finance Ministers (EcoFin) has the final say over interventions in foreign exchange markets (by unanimity), can conclude monetary agreements with third countries (by qualifiedmajority), and will decide the position of the EU in international relations on issues relating to EMU (by qualifiedmajority).
- *The role of the Council in economic policy* – EcoFin also undertakes 'multilateral surveillance', through the adoption of common economic policy guidelines (drafted in cooperation with the Commission) and the collective scrutiny of how the governments implement these guidelines, and EcoFin is responsible for imposing fines on member states who run 'excessive budget deficits'.

Who qualifies? Meeting (and fudging) the convergence criteria

Before the Maastricht Treaty came into effect in November 1993, the EMS was hit by an international currency crisis which threatened to disrupt the carefully laid plans. It soon became clear that a majority of member states would not meet the convergence criteria by the 1997 deadline. As a result, in 1996, a 'two-speed EMU' appeared to be the most likely outcome, with a small set of states whose currencies were closely linked to the Deutschmark (Germany, France, Netherlands, Luxembourg, Austria and Belgium) going ahead in 1999, and the states with weaker currencies (Spain, Italy, Portugal, Ireland, Greece and Finland) joining at some later date. In the meantime, the Swedish, Danish and British governments indicated that they were unlikely to join due to concerns over national sovereignty and anti-European feeling amongst their publics (Denmark and Britain had negotiated an 'opt-out' from the EMU plans in the Maastricht Treaty).

However, the crises strengthened the belief amongst all member states' political and administrative elites that fixed exchange rates and the delegation of monetary policy to a supranational central bank would reduce domestic political risk. Moreover, rather than abandon the project, the likely second-tier governments were more determined than ever to join EMU, as a way of constraining the power of international currency speculators once and for all (Cobham, 1996; Sandholtz, 1996; Jones, Frieden and Torres, 1998). As a result, the Spanish, Portuguese and Italian governments introduced heroic budgetary cuts: the Italian government reentered the ERM in November 1996 and introduced a one-off 'Europe tax' to reduce the budget deficit to below the 3 per cent target; the Finnish government joined the ERM and introduced a series of macroeconomic reforms; and Ireland became the fastest growing economy in Europe, which allowed the government to reduce its public debt and to revalue the currency in the ERM. Consequently, at the Brussels European Council in May 1988, the heads of government supported the Commission's proposal that EMU should be launched between 11 member states.

However, as Table 10.1 shows, only three states met all the convergence criteria. The Commission nonetheless argued that the public debt criteria was less important than the deficit criteria, and that it was more important that gross public debt figures were 'moving in the right direction' – in other words, falling between 1995 and 1997. Belgium and Italy clearly did not meet this interpretation. But, Belgium was already in a currency union with Luxembourg (which would have to be broken up if it did could not join EMU), and Belgium is a relatively small economy compared to the size of the Euro-zone. On the other hand, Italy was a bigger problem. Opinion in the German Bundesbank and the German government was divided over whether Italy should be allowed to join: with several leading figures arguing that Italian entry would undermine the stability of the new currency, and that the convergence criteria should be strictly applied. However, backed by the Commission and the French government (who feared a devaluation of the Lira if Italy remained outside EMU), Italian prime minister Romano Prodi managed to persuade the other governments that he could implement a budgetary plan that would significantly reduce Italian debt by 2002. This was clearly a political compromise. Greece, however, was the only member state that wished to join EMU but was excluded, as it clearly did not meet the convergence criteria.

Table 10.1 Qualification for Economic and Monetary Union

Criteria:	Inflation rate, 1997 (%)	Interest rates, 1997 (%)	Government budgetary position			Exchange rate (in ERM, March 1998)
			Deficit, 1997 (% of GDP)	Debt (% of GDP) 1997	Change from 1995	
Target	2.7	7.8	≤ 3.0	≤ 60.0		Yes
Members of EMU						
Luxembourg	1.4	5.6	− 1.7	6.7	+ 1.0	Yes
Finland	1.3	5.9	0.9	55.8	− 3.7	Yes
France	1.2	5.5	3.0	58.0	+ 9.5	Yes
Germany	1.4	5.6	2.7	**61.3**	+ 11.0	Yes
Portugal	1.8	6.2	2.5	**62.0**	− 1.8	Yes
Austria	1.1	5.6	2.5	**66.1**	+ 0.7	Yes
Ireland	1.2	6.2	− 0.9	**66.3**	− 22.8	Yes
Spain	1.8	6.3	2.6	**68.8**	+ 6.2	Yes
Netherlands	1.8	5.5	1.4	**72.1**	− 5.7	Yes
Italy	1.8	6.7	2.7	**121.6**	− 3.3	Yes
Belgium	1.4	5.7	2.1	**122.2**	− 11.2	Yes
Did not qualify for EMU						
Greece	**5.2**	**9.8**	**4.0**	**108.7**	− 0.7	Yes
Political decision not to Join EMU						
United Kingdom	1.8	7.0	1.9	53.4	+ 3.0	No
Denmark	1.9	6.2	− 0.7	65.1	− 13.1	Yes
Sweden	1.9	6.5	0.8	76.6	− 2.4	No

Note: The figures in bold indicate that a member state DID NOT meet the convergence criteria as set out in the Maastricht Treaty.
Source: European Commission (1998b).

Resolving other issues: appeasing an unhappy French government

But this was not the end of the story; a number of other issues remained to be resolved. First, now that more member states would join EMU than the German government had originally expected, German finance minister Theo Waigel proposed a 'Stability Pact', to prevent governments from running large public deficits once EMU was launched (see below). This was immediately opposed by the French Socialist government, which was elected on 1997 on a platform that was broadly critical of the 'monetarist' rules of EMU. In late 1997, a compromise was reached. In return for the imposition of fines on wayward governments, the French secured that these could only be imposed by a political decision, and that for cosmetic reasons the agreement should be called the 'Growth and Stability Pact'.

Second, the French government managed to secure support for another measure to introduce a 'political' element to EMU. In 1997, French finance minister Dominique Strauss-Kahn proposed a special 'Euro-X Committee', of only the finance ministers of the member states joining EMU, to oversee the management of the single currency (which hence became the 'Euro-11' committee). His intentions were clear when he described this as the 'economic government of the Euro'. However, the German government insisted that this committee could not compromise the independence of the ECB, and the British government feared that this would gradually replace EcoFin as the main economic policy organ of the EU. In a final compromise, the governments agreed that the Euro-11 committee will focus on technical issues and policy questions specific to the euro-zone states (such as international monetary cooperation), whereas EcoFin will remain the main forum for macroeconomic policy coordination. However, unlike the solution on the Growth and Stability Pact, this was seen as a victory for the French government, as it was clear that the Euro-11 committee would become the main macroeconomic policy arena in EMU.

Nevertheless, the French government lost out on the issue of the first head of the ECB. Until late 1997, most member states accepted that Wim Duisenberg, the ex-Dutch central bank governor and president of the EMI, would become the first president of the ECB. But French president Jacques Chirac and prime minister Lionel Jospin jointly proposed Jean-Claude Trichet, the French central bank governor, as a rival candidate. The French claimed that there had been an informal agreement between Mitterrand and Kohl that in return for the putting the ECB in Frankfurt, the first president would be French. However, the German government did not acknowledge this deal. The French government threatened to veto Duisenberg, but a compromise was reached in May 1998. Chirac accepted

Figure 10.1 *Krugman's theory of the costs and benefits of monetary union*

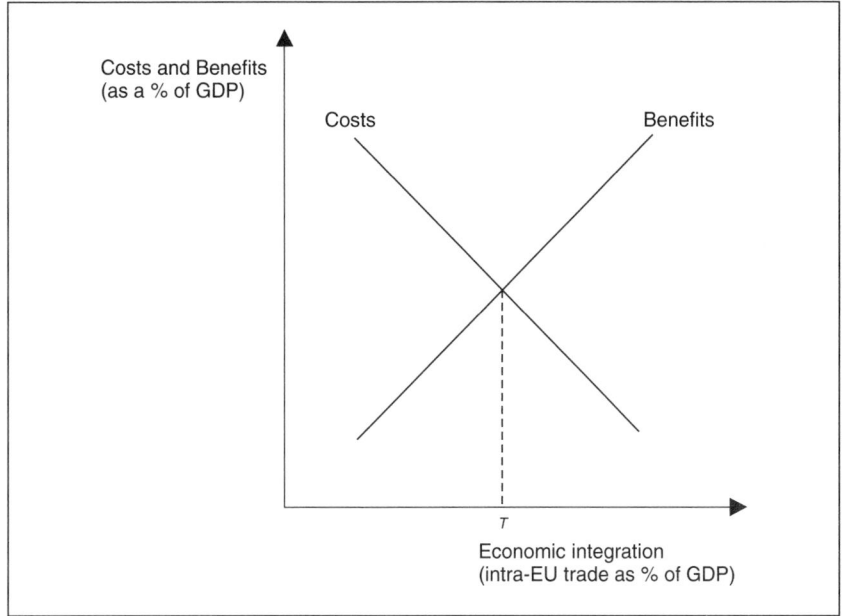

Duisenberg in return for an informal agreement from Duisenberg that he would retire half-way through his tenure, to presumably make way for Trichet. After this agreement, however, Duisenberg declared to the press that he intended to complete his full term.

Explaining economic and monetary union

Several aspects of the story so far need to be explained. For example:

- why was monetary union launched at the time it was;
- why was it designed the way it was – in terms of the three-stages, the convergence criteria, an independent Central Bank, the goal of price stability, and the growth and stability pact; and
- why did certain states join and not others?

To answer these questions, scholars of the EU have proposed four main explanations: (1) economic rationality; (2) inter-state bargaining; (3) agenda-setting by non-state interests; and (4) the dominance of neo-liberal ideas about monetary policy.

Table 10.2   *Trade integration in EU and openness to the world economy, 1994*

	Intra-EU trade (total imports and exports as a % of GDP)	Non-EU trade (total imports and exports as a % of GDP)
Belgium & Luxembourg	83.6	29.3
Ireland	80.2	34.1
Netherlands	65.0	27.7
Portugal	39.6	12.5
Denmark	35.4	17.3
Austria	33.7	16.8
Sweden	33.6	23.8
Finland	30.4	24.0
United Kingdom	24.1	18.7
France	23.6	13.5
Germany	23.1	16.3
Spain	22.8	11.5
Italy	20.9	14.5
Greece	20.8	11.4

Source: Eurostat (1997).

Figure 10.2   *Is the EU an optimal currency area?*

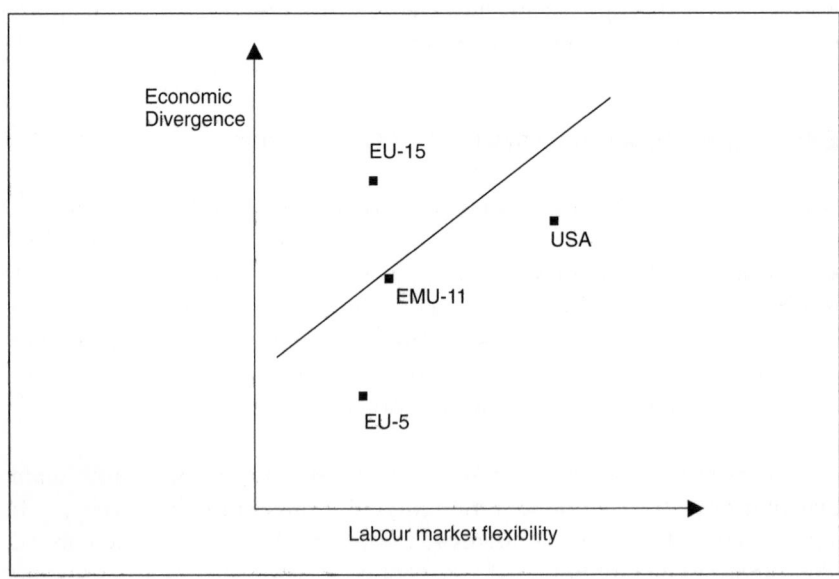

Source: Adapted from De Grauwe (1997).

Economic rationality: economic integration and a core OCA

Krugman (1990) argues that the costs and benefits of forming a single currency union vary according to the level of 'economic integration' of the states involved. The *benefits* of monetary union increase as trade between the states increases (cf. Cameron, 1997). For example, more economic integration means more benefits from the removal of transactions costs of currency exchange. In this situation, firms involved in intra-EU trade, such as manufacturing industries or the service sector that supply markets elsewhere in the EU, will lobby governments to join a single currency. On the other hand, as trade increases, the *cost* of surrendering the exchange rate as an instrument of national macroeconomic policy falls. As the structural conditions of the economies level out, with the more efficient allocation of resources as a result of a single currency and the gradual synchronization of the economic cycles, the likelihood of asymmetric shocks declines. As a result, the need to use an independent exchange rate recedes. In this situation, firms who produce predominantly for the domestic market will be less averse to joining a currency union.

Consequently, as Figure 10.1 shows, as expected benefits increase and expected costs fall, the lines are bound to intercept at a certain point in time. At this point (T), it makes rational economic sense to form or join a currency union, as any time after this point will see more benefits than costs for the member state concerned – a situation economists call 'bliss'!

However, it is difficult to tell when exactly this point was reached for the EU member states. As Table 10.2 shows, in the mid-1990s the level of imports and exports in goods (excluding services) between the EU member states varied considerably. For the larger economies intra-EU trade accounts for less than one-quarter of total GDP, while in contrast, for many of the smaller economies intra-EU trade accounts for more than half of total GDP. Moreover, for Germany, the core economy of the EU, trade with the rest of the world is almost as large as trade with the rest of the EU. In other words, when the decision was taken to launch EMU on the basis of simple economic cost–benefit calculations, the smaller states were more likely to benefit than the larger states.

In addition, empirical analyses of the EU economy suggest that the EU is not an optimal currency area, particularly when compared to the United States (see for example Eichengreen, 1990; Feldstein, 1992; Caporale, 1993; De Grauwe and Vanhaverbeke, 1993). First, there is a high degree of divergence in economic cycles amongst the 15 EU member states, so that asymmetric shocks are likely to be frequent. Second, there is a relatively low level of labour market flexibility in the European economy, both in terms of labour mobility between states, and in terms of wage and regulatory flexibility (see below). Hence, in the presence of an asymmetric shock, labour is unlikely to move or allow wages to be reduced to attract capital.

Nevertheless, an OCA may exist between the 'core' EU economies (Dornbusch, 1990). As Figure 10.2 shows, although the labour market may not be flexible, the economic cycles of Germany, France and the Benelux (EU-5) are closely linked. The situation for the 11 states that joined EMU (EMU-11 in the figure) is less clear-cut: the labour markets are as rigid as in the five core states, but the economies are more divergent.

In sum, economic logic may be able to explain why EMU was launched in the 1990s, but it only offers a partial explanation of why certain states joined and not others. Economic logic would suggest that EMU should have been launched between only the core member states. Also, most economists accept that economic analysis cannot explain why EMU was designed in a particular way: with three stages, the convergence criteria, and a specific institutional structure (for example Artis, 1996; Crowley, 1996). These questions are more convincingly answered through analyses of political interests, strategies and calculations.

Inter-state bargaining: a Franco-German deal

The institutional design of EMU was the product of an intergovernmental bargain between the governments of the EU, in the IGC that agreed the Maastricht Treaty. Two inherently contradictory forces operate in this strategic context. First, the government that has the least to lose from non-agreement on a policy is most likely to secure the type of agreement that it wants. If it has nothing to lose, it does not need to compromise. In contrast, a government that has a lot to lose from non-agreement will be willing to make significant concessions to achieve a successful bargain. Second, however, because agreement has to be reached by unanimity between the governments, the result is usually a 'package-deal' (or a 'log-rolling agreement'). This involves including other issues on the agenda so that each government can get something of what it wants in the final agreement. In this situation, the state with the least to lose may be forced to compromise to secure its interests in other areas.

Both of these dynamics were important in the politics of EMU (Sandholtz, 1993). First, the design for EMU in the Maastricht Treaty was essentially German (Moravcsik, 1993): the aim of the convergence criteria, the establishment of a European Central Bank independent from political control, and the central goal of price stability, were all supported by the German government as conditions for it to give its approval for EMU. Through these conditions, the German government hoped that EMU would be an OCA, as only a few states would be likely to meet the conditions, and the Euro would be as stable as the Deutschmark. The German government, backed by the Bundesbank, was prepared to veto the whole project and continue with the EMS, which was effectively run by the Bundesbank. The hegemony of Germany in the system was illustrated in the ERM crisis of 1992–93, when the Bundesbank dictated which states should leave the ERM and the price to be paid by the remaining members (Cameron, 1993; Smith and Sandholtz, 1995). Moreover, the other member states were prepared to pay the German price to regain some say over monetary policy. In EMU, the common interest rate would be set for the European economy as a whole, and their central banks would have an equal say in this decision alongside the Bundesbank.

However, certain aspects of the package deal, and the final outcome of EMU as it was launched in 1999, were not completely to Germany's liking. The French government extracted painful concessions from Germany. In the institutional design, Germany accepted an ECB Governing Council where the ECB Executive Board could potentially be outvoted by national central bank governors, and a political role for EcoFin in the management of external exchange rate policy (Garrett, 1994). And, in the final preparations in 1998, the German government may have got its way on the Growth and Stability Pact, but the French government extracted concessions from Germany over the creation of the Euro-11 committee and forced the governments to politicize the choice of the ECB president.

Finally, Germany in fact had little to gain from monetary union with high inflation countries such as Italy, Spain and even France (if long-term figures are taken into account). It could be argued, however, that Germany was willing to allow EMU to go ahead and to concede on the precise design of the process because it had broader political interests in maintaining the pace of political integration in Europe, following German unification and the collapse of the Soviet Union (Dyson, Featherstone and Michalopoulis, 1994; Woolley, 1994; McKay, 1996, pp. 84–95). In this interpretation, EMU is part of a broad historic deal between France and Germany: French support for German unification, in return for Germany giving up the Deutschmark and Bundesbank control of the European economy (Tsoukalis, 1997, pp. 164–72).

Agenda-setting by non-state interests: the Commission and central bankers

An alternative view, though, is that the timing and institutional design of EMU were the result of agenda-setting by non-state actors, interests and strategies beyond the control of the intergovernmental bargaining process. The most influential non-state actor in setting the agenda of EMU was the

European Commission (see for example Sandholtz, 1993; Dyson, 1994, pp. 114–48; Smith and Sandholtz, 1995). Ever since the 1960s, several commissioners and prominent figures in the Commission's administration had argued for monetary union, but it was not until the presidency of Jacques Delors that the Commission openly pursued a strategy to promote and secure EMU. Jacques Delors had considerable experience in the field of monetary policy, as the French finance minister that had managed the u-turn in French monetary policy in the early 1980s. He was also ideologically committed to the goal of monetary union, and advocated this goal at every opportunity. Delors argued that the member states should set up a committee under his leadership to prepare the plan for EMU; he chaired the Delors Committee and presented its proposals to the heads of government; his Commission published the *One Market, One Money* report; and he presented the Commission's institutional strategy for EMU to the IGC negotiating the Maastricht Treaty.

One concrete example of the impact of Delors was his idea that EMU should progress in a series of stages, where economic convergence would be pursued in parallel to the technical and institutional preparations for the launch of a single currency, and where once each stage had been reached it would be politically very difficult to take a step backwards – because of the impact of such a decision on the credibility of the EU as a whole. Most economists argued that this strategy did not make economic sense (see for example Eichengreen, 1993), and few member states supported the idea at its inception. However, through Delors's persistence, this model was institutionalized as the collective strategy for EMU.

The other main non-state actors that played an important role in EMU were the central bank governors of the member states, who shared common strategic interests in the project. EMU would guarantee their independence from political instruction from national finance ministries, and they would each participate in making EU monetary policy in the ECB Governing Council. These actors also shared similar policy ideas about how monetary policy should be managed (see below). Moreover, central bank governors had a monopoly of expertise about numerous technical issues in the transition to EMU: such as how a payments system should be designed and ran. On the one hand, central bankers sought to promote EMU by giving advice to their national governments; on the other hand they were given the opportunity to promote the project because governments chose to delegate particular responsibilities to them. All the central bank governors sat on the Delors Committee, and the Committee of Central Bank Governors proposed the draft statute of the European System of Central Banks, which was incorporated in a Protocol annexed to the Maastricht Treaty without amendment. It was in the interests of governments to secure credible technical advice and to ensure that EMU was supported by the people who would be running EU monetary policy. However, once delegation had been made, governments had little control over the behaviour of the central bankers and the ideas they put forward.

The power of ideas: the neo-liberal policy consensus

Finally, Kathleen McNamara (1998) argues that a key factor in explaining the almost unanimous agreement between the EU governments and the various non-state actors on the goal and design of EMU was the emergence of a 'neo-liberal policy consensus' in Europe by the end of the 1980s. The main reason for this new consensus was that a majority of European governments experienced 'policy failure' in the 1970s, when Keynesian demand-management policies proved inadequate for coping with slow growth, high unemployment and high inflation. At the same time, 'monetarism' emerged as an alternative economic 'paradigm' which was both theoretically coherent and an empirical success. At a theoretical level, among other things, monetarism offered a convincing critique of why there was no inherent trade-off between unemployment and inflation – as was predicted by the Phillips Curve (Friedman, 1968). At an empirical level, monetarism had a powerful and successful example in German economic growth in the 1970s and early 1980s as a result of monetarist policies. Centre-right parties now had a 'big idea' against the Keynesian hegemony of the 1960s and 1970s. As Keynesian policies failed, as monetarist policies were increasingly accepted by mainstream parties and international organizations like the OECD (e.g. McCracken, 1977), and as centre-right parties won elections across Europe in the early and mid-1980s, centre-left parties began to reject their old policies and accept the 'new economic orthodoxy'.

Monetarism also had a particular policy prescription on the issue of exchange rates. Monetarist economists argued that manipulating exchange rates (much like Keynesian demand-management) would only have short-term benefits, and that the long-term impact would be wage and price inflation. As a result, monetarists advocated stable or even fixed exchange rates, and wage flexibility and labour market reforms instead of currency devaluation as the only long-term cure of low productivity.

To explain what this meant for EMU consider the two graphs in Figure 10.3 showing the Keynesian and Monetarist interpretations of the costs and benefits of monetary union (De Grauwe, 1997). In Figure 10.3A, the Keynesian view is that the world is full of rigidities – wages and prices are stable, labour is immobile – so the exchange rate is a powerful tool of macroeconomic management. Consequently, in this interpretation the cost of fixing exchange rates falls slowly as trade integration increases

Figure 10.3   *Monetarist and Keynesian views of monetary union*

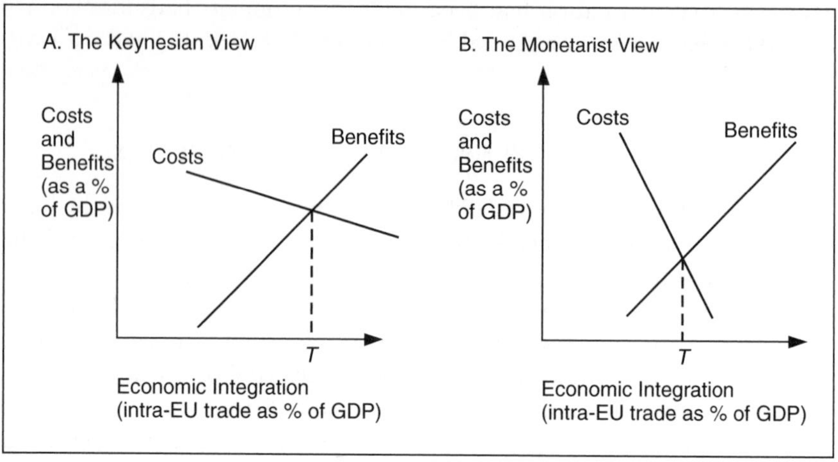

Source: De Grauwe (1997).

(cf. Minford, 1996). In contrast, as Figure 10.3B shows, in the Monetarist view the exchange rate is an ineffective tool, so that the costs of losing it fall rapidly as trade increases. The result is that Monetarists support fixed exchange rates in a monetary union at much lower levels of economic integration than Keynesians (cf. Bofinger, 1994).

These ideas gradually gained force from the end of the 1970s, through the 1980s to the 1990s. As early as 1975, *The Economist* published the 'All Saint's Day Manifesto', which was written by several prominent Monetarist economists, and which publicly called for a revival of the idea of EMU (*The Economist*, 1975). The German government, supported by the Bundesbank, used similar ideas to justify the EMS. In the 1980s, the Commission DG in charge of economic and monetary affairs was full of modified Monetarists who prepared the Commission's strategy in the Delors Committee and wrote the *One Market, One Money* report.

In the 1980s and early 1990s, governments across Europe introduced 'sound money' policies and gave independence to central banks to manage stable exchange rates. And, once this orthodoxy had been accepted, it was a small step to fixing exchange rates and delegating monetary policy to an independent supranational central bank. This made sense on both economic grounds – in terms of increased individual and collective welfare – and political grounds, in terms of limiting macroeconomic policy uncertainty for national decision-makers (Østrup, 1995; Cameron, 1997).

Making monetary and economic policy in EMU

Until now this chapter has focussed on understanding how and why EMU was established. The rest of the chapter looks at a different issue: how monetary and economic policy is made in EMU. Essentially, will the design of EMU produce a stable currency? How will EMU work in the face of a major asymmetric shock? And, how will EMU change the role of the EU in the global economy?

Independence, credibility and reputation of the ECB

There is a natural inflationary bias in the making of monetary policy (Barro and Gordon, 1983). Even if the main goal is price stability, the makers of monetary policy can gain a benefit from 'surprise inflation'. If decision-makers can produce an inflation rate that is higher than was expected by businesses and trade unions – when borrowing money and negotiating wages – there will be a short-term increase in output and employment. Growth and higher employment wins votes. So in the build-up to an election there is an incentive to 'pump-up' the economy by cutting interest rates. Private actors will be aware that governments are supplying this 'surprise inflation', and that the long-term effect will be an increase in interest rates to curb inflation. However, to preempt this strategic behaviour, governments can supply a surprise rate of inflation beyond the wildest expectation of firms. The long-term effect is consistently higher rates of inflation than are optimal for the performance of the economy, and a government policy that is not credible with national or international currency consumers.

The solution is to 'bind the hands' of governments, by providing them with incentives not to pursue these goals. This can be achieved through several mechanisms (cf. Cukierman, Webb and Neyapti, 1993; Grilli, Masciandro and Tabellini, 1991):

- The delegation of monetary policy (setting interest rates) to an independent central bank.
- The central bank can also be responsible for setting inflation and/or money supply targets.
- The goal of price stability can be set out in a constitution rather than simply a legislative act, to avoid alteration of the goal by future electoral majorities.
- The terms of office of the central bank officials can be longer than the terms of office of the political representatives who appoint them (which are usually four or five years).

- Sanctions can be used if the central bank fails to meet the price stability objective (such as automatic dismissal of the president if an inflation target is missed).

Empirical research shows that there is a significant correlation between the level of central bank independence and the average long-term inflation rate: with the most independent banks producing the lowest inflation rates (see for example Cukierman, 1992; Alesina and Summers, 1993).

In EMU, the design of the ECB meets most of these criteria (Kaufmann, 1995). The ECB is solely responsible for implementing monetary policy, without interference from the Council or from national governments; the ECB is also free to decide monetary policy goals, such as inflation or money-supply targets; the goal of price stability is set out in the Treaty, which makes its very difficult for governments to revoke; and the terms of office of the ECB officials are eight years. However, there are few sanctions if the ECB president fails to meet the price stability objective.

However, credibility is not enough to secure an independent and stable monetary policy. A central bank also needs to be legitimate – what economists call 'reputation' (Winkler, 1996). Reputation enables markets and the public to accept monetary policy decisions that might seem unpopular in the short term. Without a history of stable currency and economic growth as a result of its decisions, the markets and the public may be fickle in the face of inflation or recession. Consequently, there is a particular problem for the ECB; as a new institution managing a new currency. Without an established reputation, public opinion in states that suffer asymmetric shocks are likely to turn against the ECB quicker than they would against a national central bank with a history of independence (such as the Bundesbank). Faced with this situation, governments in these states are likely to demand a political direction of monetary policy.

Interest-rate policy of the ECB: accountability versus political bargaining

The decisions of the ECB board are carefully scrutinized: the ECB president presents an annual report to EcoFin and the Monetary Committee of the European Parliament, and the European Parliament committee can request to hear evidence from the ECB President as often as it likes. The European Parliament has consciously modelled the operating procedures of this committee on the US Senate committee hearings of the US Federal Reserve chairman. Also, the European press will carefully watch the weekly meetings of the ECB. The minutes of the meetings are not available to the public. But, as a result of rumours and hearsay, and with the eventual disclosure of debates, the media and academic commentators will be able to work out which members of the ECB Executive Board and Governing Council are eager for lower interest rates (the 'doves') and which are more stubborn (the 'hawks'). And, this will provoke governments to put pressure on their central bank governors if they are seen to be acting against the member states' interests.

Although governments cannot force the ECB to pursue a particular monetary policy, they can influence the ECB through the appointments process. When the term of office of a national central bank governor ends (after five years), a government may appoint someone who is more likely to represent their national public's views in the ECB Governing Council. And, with staggered terms of office of the ECB Executive Board, the Council may collectively decide to appoint inflation-adverse persons to the ECB board and remove hard-nosed Monetarists.

Political scrutiny of ECB decisions is unlikely to conflict with the policy of the ECB if the national economic cycles are synchronized. In these circumstances, the ECB Governing Council will have little difficulty agreeing a 'one-size-fits-all' interest rate. But, if there is an asymmetric shock, when some national economies are growing while others are declining, a common ECB position will be more problematic. In this situation, the six members of the Executive Board are likely to propose an interest rate that is the 'ideal rate' for the EMU economy as a whole (or slightly above this rate, to maintain a restrictive reputation). However, under pressure from national publics and governments, the central bank governors from the economies in recession will want a lower interest rate, while those with high growth rates will want a higher interest rate. This was often the case in the early years of the US Federal Reserve, where state central banks sought different monetary policies from the Federal Reserve chairman (Eichengreen, 1991). The Treaty specifies that decisions of the ECB Governing Council are taken by a simple majority (eight out of the 17 members). With this voting rule the Governing Council is likely to agree on the interest-rate preference of the 'median' member of the Governing Council, as this member will be pivotal in turning the preferences either side of him/her into a winning majority.

In other words, there is an inherent tension between accountability and independence. Increased transparency and accountability will enable the ECB to establish legitimacy and reputation, but it is also likely to provoke a politicization of ECB decisions and internal ECB bargaining.

Labour mobility and labour-market flexibility

The pressures for politicization will depend on how the European economy and national governments behave in the face of a major asymmetric shock. According to the OCA theory, a monetary union should be able to adapt either through labour movement, from states in recession to states in high growth, or through labour-market flexibility, with a reduction of wage and labour costs in states in recession to attract capital investment.

On the issue of *labour mobility*, there is far less labour movement across borders in the EU than in the United States (see Chapter 11). In certain sectors, such as the building industry, the service sector and the informal economy, migrant workers do follow capital investments – such as Irish, British and Portuguese workers employed in the fast-growing building sector in Berlin and the former eastern Germany (Eichengreen, 1993b). However, it is hard to imagine a situation in Europe similar to that in the USA in the 1930s and 1940s, when there was a mass labour movement of unemployed and underemployed in the southern states to the north-east states and the fast-growing car industry, based around Detroit.

Nevertheless, there is less labour mobility within existing European nation-states than in the United States. Political upheaval is avoided because European states have been able to manage internal demand and supply shocks through mechanisms other than labour movement: such as wage reductions in low-demand regions and fiscal transfers from high-demand to low-demand regions (as in the Germany following unification in 1990) (Eichengreen, 1993a).

Also, the issue of labour mobility is different for different states in the EU. For example, the success of the Irish economy in the 1990s was attributed to its open labour market, with high levels of both immigration and emigration in both low and high-wage jobs – more like a 'regional economy' in the USA than a national economy in Europe (Krugman, 1997). Consequently, although Ireland is a peripheral economy in EMU, and was already out of synch with the core economies at the start of EMU, it is likely to be able to adapt to an asymmetric shock. However, the situation is more problematic in Portugal. It too is a peripheral economy and was growing faster than the core economies when EMU was launched. But, unlike Ireland, Portugal has high unemployment amongst skilled workers (because they have not tended to emigrate) and a shortage of low-skilled workers (because low-skilled workers have not immigrated from elsewhere in the EU) (Munchau, 1998; Torres, 1998).

In addition, on the subject of *wage flexibility*, Europe is unlikely to be able to use labour market flexibility to tackle an asymmetric shock. As Table 10.3 shows, there is considerable variation in the level of labour costs in the EMU states: with the periphery economies much cheaper than the core economies. However, the table also shows that these labour costs are generally a reflection of productivity rates rather than of demand and supply shocks. For example, Spain has a high level of unemployment despite the fact that its labour costs are relatively low. To resolve this

Table 10.3 *Productivity, labour costs and unemployment in the EMU-11, 1997*

	Productivity (as a % of the west German rate)	Labour costs (as a % of the west German rate)	Unemployment (%)
Austria	90.9	89.5	4.4
Belgium	97.6	107.6	9.2
Finland	81.4	93.8	14.0
France	95.3	95.6	12.4
Germany	92.9	95.3	9.7
West	100.0	100.0	8.3
East	60.4	74.4	15.7
Ireland	69.5	71.8	10.2
Italy	85.3	79.9	12.1
Netherlands	85.4	94.4	5.2
Portugal	34.5	37.4	6.8
Spain	62.0	66.9	20.8

Source: Kiel Institute of World Economics, reported in Norman (1998).

situation in EMU, either Spanish productivity would need to increase or labour costs would need to be reduced relative to the European average.

Ultimately, the issue of labour market flexibility comes down to political commitment to EMU by governments and publics. If there is a high level of public support for EMU, governments will be able to introduce labour market reforms, and trade unions will be able to allow flexible wage rates to be negotiated. As we saw in Chapter 5, public support for the EU is high in Portugal, Ireland, Spain and Italy. Consequently, the real problem will come if an asymmetric shock hits either France or Germany, where public support for the EU is relatively soft, and where the economies are large enough to have a major impact on the rest of the EMU economy. If this happens, there will be considerable pressure on the ECB to pursue a more inflationary policy by cutting interest rates.

Fiscal policies: national deficits, fiscal federalism and tax harmonization

Political pressures on the ECB will also result from constraints on national fiscal policies in EMU. A negative demand shock in one state will increase a government's budget deficit, as there will be a reduction in tax revenues and an increase in unemployment and social security expenditure. However, experience of the 1970s and 1980s suggests that large budget deficits lead to unsustainable long-term debts, as was the case in Italy, Belgium and Greece. And, within EMU, there is the possibility that a government can 'free ride' on the sound monetary policies of other states, by running a high public deficit with only a moderate threat to the value of the common currency, and hence to the value of its bonds (Horstmann and Schnieder, 1994).

The convergence criteria were consequently designed to ensure that budget deficits were minimized before entering EMU. And to give credibility to these constraints once EMU began, the Treaty included provisions to combat 'excessive deficits' and the Growth and Stability Pact was agreed. The main elements of the Pact are:

- governments will aim to achieve a balanced budget;
- countries with a budget deficit exceeding 3 per cent of GDP will be fined up to 0.5 per cent of GDP;
- these fines will not be applied if there are exceptional circumstances, such as a natural disaster or a decline in GDP of more than 2 per cent in one year; and
- in cases where the drop in GDP is between 0.75 per cent and 2 per cent, the application of the fine will be decided by EcoFin (by a qualified majority).

These rules will mean that expansion of the welfare state will only be able to be financed through raising revenue through taxation. However, this presents a particular problem in the event of an asymmetric shock, where, instead of running a budget deficit, governments will have to find ways to cut other expenditure programmes or to raise taxes (Buiter, Corsetti and Roubini 1993; Eichengreen and Von Hagen, 1996). Raising taxes, however, will increase production and wage costs, and consequently reduce the competitiveness of the economy.

This is likely to lead to political demands for more inter-state fiscal transfers in the EU (Sala-i-Martin and Sachs, 1991; Eichengreen 1994). With an EU budget of only 1.27 per cent of EU GDP, the redistributive capacity of the EU is small (see Chapter 9), and in the 1970s it was widely argued (for example in the McDougall Report for the Commission) that EMU would not be possible under the terms of the Werner Report without a significant increase in the EU budget (McDougall, 1977). Also, in most currency unions asymmetric shocks have been tackled with a greater centralization of budgets, as in the USA after the New Deal and at the domestic level in Europe. In the event of a demand-shock in EMU, the member states in recession are likely to demand an increase in expenditure under the EU's structural funds, and a gearing of this expenditure to short-term EMU-related shocks. However, such a decision would have to be taken by unanimity, and the net contributor member states may not wish to see the EU budget increased. Nevertheless, if there is a threat that EMU could collapse as a result of the political implications of downward pressure on a particular member state's welfare expenditure, the publics in the net contributor states may agree to pay more into the EU budget to preserve a stable single currency.

Alternatively, the states in recession could demand a harmonization of tax rates (Radaelli, 1996). With varying rates of tax on capital and labour between the EMU states, governments could choose to cut taxes to attract investment, and this would put pressure on other governments to do the some. The effect would be a collective reduction in tax revenues which, as a result of the Growth and Stability Pact, would have to be met with a similar reduction in welfare expenditure. Again, in the event of an asymmetric shock the recession-hit states are likely to demand that other states maintain high tax rates to enable them to raise taxes to meet their own budget short-falls. The Treaty already has provisions for the harmonization of tax rates.

In December 1997, on the eve of the launch of EMU, the new German Socialist government raised the issue of tax harmonization and policies to prevent 'tax competition'. On the initiative of Oskar Lafontaine, the German finance minister, the issue was debated at the Vienna European Council, and the EU heads of government concluded that:

> The European Council . . . emphasises the need to combat harmful tax competition. Co-operation in the tax policy area is not aiming at uniform tax rates and is not inconsistent with fair tax competition but is called for to reduce the continuing distortions in the single market, to prevent excessive losses of tax revenue or to get tax structures to develop in a more employment-friendly way.

As with budgetary reforms, tax harmonization requires unanimity in the Council to be passed. However, if the EMU governments are determined to harmonize corporate tax rates they may try to invoke the 'flexible integration' provisions in the Amsterdam Treaty, which allow certain member states to unilaterally agree to new policy instruments.

The external impact of EMU

Finally, the Euro is likely to challenge the US Dollar as the dominant global reserve currency. As Table 10.4 shows, the size of the EU economy is comparable to that of the USA in terms of share of world GDP and global trade. However, without a single currency in Europe, the US Dollar is used far more than all the European currencies put together in world trade transactions, for managing world debt and in global currency reserve holdings and transactions.

Table 10.4 The Euro in the global economy

| | Economic size | | World trade, 1992 (%) | Use of currencies | | | |
	Share in world GDP, 1996 (%)	Share in world exports, excl. intra-EU, 1996 (%)		World debt securities, 1996 (%)	Developing country debt, 1996 (%)	Foreign exchange reserves, 1995 (%)	Foreign exchange transactions, 1995 (%)
EU15	20.4	14.7	31.0	34.5	15.8	25.8	35.0
US	20.7	15.2	48.0	37.2	50.2	56.4	41.5
Japan	8.0	6.1	5.0	17.0	18.1	7.1	12.0

Source: International Monetary Fund, reported in Wolf (1998).

With the newness of the ECB compared to the reputation and stability of the US Federal Reserve, it may take some time before non-European companies and governments choose to deal in the Euro rather than the Dollar. However, the emergence of the Euro as a major world currency may be faster than expected (Kenen, 1995, pp. 108–23; Portes and Rey, 1998). If the Euro is more stable than the Dollar, it will be attractive as a store of value, and furthermore, the emergence of the Euro will make European financial markets more liquid, which will make the Euro cheaper to hold in reserve than any current European currency. And, for political reasons, some developing countries may prefer to hold their debts in a European currency rather than in US Dollars, and the Euro will give them the first opportunity to do so without any significant additional transactions costs.

This change in the global currency balance will have political ramifications for the EU, both internal and externally. On the internal side, the Euro-zone, like the USA, will be less open to the world economy than the European national economies were before EMU. As a result, a devaluation of the Euro versus the Dollar will not have a large inflationary effect on the European economy. Several European governments and multinational European firms who export outside Europe may see this as an attractive option, and such a decision will be up to EcoFin rather than the ECB.

On the external side, the Euro will enable the USA and Europe to cooperate more closely in managing the global economy (see Chapter 12). For example, with the two dominant global reserve currencies, the USA and the EU will be more able to agree common strategies to manage Third World debt. And, on a more pertinent issue for the politics of monetary union within the EU, in the face of global recession, the US Federal Reserve and the European Central Bank could coordinate a joint reduction in interest rates to boost global economic growth.

Conclusion: political commitment and political flexibility

With an independent central bank pursuing the primary goal of price stability, and with the transaction-costs benefits and potential growth impact of a single currency, the Euro is likely to be a stable currency with a favourable interest rate. However, there is significant economic divergence in the 11 member states in EMU. The real test will be how this divergence is managed in EMU, especially in the face of a major asymmetric demand shock or a European-wide recession.

Labour mobility in the EU is low and there is insufficient wage flexibility. As a result, the 11 EMU states do not constitute an 'Optimal Currency Area'. However, according to the strict interpretation of the

OCA, neither the United States nor most domestic economies in Europe are OCAs. In a world of global trade and global financial markets, the benefits of an independent exchange rate, and hence the costs of joining a monetary union, are lower than the original theory suggests. Moreover, other policy tools can be used to overcome asymmetric shocks. Governments can introduce labour market reforms to enable wage and price flexibility in the single currency area, or the EU budget can be increased to allow for more fiscal transfers in the instance of a demand shock.

However, these policies are not automatic; they depend on the level of political commitment to EMU by governments and publics. National governments must be willing to abide by the fiscal rules, to reform their labour markets, not to interfere in ECB decisions, and to agree to supranational fiscal transfers when necessary. Publics must support structural reforms, be prepared to negotiate flexible wage rates, and be willing to cross borders to take up jobs.

Nevertheless, in the case of a major economic recession in Europe, and if the political costs of tight monetary policy are too high for governments and publics to bear, the system has several 'safety valves'. First, the ECB is not immune from outside pressure. Without an established reputation, the ECB will have to secure legitimacy in the eyes of the European public. The ECB will also be constrained through the transparency of its internal decisions and through the appointments procedures for selecting the ECB board and the national central bank governors.

Second, EcoFin and the Euro-11 committee have considerable economic policy tools at their disposal. Unlike many federal governments in currency unions, the Council has the power to overhaul the EU budget, to allow derogations from restrictive fiscal rules (even to abolish the Growth and Stability Pact), to harmonize taxation rates, and to devalue the Euro in the global economy.

Chapter 11

Citizen Freedom and Security Policies

Theories of citizenship and the state
Freedom and security policies of the EU
Explaining EU freedom and security policies
Conclusion: skeleton of a pan-European state

A main aim of the modern state is to grant and protect citizens' rights and freedoms. In a similar way, the Amsterdam Treaty commits the EU to 'maintain and develop an area of freedom, security and justice'. This chapter seeks to analyse and explain how far the EU has been able to establish European-wide citizenship rights, yet protect existing rights and freedoms as the borders between the member states are being removed. To help in this task we shall first look at general theories of the relationship between citizenship and the state.

Theories of citizenship and the state

In liberal democracies, citizens are entitled to a variety of rights and freedoms. These fall into four main categories (cf. Berlin, 1969; Rawls, 1971; Walzer, 1983):

- *Civil rights* – such as the freedom of movement, the right to privacy, the freedom of religion, and the freedom from torture.
- *Political rights* – such as the right to association, the freedom of speech, the right to vote in elections, and the right to stand as a candidate and be elected.
- *Economic rights* – such as the right to private property, the freedom to work, the right to trade, and the right to provide or receive services.
- *Social rights* – such as the right to equality (of opportunity and/or of outcomes), the right to education and health care, and the right of employment.

The traditional 'liberal' (or enlightenment) view is that these rights and freedoms are inextricably linked to the modern nation-state. For example, according to Tilly (1990), European states developed through two separate 'trajectories' (cf. Moore, 1967): either they emerged to protect the economic rights and interests of the bourgeoisie, or they emerged to promote and protect the rights of the monarchy, the landed aristocracy and the administrative elites. In both trajectories, then, citizenship rights were initially the preserve of privileged classes. Moreover, these rights were guaranteed and protected through a 'monopoly of the legitimate use of physical force' of the state (Weber, 1946 [1919], p. 78). Similarly, the expansion of citizenship went hand-in-hand with the expansion of state powers. Modern constitutions, courts and police forces and border controls emerged in the nineteenth century in response to middle-class demands for the protection of private property against the state, criminal activity and immigration.

In the same vein, the European nation is traditionally viewed as a vehicle for the establishment of political and social rights (Smith, 1991). First, democracy cannot exist without nationhood: a single political 'will' (public opinion) cannot be formed without a single national language and mass media, and majority rule is not legitimate without a single national culture (see Chapter 6). Second, 'social citizenship' requires cross-class 'social solidarity' (Marshall, 1950), with a common national destiny and the ruling class willing to allow economic redistribution and grant social rights to the working class. As a result, the welfare state in most of Europe and in America only developed once 'the nation' had been established as the dominant focus of political identification (Flora and Heidenheimer, 1981). Consequently, this traditional connection between the nation-state and citizenship suggests that 'transnational citizenship' in the EU – which is neither a state nor a nation – is impossible (Aaron, 1974; cf. Meehan, 1993). However, this is not the end of the story.

At a theoretical level, the connection between the nation-state and citizenship is a particular geographical and historical ideal type. First, the classic, homogenous nation-state only developed in a few states in western Europe (such as Britain, France and Spain), and the fully democratic welfare state only emerged in the mid-twentieth century (Birnbaum and Badie, 1979). However, citizenship rights existed in non-state and non-national settings well before this period. For example, in city-state Europe, economic rights, such as the right to trade, were granted to non-residents well before the nation-state was established; and in multiethnic polities, such as Belgium and Switzerland, redistributive welfare states were founded without strong sociocultural solidarity bonds.

Second, on the issue of democracy and democratic political and civil rights, it is not clear which came first: the nation-state or democracy. The traditional view holds that democracy was only founded after a national *ethnos* and a political state had been established. However, in most European systems and in the United States, the practice of democracy preceded the nation-state. In other words, national identity and the institutions of the nation-state were products of the development of universal democratic citizenship rights, rather than vice versa (see for example Rokkan, 1973; Skowronek, 1982).

At an empirical level, the reality of citizen rights today is very different from the experience of the mid-nineteenth century and even the immediate postwar period. The growth of political and economic migration in the late 1980s and throughout the 1990s has forced western nation-states to 'reconfigure' their traditional citizen policies (Brubaker, 1992; Habermas, 1992; Hollifield, 1992; Favell, 1997a). For example, as a result of global free trade and capital flows, economic rights have been extended to non-residents and residents who are not nationals, such as 'guest workers'. Also, the boundary of political rights is increasingly blurred with the emerging practice of 'dual nationality' and the extension of voting rights to first and even second-generation 'ex-patriots'. Finally, western societies are no longer homogenous 'nations': successive waves of immigration have produced 'multicultural' polities, which have forced states to develop new definitions of citizenship and new social and political rights, such as racial equality and minority representation (Kymlicka, 1995).

In other words, there is a tension in citizenship politics. On the one hand, citizenship requires the institutions of a state to guarantee positive freedoms (through courts) and to secure and protect negative freedoms (through police and security forces). For example, markets, including the European single market, cannot exist without the establishment and protection of property rights. On the other hand, as Soysal (1994, pp. 163–4) argues, in the world of global capitalism, global labour movements and multiethnic societies:

> the classical formal order of the nation-state and its membership is not in place. The state is no longer an autonomous and independent organization closed over a nationally defined population . . . Rights, participation, and representation in the polity, are increasingly matters beyond the vocabulary of national citizenship.

This tension is central to the politics of citizenship in the EU: by establishing 'transnational citizenship' rights, the EU undermines the traditional nation-state; but to define and secure transnational citizenship, new state powers and security mechanisms are being reinvented at the European level (Bauböck, 1994; Martiniello, 1995).

Freedom and security policies of the EU

The policies of the EU relating to citizen rights and internal security fall into four main areas:

- *the free movement of persons* between the EU member states, from work and residency rights to the removal of border controls between the member states;
- *citizenship rights* for EU nationals in other member states, such as equal opportunities, political and civil rights;
- *immigration policies*, through cooperation on refugees and asylum policies and common policies towards other 'third-country nationals'; and
- *police and judicial cooperation*, to combat drug-trafficking, terrorist activities, cross-border crime, and illegal immigration.

The first two areas infer rights on citizens of the EU member states in other EU member states. In contrast, the second two areas relate to how the member states and the EU institutions decide who has access to national and EU citizenship rights, and how these rights should be guaranteed and protected.

Free movement of persons: towards open borders

The Treaty of Rome established the 'free movement of persons' as a fundamental objective of the European Economic Community, but this provision originally applied only to cross-border economic activity. A national of one EU member state has the right to seek work, to reside, and to provide or receive a service in another member state, and secondary legislation has extended entry and residency rights to the 'economically independent' – people who have sufficient funds and resources not to be a burden on the recipient state, such as students, company employees and the self-employed. However, there are two limitations on these rights. First, in the late 1960s the ECJ confirmed that these rights do not apply to 'third country nationals', even if they are married to EU citizens. Second, the Treaty of Rome allowed any member state to deny entry by another EU national if they pose a potential threat to national security, public health or public policy. The member states consequently maintained their border controls, arguing that this was essential to ensure that free movement only applied to EU nationals involved in economic activities, and so that national security could be protected.

However, the removal of 'physical barriers' to the free movement of goods and persons became a central part of the single market programme. The 1985 Commission White Paper on *Completing the Internal Market* suggested that this implied the complete elimination of internal frontier controls and borders by 31 December 1992 (see Chapter 8). The Council adopted several measures to remove controls on the free movement of goods by this date. However, little progress was made on the removal of controls on the free movement of persons. Most member states were reluctant to remove internal borders without harmonized rules on the crossing of the external boders of the EU – such as visa requirements and asylum policies. And, due to domestic sensitivities and the requirement of unanimity, these were not agreed by 1992 (see section on immigration policies, below).

In the meantime, in 1985 France, Germany and three Benelux states signed the Schengen Accord. This was an intergovernmental agreement, formally outside the EU Treaty, for the complete elimination of border controls between the signatory states. An Implementation Convention was subsequently adopted in 1990. Italy, Spain, Portugal and Greece signed the Accord in 1992, and the members of the Nordic passport union – Denmark, Sweden, Finland and Norway (although not in the EU) – joined in 1995. On 26 March 1995, the Implementation Convention entered into force with only France refusing to remove all border controls, on the grounds that Belgium and the Netherlands had not undertaken policies to prevent drug-trafficking.

Nevertheless, in signing the Amsterdam Treaty in June 1997, the member states agreed to two major changes in the area of freedom of movement of persons. First, the Amsterdam Treaty introduced a new Title (IV) in the EC section of the EU Treaty on the free movement of persons. Article 62(1) of the EC Treaty consequently commits the Council to remove 'controls on persons, be they citizens of the Union or nationals of third countries, crossing internal borders' within five years of entry into force of the Amsterdam Treaty. In this five-year period, policies will be adopted through the consultation procedure (see Chapter 3), but with unanimity in the Council. If this goal is not achieved by the five-year deadline, the Council shall decide (by unanimity) whether legislation in this area can be passed using the codecision procedure with qualified-majority voting in the Council (see Chapter 3). Nevertheless, the Commission was granted a right of initiative (shared with the member states) for the first time, and legislation adopted under this Title is immediately binding on the member states.

Second, through a Protocol attached to the EU Treaty, the Amsterdam Treaty incorporated the 3000 pages of the Schengen *acquis* into the legal framework of the EU. The Council, acting by unanimity, became the main executive body under the Schengen rules, and the Schengen secretariat became part of the Council's general secretariat. The ECJ was granted jurisdiction over some decisions. But, as with the Schengen Accord, decision-making in this area remains highly secretive. The EP has no formal right of consultation, and the Schengen Protocol explicitly excludes the ECJ from exercising jurisdiction on matters of law and order or internal security arising from the Schengen Convention.

In addition, these provisions do not apply to all member states. Through a series of Protocols attached to the Amsterdam Treaty, the United Kingdom, Ireland and Denmark have negotiated 'opt-outs'. First, the United Kingdom and Ireland chose to be excluded from all aspects of the new Title IV and from the Schengen *acquis*. But, these states can choose to 'opt in' to individual proposals on an *ad hoc* basis. And in a separate provision of the Treaty, Ireland declared that it intends to participate as fully as possible while remaining in the passport union with the United Kingdom. Denmark, on the other hand, has opted out from Title IV with no possibility of opting in to individual proposals. Nonetheless, Denmark is a member of Schengen (but reserves the right to opt out on any new policy proposal), and has decided to participate in the provisions on common visa policies (see below). The result is a multispeed approach to the removal of internal borders, with the potential for complex legal arguments over which aspects of internal border and external frontier policies apply in the three 'laggard' states.

Citizenship: from economic to political rights

In addition to the freedom of movement, the Treaty of Rome established other 'economic rights' for citizens of the EU member states. Through the rules on state aids, the common market and competition policy, the Treaty placed limits on how far the state can intervene in private economic interaction. The Treaty also outlawed economic discrimination (such as in the granting of contracts and in pay and conditions) on the grounds of nationality and gender. Everson (1995) consequently argues that in combination with the establishment of the 'direct effect' of EU law (see Chapter 4), these provisions turned EU nationals into 'market citizens', not only in other member states of the EU, but also in their own states.

However, individual attachment to the EU institutions cannot be guaranteed through purely economic rights. In 1974, the Paris Summit first discussed the idea of adding political and civil rights to these economic rights. Then, in the preparation of the Single European Act in 1984, the Adonnino Report argued that a 'People's Europe' – such as cultural, educational and identity policies – should be pursued in parallel to the completion of the single market. Finally, in 1990, at the Rome European Council that launched the Intergovernmental Conference (IGC) that negotiated the Maastricht Treaty, the Spanish prime minister, Felipé

González, secured a commitment from the other EU heads of government that the EU Treaty should establish 'EU citizenship'.

As a result, Part Two of the EU Treaty defines 'Citizenship of the Union' as follows:

- EU citizens are nationals of the EU member states ('Citizenship of the Union shall complement not replace national citizenship');
- EU citizens have the right to reside freely anywhere in the EU;
- EU citizens have the right to vote or stand as a candidate in local and EP elections wherever they reside in the EU;
- EU citizens in third-countries have the right to consular protection by the embassy of any EU member state; and
- EU citizens have the right to petition the EP, to complain to the EU Ombudsman, and to write to any EU institution in any of the official languages of the EU.

Despite the symbolic value of declaring 'EU citizenship', these provisions are limited. First, the provisions do not mean that all EU citizens have the same rights in every member state: each member state has their own set of civil, economic, political and social rights which are selectively granted to non-nationals from other EU member states. For example, EU nationals residing in another state cannot vote in national elections, and an ethnic-minority EU citizen who resides in another member state does not have the same racial equality rights as minorities who are nationals of that member state. The Amsterdam Treaty introduced a general non-discrimination clause in the EU Treaty (article 12 [ex 6a]), on combating 'discrimination based on sex, racial or ethnic origin, religion or belief, disability, age or sexual orientation'. However, this article does not have direct effect, as it requires the Council (acting by unanimity) to apply this article through secondary legislation.

Second, EU citizenship rights only apply to EU nationals. An implication of this is that the member states retain the right to decide who is an EU citizen, and hence who has access to the economic and political rights granted under the EU Treaty. Moreover, by restricting the rights to EU nationals, millions of legal residents in the territories of the EU (who are not third-country nationals) are specifically excluded from receiving these rights. A third-country national who has the right to reside and work in one member state does not have these same rights in any member state of the EU.

Third, the EU citizenship provisions do not set out a charter of 'fundamental rights' for EU nationals or residents in the EU (O'Leary, 1995, pp. 303–14). The EU does not have a 'bill of rights'. As a result, the basic human rights set out in the constitutional provisions of the EU member states, and through the signature of the European Convention on Human Rights (ECHR) by all the EU member states, do not apply to residents who are nationals of other member states. In the IGC that negotiated the Amsterdam Treaty, several member states proposed that the EU sign the ECHR using article 235. However, the ECJ ruled (opinion 2/94) that this would be unconstitutional.

As a result, EU citizenship is not the same as national citizenship, in that it does not establish full and equal economic, political, civil and social rights for all individuals regardless of where they reside in the EU. Nevertheless, it is the first step towards a genuine 'post-national citizenship' in Europe: where the right to reside, seek work, receive welfare benefits, pursue educational opportunities, participate in society and politics, and have one's identity and culture protected, is no longer the independent preserve of the European nation-states but is the subject of collective agreement between the member states and policy-making by the supranational EU institutions (Shaw, 1997; Weiler, 1997c; Wiener, 1997).

Immigration policies: third-country nationals and refugees

Without internal borders, any person granted entry or citizenship in one member state can move freely within the territory of the EU. Consequently, the goal of removing physical barriers on the movement of persons in the single market forced the member states to address the issue of the movement of persons across the external borders of the EU. In 1986, the EU governments established the *Ad hoc* Working Group on Immigration (AWGI), which was an intergovernmental body of officials from interior ministries outside the EU institutional structure. Through this informal intergovernmental cooperation, the EU governments agreed two conventions in the area of immigration policy: the Dublin Convention on Asylum, in 1990; and the External Frontiers Convention, in 1991.

The Dublin Convention aims to prevent multiple asylum applications. This would be achieved through several provisions: the mutual recognition of each states' asylum regulations, asylum applications can only be processed by the member state in which the asylum-seeker first arrives in the EU, and other member states are not obliged to process an application once it has been filed in another member state. The External Frontiers Convention provides for the mutual recognition of visas for non-EU nationals, and abolishes the need for third-country nationals who are legal residents in one member state to obtain a visa to travel to another EU state for a period of less than three months. However, these conventions had to be transposed into national legislation in all EU member states before they entered into force. Several member states refused to ratify the Dublin Convention, and Britain and Spain refused to sign the External Frontiers Convention due to an ongoing disagreement over Gibraltar.

Nevertheless, the Maastricht Treaty brought the work of the AWGI into the framework of the EU, in the provisions for cooperation in the fields of justice and home affairs (JHA) – the 'third pillar' of the EU. The JHA established asylum policy, crossing of external frontiers, immigration policy, and policy towards third-country nationals as areas of 'common interest' of the member states. However, this development was more an institutionalization of the existing intergovernmental provisions than a new 'supranational' competence: the AWGI simply became a sub-committee of the Council committee responsible for JHA issues (the K.4 committee); decision-making remained by unanimity; the Commission still had no right of initiative; and there was no role for the EP or the ECJ. Also, the Maastricht Treaty lumped together immigration policies and police and judicial cooperation, which ensured that these issues continued to be addressed as 'security' questions rather than as issues of citizens' rights and freedoms.

Under the JHA provisions, justice and home affairs ministers began to meet on a more regular basis and to adopt more common policies. However, these policies tended to be through non-binding resolutions and recommendations rather than through directly-effective joint actions or decisions (Guild and Niessen, 1996); for example, in June 1993 the Council adopted a recommendation on the harmonization of national policies on family reunification. The few joint actions of note have covered easing travel restrictions on third-country nationals studying in the EU, a system of common transit visas in all member states, a uniform format for residence permits, and burden sharing with regard to the admission and residence of refugees. However, several member states refuse to be bound by joint actions. Also, decisions tended to be reserved for information-exchange issues; for example, a decision in November 1992 set up two clearing-houses for data exchange on asylum rules, asylum applications and immigration developments – the Centre for Information, Discussion and Exchange on Asylum (CIREA), and the Centre for Information, Discussion and Exchange on the Crossing of External Borders and Immigration (CIREFI).

Nevertheless, the Amsterdam Treaty brought immigration and asylum issues into the EC section of the EU Treaty, and in so doing combined them with the provisions for the removal of internal borders and separated them from the provisions on police and judicial cooperation on criminal matters. The new Title (IV) commits the Council to adopt common policies in the following areas:

- standards and procedures for checks on persons crossing the EU's external borders;
- rules on visas for stays longer than three months, including a single list of countries whose citizens require visas to visit the EU;
- conditions under which third-country nationals shall have freedom to travel in the EU for up to three months;
- standards and procedures for granting and withdrawing asylum and refugee status, including minimum standards for the reception of asylum seekers and refugees;
- minimum standards for the temporary protection of displaced persons (*de facto* refugees rather than asylum-seekers);
- measures on immigration policy, including common conditions of entry and residence and common rules on illegal immigration and repatriation; and
- measures defining the rights and conditions under which third-country nationals can work and reside anywhere in the EU.

Policies are still adopted through intergovernmental procedures, as the Council must agree by unanimity, and any government can initiate a policy proposal. However, the Commission shares the right of initiative with the Council, and the Council can adopt legally-binding and directly-effective directives or regulations. Decision-making is also more transparent, as the EP must be consulted. The ECJ has jurisdiction over these areas, but only if all national legal remedies have been exhausted (which places a financial burden on individuals who wish to pursue cases under these provisions at the European level). And, in most areas there is a five-year deadline, after which the Council shall decide by unanimity whether policies can be adopted by qualified-majority voting and the codecision procedure. Finally, if one or more member states faces a migration emergency, the Council can adopt temporary immigration and refugee polices through qualified-majority voting.

Police and judicial cooperation: fighting 'drugs and thugs'

In 1975, the European Council set up a forum for co-operation between interior ministries and police agencies to combat terrorism. This new intergovernmental group, the 'Trevi' group (cryptically named after its first chairman, A.R. Fonteijn, and the fountain in Rome, where it first met), was not formally part of the EU institutions. Its main activities involved information exchange about terrorist activities, about the security aspects of air traffic systems, nuclear plants and other vulnerable targets, and cooperation in the development of tactics and equipment to fight terrorism. In the 1980s, the mandate of Trevi was widened to include cooperation to fight football hooliganism and serious international organized crime, such as drug-trafficking, arms-trafficking and bank robbery, and in 1988 the 'Trevi 1992' project was launched to study the consequences of the single market programme on cross-border security issues.

With the creation of the third pillar, the Maastricht Treaty brought the Trevi framework formally into the EU structure, in the justice and home affairs provisions. In addition to immigration and asylum issues, the third pillar covered combating drug addiction, international fraud, judicial cooperation on civil matters, judicial cooperation on criminal matters, customs cooperation, police cooperation to prevent terrorism, drug-trafficking and other forms of serious international crime, and the creation of the European Police Office (EUROPOL). As with immigration and asylum issues, this was an institutionalization of the existing intergovernmental practices. The committees around the Trevi ministers meetings (such as the *Ad hoc* Group on Organized Crime) simply became working groups of COREPER, under the K.4 committee. Also, decision-making remained by unanimity, and the Commission, the EP and the ECJ remained excluded.

As with immigration policies, progress on police and security was slow and through non-binding instruments. Justice and home affairs ministers adopted action plans to fight drug addiction and organized crime, and on drug addiction this led to joint actions on approximating laws and practices to combat drug addiction, to prevent drug-trafficking, and to promote information exchange. On organized crime, however, ministers were only able to adopt one joint action, for peer evaluation by the member states of the implementation of international commitments to combat organised crime. Joint actions were also agreed on trafficking in human beings and the exploitation of children, and on the control of large groups of people who pose a threat to law and order (in other words, football hooligans). Most significantly, in December 1991 the Council passed the EUROPOL Convention, but this was not signed by all member states until July 1995, and due to problems in the ratification of the Convention, EUROPOL did not finally come into operation (in The Hague) until late 1998.

Nevertheless, unlike immigration and asylum policies, the Amsterdam Treaty did not move police and judicial cooperation policies to the first pillar; instead, these policies were left in a revamped third pillar. Under these provisions, these member states are committed to adopting common policies in the following areas:

- the prevention, detection and investigation of criminal offences;
- the collection, storage, processing, analysis and exchange of information on criminal offences, subject to the appropriate protection of personal data;

- enabling EUROPOL to support cross-border investigations, to undertake investigations in specific cases, and to establish a data-base on cross-border crime;
- facilitating extradition between the member states;
- preventing conflicts of jurisdiction between the member states; and
- the approximation of rules on criminal matters.

Council decision-making is still by unanimity, but the Commission shares the right of policy initiation with the Council, and the EP must also be consulted before the Council can act. The joint action was replaced by two new legal instruments: decisions, and framework decisions. Decisions are similar to regulations in the EC pillar, and framework decisions are similar to directives, in that they apply to the approximation of laws.

Moreover, and perhaps most significantly, the ECJ has limited jurisdiction. The ECJ cannot review the validity of acts undertaken by national police and administrative agencies in carrying out the objectives of the new third pillar. However, the ECJ has the power of judicial review over decisions and framework decisions, and can also rule on a dispute between member states regarding interpretation of acts under the third pillar. Finally, and most contentiously, member states can voluntarily accept the jurisdiction of the ECJ to make preliminary rulings. However, this means that once a member state has accepted an ECJ jurisdiction, and referred an issue to the Court, the subsequent ruling of the ECJ is binding on all courts in all EU member states. It is unlikely that most EU governments were aware of this implication at the time of singing the Amsterdam Treaty.

Explaining EU freedom and security policies

Following from the above discussion there are several issues in the development of EU freedom and security policies that need to be explained:

- why are policies to promote the free movement of persons less advanced than policies to promote the free movement of goods, services and capital;
- why (until the Amsterdam Treaty) were immigration and asylum policies dealt with under the same decision-making mechanisms as police and judicial cooperation; and
- why in the Amsterdam Treaty was a major integrationist step taken in this area – with a new Title in the EC section of the Treaty, with significant supranational elements?

Unlike most of the other areas of EU policy discussed in this book, political scientists have come late to this policy area. Instead, discussion and analysis of free movement and internal security issues has been dominated by legal scholars, public policy analysts, and policy practitioners in national administrations in and around the EU institutions (see for example Monar and Morgan, 1994; Bieber and Monar, 1995). Nevertheless, this literature has produced four main types of explanations of the development of EU citizen and security policies: (1) exogenous changes in European and global society; (2) strategic behaviour of EU governments; (3) strategic behaviour of administrative elites; and (4) interests and arguments of supranational actors.

Exogenous pressure: immigration and international crime

Since the early 1980s, western European states have become increasingly multiethnic. As Table 11.1 shows, in 1993 there were over 1 million legal immigrants to the EU, and in the mid-1990s almost 6 per cent of EU residents were racial, ethnic or religious minorities. France, Britain, Belgium and the Netherlands, who had colonial empires, have had significant minority populations since the 1950s, and Germany welcomed successive generations of 'guest workers' in the 1960s and 1970s (mostly from Turkey). By the 1990s, however, it was clear that these guest workers were permanent immigrants, whose children (and children's children) were born in Germany, but did not have German citizenship. Moreover, in the 1990s many other EU states became net-immigration states for the first time, such as Italy, Spain, Portugal, Greece and Ireland.

In addition to minority residents, the early 1990s saw a new wave of refugees to western Europe from central and eastern Europe, the former Yugoslavia, North Africa, the Horn of Africa (Ethiopia and Somalia) and the Great Lakes region of Africa (especially Rwanda and Burundi). Some of these persons could claim asylum status under the 1951 UN Convention on Asylum, but many could not as they could not prove personal persecution. They were, nonetheless, *de facto* refugees, as a result of flight from economic deprivation, political crisis or environmental destruction, who had to be offered some form of protection, either permanent or temporary. As the table shows, not all states were equal recipients of these *de jure* and *de facto* refugees. In particular, in 1993 Germany, with 22 per cent of the EU population, received over 60 percent of all refugees and asylum seekers to the EU.

In response to these developments, EU governments introduced new immigration and societal integration policies (Baldwin-Edwards and Schain, 1994; Papademetriou and Hamilton, 1996; Joppke, 1998). Throughout Europe, attacks on immigrants began to rise, as did support

Table 11.1 *Minorities, migrants and refugees in the EU*

Member state	Ethnic minorities, 1994 (% of pop'n)	Residents from other EU states, 1993 (% pop'n)	Non-EU immigrants, 1993 (Total)	Asylum seekers and refugees, 1993		Total pop'n, 1996 (% of EU pop'n)
				(Total)	(% of EU)	
Austria	5.1	1.0	n/a	5 900	1.1	2.2
Belgium	9.8	5.4	25 500	27 100	4.9	2.7
Denmark	5.0	0.8	13 200	15 100	2.8	1.4
Finland	0.8	0.2	9 900	2 000	0.4	1.4
France	8.3	2.3	79 100	27 600	5.0	15.6
Germany	7.4	2.1	852 300	339 000	61.8	22.0
Greece	8.2	0.6	10 500	900	0.2	2.8
Ireland	1.1	1.9	5 400	100	0.0	1.0
Italy	2.6	0.3	n/a	1 400	0.3	15.4
Luxembourg	11.5	n/a	1 800	200	0.0	0.1
Netherlands	6.4	1.2	66 000	45 700	8.3	4.2
Portugal	1.7	0.3	7 800	2 100	0.4	2.7
Spain	2.9	0.5	11 100	12 700	2.3	10.5
Sweden	2.5	2.2	47 100	38 700	7.1	2.4
United Kingdom	6.3	1.3	95 000	30 100	5.5	15.7
Total EU	5.9	1.5	>1 200 000	548 600	100.0	100.0

Source: Date on ethnic minorities from Minority Rights Group (1997). Data on residents from other EU states, immigrants, and asylum seekers and refugees from Eurostat (1995a). Data on EU population from Eurostat (1997).

for anti-immigration parties, and publics demanded a stop to further immigration and asylum (European Parliament, 1985, 1991; Lahav, 1997). In response, and despite differing philosophies about citizenship and society, most European governments pursued a two-pronged strategy: policies to promote the 'social integration' of existing minority populations, through equal opportunities and other race-relations policies; and greater 'controls' on immigration and asylum (Cornelius, Martin and Hollifield, 1994; Migration Policy Group, 1996; Favell, 1997a).

The late 1980s and early 1990s also saw a growth of international organized crime: 'crimes perpetrated by groups and organizations moving across the various national jurisdictions in which they are defined as a violation of the criminal code' (Anderson *et al.*, 1995, p. 14). This category of crime covers a variety of activities: from serious crimes such as terrorism, drug trafficking, money laundering, Mafia activities, arms-trafficking, and fraud against private corporations and governmental (national and EU) budgets; to lesser crimes such as football hooliganism, smuggling of tax-free goods and national cultural treasures, and the distribution of banned racist and pornographic publications (cf. Martin and Romano, 1992). It is difficult to ascertain exactly how far international crime has increased. However, the limited statistics that do exist suggest a moderate increase in international organized crime in all states of the EU (Alvazzi del Frate, Zvekic and van Dijk, 1993).

The EU single market does not necessary facilitate more migration and more organized crime. As Table 11.1 shows, in 1993 only 1.5 per cent of the EU population was living in another EU member state. The demand for migration arises from the collapse of communism, conflicts in the Balkans, and crises in northern, eastern and central Africa. Similarly, organized crime in Europe is a part of global criminal activities and is affected by the globalization of capital flows and national policies unrelated to the EU, such as the liberalization of laws on soft drugs such as cannabis. Nevertheless, the removal of physical controls on the movement of goods, services and ultimately persons makes it very difficult for national governments to pursue independent policies to control international crime. Also, open borders in the EU mean that one government's immigration policy potentially has a direct impact on the policies of other EU governments. For example, in the early 1990s Portugal granted Portuguese passports to more than 100 000 citizens of Macau. The return of this Portuguese colony to China in 1999 allows these citizens to come to anywhere in the EU and enjoy the same economic and civil rights as other EU citizens. Also, since the second language of Macau is English rather than Portuguese (their first being Chinese), the people who choose to leave Macau are more likely to come to Britain and Ireland than Portugal.

Governments' interests: high politics, regulatory failure, voters' concerns

The changing nature of European society and cross-border crime consequently presents governments with particular functional incentives to
tackle these issues at European level. However, there are also significant
countervailing forces. In the historical development of the European
integration, governments have often differentiated between 'high politics'
and 'low politics' (Hoffmann, 1966). High-politics issues are those which
touch on the fundamental definition, identity and security of the nation-
state. Low politics, in contrast, are issues that are not as threatening to
the viability of the nation-state, such as European economic integration,
the single market programme, and EU social and environmental regulation. As a result, governments are more likely to allow supranational
policy competences on low-politics issues than high-politics issues. The
free movement of persons, and the related issues of immigration and
policing, are such high-politics issues. They are central to the definition of
the nation-state: relating to who is part of the social contact between the
state and the citizens; who has the rights and freedoms of national
citizenship; and who has the right to be protected by the forces of the
state.

Consequently, as part of the single market programme governments
were less willing to remove physical borders on the movement of persons
than on the movement of goods, services and capital. Moreover, when they
could no longer resist the pressures for common action, governments were
eager to pursue cooperation through informal intergovernmental measures
– first through informal mechanisms and then in a separate 'intergovernmental pillar' in the EU. Under these arrangements, national sovereignty is
preserved in two ways: (1) decisions are taken by unanimity, which allows
any government to veto a measure that threatens a vital national interest;
and (2) decisions do not have direct effect in domestic law – they need to be
transposed into domestic law by parliaments and are justiciable only in
domestic courts.

However, in the mid-1990s the political calculations of EU governments
changed for two reasons. First, governments were forced to face up to the
failure of intergovernmental regulation of migration and policing issues.
As we have seen, the EU single market produced 'negative externalities' on
immigration, asylum and policing policies, as governments are affected by
each other's decisions about refugees, border controls and immigration. As
a result, governments have a collective interest in developing frameworks
to discuss each other's policies and develop common strategies, despite this
being an area of 'high politics'. The EU member states consequently
established institutions for such collective decision-making with the Trevi

framework, the Schengen Accord and the justice and home affairs provisions of the Maastricht Treaty.

However, the intergovernmental nature of these institutions obstructed coherent policy development. In addition to the unanimity requirement, there was no independent agenda-setter: governments had to rely on each other to come up with legislative proposals, and these inevitably tended to promote the individual interests of the particular government holding the Council presidency, rather than the collective interests of the EU. And, once adopted, there was no guarantee that non-binding actions (such as conventions) would ever be enforced. Moreover, each member state had an incentive not to implement agreements once they had been adopted: as they are costly to enforce on unwilling publics, and their citizens can 'free ride' on the liberal policies of other states. The result was a classic collective action problem (a 'joint-decision trap') with a sub-optimal outcome: of few collective policies, and a low level of implementation (Ireland, 1995; Ugar, 1995). By the mid-1990s, then, most EU governments argued that this problem could only be overcome by replacing the intergovernmental rules with a genuinely supranational regime (Monar, 1997; Governments of Belgium, the Netherlands and Luxembourg, 1996; Hix and Niessen, 1996).

Second, in the mid-1990s, governments were forced to respond to new *voter concerns* (cf. Ugar, 1995). In democratic systems, the primary goal of governments is to be reelected (Downs, 1957). In other words, a reason for them not to delegate high-politics issues to the EU level is that voters would be opposed to that policy. However, voters can change their minds, and allow the erosion of national sovereignty as a means of securing other individual and collective goals: such as personal freedom in the single market, and collective (European-wide) security from cross-border crime.

This was precisely what began to happen across Europe immediately before and during the IGC that produced the Amsterdam Treaty. In the Spring 1996 *Eurobarometer* survey (see Chapter 5), EU citizens were presented with a list of 34 issues and asked whether each was of 'high priority' or 'low priority' for the EU in the next 10 years. As Table 11.2 shows, free movement and internal security issues were high on the list of EU voters' demands for EU action. The top two issues and five of the top 10 issues were from this policy area, and one of the lowest issues of concern was one that had previously stopped governments from pooling sovereignty in this area: border controls between the EU member states. Moreover, for the first time these issues were salient in all the larger member states. As a result, German voters now had support for their demand that Europe should be taking action to stem the flow of asylum seekers and illegal immigrants into the EU, and to address the issue of organized crime in the EU single market.

Table 11.2   *What Europe's voters think are 'high priorities' for the EU*

Top 10 and bottom 10 issues (out of 34 in total) (third pillar and free movement issues in bold)	No. of persons who think the issue should be a 'High Priority' for the EU in the next 10 years (%)
1. Fighting organized crime	87
2. Fighting drug trafficking	86
3. Cooperation in the fight against Cancer/AIDS etc.	86
4. Joint programmes to fight unemployment	85
5. Joint efforts to protect the environment	83
6. Defence of human rights	81
7. Peace-keeping by firm intervention	79
8. Dealing with immigration	76
9. Providing opportunities to find jobs anywhere in the EU	76
10. Citizens able to live, work and study anywhere	73
25. No imports from countries with poor working conditions	61
26. Strong European currency	61
27. Better opportunities for smaller EU member states	59
28. Help to people in the Third World	57
29. Increased border controls	57
30. Protect EU products from non-member states	56
31. Less attention to economy, more to social justice	55
32. Protection from non-EU competition	54
33. Protecting European cultures	51
34. European army for common defence	41

Source: Eurobarometer No. 45, Spring 1996 (European Commission, 1996a).

Consequently, in the Amsterdam Treaty governments took a decisive step towards supranational decision-making on free movement and internal security issues: by delegating agenda-setting powers to the Commission, establishing some provisions for the possibility of adopting policies by qualified-majority voting (after five years), and granting limited monitoring and enforcement powers to the Commission and the ECJ. Britain and Ireland chose to opt out from these provisions as they were more able to impose *de facto* controls at borders than continental states, and hence did not suffer the same negative externalities of the single market. However, unanimity was kept as the main decision rule. This reflected the deep-seated concern amongst most governments (including Germany) that in a policy area that is central to the definition of the nation-state, governments are unlikely to enforce an agreement if they are outvoted (Moravcsik and Nicolaïdis, 1998, pp. 28–31).

Bureaucrats' strategies: bureau-shaping and the 'control' paradigm

Governments are not unitary actors, and within governments politicians and bureaucrats have different interests. Whereas politicians seek reelection, bureaucrats seek more influence over policy outcomes – through higher budgets (Niskanen, 1971), or through greater freedom to 'shape' their own organizational structures and policy choices (Dunleavy, 1991) (see Chapter 2). As a result of these interests, senior administrative elites in the immigration and internal security fields – in national justice, interior (home affairs), and customs and excise departments – sought collaboration on the development of common policies to monitor and control the movement of people and to prevent cross-border crime.

The single market programme represented a major threat to the status and resources of interior and justice ministries in Europe (Bigo, 1994). The removal of border controls on the movement of goods, services, capital and labour implied that fewer resources would need to be spent in interior and justice ministries. Also, without customs and excise duties, these departments would receive fewer revenues. As mentioned, the statistical evidence reveals only a moderate increase in cross-border crime and the movement of persons as a result of the single market, but interior and justice ministers across the EU produced reports designed to scare politicians into dedicating resources to their ministries to fight the spectre of 'Euro-crime' (Clutterbuck, 1990; Latter, 1991; Heidensohn and Farrell, 1993). The answer, so administrative elites claimed, was a 'European internal security field': with new contacts and networks between administrative elites to address the common threat (*ibid.* pp. 162–7).

This new discourse for policy-making on immigration and policing issues promoted the interests of senior bureaucrats in justice and interior ministries in two main ways. First, the aim of a European internal security field enabled the original EC Treaty aim of 'freedom' to be replaced with a concern for 'control'. Whereas 'freedom' implies a reduction of the state's role in regulating the movement and rights of persons, 'control' implies a legitimate role for the state and state officials in monitoring the movement of persons and preventing activities that threaten state security. For example, at the domestic level and in meetings at the European level, interior ministries argued that 'social integration' was best achieved through controls on immigration and asylum rather than through the promotion of race relations or anti-racism policies (see for example King, 1994; Geddes, 1995; Baldwin-Edwards, 1997). In the same way, EU immigration and asylum policies became a sub-set of 'security policies' in the Trevi, Schengen and Maastricht frameworks.

Also, through this interaction at the European level, interior ministry officials developed a common policy goal for their actions: 'controlling population rather than territory' (Chalmers, 1998). Traditionally, the state maintained internal security through controls on who enters the territory of the state. In a single market with open borders, this is no longer feasible. However, security forces can also control populations regardless of where they reside, through information exchange on criminal activities and asylum seekers, common strategies on identity cards and police stop-and-search policies, and cooperation between civil and judicial authorities (cf. den Boer, 1994; Anderson *et al.*, 1995, pp. 131–40). These 'compensatory measures' were first discussed within Trevi and Schengen and are the basis of EUROPOL. As result of this new policy idea, justice and interior ministries and securities agencies were able to maintain their levels of public funding despite the removal of border controls.

Second, cooperation at the EU level offered administrative elites a new level of independence from political interference: from party leaders and parliamentary scrutiny. There is nothing a bureaucrat likes more than to carry on his/her business without wasting time and resources answering to 'meddling' politicians and the media. The *ad hoc* intergovernmental settings were perfect for this: an opportunity to get together with like-minded officials facing similar budgetary and political constraints, with no official records of the meetings, and beyond the attention of parliaments and publics. This 'freed senior civil servants . . . from national and/or political constraints which often make it difficult to deal with controversial matters which nonetheless have to be settled speedily' (Bigo, 1994, pp. 164–5). For example, security elites could avoid issues present in domestic debates that undermine coherent control policies, such as the counter-productivity of repression or the economic incentives for employers to hire cheap labour.

However, not all bureaucratic interests benefit from the 'Europeaniza-tion of control'. As Bigo (1994, p. 172) argues:

> Those most favourable to Europe are inside ministerial cabinets or in the informal co-ordination structures between major services; their role gives them power over the services which they co-ordinate, and they have their own correspondents, interests, and political outlook.

As a result, agencies that are disconnected from national security elites, not involved in cross-agency collaboration, and absent from European-wide collaboration (such as the British HM Customs and Excise, the HM Immigration Service, the French Gendarmerie, and the Spanish Guardia Civil) tend to be opposed to common EU internal security policies. Nevertheless, the agencies who are in favour of EU policies (such as British and French drugs police) have consistently argued for cuts in the budgets of anti-European agencies, who they claim do not 'fit' with the new security environment in Europe.

Supranational entrepreneurship: supplying credibility and accountability

The institutional outcome in the Amsterdam Treaty was also a product of deliberate strategies by supranational actors, outside the control of national governments and administrative elites. As a result of the activities and policy ideas promoted by the EU institutions and nongovernmental organizations, the EU governments were persuaded that replacing intergovernmental procedures with supranational mechanisms would increase the credibility and accountability of policy-making, particularly on immigration and asylum policies.

The first and most influential amongst these interests was the European Commission. Under the Maastricht Treaty the Commission was virtually excluded from influencing policy-making in the justice and home affairs field. But following the ratification of the Treaty the Commission strengthened its ability to develop JHA policy ideas – with a new division in the Secretariat-General monitoring and supporting the third pillar; and a JHA policy portfolio with one of the commissioners (Anita Gradin). This was a long-term institutional strategy. Despite the absence of formal agenda-setting powers, the Commission sought to develop credible policy ideas in the expectation that this would tempt the EU governments to delegate this function to the Commission in the next round of institutional reform. As a result, between 1994 and 1996 the Commission undertook several policy initiatives, such as 'think papers' on several JHA issues, a number of policy proposals (such as trafficking in persons), the funding of independent research on national immigration and social integration policies, and negotiations with the US State Department on possible US–European cooperation on international migration and crime issues (for example, on a transatlantic temporary protection regime for refugees from the former Yugoslavia). The Commission also argued in the IGC that a central reason for the lack of policy development in this area was because it did not have an agenda-setting role (European Commission, 1996b). This strategy paid off. Having seen that the Commission had expertise in these areas and could develop credible and independent policy ideas, the EU governments agreed in the Amsterdam Treaty to delegate the right of initiative to the Commission.

The second supranational actor with a vested interest in further policy integration in this area was the EP. Since the establishment of the Trevi and Schengen groups, the EP had been critical of the secretive nature of intergovernmental cooperation on migration and security issues. The EP was also critical of the Maastricht Treaty provisions, despite the new ability to ask questions to the Council presidency regarding JHA developments. The EP argued that the decision procedures removed accountability of policy-making from national parliaments, without replacing it with effective powers of scrutiny for the EP (cf. Monar, 1995). As a result, in the EP's report to the 1996 IGC, and through the two EP representatives in the IGC Reflection Group, the EP argued that legislation should be adopted in this policy domain using the consultation procedure (European Parliament, 1995b). This was a 'minimalist' strategy, as the EP did not demand full legislative rights with the Council, simply a right to issue an opinion on policy proposals which gives them a limited power of delay (see Chapter 3). The EU governments agreed. This seemed a small price to pay to satisfy domestic and European-level demands for more transparency and accountability of policy-making – which the EU heads of government had established as one of the main aims of the IGC in all policy areas.

Third, in its submission to the IGC, the ECJ was tactful not to propose any concrete measures for reform (European Court of Justice, 1995). However, it argued that there was a clear clash of jurisdictions in the Maastricht design. Under the citizenship provisions in the first pillar, the ECJ must protect the fundamental rights of EU citizens. However, the ECJ pointed out that the policy areas tackled under the third pillar touched on these issues, but that neither it nor national courts have jurisdiction over Council decisions on justice and home affairs. The ECJ (*ibid.* p. 5) consequently argued that:

> judicial protection . . . especially in the context of co-operation in the field of Justice and Home Affairs, must be guaranteed and structured in such a way as to ensure consistent interpretation and application of both

Community law and of the provisions adopted within the framework of such co-operation.

The Court went on to suggest that the IGC should determine the limits of EU action in the JHA field, and establish proper legal instruments and mechanisms for legal oversight of Council decisions (cf. Neuwahl, 1995). A few months later, in March 1996, the ECJ issued an opinion (2/94) on a request from the Council, arguing that article 235 was an insufficient basis for accession of the EU to the European Convention on Human Rights. This opinion was against the views of a number of pro-integrationist member states, such as the Benelux. However, this mixed strategy – critical analysis yet moderation – paid off in the Amsterdam Treaty which extended ECJ jurisdiction on all migration and security issues.

Finally, during the IGC a number of nongovernmental organizations (NGOs) and quasi-governmental organizations lobbied for more supranational policy-making on migration and security issues (cf. Ireland, 1991; Favell, 1997b). These included Brussels-based groups such as the European Council of Refugees and Exiles, Migrants Forum, the Churches' Commission for Migrants in Europe, Migration Policy Group, and the Starting Line Group (which brought together national NGOs to campaign for a general anti-racism clause in the EU Treaty). They also included national groups such as the Dutch Standing Committee of Experts on International Immigration, Refugee and Criminal Law, and the British Commission for Racial Equality (CRE) and the Federal Trust. Despite varying perspectives, these groups were unanimous in there criticism of the secretive nature of intergovernmental decision-making, in the lack of judicial and parliamentary control, and in the subordination of migration issues to 'crime' policies (see for example Hix, 1995b; Federal Trust, 1996; Hix and Niessen, 1996; Meijers *et al.*, 1997; Chopin and Niessen, 1998). These demands were particularly effective against centre-left governments, who were part of the same social milieu as the leaders of these NGOs. For example, under pressure from the CRE, the new British Labour government changed its position on a general anti-racism clause in the Treaty, and allowing the other EU member states to integrate their immigration policies, to which Britain could then chose to 'opt in'.

Conclusion: skeleton of a pan-European state

Through the development of EU policies on citizen freedoms and security, a 'social contract' is emerging between EU citizens and the Euro-polity. Unlike the traditional state, the EU does not have the exclusive right to decide who can be an EU citizen. However, with the single market, the EU institutions have established and are responsible for governing a set of common economic rights for nationals of the EU member states: based on the freedom to move, to seek employment, to trade, and to provide and consume services. Furthermore, with the establishment of 'EU citizenship' in the Maastricht Treaty and the extension of these provisions in the Amsterdam Treaty, the EU member states are no longer independent from the EU polity in determining who can receive social, civil and political rights in the domestic system.

Also unlike a traditional state, the EU does not have a legitimate monopoly on the use of violence to guarantee, protect and secure individual and collective rights. However, through the development of EU competences on immigration and asylum, and on police and judicial cooperation, the EU governments have chosen to cooperate in deciding how domestic security forces operate to secure these goals. In addition, through the delegation of agenda-setting powers to the Commission, the right of consultation and the power of delay for the EP, and the right of judicial review in the ECJ, the Amsterdam Treaty established a new policy regime: in which the EU institutions have a say in fighting cross-border crime and directing the domestic security agencies that make asylum and immigration decisions.

This novel formation has developed as a result of a mixture of factors. The development of multiethnic societies in Europe, the increase in global migration, the globalization of capital, and the single market programme, all undermine the ability of European governments to pursue independent migration and policing policies, and undermine the administrative capacity and funding potential of bureaucrats in justice and interior ministries. In response, EU governments and administrative elites have established intergovernmental mechanisms to facilitate information-sharing and the development of collective migration and security strategies: first through mechanisms outside the EU framework (such as Trevi and Schengen), then in the third pillar of the EU (in the Maastricht Treaty).

However, this does not explain why EU governments agreed in the Amsterdam Treaty to inject a significant dose of supranational agenda-setting, scrutiny, adoption and enforcement in this policy area. This can only be explained as a result of a common response by governments to several forces. First, new demands amongst the electorate for immediate action to fight cross-border crime and to control immigration gave EU governments a window of opportunity to integrate an area of high politics. Second, pressure from non-governmental organizations, the EP and the ECJ forced EU governments to address the issues of transparency and accountability of decision-making. Finally, the establishment of policy expertise by the Commission gave the EU governments the opportunity to delegate agenda-setting and enforcement powers to an independent and credible institution – and, in so doing, to solve a collective action problem.

Chapter 12

Global Policies

Theories of international relations/political economy
External economic policies: free trade or 'fortress Europe'?
External political relations: a common foreign policy?
Explaining the global policies of the EU
Conclusion: economic heavyweight but political lightweight

The EU pursues two main types of policies towards the rest of the world: economic policies, through trade agreements and development and humanitarian aid; and foreign and security policies, through the Common Foreign and Security Policy (CFSP) and defence policy cooperation. This chapter seeks to understand and explain why the EU is able to act with a single voice on the global stage on some issues but not others. To help answer this question we shall first consider some theoretical issues in the fields of international relations (IR) and international political economy.

Theories of international relations/political economy

There are two main theoretical frameworks in the contemporary field of international relations: realism and liberalism (cf. Woods, 1996) (there are, of course, several other theoretical approaches in IR, such as idealism, reflectivism and Marxism, but these are the dominant two frameworks in contemporary IR). *Realism* sees international relations as a continuous struggle for power and domination between states in a system of anarchy: what Bismarck called Realpolitik (see for example Morgenthau, 1948). In the contemporary 'neo-realist' version, this approach has three core assumptions:

1. states are unitary actors, where the political elite and the mass public have a single conception of the 'national interest';
2. this interest is defined in geopolitical/security terms, such as the territorial integrity of the state and the structure of the political order, rather than in economic terms; and
3. the state acts upon this interest in a rational manner, by seeking to maximize its security interest given the relative 'balance of power' between states (for example Waltz, 1979; Keohane, 1986).

Realists consequently argue that because states have stable territorial and socio-political structures, their geopolitical and security preferences are also stable. As a result, in the realist account, rival actors in the international system can predict how each other are likely to behave. Moreover, because security interests are perceived to be in conflict rather than complementary, inter-state politics tends to be a 'zero-sum game': where if one state wins, another must lose. Cooperation between states is consequently unlikely as there is little opportunity for the provision of a common public good, and there are no credible enforcing agents in a system of anarchy. Hence, once created, international institutions (such as the United Nations) are weak.

Liberalism, on the other hand, sees international relations as driven by global economic interdependence. This rival approach starts from a different set of assumptions about state preferences and behaviour:

1. states are not unitary actors, as state preferences are formed through competition between domestic interests and ideologies, where social groups seek to capture the state to promote their private interests ('rent seeking') and elites seek to protect their positions of power by trading-off the international and domestic system in a 'two-level game' (Evans, Jacobson and Putnam, 1993; Milner, 1997);
2. in this competition between societal actors and elites, individual preferences are driven by economic interest (wealth) rather than geopolitical concerns (for example Rosecrance, 1986); and
3. in the international system state officials act rationally to pursue these economic preferences, but these preferences are shaped in response to developments in other systems (interdependence) and the behaviour of international and supranational institutions (for example Keohane and Nye, 1989).

As a result, in contrast to realists, liberals predict that state preferences are not stable. States' interests in the international system change as a result of two factors: first, different societal actors win in domestic competition, for example when different political parties are elected; and, second, individual economic interests and opportunities are redefined in the face of changes in the global system (Moravcsik, 1997). In addition, liberals predict more inter-state cooperation and international institution-formation than realists do. Because interests are defined economically and because economic independence increases with globalization, states have a strong incentive to solve collective action problems. This results in 'international regimes' (rather than anarchy) and the delegation of enforcement functions to international institutions, such as the World Trade Organization (see for example Krasner, 1983; Keohane, 1984; Greico, 1990).

This realist/liberal divide has specific application in the field of *international political economy* (IPE) (cf. Frieden and Lake, 1995). In global economic relations, realists assert the primacy of politics over economics. International economic policies are pursued to achieve geopolitical goals: such as state security and political hegemony, and as a result states sacrifice economic gain to strengthen their position in the global balance of power. For example, trade protection often reduces a state's long-term welfare, but may increase a state's leverage in the international system. Conversely, free trade agreements can emerge. However, realists observe that this is usually a result of 'hegemonic stability': where a single dominant actor has the power to construct an economic regime to suit its own political interests at the expense of the political interests of its partners.

Liberals, on the other hand, assert the primacy of economics and societal economic interests over politics and power relations. Most liberals accept the assumption in neo-classical economics that the free market is the most efficient way of allocating resources. For example, rather than competing in the production of the same goods, welfare will be maximized if states specialize in the production of goods in which they have a 'comparative advantage'. Liberals consequently argue that in a world where individual economic interests drive politics, states should recognize the potential 'gains from trade', and pursue free trade rather than protectionist policies. Nevertheless, liberals accept that government is important for the provision of 'public goods' – goods and services that would not be supplied to a sufficient level by the market (see Chapter 8). As a result, global governance institutions are necessary to supply the conditions for free trade and competitive global markets, such as stable property rights and rules against protectionism and unfair competition.

These two approaches consequently predict different things about the EU's global policies. From the realist perspective, because the EU is not a state it will not have a clear and indivisible 'national interest'. As a result, the global policies of the EU will be dominated by the (stable) geopolitical and security concerns of the EU member states. Ironically, however, this is similar to the liberal prediction that EU preferences will be determined by competition between rival economic interests in the EU's 'domestic' arena. Nevertheless, unlike the realist approach, liberals argue that non-state economic actors (such as multinational firms) will compete with the member states in shaping EU global policies. Liberals also predict that the preferences of these domestic EU actors will be defined in economic rather than geopolitical terms and will change in response to changes in the international environment. Finally, where liberal theory predicts that the EU external economic policies will determine how the EU acts in foreign and security policies, realist theory predicts the opposite.

External economic policies: free trade or 'fortress Europe'?

The EU has developed common external economic policies in parallel to the development of internal economic integration. Part of this has been out of necessity: to preserve the coherence of the single market. However, it has also been out of choice: to promote EU economic interests in the global arena. The result is three types of external economic policies:

- a single set of rules on the import of goods into the EU;
- bilateral and multilateral trade agreements between the EU and other actors; and
- trade, aid and cooperation with developing countries.

But before discussing these policies, it is important to understand the pattern of EU trade.

The pattern of EU trade

With a population of over 370 million, the EU is the world's largest market, and it is also the world's largest trader. In 1996, exports and imports from the EU (excluding trade between the EU member states) accounted for approximately 21 per cent of total world trade, whereas the United States accounted for 16 per cent and Japan for 12 per cent. Moreover, since the 1960s EU external trade has grown faster than EU GDP, with the result that in the late 1990s external trade contributes 19.4 per cent of total EU GDP, compared to 17.9 per cent of US GDP and 10.4 per cent of Japanese GDP. As Table 12.1 shows, most of the EU's trade is with developed countries, such as the United States, Switzerland and Japan. One-fifth of EU trade is with the North American Free Trade Area (NAFTA) – of the United States, Canada and Mexico. Overall, until the mid-1990s the EU ran a small trade deficit (of more imports than exports) with the rest of the world, after which it has managed a modest surplus. In contrast, in the 1990s the USA has experienced a growing trade deficit and Japan a growing trade surplus.

In terms of the composition of EU trade, the bulk is intra-industry trade (where the same products are imported as exported) in the manufacturing sector (such as machinery, chemicals and other manufacturing goods). Although not included in the statistics on commodities trade, EU trade in services (such as financial services, tourism and transport) has risen to almost one-third of total EU trade in commodities. In terms of the trade balance by sector, like other advanced industrial economies, the EU is a net importer of raw materials for manufacturing (such as minerals and fuels, and crude materials, oils and fats) and a net exporter of finished products from the manufacturing process. However, the trade surplus in some

Table 12.1 External trade of the EU, 1995

	Imports to the EU (bn. €)	Exports from the EU (bn. €)	Proportion of total external EU trade (%)	Trade balance (exports minus imports) (bn. €)
With individual states (top 6 states)				
United States of America	103.6	100.9	18.4	− 2.7
Switzerland	43.8	51.0	8.5	+ 7.2
Japan	54.3	32.9	7.9	− 21.9
Norway	25.4	17.3	3.9	− 8.1
China	26.3	14.6	3.7	− 12.0
Russia	21.9	16.1	3.4	− 5.8
With trade blocs				
North American Free Trade Area (NAFTA)	118.5	115.5	21.0	− 3.0
Association of Southeast Asian Nations (ASEAN)	36.5	34.5	6.4	− 2.0
Commonwealth of Independent States (CIS)	25.3	20.8	4.1	− 4.5
Africa, Caribbean, Pacific Group (ACP)	19.8	17.4	3.3	− :2.4
Mercosur	15.0	16.6	2.8	+ 1.6
By commodity				
Machinery and equipment (Sector 7)	173.3	255.7	38.5	+ 82.4
Other manufactured goods (Sectors 6 + 8 + 9)	182.4	174.9	32.0	− 7.5
Chemicals (Sector 5)	40.9	75.7	10.5	+ 34.8
Food products, beverages & tobacco (Sectors 0 + 1)	43.2	38.9	7.4	− 4.3
Minerals and fuels (Sector 3)	64.7	10.2	6.7	− 54.5
Crude materials, oils and fats (Sectors 2 + 4)	40.2	13.7	4.8	− 26.5
Total external EU trade	544.7	569.0	100.0	− 24.3

Source: Eurostat (1997).

manufacturing sectors (such as steel and textiles) has declined since the 1980s. As a result of the CAP, the EU is almost self-sufficient in agricultural products, and consequently the EU exports almost as much food products, beverages and tobacco as it imports.

However, whereas these patterns are generalizations about the EU as a whole, there are significant differences between the member states. As Tsoukalis (1997, p. 230) puts it, the EU member states 'tend to squint in different directions'. For example, in terms of the geographic orientation of trade, Britain, Ireland and the Netherlands export more to the United States than the EU average. A similar situation exists between Germany and Austria and central and eastern Europe, and Britain, France and Spain and the developing world. In terms of the product orientation of trade, the structure of trade for Portugal and Greece is similar to developing countries, whereas Germany accounts for almost 30 per cent of EU exports in manufactured goods, and the UK is the main EU exporter of financial services.

The Common Commercial Policy

Articles 131–134 [ex 110–116] of the EU Treaty set out the Common Commercial Policy (CCP) of the EU. The CCP has an underlying liberal objective: to promote 'the harmonious development of world trade, the progressive abolition of restrictions on international trade and the lowering of customs barriers' (article 131 [ex 110]). However, the CCP operates through several 'protectionist' policy instruments, the four main instruments of which are as follows:

- *The Common External Tariff* – With the establishment of the common market, the EU states agreed to apply the same tariff on goods entering their country from outside the EU. In 1995, the average tariff was approximately 10 per cent of the import value, but this varied between 26 per cent on agricultural goods and zero per cent on most industrial goods. As part of the multilateral General Agreement on Tariffs and Trade, by 2000 the EU will reduce tariffs by approximately one-third, to 18 per cent on agricultural goods and zero per cent on computer and telecoms products.
- *Import quotas* – As a result of the single market, the member states were forced to replace national quotas with EU-wide restrictions on the import of certain goods (as monitoring of national quotas is impossible without border controls on goods). These quotas apply to a wide variety of products, including textiles, agricultural products, and iron and steel. But, as a result of the multilateral multi-fibre agreement, by 2005 quotas will be phased out on textiles and clothing.

- *Anti-dumping measures* – The Commission has the power to impose import tariffs and minimum price levels if exporters to the EU are selling at discriminatory prices that are likely to injure domestic producers. In 1993, the EU's anti-dumping procedures were modified in line with the General Agreement on Tariffs and Trade. However, according to the World Trade Organization, the EU is the most frequent user of anti-dumping measures: about 150 per year in the 1990s. One of the most high-profile examples of these measures are the minimum prices on semiconductors from Japan and South Korea, which were first imposed in 1983.
- *Voluntary Export Restraints (VERs)* – VERs are agreements between an exporter and an importer, where the exporter agrees to limit the volume of goods consigned to the importer. VERs usually result from political pressure, such as the threat of anti-dumping measures by the importer. However, they can also be established to protect the interests of both exporters and import-competing domestic producers (by allowing an increase in price), at the expense of consumers in the import country. The most high-profile VER was the 1991 agreement with Japan to limit car exports to the EU. However, this agreement expires in 1999.

In addition to these instruments, the EU uses several minor measures that are also designed to restrict free trade: *export promotion measures*, where the Commission organizes EU trade fairs and coordinates national initiatives; *trade sanctions*, which are usually imposed for political reasons and are based on decisions of the UN Security Council; *countervailing duties*, which the EU imposes if there is evidence of export subsidies in third countries; *safeguard clauses*, which allow the signatories of GATT to suspend normal rules to protect a vital interest; and *rules of origin*, which determine the proportion of a product that must be added locally for a product to qualify as originating from the EU or from a state covered by a preferential trade agreement.

Under the CCP decision-making rules, the Commission has a monopoly of legislative initiative, and is responsible for managing the execution of the policy. The Commission negotiates all external trade agreements on behalf of the Council (rather like the US president's 'fast track' mandate from the US Congress). And, the Commission has the power of executive decree: to adopt anti-dumping measures, countervailing duties and other import restrictions, which have to be reviewed by the Council after a set time period. The Council, on the other hand, is the main legislative body and acts by qualified majority in all areas except in the adoption of Association Agreements, which require unanimity. The Council scrutinizes legislative initiatives and oversees the Commission's actions in a special committee of COREPER, known as the 'Article 113 Committee'. The EP has no formal role in the day-to-day adoption of legislation under the CCP, but the assent procedure (which gives the EP a power of veto) is used for the adoption of multilateral or bilateral trade agreements (article 300 [ex 228]).

Multilateral trade agreements: GATT and the WTO

The EU has been one of the key players in the negotiation and establishment of the multilateral global trading regime, which has gradually led to the liberalization of world trade. The General Agreement on Tariffs and Trade (GATT) was first agreed in 1948 and since the Dillon Round in 1960–62 the EU has attempted to coordinate a common stance in successive negotiations to reform the GATT. With the Commission as the EU's negotiator, the EU acted with a single voice in each of the subsequent negotiations: the Kennedy Round in 1964–67, the Tokyo Round in 1973–79, and the Uruguay Round in 1986–93. The Uruguay Round culminated with the establishment of the World Trade Organization (WTO), based in Geneva.

The Uruguay Round covered a number of sensitive areas for the EU, including services, intellectual property, agriculture and textiles. The EU was also a central cause of a delay of the negotiations beyond the original 1990 deadline: the problem was a protracted disagreement between the EU, the USA and the Cairns Group (a group of states in favour of agricultural free trade led by Australia) over the liberalization of trade in agricultural products, which included limits on domestic export subsidies. Without the support of the EU, the largest trade bloc, the WTO could not function. With this powerful veto threat, the EU was able to extract some important concessions from the USA in the area of farming subsidies, in return for a promise of a modest reform of the CAP (see Chapter 9).

Nevertheless, since the establishment of the WTO, the EU has been one of its strongest defenders. Leon Brittan, the EU commissioner responsible for relations with the WTO, has consistently argued to his colleagues in the Commission and to the EU governments that because the EU is the largest trader it has the most to benefit from the liberalization of world trade. Moreover, if the EU does not abide by the WTO rules, there will be little incentive for the United States to do the same. This was a particular concern in 1996–98, when there was a strongly 'isolationist' US Congress. Also, the Commission has been one of the main protagonists before WTO committees against export subsidies by other states; and when the WTO has ruled against the EU, the Commission has pressed the Council to reform the single market or CCP rules instead of challenging the WTO ruling.

Bilateral preferential trade agreements

The EU has many different types of preferential trade agreements with a wide range of countries and regions of the world. In terms of the degree of access to the single market granted by these agreements, the hierarchy is as follows (with the most privileged at the top):

- The European Economic Area (EEA), with Norway, Iceland and Liechtenstein.
- Customs union agreements, with Turkey, Malta and Cyprus.
- Europe Agreements, with the central and eastern European states that have applied for EU membership (Bulgaria, Czech Republic, Estonia, Hungary, Latvia, Lithuania, Poland, Romania, Slovakia and Slovenia).
- Free trade agreements, with Israel and Switzerland.
- Euro-Mediterranean Accords, with Egypt, Jordan, Morocco, Tunisia, Algeria, Lebanon and Syria.
- The Lomé Convention, with 70 African Caribbean and Pacific former colonies of the EU (see below).
- The Generalized System of Preferences, which gives privileged access to the single market for certain products from 145 developing countries.
- Mutual recognition agreements, with the United States and Canada.
- Partnership and Cooperation Agreements, with the 10 members of the Commonwealth of Independent States.
- Inter-Regional Agreements, with the members of the Andean Pact, Mercosur, the Central American customs union, the Gulf Cooperation Council and the Association of Southeast Asian Nations.
- A variety of trade agreements with other countries, including Australia, New Zealand, South Africa, Argentina, Brazil, India, Pakistan and South Korea.

The different level of access to the single market in these agreements reflects the political priorities of the EU. For example, the EEA allows the states who would be eligible to join the EU but have chosen to remain outside to be part of the EU single market – in a similar relationship to that between a 'Commonwealth of the USA' (such as Puerto Rico) and the US market. The Europe Agreements, on the other hand, are specifically designed to prepare the central and eastern European states for EU membership. Also, the Commission has argued that the agreements with the USA and Canada for the 'mutual recognition' of product standards in a number of product areas (based on the same principles as in the EU single market) could be the basis for a general free trade agreement between the EU and NAFTA. Below this hierarchy of access to the single market are the general members of the WTO (such as Japan), and at the bottom of the EU's priority list are non-members of the WTO (such as China).

Development policies: trade and aid

The EU also uses its external economic policies to promote political and economic progress in the developing world. All EU member states except Greece are also members of the Organization for Economic Cooperation and Development's (OECD) development assistance committee (DAC), which seeks to coordinate national aid and development policies. The member states have also delegated a responsibility to the European Commission to participate in the activities of the DAC and to coordinate the positions of the EU states in this committee. Together, the EU member states provide just over 50 per cent of all global development aid, compared to 22 per cent by the United States and 17 per cent by Japan. This amounts to an average of 0.4 per cent of EU GDP, with Denmark and Sweden being the highest donors (around 1 per cent). In addition, approximately 3 per cent of the EU budget is spent on development assistance.

The most prominent EU development activity is the Lomé Convention, which was signed in 1975 and now covers 70 former colonies of the EU member states in Africa, the Caribbean and the Pacific (ACP). The Convention combines preferential trade (zero tariffs on 99 per cent of imports from these states) with grants and loans worth €12bn for the 1995–2000 period. This budget accounts for 55 per cent of total aid from the EU member states, and is managed separately from the EU budget. However, the fourth Lomé Convention expires in 2000, and there is growing pressure on the EU from the WTO and the EU's other main trading partners to introduce substantial reforms to the preferential trade aspect of the policy.

The EU also pursues development policies towards central and eastern Europe and the former Soviet Union. In addition to signing trade agreements, the EU and its member states have been the main suppliers of technical and financial assistance to promote the transition to democracy and a free-market economy in this region. The EU member states provided a total of €33.8bn in aid to central and eastern European states between 1990 and 1994, which was 45 per cent of the total assistance they received. Part of these funds, to a value of €5.3bn, was channelled through the EU's PHARE programme, which provides technical assistance to state officials and public and private enterprises. A similar programme – TACIS – was set up for Russia, which involved €790m between 1991 and 1995, and focused on restructuring state enterprises, reforming public administration and developing the private sector.

In addition, through the European Community Humanitarian Aid Office (ECHO), which is managed by the Commission, the EU provides emergency humanitarian and food aid to many parts of the world.

Although the amounts involved compared to EU development assistance are small, the EU's humanitarian aid policy has raised the profile of the EU on the international stage. Part of this has been through the headline-grabbing strategies of commissioner Emma Bonino, responsible for ECHO, who among other things was kidnapped while on an EU aid mission in Afghanistan.

In sum, the EU's external economic policies are inconsistent. A central aim of the single market and of the CCP is to favour domestic producers over producers in third countries; and through preferential trade agreements the EU has consciously tried to distort international trade to favour certain exporters – such as former colonies and prospective EU member states. However, the assertion that the EU is a 'fortress Europe', which was a popular view outside the EU in the mid-1980s, is not wholly true. The EU imports and exports more goods and services than any other market in the world. In most sectors, EU import duties are small relative to some of the EU's competitors, and the EU is also an active promoter of the liberalization of free trade through its activities in the successive GATT negotiations, in the WTO, and in the EU's various bilateral free trade agreements.

External political relations: a common foreign policy?

The Maastricht Treaty, adopted in December 1992, introduced a new aim for the EU:

> to assert its identity on the international scene, in particular through the implementation of a common foreign and security policy including the eventual framing of a common defence policy, which might in time lead to a common defence. (Article 2 [ex B])

However, common external 'political' relations have been considerably more difficult to achieve than common external economic relations.

Development of foreign policy cooperation and decision-making

The West European Union (WEU) was set up in 1948 between the European members of the North Atlantic Treaty Organization (NATO), but this included the United Kingdom, which was not a signatory of the Treaty of Rome. The six founding states of the EU subsequently agreed a plan for a European Defence Community (EDC) in 1952. However, the French National Assembly rejected this plan over concerns about national sovereignty.

This rejection meant that it was not until the attempts to 're-launch European integration' at the Hague Summit, in 1969, that the EC member states sought to add a political dimension to the process of economic integration. The Hague Summit set up European Political Cooperation (EPC). This was a forum for cooperation on foreign policy issues between the EC member states, but was outside the legal structure of the EC treaties. EPC enabled EC foreign ministers and heads of government to debate broader political and security issues alongside their regular EC meetings: respectively, the General Affairs Council and the European Council. The day-to-day business of EPC was managed by a network of committees of national bureaucrats, under the responsibility of the 'political directors' – who were senior officials from the member states' foreign ministries.

EPC actions were taken through 'common positions' of the EC foreign ministers or heads of government. These were not binding, but the governments agreed that they would try not to undertake national actions that would contradict a common position. In 1981, in the London Report, the governments strengthened this structure: providing a new role for the rotating presidency of the Council, formalizing a 'Troika' system (where the previous, current and next presidents can act together on behalf of the EC), establishing a consultation role for the Commission, and allowing for common positions to be adopted in a number of new areas (such as on economic and trade sanctions).

The institutionalization of foreign policy cooperation was further enhanced when EPC was brought into the EC Treaty framework in the 1987 Single European Act. This was still separate from the institutions and policies of the EEC. However, linking EPC to the EC framework provided a 'legal' framework for EPC actions, formalized the relationship between the EPC and the General Affairs Council, and gave more freedom to the EP to scrutinize the actions of national officials and the foreign ministers under EPC. Also, as part of this integration into the EC Treaty, the member states introduced a new decision-making norm: that decisions should be by consensus, but that if a consensus cannot be reached, governments in the minority should try to abstain rather than vetoing an agreement. This became known as 'constructive abstention', which has remained a central decision-making norm in the area of foreign policy cooperation.

However, at the beginning of the 1990s, foreign and security policy issues were pushed to the top of the EC agenda with the revolutions in central and eastern Europe, the collapse of the Soviet empire, and the sudden end of the cold war. The inadequacy of the EPC structure, even within the SEA framework, was further highlighted by the outbreak of the Gulf crisis in August 1990 and the civil war in Yugoslavia in June 1991. In response, Europe's leaders agreed in June 1990 that an intergovernmental conference (IGC) on 'political union' should be convened in parallel to the one preparing institutional reforms for 'economic and monetary union'. The political union IGC, which was concluded in December 1991 with the Maastricht Treaty, transformed EPC into the CFSP: the 'second pillar' of the EU.

The Maastricht Treaty set out five objectives of CFSP:

- to strengthen the common values, fundamental interests and independence of the Union;
- to strengthen the security of the Union and its member states in all ways;
- to preserve peace and strengthen international security, in accordance with the principles of the United Nations Charter as well as the principles of the Helsinki Final Act and the objectives of the Paris Charter;
- to promote international cooperation; and
- to develop and consolidate democracy and the rule of law, respect for human rights and fundamental freedoms.

To achieve these goals, the decision-making procedures and instruments of foreign policy cooperation were reformed. Foreign policy issues became a normal part of Council business: the EPC meetings of foreign ministers were subsumed within the General Affairs Council; the Political Committee (of the political directors) became part of the Committee of Permanent Representatives (COREPER); and the EPC secretariat joined the Council secretariat. The Commission became 'fully associated with the work carried out in the CFSP field'. The Commission does not have a right of initiative, but it has free reign to generate policy ideas. The Commission consequently created a new directorate-general for external political affairs (DG1A) to manage this responsibility.

The European Parliament was not given a role in CFSP decision-making, but the presidency of the Council is committed to consulting the EP on the main aspects of CFSP, to ensuring that the EP's views are taken into account, and to answer all EP questions relating to the CFSP field. In addition, the EP's Committee on Foreign Affairs, Security and Defence Policy holds special 'colloquia' four times a year with the chairman of the Political Committee (the political director from the member state holding the Council presidency).

The Maastricht Treaty also established two CFSP policy instruments. The first, and main, instruments are common positions. These are adopted in the Council by consensus, but with the informal constructive abstention rule applying. As with the EPC, the member states must ensure that their national policies conform to common positions, but a new innovation was that these common positions commit the member states to common actions in international organizations and international conferences, such as in the United Nations Security Council. But the EU does not possess legal sanctions to enforce national compliance with common positions.

The second instruments are joint actions. The General Affairs Council adopts these after the European Council has agreed that a matter should be the subject of a joint action. The member states may decide (by unanimity) that any matter covered by a joint action can be adopted by a qualified majority in the Council. This was the first time that the Treaty provided for the use of a qualified majority in the foreign policy field. Also, joint actions are more binding than common positions. Like common positions, the member states committed to changing their policies in accord with a joint action. But under joint actions they must also inform and consult the Council on how joint actions have been implemented. And, if a member state is unable or unwilling to implement a joint action, it must justify this position to the other member states.

In addition, the Maastricht Treaty brought the issue of defence policy into the EU framework for the first time. In so doing, the Treaty represented a compromise between the 'Atlanticists' who favour strong ties with the United States (such as Britain and the Netherlands), the 'Europeanists' who favour a European defence policy independent of NATO (mainly France), and the neutral member states of the EU (Ireland and Denmark at that time). The Treaty recognized WEU as 'an integral part of the development of the EU' and provided for the foreign and defence ministers of the WEU member states to discuss defence issues within the framework of the EU Council; and to address the fears of the Atlanticists, the Treaty asserted that the aim is to 'strengthen the European pillar of the Atlantic Alliance'. However, having adopted this bargain, the EU heads of government decided that the reform of the CFSP should be a central issue for the 1996 IGC. The resulting Amsterdam Treaty consequently made several significant changes.

First, a new vehicle for CFSP cooperation was introduced: 'common strategies'. These strategies are to be adopted at the level of the European Council, on the basis of proposals from the foreign ministers, and will then be transformed into actions (through common positions or joint actions) by the Council. The intention is that this will give a clearer focus to EU foreign policy negotiations.

Second, the Treaty established a clearer distinction between common positions and joint actions. Joint actions are meant to be used where specific operational action is required, whereas common positions are meant for less-clearly-definable situations, 'of a geographic or thematic nature' (article 15 [ex J.5]).

Third, Amsterdam formalized and clarified the practice of agreement through 'constructive abstention'. The Treaty asserts that: 'All CFSP decisions are taken by unanimity'. However, abstentions do not count as votes against, and to encourage governments to abstain rather than veto an agreement, governments are allowed to qualify an abstention in a formal declaration. Also, governments who abstain are not bound to participate in the implementation of a decision, although they must still refrain from taking an action directly contrary to the decision.

Fourth, the Treaty formalized the use of qualified-majority voting on issues relating to policy implementation. When a common strategy has been adopted (by unanimity) in the European Council, the Council is then required to adopt common positions or joint actions implementing this decision by qualified-majority. Qualified majority voting can also be used to adopt decisions implementing other common positions or joint actions. However, if a member state objects to the use qualified-majority voting for 'important and stated reasons of national policy', it can request that the matter be referred to the European Council for a decision by unanimity.

Fifth, the Amsterdam Treaty enhanced the capacity of the EU to project a single voice on foreign policy issues. The Council presidency was granted several new powers: to convene an extraordinary Council meeting with 48 hours notice (or shorter, in an emergency); the possibility of being mandated to negotiate on behalf of the EU in international negotiations; and an enhanced responsibility for ensuring the implementation of EU actions. In the preparation of the IGC, the Reflection Group proposed the creation of a new post, to which an individual would be appointed to represent the EU on CFSP matters: a 'Mr. or Ms. CFSP'. The Commission argued that this should be one of the commissioners responsible for external political relations. However, the EU governments agreed that such a post should be part of the Council structure: where the secretary-general of the Council would also be the high representative for CFSP. To increase policy information and coordination, the high representative was given responsibility for managing a new policy-planning and early-warning unit, located in the secretariat general of the Council.

Sixth, the Amsterdam Treaty further integrated defence policy cooperation into the EU. The European Council was granted the competence to elaborate and implement common defence policies, particularly relating to armaments. To appease the Atlanticists, however, the Treaty explicitly stated that these policies must not jeopardise NATO, and the right to remain neutral, which was demanded by Sweden, Austria, Finland and Ireland, was also guaranteed. However, no decision was taken as to what to do with the WEU once the WEU Treaty expired in 1998.

Consequently, there has been a gradual establishment of foreign policy competences at the European level and a progressive movement towards supranational decision-making: with a limited agenda-setting role of the Commission; increased policy coordination by the presidency; the possibility of majority voting; and instruments to ensure that the EU acts as a united force in world affairs. Nevertheless, CFSP remains essentially an intergovernmental policy area: the General Affairs Council is the dominant executive and legislative body, and 'governance by consensus' is the main decision-making norm.

Policy success and failure: the 'capability-expectations' gap

Despite this institutional integration, the record of EU action in the area of foreign and security policy is far from consistent. There were some early policy successes under the EPC. For example, the EC first presented a common stance in the negotiations on the Conference on Security and Cooperation in Europe in the early 1970s.

However, the inadequacy of EPC was soon realized when the EC attempted to negotiate a broad political and economic agreement with the USA through EPC. First, the EPC was insufficiently flexible to enable the USA to take part in the intra-European negotiations on the future of western European security. Henry Kissinger, the US Secretary of State, claimed that this was antithetical to the basic assumptions of the Atlantic Alliance: where in return for US military protection, the USA had a right to participate in European security decision-making. The problem for the EPC is that it tended to facilitate positions that were then presented to the US as *fait accomplis* (Featherstone and Ginsberg, 1996, p. 85). Second, and related to this issue, the EPC prevented the EC from negotiating with her partners with a single voice. Following a series of visits to Washington by different EC foreign ministers, each claiming to speak for the EC, Kissinger made his now legendary remark: 'Who speaks for Europe?' (Dinan, 1994, p. 85).

Another area where initial success was replaced by policy intransigence was over economic sanctions against the apartheid regime in South Africa (Holland, 1988). In 1977, the EC adopted a 'Code of Conduct' regulating the employment practices of European firms with subsidiaries in South Africa. In 1985 and 1986, this was reinforced with a series of sanctions on trade between the EC member states and South Africa in oil, iron and steel, paramilitary goods and sensitive technologies, and the banning of cultural, sporting and scientific contacts and military and nuclear cooperation. However, towards the end of the 1980s internal disputes over how best to tackle the South African regime undermined Europe's status as the leader of the global anti-apartheid movement.

Similarly, within a few months of the implementation of the Maastricht

Treaty, the Council adopted a series of joint actions. However, this was less a result of a new institutional capacity, and more to do with the consensual nature of the issues involved. For example, one of these covered South Africa, where common action was now possible because the member states were united in their support for democracy, where before they had been divided over how best to bring down apartheid (Holland, 1995). Most of the other joint actions addressed 'soft' foreign policy issues: such as support for the Middle East peace process; the dispatch of a team of observers for the parliamentary elections in Russia; and humanitarian aid for Bosnia.

However, when it came to 'hard' issues, such as the conflict in the former Yugoslavia, the EU was patently incapable of acting in a clear and decisive manner. Whereas the EU could agree to send humanitarian aid, the EU member states were divided over when to recognize the sovereignty of Croatia, whether to maintain a blockade on the provision of arms to the Bosnian Muslims, and whether to intervene against Serbian oppression and ethnic cleansing. Part of the problem was that the CFSP could be used to prevent a member state from using military force against a common EU policy, but it could not be used to agree a common military strategy and direct the use of force. The EU consequently found itself in an embarrassing position, of initially telling the USA to keep out of Europe's 'backyard', but then relying on the USA to force the sides in the conflict to sit down (in a small town in the US Midwest) and negotiate a peace agreement.

The fundamental problem for the EU in the area of external political and security relations is what Christopher Hill (1993) calls a 'capability-expectations gap'. On the one hand, the EU public and the EU's partners (notably the United States) demand that the EU takes a more active role in world affairs: as a pacifier of regional conflicts; as an intervenor and mediator in global conflicts; as a facilitator of North–South cooperation; and as a joint supervisor of the world economy. On many of these issues the EU is regarded as 'a panacea, a cross between Father Christmas and the Seventh Cavalry' (ibid., p. 322). However, the EU does not have the institutional resources or the political legitimacy to take on these roles. The reforms of Maastricht and Amsterdam may have reduced the institutional constraints on the capacity for common action, but the rival historical and political interests of the EU member states prevent the definition of a common European security identity, and undermine any possibility of acting upon this identity as a united front.

Nevertheless, foreign policy-making for any actor in the international system is more complex at the turn of the century than in the bipolar world of the 1950s to 1980s. As Piening (1997, p. 44) points out:

what have sometimes been perceived as failures of the CFSP (such as the EU's role in Bosnia) are not necessarily a reflection on the policymaking apparatus itself but rather on the intrinsic difficulties in finding solutions to complex problems. After all, it is not as if the finely tuned foreign policy machines of Foggy Bottom, the Quai d'Orsay, or Whitehall have proved any more adept at dealing with issues like Bosnia, Rwanda/Burundi, or Iraq.

In the post-cold war world, without an overarching global balance-of-power or security architecture, the definition of actors' policy preferences is more complex and the final result of policy actions is less predictable. In other words, the EU is not alone in suffering from a capability-expectations gap. The problem is simply that this gap is larger for the EU than for some other actors in the international system.

Explaining the global policies of the EU

Among a number of possible questions arising from this survey of EU global policies, several issues stand out:

- why has the EU been more successful in pursuing a single common economic policy than a single foreign security policy;
- why has the EU pursued a relatively liberal global trade and economic policy despite pressures for and fears of a 'fortress Europe'; and
- why has the EU been able to adopt and implement common foreign and security policies on some issues but not others?

The extensive literature on the EU's global policies offers four main perspectives on these questions: (1) the importance of global economic and geopolitical relations in driving the EU's agenda and decision-making; (2) the dominance and intransigence of European nation-states' security interests; (3) the role of 'domestic' economic interests in the EU, which includes the EU governments and private actors; and (4) how the design and context of the EU's institutional framework shapes agendas and outcomes.

Global economic and geopolitical (inter)dependence

Western Europe is more a recipient of global economic and geopolitical developments than it is a shaper of these developments. Global developments beyond the EU's control determine the agenda and timetable of EU global policies, and the possible options available to EU policy-makers. For example, in the 1980s and 1990s the EU was forced to react to two powerful exogenous developments: (1) economic globalization; and (2) the end of the cold war.

In terms of economic globalization, between 1970 and 1990 there was a dramatic expansion in cross-border trade and capital movements. First, import volumes as a percentage of GDP of advanced industrial countries, which remained steady at 10–16 per cent between 1880 and 1972, increased to almost 22 per cent between 1973 and 1987 (McKeown, 1991, p. 158); and whereas internal demand grew at approximately 2 per cent per year, trade grew at almost 5 per cent per year. In other words, trade grew between the 1970s and 1990s at a rate of about 66 per cent higher than growth in domestic demand. Second, cross-border capital flows have increased faster than domestic demand for capital. For example, international capital flows to the advanced industrial countries rose from an annual average of $99 billion in 1975–77 to $463 billion in 1985–89 (Turner, 1991; p. 23). Also, total net lending in world markets grew from $100 billion a year in the late 1970s to $342 billion a year in 1990; and foreign exchange trading more than quadrupled between 1982 and 1992 to $1000 billion a day, or 40 times the average daily volume of world trade.

This economic globalization has two main effects (Milner and Keohane, 1996; Frieden and Rogowski, 1996; Garrett and Lange, 1996). First, globalization facilitates global convergence in the price of goods, services and capital. This consequently puts pressure on the EU states to reform their internal policies to allow convergence with its global competitors. Second, globalization favours some domestic interests and disadvantages others: namely financial services, importing firms, and firms involved in production for global markets are favoured at the expense of producers for the domestic market (Frieden, 1991). As a result, as trade and capital flows grow, there is greater pressure from organised interests for policies that promote more free trade, and so on. For example, in the Uruguay Round negotiations, the issue-linkage between trade liberalization and CAP reform meant that pro-free-trade EU states and domestic economic interests argued for CAP reform as a means of promoting greater trade liberalization (cf. Devuyst, 1995; Patterson, 1997; Meunier, 1998).

Similarly, the fall of the Berlin Wall, the democratic revolutions in central and eastern Europe, and the collapse of the Soviet Union and its empire created a new strategic environment for western Europe (Knudsen, 1994; Sperling and Kirchner, 1997). The EU member states were immediately forced to address a series of interrelated security, political and economic issues, which had not been on the EU agenda. These included, *inter alia*, how to incorporate a united Germany into the western alliance, how to stabilize democracy and the free market in the new democracies in central and eastern Europe, how to involve these states in a broader

'European house' without antagonizing Russia, and how to tackle the potential large influx of economic migrants (Smith, 1996; Heiberg, 1998).

Furthermore, the choices available to the EU on many items on this agenda were constrained by the policy of the United States. The EU was dependent upon how far the USA would 'pull the troops out', whether the US Congress would retreat into isolationism, and how fast the US administration wanted to enlarge NATO to the east (Ullrich, 1998). For example, in the Maastricht Treaty negotiations, the US government played a crucial role in determining the shape of the rules on defence cooperation in the final Treaty (van Staden, 1994; Duke, 1996).

Security identities/interests of the western European nation-states

However, as discussed in the previous chapter, not all issues are of the same political salience and sensitivity for states. Hoffmann (1966) distinguishes between two issue types: (1) 'high politics', that touch on the fundamental definition, identity, security and sovereignty of the nation-state; and (2) 'low politics', that are not as threatening to the viability of the nation-state, such as European economic integration and EU regulatory policies. Consequently, because foreign and security policies are central to the concept of national identity and national security, the EU member states have been less willing to develop supranational forms of decision-making in this area than in the less-politically-sensitive area of external economic and trade policies.

The underlying reason for this dichotomy is that the European nation-states have divergent political/security interests and conceptions of how best to protect these interests. Waever (1996) argues that there are four different types of 'security identities': societal, political/military, economic and environmental. Each of these 'dialectics' has a different 'referent object' and a different notion of how this object can be protected. As a result, Waever argues that whereas the referent object of political/military security is the 'state', which is best protected through state 'sovereignty', the referent objects of economic security are firms, who have varying chances of survival in the face of liberalization and national protectionism. From the realist perspective, then, economic security is subservient to political security because 'the state' and 'sovereignty' are more powerful forms of identification than private firms.

As a result, the history of the development of the EU's common foreign and defence policies is a history of competition between rival nation-states' interpretations of how best to defend their security (Hill, 1996; Pfetsch, 1994). The western European nation-state remains the sovereign actor in foreign policy issues. As a result, instead of the EU developing an autonomous identity and capacity on the global stage, the EU is simply a vehicle through which the member states pursue those parts of their foreign policies that coincide. Where the interests of the state diverge, the EU becomes incapacitated and the member states pursue their interests independently of the EU. In this interpretation, the institutional design of the CFSP is largely irrelevant (Stavridis, 1997). What matters is the political commitment of the member states, which cannot be overcome with more 'effective' decision-making procedures. The only hope for the EU is that security interests may coincide in the long term, and that this process may be facilitated by continued bargaining in the CFSP and institutions like the early-warning unit in the Council secretariat. However, from a realist perspective this is unlikely, as security interests are invariable.

Finally, the member states' security identities in the foreign policy field also determine the global economic policies of the EU. The member states allow supranational institutions and common policies in external economic affairs because they share certain common economic interests. However, where security interests diverge, external trade policy preferences also diverge. For example, states that favour an independent European defence identity are reluctant to allow the European economy to become dependent on transatlantic trade. Conversely, states that favour a transatlantic defence community have been at the forefront of attempts to tie the EU economy into a broader transatlantic economic community. In other words, the free trade/protectionism cleavage in trade policies follows the Atlanticist/Europeanist cleavage in security policies.

'Domestic' economic interests: EU governments and multinational firms

From a liberal perspective, however, the determination of policy choices is the other way round: security interests are derived from economic interests. These interests can be defined at the national level, where governments define their preferences to cater to the median voter or the most powerful domestic economic interests. Alternatively, they can be defined and articulated at the European level by private economic actors who have no specific 'national allegiance', such as multinational corporations and sectoral associations (Junne, 1994). In either case, EU global policies change as different domestic economic interests come to power or change their own preferences in light of exogenous developments (such as globalization and the emergence of new markets in central and eastern Europe).

First, economic interests play a vital role in shaping the external economic policies of the EU. For example, multinational corporations, not only from the EU member states but also from non-EU states in Europe (such as Sweden), played a pivotal role in shaping the EU's agenda in the Uruguay Round negotiations. Also, the European Round-Table of Industrialists and the EU Committee of the American Chamber of Commerce launched a campaign to persuade anti-free-trade EU governments to support trade liberalization, and supplied the Commission with arguments to strengthen their position in Council bargaining. Similarly, a group of European and American multinational corporations formed the Trans-Atlantic Business Dialogue (TABD) in 1994 to campaign for greater transatlantic free trade. In a series of committees composed of representatives of these firms, the TABD drew up detailed proposals for the mutual recognition of standards in a number of product areas. The Commission and the US government subsequently adopted these proposals almost in their entirety.

Second, economic interests are also a key factor in explaining the external political and security policies of the EU (cf. Praet, 1987). For example, German businesses were the largest investors in central and eastern Europe following the collapse of communism, so that Germany had both an economic and a strategic interest to promote the development of stable markets in its neighbours. In this instance, economic interest went hand in hand with security interests. In other situations, however, collective economic interest has overridden competing security concerns. For example, the need to defend the credibility of GATT and the WTO is forcing the French and British governments to redefine and reform their historical relations with their former colonies, many of whom have been kept for security and military reasons. Administrative elites may oppose this threat to national identities and security interests, but domestic economic groups are less interested in these concerns than in their own material well-being, and governments are ultimately accountable to the median voter. Hence, in the liberal interpretation, if a state is faced with a choice between free trade and protection of a security interest, and there is a large portion of the electorate employed in globally-competitive industries, the government will chose free trade.

As a result, in almost direct contrast to the above claims of the determinacy of security interests, from this perspective the external economic implications of the EU single market have played a major role in determining the pace of institutional integration and the type of policy outcomes in the foreign and security policy field. As Smith (1998a, p. 93) explains: 'The strategic framework is provided by the EU but the agency and action are provided by the EC'. Part of the reason for this is that trade policy is managed in the first pillar through a division of competences along regional lines in the Commission and in the agenda of trade ministers: such as, EU–US relations, EU–Asia relations, and EU–Mediterranean. When these external economic issues touch on political and security concerns, they are passed on to foreign ministers. However, this forces the governments to tackle many political/security issues on an agenda and timetable that is set by the EU's single market and external economic policy agenda.

Supranational institutional context: decision-rules and agenda-setting

Finally, and related to this perspective, is the argument that the EU's global policies are determined by the institutional context at the European level. Against the sceptical opinion of realists, liberal-institutionalists maintain that the supranational institutional framework shapes EU global policies in three ways: (1) through the existence of a supranational actor – the Commission – with certain agenda-setting powers and a vested interest in promoting political integration and other policy outcomes; (2) through the institutional design of trade policy-making, which limits the ability of anti-free-trade states to block a liberal policy outcome; and (3) through the decision-rules and institutional norms in the CFSP field, which have promoted policy movement despite deep disagreement.

First, the European Commission has particular policy preferences in the area of EU global policies. On the one hand, the Commission has institutional interests: further economic and political integration in Treaty reforms, and designs that grant it significant agenda-setting power and policy discretion (see Chapter 2). On the other hand, the Commission has political preferences: there is a free-trade majority in the College of Commissioners, but the Commission also favours the EU playing a greater (interventionist) role in global political and economic affairs. In the making of EU trade policy, the Commission has used its powers of agenda-setting and policy implementation to maximum effect (Smith, 1997b). The Commission has successfully promoted multilateral and bilateral free-trade agreements against the preferences of important member states (notably France), and has been able to place new issues on the agenda such as the mutual recognition agreements with the USA and the organization and promotion of the EU–Asia summits. In some respects the Commission has successfully 'captured' the external trade policy of the EU. This facilitated free trade in the 1980s and 1990s. However, under a different set of political preferences in the Commission or through the mobilization of anti-free-trade 'Euro-champions', policy capture by the Commission might lead to trade protectionism by the EU in the future (Bilal, 1998).

In the making of foreign and security policies, the Commission does not have the same agenda-setting capabilities as in trade policies. Nevertheless, the Commission has been able to influence policy outcomes through informal agenda-setting, such as the generation of policy ideas (Nuttall, 1997). The Commission has also used its powers in external trade policy to promote explicitly political goals, as in the development of the EU's policy towards the Mediterranean (see for example Piening, 1997; Gomez, 1998). Consequently, the Commission's potential for policy-activism in such a sensitive policy area is one of the key reasons why the EU governments have been reluctant to delegate full agenda-setting powers to the Commission (Nuttall, 1996).

Second, Hanson (1998, p. 81) argues 'that trade policy liberalization is largely the result of changes in the institutional context of trade policy-making'. By delegating trade policy-making to a supranational institutional setting, only those actors with the most resources can influence the policy agenda (see Chapter 7) (cf. Nicolaides, 1995). Also, through the use of the consultation procedure the Council only requires a majority to adopt the (free-trade) policy proposals of the Commission, but unanimity to reject them (see Chapter 3). Hence, the protectionist majority is repeatedly outvoted. The result is that 'trade policy outcomes have become divorced from their relationship to underlying preferences of state and societal actors for some of the large and important member states', most notably France (Hanson, 1998, p. 81).

Third, the design of decision-making in foreign and security policies has promoted policy convergence and consensus and restricted competition and divergence. For example, Bulmer (1991) argues that even the limited institutional structure of European political cooperation created a relationship between the member states akin to 'cooperative federalism': where the member states recognize that foreign policy-making should be 'shared' between the European and the national level. Moreover, the establishment of a new institutional framework for the CFSP produced several policy changes immediately, such as an increase in the number of common positions agreed, a use of the new joint-action policy instrument, and an integration of CFSP issues into the general EU timetable (Cameron, 1998). Indeed, Michael Smith (1998, p. 332) argues that the development of the EU's foreign policy shows that:

> intergovernmental systems can still be altered with rules that are more powerful than analysts appreciate, and that neither the ECJ nor the Commission are necessarily needed to develop and reinforce them.

Moreover, once states learned that using supranational modes of decision-making – such as qualified-majority voting and agenda-setting by the Commission – do not present a fundamental challenge to national security identities, they were willing to accept a development of these rules at the Amsterdam Treaty.

Conclusion: economic heavyweight but political lightweight

The EU has the potential to be a major force in shaping global events. But the EU has lived up to this potential in the economic sphere more than in the political and security spheres. The EU is the world's largest trader, and through the Common Commercial Policy it has used its power to promote global free trade. The single market has been opened to the world through multiple trade agreements with almost every region of the world, and the EU also played a crucial role in the establishment of the WTO, and has worked to promote and defend its legitimacy.

The EU has been less capable of speaking with a single and consistent voice on global political and security issues. The EU governments have progressively strengthened the institutional capacity of the EU to agree and implement foreign policy actions, and these procedures have facilitated the definition of collective interests, the adoption of policy compromises, the prevention of national actions that undermine common policies, and the representation of these views in a coherent manner to the outside world. The EU has taken action on a number of non-sensitive issues, such as political and economic support for new democracies in central and eastern Europe, but it has been incapable of acting coherently and decisively when faced with fundamental challenges to EU security, as was demonstrated in the EU's response to the conflict in the former Yugoslavia. As a result, the United States has grown increasingly impatient with western Europe's inability to share the burden of the 'global policeman'.

But, why does this dichotomy exist? The answer lies in a mixture of the liberal and realist theories of international relations and international political economy. The liberal theory appears to explain EU global economic policies. In this area, policies have been driven more by economic than security interests. As the world's largest trader, global free trade is in the EU's rational economic interest. Moreover, free trade outcomes are partly due to the organizational power of multinational businesses, who are inherently more able to organize at the EU level than producers for domestic markets. Supranational institutions have also played a part. The Commission has had an institutional incentive to facilitate global free-trade institutions as a means of increasing its negotiating mandate and policy freedom from EU governments.

However, realist theory is more helpful in explaining EU foreign and security policies. The deep historical and cultural roots of the rival European nation-states' security identities have undermined the ability of the EU to define and project a single 'European foreign policy'. In fact, Piner Tank (1998) argues that the loss of economic sovereignty as a result of economic integration and common trade policies in the first pillar strengthens the resolve of the member states to defend their sovereignty over foreign and security policies in the Common Foreign and Security Policy. Consequently, the mix of supranational and intergovernmental decision rules, as set up by the Maastricht and Amsterdam Treaties, may be necessary to enable common policies to be adopted, but these rules are certainly not sufficient to produce decisive actions.

Conclusion: Rethinking the European Union

What does political science teach us about the EU?
What does the EU teach us about political science?

This book thinks about the EU in a different way to the traditional approaches to European integration and EU studies. It does not propose a new 'integration theory', nor does it attempt a detailed description of particular events or developments in Brussels. Instead, it argues that we can improve our understanding of how the EU works by applying our general understanding of the main processes in modern political systems to the EU. The key underlying assumption, then, is that the EU is already a fully-functioning political system. Because of this, political science has a lot to teach us about the EU. Conversely, since the EU is an unusual political system, we can also improve our general understanding of political science. In so doing, this book attempts to integrate research and teaching on the EU into the mainstream study of politics.

What does political science teach us about the EU?

Operation of government, politics and policy-making in the EU

Political science tells us a considerable amount about each of the processes analysed in this book. In the area of executive politics, the Council delegates agenda-setting and policy implementation tasks to the Commission primarily to reduce transactions costs and facilitate policy credibility. However, the Commission is not simply a neutral actor. Like all political executives, commissioners have their own career and partisan/ideological goals; and, like all bureaucracies, the Commission administration has incentives to expand its fiscal resources, its political and regulatory powers, and its autonomy from political control. But, the EU governments can predict this. To preempt this 'bureaucratic drift', the Council has established mechanisms to constrain the Commission: such as control over the appointment of commissioners and the comitology system.

In the area of legislative politics, both the Council and the EP have established internal institutions to improve legislative decision-making: the

357

Council presidency and the EP leadership structures improve agenda-organization; and sectoral Councils and EP committees facilitate bargaining on an issue-by-issue basis. As we expected, different legislative coalitions form on different policy dimensions (such as the pro-/anti-integration dimension and the left–right), and actors have different powers under the various legislative rules (QMV/unanimity and cooperation/co-decision).

In the area of judicial politics, the EU governments established the ECJ to overcome a collective action problem: the disincentive for each member state to implement market liberalization without an external threat. However, several actors had incentives to promote the subsequent 'constitutionalization' of the Treaties: the ECJ developed doctrines to increase its institutional autonomy and influence over policy outcomes; national courts accepted EU law to strengthen their powers against national parliaments and governments; and private litigants sought EU norms to further their private interests. Moreover, the institutional design of the EU made it difficult for anti-integrationist forces to reign in the ECJ.

In the area of public opinion, EU society is primarily divided along national lines. However, citizens also form their attitudes towards the EU on the basis of personal economic interests and political values and as a result individuals from the same social group in different member states share similar views on EU integration. The result is a complex political environment for EU political elites. If EU leaders mobilize the national divisions, the integration project will come to a standstill. But, it will be difficult for political parties to mobilize around EU issues that divide groups along socioeconomic lines (left–right issues), because both the working class and the middle class are internally divided over the EU.

Turning to parties and elections, EP elections do not allow voters to throw out the EU executive or choose the EU policy agenda. This is not because the EP lacks the power over the Commission or in the legislative process. Rather, EP elections do not work because national parties have an incentive to use them in the competition for domestic government office. Nevertheless, as elites have coalesced with like-minded actors in the EU policy process, nascent 'Euro-parties' have begun to compete to influence the EU policy agenda (in the EP party groups and party leaders' summits).

In the area of interest representation, groups that can secure selective benefits from the EU (such as businesses and farmers) have more of an incentive to organize at the EU level than groups where the benefits or costs of EU policies are diffuse (such as consumers, taxpayers, workers and environmentalists). Nevertheless, the Commission and the EP have incentives to promote the organization and subsidy of under-represented groups, to gain policy expertise, to establish policy credibility, to secure legislative adoption in the Council, and to develop a wide support base.

On regulatory policies, the single market is a classic regulatory project: its aim is positive-sum rather than zero-sum. However, EU regulatory policies do have 'indirect' redistributive consequences. The deregulation of national rules favours producer groups, whereas the harmonization of 'process standards' protects workers, environmentalists and consumers. Nevertheless, on some regulatory issues governments prefer any EU regulation to none (the status quo), and as a result the EU is more able to adopt deregulatory policies and common product standards (such as environmental labelling) than common process standards (such as workers' rights).

As regards redistributive policies, the member states that benefit most from the single market and EMU are willing to grant 'side payments' to the losers in the EU project. However, because receipts are concentrated whereas payments are diffuse, social groups that benefit under each EU programme have more of an incentive to mobilize to protect their subsidies than groups who pay into the budget. Also, redistributive policies tend to facilitate 'iron triangles': where executive officials (such as the Agriculture DG in the Commission), legislators (such as agriculture ministers), and private interests (such as the farm lobby) share an interest in promoting and protecting expenditure in their policy area.

In the operation of economic and monetary union, the EU is not an 'optimum currency area', and as a result the Euro-zone is likely to experience asymmetric shocks. However, the EU is ill-equipped to address these shocks: there is little labour movement between the states, fiscal transfers through the EU budget are small, and the Euro-11 governments cannot run fiscal deficits. But, the institutional design of EMU allows for policy flexibility. The member states can implement labour market reforms; the ECB will not be completely immune from political pressure; and finance ministers can introduce tax harmonization, reform the fiscal rules, allow more fiscal transfers and devalue the Euro.

In the area of citizen freedom and security policies, governments responded to voter demands for action to combat the perceived threat of cross-border crime and illegal immigration as a result of the free movement of persons in the single market. Bureaucrats in interior ministries also sought to increase their capacity to control the movement of persons. On the other side, the EU institutions demanded institutional reforms to improve policy accountability (which would also increase their influence), and as a result governments introduced majority voting, established new EP and ECJ powers, and delegated agenda-setting powers to the Commission.

Finally, on global policies, the EU is more able to agree common external economic policies than common external political/security policies. On economic issues, policies tend to be driven by economic interests. As the world's largest trader, global free trade is in the EU's collective economic interest, and multinational firms (who benefit from free trade) are more able to lobby the EU than are domestic producers (who gain from protectionist policies). On political and security issues, in contrast, the member states have competing geo-political interests and identities, and private non-state actors have little incentive to push for genuine common EU foreign or defence policies.

Connections between government, politics and policy-making in the EU

Political science also teaches us about how the processes of government, politics and policy-making are interconnected in the EU. In the connection *from politics to government*, EU governments are composed of national political parties whose primary goal is to be reelected. This has two effects. First, governments seek EU policies that are in line with their electoral commitments, accord with their domestic public opinion, or directly benefit their voters and supporting interest groups. Second, governments have limited time horizons – the long-term impact of EU decisions is less important than the short-term political salience and impact of EU decisions.

In contrast, the supranational institutions – the Commission, the EP and the ECJ – are relatively isolated from short-term electoral considerations. Individual commissioners may wish to have their terms renewed, which encourages them to remain connected to their domestic governing and party elites. However, this is unpredictable as governments and party elites change. Similarly, because European elections are fought as national contests, the reelection of MEPs depends on the electoral success of their domestic party rather than their individual or party-group performance in the EP. The national content of European elections also leads to party fragmentation in the EP. Nevertheless, the supranational interests are not completely isolated from public opinion. If the EU governments are to grant them more powers, they need the support and confidence of EU citizens. As a result, the Commission has often proposed 'populist' measures, the ECJ was less activist after the rise of 'Euro-scepticism' in the mid-1990s, and the EP has tried to raise its profile on the eve of European elections (to achieve a higher turnout in the elections).

In the connection *from politics to policy-making*, public opinion and party competition shape the preferences and strategies of actors in the policy-making process. For example, governments are weary of delegating powers to the Commission and the ECJ in areas where their electorates have opposed EU actions. And, on highly-salient issues (such as key pieces of legislation or the candidate for the Commission president), parties in government put pressure on their MEPs to back their government's position in the Council. In contrast, on issues where there is high public support for EU actions (as in the environmental field), and on low-saliency issues (such as the single market programme), governments are more willing to allow policy outcomes that might strengthen the powers of the EU institutions in the long term.

The structure of interest representation also shapes policy outcomes. Groups that can secure selective or concentrated benefits from the EU policy process have the most incentive to mobilize. As a result, business interests lobbied for the single market programme and against high environmental and social regulations; regions lobby to maintain cohesion expenditure; and farmers lobby to maintain the CAP. Nevertheless, diffuse interests (such as environmentalists, consumers and trade unions) have secured policies where the Commission has had an incentive to incorporate these groups; when centre-left parties have been powerful in the Council; and where the centre-left in the EP has been able to set the legislative agenda. In addition, transnational social divisions, domestic party competition and interest group organization have all contributed to the emergence of a new 'left–right' dimension in the EU policy process. The traditional 'integration dimension' remains: between groups and institutions seeking further European integration and groups in favour of maintaining national sovereignty. However, on many policy issues (such as macroeconomic questions in EMU and value-allocation questions in the governance of the single market), the battle lines are between 'regulated capitalism' (supported by parties on the left in the EU institutions) and 'neo-liberalism' (supported by parties on the right in the EU institutions).

In the connection *from government to policy-making*, the institutional rules of EU government facilitate particular policy outcomes. For example, the delegation of executive and judicial powers to the Commission and the ECJ has 'locked-in' the policy of 'ever-closer union'. The Commission and the ECJ have used these powers to protect their own institutional interests in the EU system and to secure the interests of their support groups (the interests organized around the Commission, and national courts and the legal community around the ECJ). Also, governments were unable to predict these outcomes because of a lack of information and because of short time-horizons. And, because Treaty reform requires unanimity, this delegation has always been 'one-way traffic'.

The legislative rules have also shaped policy outcomes. Qualified-majority voting in the Council has facilitated agreement on deregulatory policies and EU-wide product standards. In contrast, unanimity voting has undermined efforts to adopt common process standards (such as workers' rights). Also, the EP has used its powers under the cooperation and co-decision procedures to promote the policies of the main party groups (such as the PES goal of high EU environmental protection), but this has usually been conditional on the majority of governments in the Council preferring any EU legislation to no common regulations. Perhaps only in the area of external political and security policies have decision-making rules been less determinant of policy outcomes than 'politics' within and between the EU governments.

However, as governments have increasingly understood the long-term relationship between institutional rules and policy outcomes, they have consciously chosen institutional designs to promote or prevent particular policy outcomes. For example, most governments have been reluctant to delegate executive and judicial powers in areas of fundamental national sovereignty (such as on foreign policy and internal security). Similarly, anti-integration and centre-right governments have fought to maintain the consultation procedure and unanimity voting in policy areas that are likely to result in federalist and left-wing outcomes (such as tax harmonization).

Finally, the connection *from government/policy-making to politics* has generally been weaker than the connections in the opposite direction. Developments at the EU level have only had a limited impact on the processes of domestic preference formation and contestation. EU citizens remain ill-informed about EU governance, and domestic political parties remain focused on the battle for domestic government office and policy outputs. As a result, whereas domestic politics can lead to new issues on the EU agenda (such as the need to combat cross-border crime and illegal immigration in the late 1990s), EU policy decisions are rarely overturned in the face of domestic opposition. For example, in the early 1990s a majority of public opinion, several major political parties and numerous powerful social groups (such as trade unions) were opposed to EMU, but governing parties were able to keep this issue off the domestic political agenda in the hope that the public would eventually 'come round' to the idea.

Nevertheless, voters' and interest groups' preferences change as their incentives and environment change. This has allowed governments and the EU institutions to use EU policy outputs to change the structure of preferences in the domestic system. For example, centre-right governments have promoted EU competition and state-aid policies to produce domestic firms with an interest in open markets and a larger private-sector middle class (which tends to support centre-right political parties). Similarly, pro-integration EU governments and the Commission have used EU regional policies to 'buy' support for the EU in periphery states.

And, things are starting to change. The end of the permissive consensus, the launch of EMU, and the rise of party-political contestation over the EU agenda all mean that EU citizens, rank-and-file party members and non-governing party elites are starting to take notice of the governing and policy-making processes at the European level. The result is increasing restrictions on the freedom of manoeuvre of elites at the EU level.

What does the EU teach us about political science?

At the *micro level*, research on the EU has made some important findings about the relationship between actors and their institutional environment. In particular, the development and operation of the EU confirms the core assumptions of the 'institutional rational choice' and 'historical-institutionalist' schools in political science.

As in all systems, policy outcomes result from strategic interaction between the actors in the EU system. The location of actors in the EU policy space determines which actors are pivotal in turning minority coalitions into winning coalitions: whether this is the Commission, the EP or the least integrationist government in the Council. However, the formal and informal institutions of the EU system are also crucially important in shaping political outcomes. The EU is a complex political system with multiple rules and procedures. These determine the order in which decisions are tackled, the time-horizons of the actors, the types of pay-offs that can be achieved in the policy process, who has agenda-setting power (and under what conditions), whether or not actors can exercise a veto, and consequently under which conditions actors are pivotal (independently of their policy preferences). Also, the informal norms of the EU system – such as the need to achieve a broad political consensus – are as important in determining political outcomes as the formal rules. Put another way, 'equilibria' in the EU system are usually 'structure-induced'.

Also, these formal and informal rules of the EU game do not come from anywhere. 'Institutional choices' are policy choices by other means. In the recurring institutional game that is EU politics, the actors have developed highly-sophisticated institutional preferences: such as which policies should be tackled at the European level, who has the right to initiate proposals under each of these policies, the internal rules of procedure of each of the institutions, the rules governing which private actors should be included in the policy process, how the implementation process should be held to account, and under which decision-making procedures policies should be implemented. In particular strategic and institutional circumstances, actors are able to choose between rules or choose new rules. This is almost always to secure outcomes that are closer to their ideal preferences. However, the EU system also shows that in a highly complex strategic and institutional setting, actors can never be certain of the ultimate (long-term) policy impact of institutional choices.

Extrapolating this to the *meso level*, research on the EU tells us something interesting about each of the cross-systemic processes discussed in this book. In the area of government, once executive, legislative or judicial powers have been delegated to independent agents – whether they are governmental agencies or courts – they are notoriously difficult to withdraw. As in the United States and at the domestic level in Europe, this has generally led to a strengthening of the power of bureaucrats and judges at the expense of directly-elected legislative representatives. Nonetheless, the growing power of the EP in the legislative process and in scrutinizing the activities of the Commission may be an important exception to this general rule.

In the area of politics, the EU tells us that citizens' opinions matter, but not as much as we might like. Governing elites in the EU are only forced to respond to public opinion when issues become highly salient, and, as a result, elites often share incentives to collude to keep issues off the political agenda. Nonetheless, the EU illustrates that in complex policy systems there are numerous opportunities for interest groups to become the key intermediaries between society and decision-makers. But, political parties are never absent for long. When agendas become politicized, party organizations, alliances and interests begin to drive the policy agenda and link the processes of mass politics, governmental bargaining and policy outputs.

In the area of policy-making, the EU shows how 'regulation' has become the key instrument of modern governance. The redistributive bargains of the democratic welfare state were struck in the immediate postwar world. The new policy battles relate to the level of state regulation of private economic and social interaction and competing agendas have begun to emerge in this new battle. The 'new right' supports freedom from regulatory 'red tape' and the delegation of regulatory policies to 'independent' institutions (such as the European Central Bank). In opposition, the 'old left' agenda of wealth redistribution is being replaced by a 'new left' agenda of high levels of 'protection' against social and economic risk and 'political' accountability and control of independent regulators.

Finally, extrapolating to the *macro level*, the EU shows that a highly-developed political system can emerge without either the full-blown apparatus of a state, or a high level of popular support and mass political participation. The key reasons for this are the outputs of the EU system: a single market, a single currency, regulatory rather than redistributive policies, and limited encroachment into the traditional areas of state power (internal and external security). These policies tend to be positive-sum rather than zero-sum: there are few clear 'losers' in the EU political system. If the outcomes were highly redistributive, the EU would either require a greater use of force to impose its policies or a greater level of democratic participation to legitimize redistributive outcomes. Ironically, then, if economic and political integration is to proceed much further, the EU is likely to need a greater state-capacity as well as genuine democratic contestation to legitimize this state power.

In sum, the key contention of this book is that to understand how the EU works we need to think about it in a more structured, systematic and scientific way. Only by doing so can we begin to answer the vital theoretical and normative questions that surround the building of this new and important political system. And, along the way, we may learn some new things about the world of politics at the start of the new century.

Decision-Making Procedures
of the European Union

Title	Issue
Treaty on European Union	
I. Common	Breach of EU principles
Provisions	Suspend rights/revoke suspension
V. Common	Adoption of decisions
Foreign and	
Security Policy	Implementation
	Procedural questions
	Open negotiations with third countries/IOs
	Agreements with third countries/IOs
	Expenditure beyond budget or for military
VI. Police and	Adoption of measures
Judicial	Implementation
Cooperation in	Flexible integration
Criminal	
Matters	Join flexible integration
	Expenditure beyond budget
	Transfer to EC pillar
VII. Closer	Common expenditure
Cooperation	
VIII. Final Provisions	Proposal for amending the Treaties
	Acceptance of new members
Schengen	Implementation
Protocol	
	Participation of UK & Ireland
	Agreement with Norway & Iceland
Treaty establishing the European Community	
Part One: Principles	Authorization/joining flexible integration
	Discrimination on grounds of nationality
	Other forms of discrimination (e.g. race)
	Guidelines for internal market sectors
Part Two: Citizenship	Right to free movement and residence
	Arrangements for voting rights

Article	Old Article	Right of initiative	Council voting rule	Parliament involvement
7(1) EU	—	C or 1/3 MS	Unanimity	Assent
7(2)/(3) EU	—	Council	QMV	None
23(1) EU	J.3	Council	Unanimity/ Constr.Abs.	None
23(2) EU	J.3	MS	QMV(10)/ veto + Un.	None
23(3) EU	None	Council	Simple Majority	None
24 EU	J.5	MS (Pres)	QMV	None
24 EU	J.5	MS (Pres)	Unanimity	None
28 EU	None	Council	Unanimity	None
34(2a,b,di) EU	K.1	C or MS	Unanimity	Consultation
34(2c,dii) EU	K.1	C or MS	QMV(10)	Consultation
40(2) EU	None	MS + C(Op.)	QMV(10)/ veto + Un.	None
40(3) EU	None	MS + C(Op.)	Unan./QMV (to delay)	None
41 EU	K.8	Council	Unanimity	None
42 EU	K.9	C or MS	Unanimity	Consultation
44(2) EU	None	Council	Unanimity	None
48 EU	N	C or MS	Unanimity + Ratification	Consultation
49 EU	O	MS + C(Op.)	Unanimity + Ratification	Assent
[2(1) Protocol]	None	Council	Unan. (of signatories)	None
[3 Protocol]	None	Council	Unan. (of signatories)	None
[5 Protocol]	None	Council	Unan. (of signatories)	None
11	None	C	QMV/veto + Un.	Consultation
12	6	C	QMV	Co-decision
13	None	C	Unanimity	Consultation
14	7a	C	QMV	None
18	8a	C	Unanimity	Co-decision
19	8b	C	Unanimity	Consultation

Title		*Issue*
Part Three: Community Policies		
I.	Free Movement of Goods	Common customs tariff
II.	Agriculture	Operation of the CAP
		New products covered by CAP
III.	Free Movement of Persons, Services and Capital	Workers:
		establish freedoms
		social security rights
		Right of establishment:
		all provisions
		amend rules of professions
		Services:
		liberalization
		Capital and Payments:
		direct investments
		threat to EMU
		urgent measures
IV.	Visas, Asylum, Immigration and Free Movement of Persons	Internal borders, asylum, immigration, extradition
		Issue of visas, rules on uniform visa
		Visa list, uniform format for visas
		Emergency measures on immigration
		Decision after 5 years to move to co-decision
V.	Transport	General transport policy
		Abolition of discrimination
		Sea and air transport
VI.	Competition, Taxation and Approximation of Laws	Competition:
		rules applying to undertakings
		State Aids:
		new categories of state aid
		general state aids policy
		Taxation:
		limited taxes on internal trade
		harmonization of indirect taxation
		Approximation of Laws:
		single market regulation (rarely used)
		single market regulation (most areas)
		prevent distortion of competition
VII.	Economic and Monetary Union	Economic Policy:
		economic policy guidelines
		rules for multilateral surveillance
		special financial assistance
		assistance for natural disasters
		privileged access to financial institutions
		guarantees against EC financial liability

Article	Old Article	Right of initiative	Council voting rule	Parliament involvement
26	12	C	QMV	None
37(2)	43	C	QMV	Consultation
37(3)	43	C	QMV	None
40	49	C	QMV	Co-decision
42	51	C	Unanimity	Co-decision
44-47	54-57	C	QMV	Co-decision
47(2)	57	C	Unanimity	Co-decision
52	63	C	QMV	Consultation
57	73c	C	QMV (Unan. to repeal)	None
59	73f	C	QMV	None
60	73g	C	QMV	None
62(1)(2a), 63, 65, 66	None	C or MS	Unanimity	Consultation
62(2bii, biv)	None	C or MS	Unanimity (5ys-QMV)	Con. (5ys-Cod)
62(2bi, biii)	None	C or MS	QMV	Consultation
64	None	C	QMV	None
67	None	C	Unanimity	Consultation
71	75	C	QMV	Co-decision
75	79	C	QMV	None
80	84	C	QMV	Co-decision
83	87	C	QMV	Consultation
87(3)	92	C	QMV	None
89	94	C	QMV	Consultation
92	98	C	QMV	None
93	99	C	Unanimity	Consultation
94	100	C	Unanimity	Consultation
95	100a	C	QMV	Co-decision
96	101	C	QMV	None
99(2)	(4)103	C	QMV	None
99(5)	103	C	QMV	Cooperation
100(2)	103a	C	Unanimity	None
100(2)	103a	C	QMV	None
102	104a	C	QMV	Cooperation
103	104b	C	QMV	Cooperation

Title		*Issue*

VII.	Economic and Monetary Union *continued*	decision of existence of excessive deficit
		implementation of excessive deficit rules
		replace Excessive Deficit Protocol
		rules for application of Ex.Def.Protocol
		Monetary Policy:
		  amendment of ECSB statutes (part)
		  amendment of ECSB statutes (part)
		  ER system with non-EU currencies
		  abandon central rates in such a system
		  general orientations for ER policy
		  international agreements & policy
		Institutional Provisions:
		  appointment of ECB officials

		provisions for composition of EFC Transition Provisions: appointment of EMI President
		confer extra tasks to EMI assistance in balance of payments crisis which states qualify for EMU
		derogation for a state from EMU set single currency conversion rates
VIII.	Employment	Annual employment policy guidelines Recommendations to member states Incentive measures for co-operation Establishment of employment committee
IX.	Common Commercial Policy	Harmonise rules on aid for exports General CCP provisions Extend CCP to intellectual property & services
X.	Customs Cooperation	Strengthen customs co-operation

XI.	Social Policy, Education, Vocational Training and Youth	Social Provisions:
		  health & safety, equality, exclusion etc.
		  social security, termination, TCNs etc.
		  implm't social agreements under 137(2)
		  implm't social agreements under 137(3)
		  equality pay for men and women
		  social security for migrant workers
		European Social Fund:
		  implementation
		Education, Vocat'l Training and Youth:
		  incentive measures on education
		  recommendations on education
		  vocational training

Article	Old Article	Right of initiative	Council voting rule	Parliament involvement
104(6)	104c	C	QMV	None
104(13)	104c	Council	W2/3(ex. subject)	None
104(14)	104c	C	Unanimity	Consultation
104(14)	104c	C	QMV	Consultation
107(5)	106	ECB/C	QMV/Unanimity	None
107(6)	106	C or ECB	QMV	Consultation
111(1)	109	C or ECB	Unanimity	Consultation
111(1)	109	C or ECB	QMV	None
111(2)	109	C or ECB	QMV	None
111(3)(4)	109	C	QMV	None
112	109a	Council	Un. (European Council)	Consultation
114	109c	C	QMV	None
117(1)	109f	Council	Un. (European Council)	Consultation
117(7)	109fC	Unanimity	·Consultation	
119	109h	Council	QMV(10)	None
121	109j	C	QMV (Euro. Council)	Consultation
122	109k	C	QMV	None
123	109l	C	Unanimity	None
128(2)	None	C	QMV	Consultation
128(4)	None	C	QMV	None
129	None	C	QMV	Co-decision
130	None	Council	QMV(10)	Consultation
132	112	C	QMV	None
133(4)	113	C	QMV	None
133.V	None	C	QMV	Consultation
135	None	C	QMV	Co-decision
137(2)	118	C	QMV	Co-decision
137(3)	118	C	Unanimity	Consultation
139(2)	118b	C	QMV	None
139(2)	118b	C	Unanimity	None
141	119	C	QMV	Co-decision
144	121	Council	QMV(10)	None
148	125	C	QMV	Co-decision
149(4)	126	C	QMV	Co-decision
149(4)	126	C	QMV	None
150	127	C	QMV	Co-decision

Title	Issue
XII. Culture	Incentive measures on culture
	Recommendations on culture
XIII. Public Health	Safety standards on organs etc.
	Recommendations on public health
XIV. Consumer Protection	General measures
XV. Trans-Euro. Networks	Guidelines and other measures on TENs policy
XVI. Industry	Specific industrial policy measures
XVII. Economic and Social Cohesion	Specific actions outside structural funds
	Define tasks, objectives and organization of funds
	Implementation decisions
XVIII. Research and Technological Development	Adoption of MFP
	Adoption of specific programmes in MFP
	Set up joint undertakings
	Implementation of MFP
XIX. Environment	General environment policies
	Taxes, development plans etc.
	Environmental action programmes
XIX. Development Coop.	General measures
Part Four: Association of Overseas Countries and Territories	
	Rules for association with EU
Part Five: Institutions of the Community	
I.1(1). European Parliament	Adoption of uniform electoral procedure
	Rules governing duties of MEPs
	Own initiative proposals
	Establishment of Committee of Enquiry
	Regulation of duties of Ombudsman
	Censure of the Commission
I.1(2). Council	Confer implementation powers
	Determine order of presidency
	Pay of commissioners & ECJ
I.1(3) Commission	Alter the number of commissioners
	Nomination of Commission president
	Appointment of individual commissioners
	Fill a commissioner vacancy
I.1(4). Court of Justice	Increase number of judges
	Increase number of advocates general
	Determine classes of action covered by CFI
	Amendment of statute of ECJ
I.1(5). Court of Auditors	Appointment of COA
	Employment conditions of COA members
I.2. Common Instit'l Prov's	Principles for access to documents

Article	Old Article	Right of initiative	Council voting rule	Parliament involvement
151(5)	128	C	QMV	Co-decision
151(5)	128	C	QMV	None
152(4)	129	C	QMV	Co-decision
152(4)	129	C	QMV	None
153	129a	C	QMV	Co-decision
156	129d	C	QMV	Co-decision
157	130	C	Unanimity	Consultation
159	130b	C	Unanimity	Consultation
161	130d	C	Unanimity	Assent
162	130e	C	QMV	Co-decision
166(1)	130i	C	QMV	Co-decision
166(4)	130i	C	QMV	Consultation
172	130o	C	QMV	Consultation
172	130o	C	QMV	Co-decision
175(1)	130s	C	QMV	Co-decision
175(2)	130s	C	Unanimity	Consultation
175(3)	130s	C	QMV	Co-decision
179	130x	C	QMV	Co-decision
187	136	Council	Unanimity	None
190(3)	138	EP	Unanimity	Abs.Majority
190(4)	None	EP	Unanimity	Abs.Majority
192	138b	EP	None	Abs.Majority
193	138c	EP(1/4)	None	Abs.Majority
195(4)	138e	EP	QMV(10)	Abs.Majority
201	144	EP	None	2/3 Majority
202	145	C	Unanimity	Consultation
203	146	Council	Unanimity	None
210	154	Council	QMV(10)	None
213	157	Council	Unanimity	None
214	158	Council	Un. (European Council)	Assent
214	158	Council	Un. (European Council)	Assent
215	159	Council	Unanimity	None
221	165	ECJ	Unanimity	None
222	166	ECJ	Unanimity	None
225	168a	ECJ	Unanimity	Consultation
245	188	ECJ	Unanimity	Consultation
247(3)	188b	Council	Unanimity	Consultation
247(8)	188b	Council	QMV(10)	None
255	None	C	QMV	Co-decision

Title		*Issue*
II.	Financial Provisions	Provisions for own resources
		Adoption of the budget
		Authorize expenditure if no budget
		Examine budget implementation
		Rules of budget implementation
		Measures countering fraud
	Part Six. General and Financial Provisions	Staff regulations for EC officials
		Measures for production of statistics
		Set up of data protection supervisory body
		Amend list of 'essential interests of security'
		Application of Treaty to remote regions
		Negotiation of international agreements by Commission
		Conclusion of international agreements
		Conclusion of Association Agreements
		Adoption of any measure not covered in the Treaty
		Suspension of voting rights/revoke of suspension

Key:

Policy Areas

CFI	The Court of First Instance
ECF	Economic and Financial Committee (of the ECB)
ECSB	European System of Central Banks
EMI	European Monetary Institute
ER	exchange-rate
IO	International Organizations
MFP	multiannual framework programme
TCNs	third-country nationals
TENs	trans-European networks

Right of Initiative

C	Commission
C(Op.)	Commission opinion is required
MS	a member state
1/3 MS	one-third of member states
Pres.	Presidency of Council
ECB	European Central Bank
EP	European Parliament
EP(1/4)	at the request of a quarter of the members of the EP
ECJ	European Court of Justice

Article	Old Article	Right of initiative	Council voting rule	Parliament involvement
269	201	C	Unanimity	Consultation
272	203	C	QMV	Budgetary
273	204	C	QMV	Assent
276	206	Council	QMV	Assent
279	209	C	Unanimity	Consultation
280	None	C	QMV	Co-decision
283	212	C	QMV	Consultation
285	None	C	QMV	Co-decision
286	None	C	QMV	Co-decision
296	223	C	Unanimity	None
299	227	C	QMV	Consultation
300(1)	228	C	QMV	None
300(2)(3)	228	C	Unanimity	Consultation
300(3)	228	C	Unanimity	Assent
308	235	C	Unanimity	Consultation
309	None	C	QMV	None

Council Voting Rule
Unan.   unanimity
QMV   qualified-majority, where votes are weighted according to Article 205
              [ex 148]
QMV(10)   qualified-majority, with at least 10 member states in favour
Const.Abs.   'constructive abstention', where a decision can be carried, with a
              member state opposed
Veto + Un.   if a m.state claims a threat to a vital national interest, it can request the
              decision be referred to the European Council, for a decision by
              unanimity
5ys-QMV   qualified-majority after five years from entry into force of the Treaty
W2/3(ex subject)   a decision of two-thirds of votes cast, weighted according to the
              usual QMV, excluding the votes of the subject member state
Un. (European Council)   unanimity required in the European Council

Parliament Involvement
Con. (5ys-Cod)   Consultation procedure, then Co-decision procedure after five
              years from entry into force of the Treaty
Abs.Majority   requires the support of majority of all members of the European
              Parliament, not simply of votes cast
2/3 Majority   requires the support of two-thirds of votes cast and a majority of all
              members of the European Parliament

Bibliography

Aaron, R. (1974) 'Is Multinational Citizenship Possible', *Social Research*, vol. 41, no. 4, pp. 638–56.

Abélès, M., Bellier, I. and McDonald, M. (1993) *Approche anthropologique de la commission européenne: Executive Summary* (Brussels: European Commission).

Alesina, A. and Summers, L. (1993) 'Central Bank Independence and Macroeconomic Performance: Some Comparative Evidence', *Journal of Money, Credit and Banking*, vol. 25.

Almond, G. A. (1956) 'Comparing Political Systems', *Journal of Politics*, vol. 18, no. 2, pp. 391–409.

Almond, G. A. (1996) 'Political Science: The History of the Discipline', in R. E. Goodin and H.-D. Klingemann (eds), *A New Handbook of Political Science* (Oxford: Oxford University Press).

Almond, G. A. and Verba, S. (1963) *The Civic Culture* (Boston: Little, Brown).

Alter, K. J. (1996) 'The European Court's Political Power', *West European Politics*, vol. 19, no. 3, pp. 458–87.

Alter, K J. (1998a) 'Explaining National Court Acceptance of European Court Jurisprudence: A Critical Evaluation of Theories of Legal Integration', in A.-M. Slaughter, A. Stone Sweet and J. H. H. Weiler (eds), *The European Court and National Courts – Doctrine and Jurisprudence: Legal Change in Its Social Context* (Oxford: Hart Publishing).

Alter, K. J. (1998b) 'Who Are the "Masters of the Treaty?": European Governments and the European Court of Justice', *International Organization*, vol. 52, no. 1, pp. 121–47.

Alter, K. J. and Meunier-Aitsahalia, S. (1994) 'Judicial Politics in the European Community: European Integration and the Pathbreaking *Cassis de Dijon* Decision', *Comparative Political Studies*, vol. 26, no. 4, pp. 535–61.

Alvazzi del Frate, A., Zvekic, U. and Dijk, J. M. van (eds) (1993) *Understanding Crime: Experiences of Crime and Crime Control* (Rome: United Nations Interregional Crime and Justice Research Institute).

Andersen, S. S. and Eliassen, K. A. (1993) 'The EC as a Political System', in S. S. Andersen and K. A. Eliassen (eds), *Making Policy in Europe: The Europeification of National Policy-Making* (London: Sage).

Anderson, C. (1995) 'Economic Uncertainty and European Solidarity Revisited: Trends in Public Support for European Integration', in C. Rhodes and S. Mazey (eds), *The State of the European Union*, vol. 3 (London: Longman).

Anderson, C. (1998) 'Attitudes Towards Domestic Politics and Support for European Integration', *Comparative Political Studies*, forthcoming.

Anderson, C. and Kalthenthaler, K. (1996) 'The Dynamics of Public Opinion Toward European Integration, 1973–93', *European Journal of International Relations*, vol. 2, no. 2, pp. 175–99.

Anderson, C. and Reichert, M. S. (1996) 'Economic Benefits and Support for Membership in the E.U.: A Cross-National Analysis', *Journal of Public Policy*, vol. 15, no. 3, pp. 231–49.

Anderson, J. J. (1990) 'Skeptical Reflections on a Europe of Regions: Britain, Germany and the ERDF', *Journal of Public Policy*, vol. 10, no. 4, pp. 417–48.

Anderson, J. J. (1995) 'Structural Funds and the Social Dimension of EU Policy: Springboard or Stumbling Block?', in S. Leibfried and P. Pierson (eds), *European Social Policy: Between Fragmentation and Integration* (Washington, D.C.: The Brookings Institution).

Anderson, M, den Boer, M., Cullen, P., Gilmore, W., Raab, C. and Walker, N. (1995) *Policing the European Union* (Oxford: Clarendon Press).

Ansell, C. K., Parsons, C. A. and Darden, K. A. (1997) 'Dual Networks in European Regional Development Policy', *Journal of Common Market Studies*, vol. 35, no. 3, pp. 347–76.

Aspinwall, M. and Greenwood, J. (1998) 'Conceptualising Collective Action in the European Union: An Introduction', in J. Greenwood and M. Aspinwall (eds), *Collective Action in the European Union* (London: Routledge).

Armstrong, K. A. and Bulmer, S. J. (1998) *The Governance of the Single European Market* (Manchester: Manchester University Press).

Artis, M. (1996) 'Alternative Transitions to EMU', *Economic Journal*, vol. 106, pp. 1005–15

Attinà, F. (1990) 'The Voting Behaviour of the European Parliament Members and the Problem of Europarties', *European Journal of Political Research*, vol. 18, no. 3, pp. 557–79.

Attinà, F. (1992) *Il Sistema Politico della Communità Europea* (Milan: Giuffrè).

Axelrod, R. (1970) *Conflict of Interest: A Theory of Divergent Goals with Application to Politics* (Chicago: Markham).

Bagehot, W. (1963 [1865]) *The English Constitution* (London: Fontana).

Baldwin-Edwards, M. (1997) 'The Emerging European Immigration Regime: Some Reflections on Implications for Southern Europe', *Journal of Common Market Studies*, vol. 35, no. 4, pp. 497–520.

Baldwin-Edwards, M. and Schain, M. (eds) (1994) *The Politics of Immigration in Western Europe* (London: Frank Cass).

Balme, R. and Jouve, B. (1996) 'Building the Regional State: Europe and Territorial Organization in France', in L. Hooghe (ed.), *Cohesion Policy and European Integration: Building Multi-Level Governance* (Oxford: Oxford University Press).

Banzhaf, J. F. (1965) 'Weighted Voting Doesn't Work: A Mathematical Analysis', *Rutgers Law Review*, vol. 19, pp. 317–43.

Bardi, L. (1996) 'Transnational Trends in European Parties and the 1994 Elections of the European Parliament', *Party Politics*, vol. 2, no. 1, pp. 99–114.

Barro, R. J. and Gordon, D. B. (1983) 'A Positive Theory of Monetary Policy in a Natural Rate Model', *Journal of Political Economy*, vol. 91, no. 4, pp. 585–610.

Bartolini, S. and Mair, P. (1990) *Identity, Competition, and Electoral Availability: The Stability of European Electorates, 1885–1985* (Cambridge: Cambridge University Press).

Bastian, J. (1998) 'Putting the Cart Before the Horse? Labour market challenges ahead of monetary union in Europe', in D. Hine and Kassim (eds), *Beyond the Market: The EU and National Social Policy* (London: Routledge).

Bauböck, R. (1994) *Transnational Citizenship: Membership and Rights in International Migration* (Aldershot: Edward Elgar).

Becker, G. S. (1983) 'A Theory of Competition Among Pressure Groups for Political Influence', *Quarterly Journal of Economics*, vol. 98, no. 3, pp. 371–400.

Bell, D. (1960) *The End of Ideology* (New York: Free Press).

Bentley, A. (1967) *The Process of Government* (Chicago: University of Chicago Press).

Berlin, I. (1969) *Four Essays on Liberty* (Oxford: Oxford University Press).

Bermann, G. (1994) 'Taking Subsidiarity Seriously: Federalism in the EC and the US', *Columbia Law Review*, vol. 94, no. 2, pp. 331–456.

Bieber, R. and Monar, J. (eds) (1995) *Justice and Home Affairs in the European Union: The Development of the Third Pillar* (Brussels: Interuniversity Press).

Bigo, D. (1994) 'The European Security Field: Stakes and Rivalries in a Newly Developing Area of Policy Intervention', in M. Anderson and M. den Boer (eds), *Policing Across National Boundaries* (London: Pinter).

Bilal, S. (1998) 'Political Economy Considerations on the Supply of Trade Protection in Regional Integration Agreements', *Journal of Common Market Studies*, vol. 36, no. 1, pp. 1–32.

Birnbaum, P. and Badie, P. (1983 [1979]) *The Sociology of the State* (Chicago: University of Chicago Press).

Blondel, J. (1984) 'Dual Leadership in the Contemporary World: A Step Towards Executive and Regime Stability?', in D. Kavanagh and G. Peele (eds), *Comparative Government and Politics: Essays in Honour of S. E. Finer* (London: Heinemann).

Bobbio, N. (1996 [1995]) *Left and Right: The Significance of a Political Distinction*, trans. A. Cameron (Cambridge: Polity).

Boer, M. den (1994) 'The Quest for European Policing: Rhetoric and Justification in a Disorderly Debate', in M. Anderson and M. den Boer (eds), *Policing Across National Boundaries* (London: Pinter).

Bofinger, P. (1994) 'Is Europe an Optimum Currency Area', Discussion Paper no. 915 (London: Centre for Economic Policy Research).

Bogdanor, V. (1986) 'The Future of the European Community: Two Models of Democracy', *Government and Opposition*, vol. 22, no. 2, pp. 344–70.

Borras-Alomar, S., Christiansen, T. and Rodriguez-Pose, A. (1994) 'Towards a "Europe of the Regions"? Visions and Realities from a Critical Perspective', *Regional Politics and Policy*, vol. 4, no. 2, pp. 1–27.

Bosch, A. and Newton, K. (1995) 'Economic Calculus or Familiarity Breeds Content?', in O. Niedermayer and R. Sinnott (eds), *Public Opinion and Internationalized Governance* (Oxford: Oxford University Press).

Bowler, S. and Farrell, D. (1993) 'Legislator Shirking and Voter Monitoring: Impact of European Parliament Electoral Systems upon Legislator-Voter Relationships', *Journal of Common Market Studies*, vol. 31, no. 1, pp. 45–69.

Bowler, S. and Farrell, D. (1995) 'The Organization of the European Parliament: Committees, Specialization and Co-ordination', *British Journal of Political Science*, vol. 25, no. 2, pp. 219–43.

Bradley, K.St.C. (1997) 'The European Parliament and Comitology: On the Road to Nowhere?', *European Law Journal*, vol. 3, no. 3, pp. 230–54.

Brams, S. J. and Affuso, P. J. (1985) 'New Paradoxes of Voting Power in the EC Council of Ministers', *Electoral Studies*, vol. 4, no. 1, pp. 135–9.

Bribosia, H. (1998) 'Report on Belgium', in A.-M. Slaughter, A. Stone Sweet and J. H. H. Weiler (eds), *The European Court and National Courts – Doctrine and Jurisprudence: Legal Change in Its Social Context* (Oxford: Hart Publishing).

Brubaker, R. (1992) *Citizenship and Nationhood in France and Germany* (Cambridge: Harvard University Press).

Brzinski, J. Bay (1995) 'Political Group Cohesion in the European Parliament, 1989–1994', in C. Rhodes and S. Mazey (eds), *The State of the European Union, vol. 3* (London: Longman).

Buchanan, J. M. and Tullock, G. (1962) *The Calculus of Consent* (Ann Arbor: Michigan University Press).

Bufacchi, V. and Garmise, S. (1995) 'Social Justice in Europe: An Evaluation of European Regional Policy', *Government and Opposition*, vol. 30, no. 2, pp. 179–97.

Buiter, W., Corsetti, G. and Roubini, N. (1993) 'Maastricht's Fiscal Rules', *Economic Policy*, April 1993.

Bulmer, S. (1991) 'Analysing European Political Co-operation: The Case for Two-Tier Analysis', in M. Holland (ed.), *The Future of European Political Co-operation: Essays on Theory and Practice* (London: Macmillan).

Bulmer, S. (1994) 'The Governance of the European Union: A New Institutionalist Approach', *Journal of Public Policy*, vol. 13, no. 4, pp. 351–80.

Bulmer, S. and Wessels, W. (1987) *The European Council: Decision-Making in European Politics* (London: Macmillan).

Burley, A.-M. and Mattli, W. (1993) 'Europe Before the Court: A Political Theory of Legal Integration', *International Organization*, vol. 47, no. 1, pp. 41–76.

Butler, D. and Ranney, D. (eds) (1994) *Referendums Around the World: The Growing Use of Direct Democracy* (London: Macmillan).

Butt Philip, A. (1985) *Pressure Groups in the European Community* (London: Universities Association of Contemporary European Studies).

Cameron, D. (1992) 'The 1992 Initiative: Causes and Consequences', in A.M. Sbragia (ed.), *Euro-Politics: Institutions and Policymaking in the "New" Europe* (Washington, D.C.: The Brookings Institution).

Caldeira, G. A. and Gibson, J. L. (1995) 'The Legitimacy of the Court of Justice in the European Union: Models of Institutional Support', *American Political Science Review*, vol. 89, no. 2, pp. 356–76.

Cameron, D. (1993) 'British Exit, German Voice, French Loyalty: Defection, Domination, and Cooperation in the 1992–93 ERM Crisis', Paper presented at the Annual Meeting of the American Political Science Association, Washington, D.C., September 1993.

Cameron, D. (1997) 'Economic and Monetary Union: Underlying Imperatives and Third-Stage Dilemmas', *Journal of European Public Policy*, vol. 4, no. 3, pp. 455–85.

Cameron, F. (1998) 'Building a Common Foreign Policy: Do Institutions Matter?', in J. Peterson and H. Sjursen (eds), *A Common Foreign Policy for Europe? Competing Visions of the CFSP* (London: Routledge).

Caporale, G. M. (1993) 'Is Europe an Optimum Currency Area? Symmetric Versus Asymmetric Shocks in the EC', *National Institute Economic Review*, no. 144, pp. 95–103.

Cappelletti, M., Seccombe, M. and Weiler, J. H. H. (eds) (1986) *Integration Through Law, Volumes 1 and 2* (Berlin: De Gruyter).

Carey, W. L. (1974) 'Federalism and Corporate Law: Reflections upon Delaware', *Yale Law Review*, vol. 83, no. 4, pp. 663–705.

Carrubba, C. (1997) 'Net Financial Transfers in the European Union: Who Gets What and Why?', *The Journal of Politics*, vol. 59, no. 2, pp. 469–96.

Carrubba, C. (1998) 'The Electoral Connection in European Union Politics', paper presented at the Midwest Political Science Association.

Catabia, M. (1998) 'The Italian Constitutional Court and the Relationship Between the Italian Legal System and the European Union', in A.-M. Slaughter, A. Stone Sweet and J. H. H. Weiler (eds), *The European Court and National Courts – Doctrine and Jurisprudence: Legal Change in Its Social Context* (Oxford: Hart Publishing).

Cawson, A. and Saunders, P. (1983) 'Corporatism, Competitive Politics and Class Struggle', in R. King (ed.), *Capital and Politics* (London: Routledge).

Cecchini, P. (1988) *The European Challenge, 1992: The Benefits of a Single Market* (Aldershot: Gower).

Chalmers, D. (1995) 'The Single Market: From Prima Donna to Journeyman', in J. Shaw and G. More (eds), *New Legal Dynamics of European Union* (Oxford: Clarendon Press).

Chalmers, D. (1997) 'Judicial Preferences and the Community Legal Order', *Modern Law Review*, vol. 60, no. 2, pp. 164–99.

Chalmers, D. (1998) 'Bureaucratic Europe: From Regulatory Communities to Securitising Unions', paper presented at the annual conference of the Council for European Studies, Baltimore, 28 February 1998.

Chopin, I. and Niessen, J. (eds) (1998) *Proposals for Legislative Measures to Combat Racism and to Promote Equal Rights in the European Union* (Brussels: Starting Line Group / London: Commission for Racial Equality.

Chryssochoou, D. (1994) 'Democracy and Symbiosis in the European Union: Towards a Confederal Consociation?', *West European Politics*, vol. 17, no. 1, pp. 1–14.

Cini, M. (1996) *The European Commission: Leadership, Organisation and Culture in the EU Administration* (Manchester: Manchester University Press).

Cini, M. (1997) 'Administrative Culture in the European Commission: The Cases of Competition and Environment', in N. Nugent (ed.), *At the Heart of the Union: Studies of the European Commission* (London: Macmillan).

Claes, M. and de Witte, B. (1998) 'Report on the Netherlands', in A.-M. Slaughter, A. Stone Sweet and J. H. H. Weiler (eds), *The European Court and National*

Courts – Doctrine and Jurisprudence: Legal Change in Its Social Context (Oxford: Hart Publishing).

Clutterbuck, R. (1990) *Terrorism, Drugs and Crime in Europe after 1992* (London: Routledge).

Cobham, D. (1996) 'Causes and Effects of the European Monetary Crisis of 1992–93', *Journal of Common Market Studies*, vol. 34, no. 4, pp. 585–604.

Coen, D. (1997) 'The Evolution of the Large Firm as a Political Actor in the European Union', *Journal of European Public Policy*, vol. 4, no. 1, pp. 91–108.

Cohen, M. A. (1992) 'The Motives of Judges: Empirical Evidence from Antitrust Sentencing', *International Review of Law and Economics*, vol. 12, no. 1, pp. 13–30.

Cole, J. and Cole, F. (1998) *A Geography of the European Union*, 2nd edn (London: Routledge).

Committee for the Study of Economic and Monetary Union (1989) *Report on Economic and Monetary Union in Europe* (the Delors Report) (Luxembourg: Office for Official Publications of the European Union).

Conzelmann, T. (1995) 'Networking and the Politics of EU Regional Policy: Lessons from North Rhine-Westphalia, Nord-Pas de Calais and North West England', *Regional and Federal Studies*, vol. 5, no. 2, pp. 134–72.

Cooter, R. and Drexl, J. (1994) 'The Logic of Power in the Emerging European Constitution: Game Theory and the Division of Powers', *International Review of Law and Economics*, vol. 14, no. 2, pp. 307–26.

Cooter, R. and Ginsburg, T. (1997) 'Comparative Judicial Discretion: An Empirical Test of Economic Models', in D. Schmidtchen and R. Cooter (eds), *Constitutional Law and Economics of the European Union* (Cheltenham: Edward Elgar).

Corbett, R., Jacobs, F. and Shackleton, M. (1995) *The European Parliament*, 3rd edn (London: Catermill).

Cornelius, W. A., Martin, P. L. and Hollifield, J. F. (1994) 'Introduction: The Ambivalent Quest for Immigration Control', in W. A. Cornelius, P. L. Martin and J. F. Hollifield (eds), *Controlling Immigration: A Global Perspective* (Stanford: Stanford University Press).

Council of the European Communities (1990) *The Council of the European Community* (Luxembourg: Office of Official Publications of the European Communities).

Council of the European Union (1995) *Draft Report of the Council on the Functioning of the Treaty on European Union* (Brussels: Council of Ministers).

Cowles, M. Green (1995) 'Setting the Agenda for a New Europe: The ERT and EC 1992', *Journal of Common Market Studies*, vol. 33, no. 4, pp. 501–26.

Cowles, M. Green (1997) 'Organizing Industrial Coalitions: A Challenge for the Future?', in H. Wallace and A. R. Young (eds), *Participation and Policy-Making in the European Union* (Oxford: Clarendon).

Cowles, M. Green (1998) 'The Changing Architecture of Big Business', in J. Greenwood and M. Aspinwall (eds), *Collective Action in the European Union* (London: Routledge).

Cox, G. W. and McCubbins, M. (1993) *Legislative Leviathan: Party Government in the House* (Berkeley: University of California Press).

Craig, P. P. (1998) 'Report on the United Kingdom', in A.-M. Slaughter, A. Stone Sweet and J. H. H. Weiler (eds), *The European Court and National Courts – Doctrine and Jurisprudence: Legal Change in Its Social Context* (Oxford: Hart Publishing).

Cram, L. (1993) 'Calling the Tune Without Paying the Piper? Social Policy Regulation: the Role of the Commission in European Union Social Policy', *Policy and Politics*, vol. 21, no. 1, pp. 135–46.

Cram, L (1994) 'The European Commission as a Multi-Organization: Social Policy and IT Policy in the EU', *Journal of European Public Policy*, vol. 1, no. 2, pp. 195–217.

Cram, L. (1997) *Policy-Making in the EU: Conceptual Lenses and the Integration Process* (London: Routledge).

Cram, L. (1998) 'The EU Institutions and Collective Action: Constructing a European Interest?', in J. Greenwood and M. Aspinwall (eds), *Collective Action in the European Union* (London: Routledge).

Crombez, C. (1996) 'Legislative Procedures in the European Community', *British Journal of Political Science*, vol. 26, no. 2, pp. 199–218.

Crombez, C. (1997) 'The Co-Decision Procedure in the European Union', *Legislative Studies Quarterly*, vol. 22, no. 1, pp. 97–119.

Crouch, C. and Menon, A. (1997) 'Organised Interests and the State', in M. Rhodes, P. Heywood and V. Wright (eds), *Developments in West European Politics* (London: Macmillan).

Crowley, P. (1996) 'EMU, Maastricht and the 1996 Intergovernmental Conference', *Contemporary Economic Policy*, vol. 14, pp. 41–55.

Cukierman, A. (1992) *Central Bank Strategy, Credibility and Independence: Theory and Evidence* (Cambridge: Massachusetts Institute of Technology Press).

Cukierman, A., Webb, S. B. and Neyapti, B. (1993) 'The Measurement of Central Bank Independence and its Effect on Policy Outcomes', *The World Bank Economic Review*, vol. 6, pp. 353–98.

Dahrendorf, R. (1959) *Class and Class Conflict in Industrial Society* (London: Routledge).

Dalton, R. J. (1988) *Citizen Politics in Western Democracies: Public Opinion and Political Parties in the United States Great Britain, West Germany and France* (Chatham: Chatham House).

Dalton, R. J., Kuechler, M. and Bürklin, W. (1990) 'The Challenge of New Movements', in R. J. Dalton and M. Kuechler (eds), *Challenging the Political Order: New Social and Political Movements in Western Democracies* (Oxford: Oxford University Press).

De Grauwe, P. (1997) *The Economics of Monetary Integration*, 3rd edn (Oxford: Oxford University Press).

De Grauwe, P. and Vanhaverbeke, W. (1993) 'Is Europe and Optimum Currency Area? Evidence From Regional Data', in P. R. Masson and M. P. Taylor (eds), *Policy Issues in the Operation of Currency Unions* (Cambridge: Cambridge University Press).

Dedman, M. (1996) *The Origins and Development of the European Union, 1945–1995* (London: Routledge).

Dehousse R. (1992) 'Integration v. Regulation? On the Dynamics of Regulation in the European Community', *Journal of Common Market Studies*, vol. 30, no. 4, pp. 383–402.

Dehousse, R. (1995) 'Constitutional Reform in the European Community: Are there Alternatives to the Majoritarian Avenue?', in J. Hayward (ed.), *The Crisis of Representation in Europe* (London: Frank Cass).

Dehousse, R. (1997) 'Regulation by Networks in the European Community: The Role of European Agencies', *Journal of European Public Policy*, vol. 4, no. 2, pp. 246–61.

Dehousse, R. and Majone, G. (1994) 'The Institutional Dynamics of European Integration: From the Single Act to the Maastricht Treaty', in S. Martin (ed.), *The Construction of Europe – Essays in Honour of Emile Noël* (Dordrecht: Kluwer).

Devuyst, Y. (1995) 'The European Community and the Conclusion of the Uruguay Round', in C. Rhodes and S. Mazey (eds), *The State and the European Union*, vol. 3 (London: Longman).

Dicey, A. V. (1939 [1885]) *Introduction Study of the Law of the Constitution* (London: Macmillan).

Dinan, D. (1994) *Ever Closer Union? An Introduction to the European Community* (London: Macmillan).

Docksey, C. and Williams, K. (1997) 'The Commission and the Execution of Community Policy', in G. Edwards and D. Spence (eds), *The European Commission*, 2nd edn (London: Catermill).

Dogan, R. (1997) 'Comitology: Little Procedures with Big Implications', *West European Politics*, vol. 20, no. 3, pp. 31–60.

Donnelly, M. and Ritchie, E. (1997) 'The College of Commissioners and the Cabinets', in G. Edwards and D. Spence (eds), *The European Commission*, 2nd edn (London: Catermill).

Dornbusch, R. (1990) 'Two-Track EMU, Now!', in K. O. Pöhl *et al.*, *Britain and EMU* (London: Centre for Economic Peformance).

Downs, A. (1957) *An Economic Theory of Democracy* (New York: Harper and Row).

Drake, H. (1995) 'Political Leadership and European Integration: The Case of Jacques Delors', *West European Politics*, vol. 18, no. 1, pp. 140–60.

Drewry, G. (1993) 'Judicial Politics in Britain: Patrolling the Boundaries', in M. L. Volcansek (ed.), *Judicial Politics and Policy-Making in Western Europe* (London: Frank Cass).

Duke, S. (1996) 'The Second Death (or Second Coming?) of the WEU', *Journal of Common Market Studies*, vol. 34, no. 2, pp. 167–190.

Dunleavy, P. (1979) 'The Urban Basis of Political Alignment: Social Class, Domestic Property Ownership and State Intervention in Consumer Processes', *British Journal of Political Science*, vol. 9, no. 3, pp. 409–43.

Dunleavy, P. (1990) *Democracy, Bureaucracy and Public Choice: Economic Explanations in Political Science* (London: Harvester Wheatsheaf).

Dunleavy, P. (1997) 'Explaining the Centralization of the European Union: A Public Choice Analysis', *Aussenwirtschaft*, vol. 52, no's 1/2, pp. 183–212.

Dunleavy, P. and O'Duffy, B. (1998) 'The Organizational Structure of the European Commission: A Bureau-Shaping Analysis', unpublished mimeo (London: London School of Economics and Political Science).

Dunleavy, P. and O'Leary, B. (1987) *Theories of the State: The Politics of Liberal Democracy* (London: Macmillan).

Dyson, K. (1994) *Elusive Union: The Process of Economic and Monetary Integration in Europe* (London: Longman).

Dyson, K., Featherstone, K. and Michalopoulis, G. (1994) 'The Politics of EMU: The Maastricht Treaty and the Relevance of Bargaining Models', Paper presented at the Annual Meeting of the American Political Science Association, New York, September 1994.

Earnshaw, D. and Judge, D. (1995) 'Early Days: the European Parliament, Co-Decision and the European Union Legislative Process Post-Maastricht', *Journal of European Public Policy*, vol. 2, no. 4, pp. 624–49.

Earnshaw, D. and Judge, D. (1997) 'The Life and Times of the European Union's Co-operation Procedure', *Journal of Common Market Studies*, vol. 35, no. 4, pp. 543–64.

Easton, D. (1957) 'An Approach to the Study of Political Systems', *World Politics*, vol. 9, no. 5, pp. 383–400.

Easton, D. (1965) *A Framework for Political Analysis* (Englewood Cliffs: Prentice Hall).

Easton, D. (1975) 'A Reassessment of the Concept of Political Support', *British Journal of Political Science*, vol. 5, pp. 435–57.

Economist, The (1975) 'All Saint's Day Manifesto', 1 November 1995, p. 33.

Economist, The (1996) 'Europe's Union: Who Pays for It?', 23 November 1996 (London: The Economist).

Edwards, G. and Spence, D. (eds) (1997) *The European Commission*, 2nd edn (London: Catermill).

Ehlermann, C.-D. and Hancher, L. (1995) 'Comments on Streit and Mussler', *European Law Journal*, vol. 1, no. 1, pp. 84–88.

Eichenberg, R. C. and Dalton, R. J. (1993) 'Europeans and the European Community: The Dynamics of Public Support for European Integration', *International Organization*, vol. 47, no. 4, pp. 507–34.

Eichener, V. (1992) *Social Dumping or Innovative Regulation? Processes and Outcomes of European Decision-Making in the Sector of Health and Safety at Work Hamonization*, EUI Working Paper SPS no. 92/28 (Florence: European University Institute).

Eichener, V. (1997) 'Effective European Problem-Solving: Lessons from the Regulation of Occupational Safety and Environmental Protection', *Journal of European Public Policy*, vol. 4, no. 4, pp. 591–608.

Eichengreen, B. (1990) 'Costs and Benefits of European Monetary Unification', Discussion Paper no. 453 (London: Centre for Economic Policy Research).

Eichengreen, B. (1991) 'Designing a Central Bank for Europe: A Cautionary Tale from the Early Years of the Federal Reserve System', Discussion Paper no. 585 (London: Centre for Economic Policy Research).

Eichengreen, B. (1993a) 'Labor Markets and European Monetary Unification', in P. Masson and M. Taylor (eds), *Policy Issues in the Operation of Currency Unions* (Cambridge: Cambridge University Press).

Eichengreen, B. (1993b) 'Thinking About Migration: Notes on European Migration Pressures at the Dawn of the Next Millennium', in H. Siebert (ed.), *Migration: A Challenge for Europe* (Ann Arbor: University of Michigan Press).

Eichengreen, B. (1994) 'Fiscal Policy in EMU', in B. Eichengreen and J. Frieden (eds), *The Political Economy of European Monetary Unification* (Boulder: Westview).

Eichengreen, B. and Frieden, J. (1994) 'The Political Economy of European Monetary Unification: An Analytical Introduction', in B. Eichengreen and J. Frieden (eds), *The Political Economy of European Monetary Unification* (Boulder: Westview).

Eichengreen, B. and Von Hagen, J. (1996) 'Fiscal Policy and Monetary Union: Federalism, Fiscal Restrictions, and the No-Bailout Rule', in H. Siebert (ed.), *Monetary Policy in an Integrated World Economy* (Mohr: Tübingen).

van der Eijk, C. and Franklin, M. (eds) (1996) *Choosing Europe? The European Electorate and National Politics in the Face of Union* (Ann Arbor: University of Michigan Press).

van der Eijk, C., Franklin, M. and Oppenhuis, E. (1996) 'The Strategic Context: Party Choice', in van der Eijk, C. and Franklin, M. (eds), *Choosing Europe? The European Electorate and National Politics in the Face of Union* (Ann Arbor: University of Michigan Press).

El-Agraa, A. M. (1998) 'The Basic Statistics of the European Union', in A. M. El-Agraa (ed.), *The European Union: History, Institutions, Economics and Policies* (London: Prentice-Hall).

Epstein, D. and O'Halloran, S. (1998) *Delegating Powers: A Transaction Cost Politics Approach to Policy Making Under Separate Powers* (Cambridge: Cambridge University Press).

Eskridge, W. N. Jr. (1991) 'Reneging on History? Playing the Court/Congress/President Civil Rights Game', *California Law Review*, vol. 38, pp. 613–84.

Esping-Anderson, G. (1990) *The Three Worlds of Welfare Capitalism* (Cambridge: Polity Press).

European Commission (1985) *Completing the Internal Market: White Paper of the Commission the European Council*, COM(85) 310 (Luxembourg: Office of Official Publications of the European Communities).

European Commission (1990) 'One Market, One Money: An Evaluation of the Potential Benefits and Costs of Forming an Economic and Monetary Union', *European Economy*, no. 44.

European Commission (1992) *An Open and Structured Dialogue between the Commission and Special Interest Groups*, Brussels, 2 December, SEC(92) 2272 final.

European Commission (1995) *The Agricultural Situation in the Community* (Luxembourg: Office for Official Publications of the European Communities).

European Commission (1996a) *Eurobarometer, no. 45, Spring 1996* (Brussels: European Commission).

European Commission (1996b) *Intergovernmental Conference 1996: Commission Opinion – Reinforcing Political Union and Preparing for Enlargement* (Luxembourg: Office for Official Publications of the European Communities).

European Commission (1998a) *European Union Financial Report, 1996* (Luxembourg: Office for Official Publications of the European Communities).

European Commission (1998b) *Report on Progress Towards Convergence and the Recommendation with a View to the Transition to the Third Stage of Economic and Monetary Union, Part 1: Recommendation*, 25 March 1998 (Luxembourg: Office of Official Publications of the European Communities).

European Commission (1998c) *Committee Procedures: Simpler, More Democratic, More Transparent*, 24 June 1998, IP/98/554 (Brussels: European Commission).

European Commission (1998d) *Single Market: New Scorecard Reflects Significant Progress*, http://europa.eu.int/comm/dg15/en/update/score/score2.htm.

European Commission (1998e) *XXVIIth Report on Competition Policy 1997*, SEC(98) 636 final (Luxembourg: Office of Official Publications of the European Communities).

European Court of Justice (1995) *Report of the Court of Justice on Certain Aspects of the Application of the Treaty on European Union*, 22 May 1995 (Luxembourg: European Court of Justice.

European Parliament (1985) *Committee of Inquiry into the Rise of Fascism and Racism in Europe: Report of the Findings of the Inquiry (Evrigenis Report)* (Luxembourg: Office for Official Publications of the European Communities).

European Parliament (1991) *Committee of Inquiry on Racism and Xenophobia: Report on the Findings of the Inquiry (Ford Report)* (Luxembourg: Office for Official Publications of the European Communities).

European Parliament (1995a) *Report on the Functioning of the Treaty on European Union with a View to the 1996 Intergovernmental Conferences*, PE212.450 (Brussels: European Parliament).

European Parliament (1995b) *Resolution on the Functioning of the Treaty on European Union With a View to the 1996 Intergovernmental Conference – Implementation and Development of the Union*, PE 190.440 (Brussels: European Parliament).

European Parliament (1997) *Progress Report, 1 August 1996 to 31 July 1997, on the Delegations to the Conciliation Committee (Fontaine, Imbeni, Verde i Aldea)*, PE 223.209 (Brussels: European Parliament).

Eurostat (1995a) *Migration Statistics 1995* (Luxembourg: Office for Official Publications of the European Communities).

Eurostat (1995b) *Statistics in Focus, Regions* (Luxembourg: Office for Official Publications of the European Communities).

Eurostat (1997) *Basic Statistics of the European Union: Comparison with the Principal Partners of the European Union*, 33rd edition (Luxembourg: Office for Official Publications of the European Communities).

Evans, R.B., Jacobson, H.K. and Putnam, R.D. (eds) (1993) *Double-Edged Diplomacy: International Bargaining and Domestic Politics* (Berkeley: University of California Press).

Everson, M. (1995) 'The Legacy of the Market Citizen', in J. Shaw and G. More (eds), *New Legal Dynamics of European Union* (Oxford: Clarendon).

Fagerberg, J. and Verspagen, B. (1996) 'Heading for Divergence? Regional Growth in Europe Reconsidered', *Journal of Common Market Studies*, vol. 34, no. 3, pp. 431–48.

Falkner, G. (1996) 'European Works Councils and the Maastricht Social Agreement: Towards a New Policy Style?', *Journal of European Public Policy*, vol. 3, no. 2, pp. 192–208.

Falkner, G. (1997) 'Corporatist Governance and Europeanisation: No Future in the Multi-Level Game?', *European Integration On-line Papers*, 1, 11, http://eiop.or.at/eiop/texte/1997-011a.htm.

Favell, A. (1997a) *Philosophies of Integration: Immigration and the Idea of Citizenship in France and Britain* (London: Macmillan).

Favell, A. (1997b) 'European Citizenship and the Incorporation of Migrants and Minorities in Europe: Emergence, Transformation and Effects of a New Political Field', paper presented at the annual conference of the European Sociological Association, Essex, 27–30 August 1997.

Featherstone, K. and Ginsberg, R. H. (1996) *The United States and the European Union in the 1990s: Partners in Transition*, 2nd edn (London: Macmillan).

Federal Trust (1996) *Justice and Fair Play*, The Intergovernmental Conference of the European Union 1996 Federal Trust Papers 6 (London: Federal Trust.

Feldstein, M. (1992) 'Europe's Monetary Union: The Case Against EMU', *The Economist*, 13 June 1992, pp. 19–22.

Felsenthal, D. S. and Machover, M. (1997) 'The Weighted Voting Rule in the EU's Council of Ministers, 1958–95: Intentions and Outcomes', *Electoral Studies*, vol. 16, no. 1, pp. 33–47.

Ferejohn, J. A. and Weingast, B. R. (1992) 'A Positive Theory of Statutory Interpretation', *International Review of Law and Economics*, vol. 12, no. 2, pp. 263–79.

Finer, S. E. (1987) 'Left and Right', in V. Bogdanor (ed.), *The Blackwell Encyclopaedia of Political Institutions* (Oxford: Blackwell).

Fiorina, M. (1982) 'Legislative Choice of Regulatory Forms: Legal Process or Administrative Process?', *Public Choice*, vol. 39, no. 1, pp. 33–66.

Fitzmaurice, J. (1978) *The European Parliament* (London: Saxon House).

Flanagan, S. C. (1987) 'Value Change in Industrial Societies', *American Political Science Review*, vol. 81, no. 4, pp. 1303–18.

Fligstein, N. and Mara-Drita, I. (1996) 'How to Make a Market: Reflections on the Attempt to Create a Single Market in the European Union', *American Journal of Sociology*, vol. 102, no. 1, pp. 1–33.

Fligstein, N. and McNichol, J. (1998) 'The Institutional Terrain of the European Union', in W. Sandholtz and A. Stone Sweet (eds), *European Integration and Supranational Governance* (Oxford: Oxford University Press).

Flora, P. and Heidenheimer, A. J. (eds) (1981) *The Development of the Welfare State in Europe and America* (New Brunswick: Transaction Books).

Frank, J. (1973) *Courts on Trial: Myth and Reality of American Justice* (Princeton: Princeton University Press).

Franklin, M. (1992) 'The Decline of Cleavage Politics', in M. Franklin, T. Mackie and H. Valen (eds), *Electoral Change: Responses to Evolving Social and Attitudinal Structures in Western Countries* (Cambridge: Cambridge University Press).

Franklin, M, van der Eijk, C. and Marsh, M. (1995) 'Referendum Outcomes and Trust in Government: Public Support for Europe in the Wake of Maastricht', in J. Hayward (ed.), *The Crisis of Representation in Europe* (London: Frank Cass).

Franklin, M., Mackie, T. and Valen, H. (eds) (1992) *Electoral Change: Responses to Evolving Social and Attitudinal Structures in Western Countries* (Cambridge: Cambridge University Press).

Franklin, M., Marsh, M. and McLaren, L. (1994) 'Uncorking the Bottle: Popular Opposition to European unification in the wake of Maastricht', *Journal of Common Market Studies*, vol. 32, no. 4, pp. 101–17.

Franklin, M., van der Eijk, C. and Oppenhuis, E. (1996) 'The Institutional Context: Turnout', in van der Eijk, C. and Franklin, M. (eds), *Choosing Europe? The European Electorate and National Politics in the Face of Union* (Ann Arbor: University of Michigan Press).

Frieden, J. A. (1991) 'Invested Interests: The Politics of National Economic Policies in a World of Global Finance', *International Organization*, vol. 45, no. 4, pp. 425–51.

Frieden, J. A. and Lake, D. A. (1995) 'Introduction: International Politics and International Economics', in J. A. Frieden and D. A. Lake (eds), *International Political Economy: Perspectives on Global Power and Wealth* (London: Routledge).

Frieden, J. A. and Rogowski, R. (1996) 'The Impact of the International Political Economy on National Policies: An Overview', in R. O. Keohane and H. V. Milner (eds), *Internationalization and Domestic Politics* (Cambridge: Cambridge University Press).

Friedman, M. (1968) 'The Role of Monetary Policy', *American Economic Review*, vol. 58, no. 2, pp. 1–17.

Frowein, J. A. (1986) 'Integration and the Federal Experience in Germany and Switzerland', in M. Cappelletti, M. Seccombe and J. Weiler (eds), *Integration Through Law: European and the American Federal Experience, Volume 1: Methods, Tools and Institutions, Book 1: A Political Legal and Economic Overview* (Berlin: De Gruyter).

Gabel, M. (1998a) *Interests and Integration: Market Liberalization, Public Opinion, and European Union* (Ann Arbor: University or Michigan Press).

Gabel, M. (1998b) 'Public Support for European Integration: An Empirical Test of Five Theories', *Journal of Politics*, vol. 60, no. 2, pp. 333–54.

Gabel, M. (1998c) 'The Endurance of Supranational Governance: A Consociational Interpretation of the European Union', *Comparative Politics*, vol. 30, no. 2, pp. 463–75.

Gabel, M. and Palmer, H. (1995) 'Understanding Variation in Support for European Integration', *European Journal of Political Research*, vol. 27, no. 1, pp. 3–19.

Gabel, M. and Whitten, G. (1997) 'Economic Conditions, Economic Perceptions, and Public Support for European Integration', *Political Behaviour*, vol. 19, no. 1, pp. 81–96.

Galbraith, J. K. (1953) *American Capitalism and the Concept of Countervailing Power* (Boston: Houghton Mifflin).

Garrett, G. (1992) 'International Cooperation and Institutional Choice: The European Community's Internal Market', *International Organization*, vol. 46, no. 2, pp. 533–60.

Garrett, G. (1994) 'The Politics of Maastricht', in B. Eichengreen and J. Frieden (eds), *The Political Economy of European Monetary Unification* (Boulder: Westview).

Garrett, G. (1995a) 'The Politics of Legal Integration in the European Union', *International Organization*, vol. 49, no. 1, pp. 171–81.

Garrett, G. (1995b) 'From the Luxembourg Compromise to Codecision: Decision Making in the European Union', *Electoral Studies*, vol. 14, no. 3, pp. 289–308.

Garrett, G. Kelemen, R. D. and Schulz, H. (1998) 'The European Court of Justice, National Governments, and Legal Integration in the European Union', *International Organization*, vol. 52, no. 1, pp. 149–76.

Garrett, G. and Lange, P. (1996) 'Internationalization, Institutions and Political Change', in R. O. Keohane and H. V. Milner (eds), *Internationalization and Domestic Politics* (Cambridge: Cambridge University Press).

Garrett, G. and McLean, I. (1996) 'On Power Indices and Reading Papers', *British Journal of Political Science*, vol. 26, no. 4, p. 600.

Garrett, G., McLean, I. and Machover, M. (1995) 'Power, Power Indices and Blocking Power: A Comment on Johnston', *British Journal of Political Science*, vol. 25, no. 4, pp. 563–8.

Garrett, G. and Tsebelis, G. (1996) 'An Institutional Critique of Intergovernmentalism', *International Organization*, vol. 50, no. 2, pp. 269–99.

Garrett, G. and Weingast, B. R. (1993) 'Ideas, Interests and Institutions: Constructing the European Community's Internal Market', in J. Goldstein and R. O. Keohane (eds), *Ideas and Foreign Policy: Beliefs, Institutions and Political Change* (Ithaca: Cornell University Press).

Gatsios, K. and Seabright, P. (1989) 'Regulation in the European Community', *Oxford Review of Economic Policy*, vol. 5, no.2, pp. 37–60.

Geddes, A. (1995) 'Immigration and Ethnic Minorities and the EU's "Democratic Deficit" ', *Journal of Common Market Studies*, vol. 33, no. 2, pp. 197–217.

Gehring, T. (1997) 'Governing in Nested Institutions: Environmental Policy in the European Union and the Case of Packaging Waste', *Journal of European Public Policy*, vol. 4, no. 3, pp. 337–54.

Gely, R. and Spillar, P. T. (1992) 'The Political Economy of Supreme Court Constitutional Decisions: The Case of Roosevelt's Court Packing Plan', *International Review of Law and Economics*, vol. 12, no. 1, pp. 45–67.

Genschel, P. and Plümper, T. (1997) 'Regulatory Competition and International Co-operation', *Journal of European Public Policy*, vol. 4, no. 4, pp. 626–42.

Gibson, J. L. and Caldeira, G. A. (1995) 'The Legitimacy of Transnational Legal Institutions: Compliance, Support, and the European Court of Justice', *American Journal of Political Science*, vol. 39, no. 2, pp. 459–98.

Gibson, J. L. and Caldeira, G. A. (1998) 'Changes in the Legitimacy of the European Court of Justice: A Post-Maastricht Analysis', *British Journal of Political Science*, vol. 28, no. 1, pp. 63–91.

Giddens, A. (1973) *The Class Structure of the Advanced Societies* (London: Hutchinson).

Goetz, K. (1995) 'National Governance and European Integration: Intergovernmental Relations in Germany', *Journal of Common Market Studies*, vol. 33, no. 1, pp. 131–44.

Golub, J. (1996a) 'The Politics of Judicial Discretion: Rethinking the Interaction Between National Courts and the European Court of Justice', *West European Politics*, vol. 19, no. 2, pp. 360–85.

Golub, J. (1996b) *Why Did They Sign? Explaining EC Environmental Bargaining*, EUI Working Paper RSC no. 96/52 (Florence: European University Institute).

Golub, J. (1996c) 'State Power and Institutional Influence in European Integration: Lessons from the Packaging Waste Directive', *Journal of Common Market Studies*, vol. 34, no. 3, pp. 313–39.

Golub, J. (1996d) 'Modelling Judicial Dialogue in the European Community: The Quantitative Basis of Preliminary References to the ECJ', Robert Schuman Centre Working Paper 96/58 (Florence: European University Institute).

Golub, J. (1997) 'In the Shadow of the Vote? Decisionmaking Efficiency in the European Community, 1974–1995', MPIfG Discussion Paper 97/3 (Bonn: Max-Plank-Institut für Gesellschaftsforschung).

Gomà, R. (1996) 'The Social Dimension of the European Union: A New Type of Welfare System?', *Journal of European Public Policy*, vol. 3, no. 2, pp. 209–30.

Gomez, R. (1998) 'The EU's Mediterranean Policy: Common Foreign Policy By the Back Door?', in J. Peterson and H. Sjursen (eds), *A Common Foreign Policy for Europe? Competing Visions of the CFSP* (London: Routledge).

Goodhart, D. (1998) 'Social Dumping Within the EU', in D. Hine and Kassim (eds), *Beyond the Market: The EU and National Social Policy* (London: Routledge).

Gourevitch, P. A. (1989) 'The Politics of Economic Policy Choice in the Post-War Era', in P. Guerrieri and P. C. Padoan (eds), *The Political Economy of European Integration: States, Markets and Institutions* (London: Harvester Wheatsheaf).

Governments of Belgium, The Netherlands and Luxembourg (1996) *Mémorandum de la Belgique, des Pays-Bas et du Luxembourg en vue de la CIG*, 7 March 1996.

Grahl, J. and Teague, P. (1990) *1992 – The Big Market: The Future of the European Community* (London: Lawrence and Wishart).

Grant, W. (1997) *The Common Agricultural Policy* (London: Macmillan).

Green, A. W. (1969) *Political Integration by Jurisprudence* (Leyden: Sijthoff).

Greenwood, J. (1997) *Representing Interests in the European Union* (London: Macmillan).

Greenwood, J. and Aspinwall, M. (eds) (1998) *Collective Action in the European Union* (London: Routledge).

Greenwood, J., Grote, J. R. and Ronit, K. (eds) (1992) *Organized Interests and the European Community* (London: Sage).

Greico, J. M. (1990) *Cooperation Among Nations: Europe, America and Non-Tariff Barriers to Trade* (Ithaca: Cornell University Press).

Grilli, V., Masciandro, D. and Tabellini, G. (1991) 'Political and Monetary Institutes and Public Financial Policies in the Industrial Countries', *Economic Policy*, vol. 13, pp. 341–92.

Grimm, D. (1995) 'Does Europe Need a Constitution?', *European Law Review*, vol. 1, no. 3, pp. 282–302.

Haas, E. B. (1958) *The Uniting of Europe: Political, Social and Economic Forces 1950–1957* (London: Stevens and Sons).

Haas, E. B. (1961) 'International Integration: The European and the Universal Process', *International Organization*, vol. 15, no. 3, pp. 366–92.

Habermas, J. (1992) 'Citizenship and National Identity: Some Reflections on the Future of Europe', *Praxis International*, vol. 12, no. 1, pp. 1–19.

Habermas, J. (1995) 'Comment on the Paper by Dieter Grimm: "Does Europe Need a Constitution"', *European Law Journal*, vol. 1, no. 3, pp. 303–7.

Hall, P. and Taylor, R. C. R. (1996) 'Political Science and the Three Institutionalism', *Political Studies*, vol. 44, no. 4, pp. 936–57.

Hallstein, W. (1972) *Europe in the Making* (London: Allen and Unwin).

Hanson, B. (1998) 'What Happened to Fortress Europe?: Trade Policy Liberalization in the European Union', *International Organization*, vol. 52, no. 1, pp. 55–85.

Hardin, R. (1971) 'Collective Action as an Agreeable N-Person Prisoners' Dilemma', *Behavioral Science*, vol. 16, pp. 472–71.

Hartley, T. C. (1986) 'Federalism, Courts and Legal Systems: The Emerging Constitution of the European Community', *American Journal of Comparative Law*, vol. 34, pp. 229–48.

Hartley, T. C. (1994) *The Foundations of European Community Law: An Introduction to the Constitutional and Administrative Law of the European Community*, 3rd edn (Oxford: Clarendon).

Hayes-Renshaw, F. and Wallace, H. (1995) 'Executive Power in the European Union: the functions and limits of the Council of Ministers', *Journal of European Public Policy*, vol. 2, no. 4, pp. 559–82.

Hayes-Renshaw, F. and Wallace, H. (1997) *The Council of Ministers* (London: Macmillan).

Heiberg, E. O. (1998) 'Security Implications of EU Expansion to the North and East', in K. A. Eliassen (ed.), *Foreign and Security Policy in the European Union* (London: Sage).

Heidenheimer, A. J., Heclo, H. and Adams, C. T. (1990) *Comparative Public Policy: The Politics of Social Choice in America, Europe, and Japan*, 3rd edn (New York: St. Martin's Press).

Heidensohn, F. and Farrell, M. (ed.) (1993) *Crime in Europe*, 2nd edn (London: Routledge).

Helgadottir, H. (1994) 'Rich Get Richer, Poor Get Poorer', *The European*, 4–10 February 1994.

Helm, D. and Smith, S. (1989) 'The Assessment: Economic Integration and the Role of the European Community', *Oxford Review of Economic Policy*, vol. 5, no. 2, pp. 1–19.

Héritier, A. (1994) '"Leaders" and "Laggards" in European Policy-Making: Clean Air Policy Changes in Britain and Germany', in F. van Waarden and B. Unger (eds), *Convergence or Diversity: The Pressure of Internationalization on Economic Governance Institutions and Policy Outcomes* (Aldershot: Avebury).

Héritier, A. (1996) 'The Accommodation of Diversity in European Policy-Making and its Outcomes: Regulatory Policy as a Patchwork', *Journal of European Public Policy*, vol. 3, no. 2, pp. 149–67.

Héritier, A. (1997) 'Policy-Making by Subterfuge: Interest Accommodation, Innovation and Substitute Democratic Legitimation in Europe – Perspectives from Distinct Policy Areas', *Journal of European Public Policy*, vol. 4, no. 2, pp. 171–89.

Héritier, A., Knill, C. and Mingers, S. (1996) *Ringing the Changes in Europe: Regulatory Competition and Redefinition of the State. Britain, France, Germany* (Berlin: De Gruyter).

Heywood, P. and Wright, V. (1997) 'Executives, Bureaucracies and Decision-Making', in M. Rhodes, P. Heywood and V. Wright (eds), *Developments in West European Politics* (London: Macmillan).

Hill, C. (1988) 'The Capability-Expectations Gap, or Conceptualizing Europe's International Role', *Journal of Common Market Studies*, vol. 31, no. 3, pp. 305–28.

Hill, C. (ed.) (1996) *The Actors in Europe's Foreign Policy* (London: Routledge).

Hinich, H. J. and Munger, M. C. (1997) *Analytical Politics* (Cambridge: Cambridge University Press).

Hix, S. (1994) 'The Study of the European Community: The Challenge to Comparative Politics', *West European Politics*, vol. 17, no. 1, pp. 1–30.

Hix, S. (1995a) *Political Parties in the European Union System: A 'Comparative Political Approach' to the Development of the Party Federations*, unpublished PhD Thesis (Florence: European University Institute).

Hix, S. (1995b) *The 1996 Intergovernmental Conference and the Future of the Third Pillar*, Briefing Paper no. 20 (Brussels: Churches' Commission for Migrants in Europe.

Hix, S. (1997) 'Executive Selection in the European Union: Does the Commission President Investiture Procedure Reduce the Democratic Deficit?', *European Integration On-line Papers*, 1, 21, http://eiop.or.at/eiop/texte/1997-021a.htm.

Hix, S. (1998a) 'The Study of the European Union II: The "New Governance" Agenda and Its Rival', *Journal of European Public Policy*, vol. 5, no. 1, pp. 38–65.

Hix, S. (1998b) 'Elections, Parties and Institutional Design: EU Democracy in Comparative Perspective', *West European Politics*, vol. 21, no. 3, pp. 19–52.

Hix, S. (1999) 'Dimensions and Alignments in European Union Politics: Cognitive Constraints and Partisan Responses', *European Journal of Political Research*, vol. 33, forthcoming.

Hix, S. and Lord, C. (1995) 'The Making of a President: The European Parliament and the Confirmation of Jacques Santer as President of the Commission', *Government and Opposition*, vol. 31, no. 1, pp. 62–76.

Hix, S. and Lord, C. (1997) *Political Parties in the European Union* (London: Macmillan).

Hix, S. and Niessen, J. (1996) *Reconsidering European Migration Policies: The 1996 Intergovernmental Conference and the Reform of the Maastricht Treaty* (Brussels: Migration Policy Group/Churches' Commission for Migrants in Europe/Starting Line Group).

Hoffmann, S. (1966) 'Obstinate or Obsolete? The Fate of the Nation State and the Case of Western Europe', *Daedalus*, vol. 95, no. 4, pp. 862–915.

Hoffman, S. (1982) 'Reflections on the Nation-State in Western Europe Today', *Journal of Common Market Studies*, vol. 21, Nos 1/2, pp. 21–37.

Hoffmann, S. (1989) 'The European Community and 1992', *Foreign Affairs*, vol. 68, no. 4, pp. 27–47.

Holland, M. (1988) 'The European Community and South Africa: In Search for a Policy for the 1990s', *International Affairs*, vol. 64, no. 3, pp. 415–60.

Holland, M. (1995) 'Bridging the Capability-Expectations Gap: A Case Study of the CFSP Joint Action on South Africa', *Journal of Common Market Studies*, vol. 33, no. 4, pp. 555–72.

Holland, S. (1980) *Uncommon Market* (London: Macmillan).

Hollifield, J. F. (1992) *Immigrants, Markets and the State* (Cambridge: Harvard University Press).

Hooghe, L. (1995) 'Subnational Mobilization in the European Union', *West European Politics*, vol. 18, no. 3, pp. 175–98.

Hooghe, L. (1996a) 'Building a Europe With the Regions: The Changing Role of the European Commission', in L. Hooghe (ed.), *Cohesion Policy and European Integration: Building Multi-Level Governance* (Oxford: Oxford University Press).

Hooghe, L. (ed.) (1996b) *Cohesion Policy and European Integration: Building Multi-Level Governance* (Oxford: Oxford University Press).

Hooghe, L. (1997) ' "Serving Europe": Political Orientations of Senior Commission Officials', *European Integration On-line Papers*, http://eiop.or.-at/eiop/texte/1997-008a.htm.

Hooghe, L. and Keating, M. (1994) 'The Politics of European Union Regional Policy', *Journal of European Public Policy*, vol. 1, no. 3, pp. 367–93.

Hooghe, L. and Marks, G. (1996) ' "Europe With the Regions": Channels of Regional Representation in the European Union', *Publius*, vol. 26, no. 1, pp. 1–20.

Hooghe, L. and Marks, G. (1998) 'The Making of a Polity: The Struggle over European Integration', in H. Kitschelt, P. Lange, G. Marks and J. Stephens (eds), *The Politics and Political Economy of Advanced Industrial Societies* (Cambridge: Cambridge University Press).

Horn, M. (1995) *The Political Economy of Public Administration: Institutional Choice in the Public Sector* (Cambridge: Cambridge University Press).

Horstmann, W. and Schneider, F. (1994) 'Deficits, Bailout and Free Riders: Fiscal Elements of a European Constitution', *Kyklos*, vol. 47, no. 3, pp. 355–83.

Hosli, M. O. (1995a) 'The Political Economy of Subsidiarity', in F. Laursen (ed.), *The Political Economy of European Integration* (The Hague: Kluwer).

Hosli, M. O. (1995b) 'The Balance Between Small and Large: Effects of a Double-Majority on Voting Power in the European Union', *International Studies Quarterly*, vol. 39, no. 2, pp 351–70.

Hosli, M. O. (1996) 'Coalitions and Power: Effects of Qualified Majority Voting in the Council of the European Union', *Journal of Common Market Studies*, vol. 34, no. 2, pp. 255–73.

Hosli, M. O. (1997) 'Voting Strength in the European Parliament: The Influence of National and of Partisan Actors', *European Journal of Political Research*, vol. 31, no. 3, pp. 351–66.

Huber, J. and Inglehart, R. (1995) 'Expert Judgements of Party Space and Party Locations in 42 Societies', *Party Politics*, vol. 1, no. 1, pp. 73–111.

Hubschmid, C. and Moser, P. (1997) 'The Co-operation Procedure in the EU: Why was the EP Influential in the Decision on Car Emissions Standards?', *Journal of Common Market Studies*, vol. 35, no. 2, pp. 225–42.

Inglehart, R. (1970a) 'Cognitive Mobilization and European Identity', *Comparative Politics*, vol. 3, no. 1, pp. 45–70.

Inglehart, R. (1970b) 'Public Opinion and Regional Integration', *International Organization*, vol. 24, no. 4, pp. 764–95.

Inglehart, R. (1977a) *The Silent Revolution: Changing Values and Political Styles Among Western Publics* (Princeton: Princeton University Press).

Inglehart, R. (1977b) 'Long Term Trends in Mass Support for European Unification', *Government and Opposition*, vol. 12, no. 2, pp. 150–77.

Inglehart, R. (1991) 'Trust Between Nations: Primordial Ties, Societal Learning and Economic Development', in K. Reif and R. Inglehart (eds), *Eurobarometer: The Dynamics of European Public Opinion – Essays in Honour of Jacques-René Rabier* (London: Macmillan).

Inglehart, R. and Rabier, J.-R. (1978) 'Economic Uncertainty and European Solidarity: Public Opinion Trends', *Annals of the American Academy of Political and Economic Science*, vol. 440, pp. 66–97.

Inglehart, R. and Reif, K. (1991) 'Analyzing Trends in Western European Opinion: The Role of the Eurobarometer Surveys', in K. Reif and R. Inglehart (eds), *Eurobarometer: The Dynamics of European Public Opinion – Essays in Honour of Jacques-René Rabier* (London: Macmillan).

Ioakimidis, P. C. (1996) 'EU Cohesion Policy in Greece: The Tensions Between Bureaucratic Centralism and Regionalism', in L. Hooghe (ed.), *Cohesion Policy and European Integration: Building Multi-Level Governance* (Oxford: Oxford University Press).

Ireland, P. (1991) 'Facing the True "Fortress Europe": Immigrant and Politics in the EC', *Journal of Common Market Studies*, vol. 29, no. 5, pp. 457–80.

Ireland, P. (1995) 'Migration, Free Movement, and Immigrant Integration in the EU: A Bifurcated Policy Response', in S. Leibfried and P. Pierson (eds), *European Social Policy: Between Fragmentation and Integration* (Washington, D.C.: The Brookings Institution).

Jachtenfuchs, M. (1995) 'Theoretical Perspectives on European Governance', *European Law Journal*, vol. 1, no. 2, pp. 115–33.

Jackman, R. (1998) 'The Impact of the European Union on Unemployment and Unemployment Policy', in D. Hine and Kassim (eds), *Beyond the Market: The EU and National Social Policy* (London: Routledge).

Jacobs, F. (1997) 'Legislative Co-Decision: A Real Step Forward?', Paper presented at the Fifth Biennial Conference of the European Community Studies Association, 29 May–1 June, Seattle.

Janssen, J. I. H. (1991) 'Postmaterialism, Cognitive Mobilization and Public Support for European Integration', *British Journal of Political Science*, vol. 21, pp. 443–68.

Joerges, C. (1994) 'European Economic Law, the Nation-State and the Maastricht Treaty', in R. Dehousse (ed.), *Europe After Maastricht: An Ever Closer Union?* (Munich: Law Books on Europe).

Joerges, C. (1997) 'The Market without a State? The 'Economic Constitution' of the European Community and the Rebirth of Regulatory Politics', *European Integration On-line Papers*, vol. 1, no. 19, http://eiop.or.at/eiop/texte/1997-019a.htm.

Joerges, C. and Neyer, J. (1997) 'From Intergovernmental Bargaining to Deliberative Political Process: The Constitutionalisation of Comitology', *European Law Journal*, vol. 3, no. 3, pp. 273–299.

Johnston, M. J. (1994) *The European Council: Gatekeeper of the European Community* (Boulder: Westview).

Johnston, R. J. (1995) 'The Conflict Over Majority Voting in the EU Council of Ministers: An Analysis of the UK Negotiating Stance Using Power Indices', *British Journal of Political Science*, vol. 25, pp. 245–54.

Johnston, R. J. (1996) 'On Keeping Touch with Reality and Failing to be Befuddled by Mathematics', *British Journal of Political Science*, vol. 26, pp. 598–99.

Jones, B. and Keating, M. (eds) (1995) *The European Union and the Regions* (Oxford: Clarendon Press).

Jones, E., Frieden, J. and Torres, F. (eds) (1998) *Joining Europe's Monetary Club: The Challenges for Smaller Member States* (London: Macmillan).

Jones, G. (ed.) (1991) *West European Prime Ministers* (London: Frank Cass).

Joppke, C. (ed.) (1998) *Challenge to the Nation-State: Immigration in Western Europe and the United States* (Oxford: Oxford University Press).

Jordan, G. (1998) 'What Drives Associability at the European Level? The Limits of the Utilitarian Explanation', in J. Greenwood and M. Aspinwall (eds), *Collective Action in the European Union* (London: Routledge).

Jordan, W. A. (1972) 'Producer Protection, Prior Market Structure and the Effects of Government Regulation', *Journal of Law and Economics*, vol. 15, no. 2, pp. 151–76.

Joskow, P. L. and Noll, R. G. (1981) 'Regulation in Theory and Practice: An Overview', in G. Fromm (ed.), *Studies in Public Regulation*, Cambridge; Massachusetts Institute of Technology Press).

Judge, D. (1993) ' "Predestined to Save the Earth": The Environment Committee of the European Parliament', in D. Judge (ed.), *A Green Dimension for the European Community* (London: Frank Cass).

Judge, D. and Earnshaw, D. (1994) 'Weak European Parliament Influence? A Study of the Environment Committee of the EP', *Government and Opposition*, vol. 29, no. 2, pp. 262–76.

Judge, D., Earnshaw, D. and Cowan, N. (1994) 'Ripples and Waves: The European Parliament in the European Community Policy Process', *Journal of European Public Policy*, vol. 1, no. 1, pp. 27–52.

Junne, G. (1994) 'Multinational Enterprises as Actors', in W. Carlsnaes and S. Smith (eds), *European Foreign Policy: The EC and Changing Perspectives in Europe* (London: Sage).

Kassim, H. and Hine, D. (1998) 'Conclusion: The European Union, Member States and Social Policy', in D. Hine and H. Kassim (eds), *Beyond the Market: The EU and National Social Policy* (London: Routledge).

Kassim, H. and Menon, A. (eds) (1996) *The European Union and National Industrial Policy* (London: Routledge).

Kaufmann, H. M. (1995) 'The Importance of Being Independent: Central Bank Independence and the European System of Central Banks', in C. Rhodes and S. Mazey (eds), *The State of the European Union*, vol. 3 (London: Longman).

Keating, M. (1995) 'A Comment on Robert Leonardi, "Cohesion in the European Community: Illusion or Reality?" ', *West European Politics*, vol. 18, no. 2, pp. 408–12.

Keating, M. and Jones, B. (1995) 'Nations, Regions, and Europe: The UK Experience', in B. Jones and M. Keating (eds), *The European Union and the Regions* (Oxford: Clarendon Press).

Keeler, J. T. S. (1996) 'Agricultural Power in the European Community: Explaining the Fate of CAP and GATT Negotiations', *Comparative Politics*, vol. 28, no. 2, pp. 127–49.

Keman, H. (1993) 'Comparative Politics: A Distinctive Approach to Political Science?', in H. Keman (ed.), *Comparative Politics: New Directions in Theory and Method* (Amsterdam: VU University Press).

Kenen, P. B. (1969) 'The Optimum Currency Area: An Eclectic View', in R. Mundell and A. Swoboda (eds), *Monetary Problems of the International Economy* (Chicago: University of Chicago Press).

Kenen, P. B. (1995) *Economic and Monetary Union in Europe: Moving Beyond Maastricht* (Cambridge: Cambridge University Press).

Keohane, R. O. (1984) *After Hegemony: Cooperation and Discord in the World Political Economy* (Princeton: Princeton University Press).

Keohane, R. O. (ed.) (1986) *Neo-Realism and Its Critics* (New York: Columbia University Press).

Keohane, R. O. and Nye, J. S. (1989) *Power and Interdependence: World Politics in Transition*, 2nd edn (Boston: Little, Brown).

Key, V. O. (1961) *Public Opinion and American Democracy* (New York: Knopf).

Kiewiet, D. R. and McCubbins, M. (1991) *The Logic of Delegation: Congressional Parties and the Appropriations Process* (Chicago: University of Chicago Press).

King, A. (1981) 'What do Elections Decide?', in D. Butler, H. R. Penniman and A. Ranney (eds), *Democracy at the Polls* (Washington, D.C.: American Enterprise Institute).

King, M. (1994) 'Policing Refugees and Asylum Seekers in "Greater Europe": Towards a Reconceptualisation of Control', in M. Anderson and M. den Boer (eds), *Policing Across National Boundaries* (London: Pinter).

Kingdon, J. W. (1984) *Agendas, Alternatives, and Public Policies* (Boston: Little, Brown).

Kirchner, E. (1992) *Decision-Making in the European Community: The Council Presidency and European Integration* (Manchester: Manchester University Press).

Kitschelt, H. (1993) 'Class Structure and Social Democratic Party Strategy', *British Journal of Political Science*, vol. 23, pp. 299–337.

Kitschelt, H. (1994) *The Transformation of European Social Democracy* (Cambridge: Cambridge University Press).

Kitschelt, H. (1995) *The Radical Right in Western Europe: A Comparative Analysis* (Ann Arbor: University of Michigan Press).

Knudsen, O.F. (1994) 'Context and Action in the Collapse of the Cold War European System', in W. Carlsnaes and S. Smith (eds), *European Foreign Policy: The EC and Changing Perspectives in Europe* (London: Sage).

Kohler-Koch, B. (1996) 'Catching Up with Change: The Transformation of Governance in Europe', *Journal of European Public Policy*, vol. 3, no. 3, pp. 359–80.

Kohler-Koch, B. (1997) 'Organized Interests in the EC and European Parliament', *European Integration On-line Papers*, 1, 9, http://eiop.or.at/eiop/texte/1997-009a.htm.

Kokott, J. (1998) 'Report on Germany', in A.-M. Slaughter, A. Stone Sweet and J. H. H. Weiler (eds), *The European Court and National Courts – Doctrine and Jurisprudence: Legal Change in Its Social Context* (Oxford: Hart Publishing).

Koole, R. and Mair, P. (eds) (1995) *Political Data Yearbook 1995*, *European Journal of Political Research*, 28, 3/4.

Krasner, S. (ed.) (1983) *International Regimes* (Ithaca: Cornell University Press).

Krehbiel, K. (1991) *Information and Legislative Organization* (Ann Arbor: University of Michigan Press).

Kreher, A. (1997) 'Agencies in the European Community: A Step Towards Administrative Integration in Europe', *Journal of European Public Policy*, vol. 4, no. 2, pp. 225–45.

Kreppel, A. (1997) 'The EP's Influence Over EU Policy Outcomes: Fantasy, Fallacy or Fact?', paper presented at the Fifth Biennial Conference of the European Community Studies Association, 29 May–1 June, Seattle.

Krugman, P. (1987) 'Economic Integration in Europe: Some Conceptual Issues', in T. Padoa-Schioppa (ed.), *Efficiency, Stability, Equity* (Oxford: Oxford University Press).

Krugman, P. (1990) 'Policy Problems of a Monetary Union', in P. De Grauwe and L. Papademos (eds), *The European Monetary System in the 1990s* (London: Longman).

Krugman, P. (1991) *Geography and Trade* (Cambridge: Massachusetts Institute of Technology Press).

Krugman, P. (1997) 'Good News from Ireland: A Geographic Perspective', in A. W. Gray (ed.), *International Perspectives on the Irish Economy*, Indecon Economic Consultants.

Krugman, P. (1998) *The Accidental Theorist and Other Dispatches from the Dismal Science* (London: Norton and Co.

Kymlicka, W. (1995) *Multicultural Citizenship: A Liberal Theory of Minority Rights* (Oxford: Clarendon).

Laderchi, F. P. R. (1998) 'Report on Italy', in A.-M. Slaughter, A. Stone Sweet and J. H. H. Weiler (eds), *The European Court and National Courts – Doctrine and Jurisprudence: Legal Change in Its Social Context* (Oxford: Hart Publishing).

Laffan, B. (1997) *The Finances of the European Union* (London: Macmillan).

Lahav, G. (1997) 'Ideology and Party Constraints on Immigration Attitudes in Europe', *Journal of Common Market Studies*, vol. 35, no. 3, pp. 377–406.

Lane, J.-E., Maeland, R. (1995) 'Research Note: Voting Power under the EU Constitution', *Journal of Theoretical Politics*, vol. 7, no. 2, pp. 223–30.

Lane, J.-E., Maeland, R. and Berg, S. (1995) 'The EU Parliament: Seats, States and Political Parties', *Journal of Theoretical Politics*, vol. 7, no. 3, pp. 395–400.

Lange, P. (1993) 'Maastricht and the Social Protocol: Why Did They Do It?', *Politics and Society*, vol. 21, no. 1, pp. 5–36.

Lange, P. and Meadwell, H. (1991) 'Typologies of Democratic Systems: From Political Inputs to Political Economy', in H. J. Wiarda (ed.), *New Directions in Comparative Politics*, 2nd edn (Boulder: Westview).

Lasswell, H. D. (1936) *Politics: Who Gets What, When and How* (New York: McGraw-Hill).

Latter, R. (1990) *Crime and the European Community after 1992* (London: HMSO).

Laver, M. J. and Budge, I. (1992) 'Measuring Policy Distances and Modelling Coalition Formation', in M. J. Laver and I. Budge (eds), *Party Policy and Government Coalitions* (New York: St. Martin's Press).

Laver, M. J., Gallagher, M., Marsh, M., Singh, R. and Tonra, B. (1995) *Electing the President of the European Commission*, Trinity Blue Papers in Public Policy: 1, Dublin: Trinity College.

Laver, M. J. and Hunt, W. B. (1992) *Policy and Party Competition* (London: Routledge).

Lee, N. (1997) 'Environmental Policy', in M. Artis and N. Lee (eds), *The Economics of the European Union*, 2nd edn (Oxford: Oxford University Press).

Lehmbruch, G. (1967) *Proporzdemokratie: Politisches System und politische Kultur in der Schweiz und in Österreich* (Tübingen: Mohr).

Lehner, F. and Homann, B. (1987) 'Consociational Decision-Making and Party Government in Switzerland', in R. S. Katz (ed.), *Party Government: European and American Experiences* (Berlin: De Gruyter).

Leibfried, S. (1992) 'Towards a European Welfare State? On Integrating Poverty Regimes into the European Community', in Z. Ferge and J. E. Kolberg (eds), *Social Policy in a Changing Europe* (Boulder: Westview).

Leibfried, S. and Pierson, P. (1995) 'Semisovereign Welfare States: Social Policy in a Multitiered Europe', in S. Leibfried and P. Pierson (eds), *European Social Policy: Between Fragmentation and Integration* (Washington, D.C.: The Brookings Institution).

Leibfried, S. and Pierson, P. (1996) 'Social Policy', in H. Wallace and W. Wallace (eds), *Policy-Making in the European Union*, 3rd edn (Oxford: Oxford University Press).

Lenaerts, K. (1991) 'Some Reflections on the Separation of Powers in the European Community', *Common Market Law Review*, vol. 28, no. 1, pp. 11–35.

Lenschow, A. (1997) 'Variation in EC Environmental Policy Integration: Agency Push Within Complex Institutional Structures', *Journal of European Public Policy*, vol. 4, no. 1, pp. 109–27.

Leonardi, R. (1993) 'Cohesion in the European Community: Illusion or Reality?', *West European Politics*, vol. 16, no. 4, pp. 492–517.

Leonardi, R. (1995) *Convergence, Cohesion and Integration in the European Union* (London: Macmillan).

Liefferink, D. and Andersen, M. S. (1998) 'Strategies of "Green" Member States in EU Environmental Policy-Making', *Journal of Common Market Studies*, vol. 5, no. 2, pp. 254–70.

Lijphart, A. (1968) *The Politics of Accommodation: Pluralism and Democracy in the Netherlands* (Berkeley: University of California Press).

Lijphart, A. (1977) *Democracy in Plural Societies: A Comparative Exploration* (New Haven: Yale University Press).

Lijphart, A. (1981) 'Political Parties: Ideologies and Programs', in D. Butler, H. R. Penniman and D. Ranney (eds), *Democracy at the Polls: A Comparative Study of Competitive National Elections* (Washington, D.C.: American Enterprise Institute).

Lijphart, A. (1984) *Democracies: Patterns of Majoritarian and Consensus Government in Twenty-One Countries* (New Haven: Yale University Press).

Lijphart, A. (ed.) (1992) *Parliamentary Versus Presidential Government* (Oxford: Oxford University Press).

Lijphart, A. (1994) 'Democracies: Forms, Performance, and Constitutional Engineering', *European Journal of Political Research*, vol. 25, no. 1, pp. 1–17.

Lindberg, L. N. (1963) *The Political Dynamics of Economic Integration* (Oxford: Oxford University Press).

Lindberg, L. and Scheingold, S. (1970) *Europe's Would-Be Polity: Patterns of Change in the European Community* (Harvard: Harvard University Press).

Lindberg, L. N. and Scheingold, S. A. (eds) (1971) *Regional Integration: Theory and Research* (Harvard: Harvard University Press).

Lindblom, C. (1977) *Politics and Markets* (New York: Basic Books).

Lipset, S. M. (1959) *Political Man* (London: Heinemann).

Lipset, S. M. and Rokkan, S. (1967) 'Cleavage Structures, Party Systems and Voter Alignments: An Introduction', in S. M. Lipset and S. Rokkan (eds), *Party Systems and Voter Alignments: Cross-national Perspectives* (New York: Free Press).

Lodge, J. (ed.) (1996) *The 1994 Elections to the European Parliament* (London: Pinter).

Loughlin, J, (1996) 'Representing Regions in Europe: The Committee of the Regions', *Regional and Federal Studies*, vol. 6, no. 2, pp. 147–65.

Lowi, T. J. (1964) 'American Business, Public Policy, Case Studies, and Political Theory', *World Politics*, vol. 16, no. 4, pp. 677–715.

Lowi, T. J. (1969) *The End of Liberalism* (New York: Knopf).

Luce, D. R. and Raiffa, H. (1957) *Games and Decisions* (New York: Wiley).

Ludlow, P. (1991) 'The European Commission', in R. O. Keohane and S. Hoffmann (eds), *The New European Community: Decisionmaking and Institutional Change* (Boulder: Westview).

Mackie, T. and Rose, R. (1991) *The International Almanac of Electoral History* (London: CQ Press).

MacMullen, A. (1997) 'European Commissioners 1952–1995: National Routes to a European Elite', in N. Nugent (ed.), *At the Heart of the Union: Studies of the European Commission* (London: Macmillan).

Madison, J., Hamilton, A. and Jay, J. (1987 [1788]) *The Federalist Papers* (London: Penguin).

Maduro, M. P. (1997) 'Reforming the Market or the State? Article 30 and the European Constitution: Economic Freedom and Political Rights', *European Law Journal*, vol. 3, no. 1, pp. 55–82.

Maher, I. (1998) 'Community Law in the National Legal Order: A Systems Analysis', *Journal of Common Market Studies*, vol. 36, no. 2, pp. 237–54.

Majone, G. (1989) *Evidence, Argument and Persuasion in the Policy Process* (New Haven: Yale University Press).

Majone, G. (1991) 'Cross-National Sources of Regulatory Policy-making in Europe and the United States', *Journal of Public Policy*, vol. 11, no. 1, pp. 79–106.

Majone, G. (1993a) 'The European Community Between Social Policy and Social Regulation', *Journal of Common Market Studies*, vol. 31, no. 2, pp. 153–70.

Majone, G. (1993b) 'The European Community: An "Independent Fourth Branch of Government"?', EUI Working Paper SPS no. 94/17 (Florence: European University Institute).

Majone, G. (1994) 'The Rise of the Regulatory State in Europe', *West European Politics*, vol. 17, no. 3, pp. 78–102.

Majone, G. (1996) *Regulating Europe* (London: Routledge).

Majone, G. (1997) 'The New European Agencies: Regulation by Information', *Journal of European Public Policy*, vol. 4, no. 2, pp. 262–75.

Majone, G. (1998) 'From the Positive to the Regulatory State: Causes and Consequences of Changes in the Mode of Governance', *Journal of Public Policy*, vol. 17, no. 2, pp. 139–67.

Mancini, F. (1989) 'The Making of a Constitution for Europe', *Common Market Law Review*, vol. 26, no. 4, pp. 595–614.

March, J. G. and Olsen, J. P. (1989) *Rediscovering Institutions* (New York: Free Press).

Marin, A. (1997) 'EC Environment Policy', in S. Stavridis, E. Mossialos, R. Morgan and H. Machin (eds), *New Challenges to the European Union: Policies and Policy-Making* (Aldershot: Gower).

Marks, G. (1992) 'Structural Policy in the European Community', in A. M. Sbragia (ed.), *Euro-Politics: Institutions and Policymaking in the 'New' European Community* (Washington, D.C.: The Brookings Institution).

Marks, G. (1993) 'Structural Policy and Multilevel Governance in the EC', in A. W. Cafruny and G. G. Rosenthal (eds), *The State of the European Community*, vol. 2 (London: Longman).

Marks, G. (1996) 'Decision-Making in Cohesion Policy: Describing and Explaining Variation', in L. Hooghe (ed.), *Cohesion Policy and European Integration: Building Multi-Level Governance* (Oxford: Oxford University Press).

Marks, G., Hooghe, L. and Blank, K. (1996) 'European Integration from the 1980s: State-Centric v. Multi-Level Governance', *Journal of Common Market Studies*, vol. 34, no. 3, pp. 341–78.

Marks, G. and McAdam, D. (1996) 'Social Movements and the Changing Structure of Political Opportunity in the European Union', in G. Marks, F. W. Scharpf, P. C. Schmitter and W. Streeck (eds), *Governance in the European Union* (London: Sage).

Marks, G., Nielsen, F., Ray, L. and Salk, J. (1996) 'Competencies, Cracks and Conflicts: Regional Mobilization in the European Union', in G. Marks, F. W. Scharpf, P. C. Schmitter and W. Streeck (eds), *Governance in the European Union* (London: Sage).

Marquand, D. (1978) 'Towards a Europe of Parties', *Political Quarterly*, vol. 49, no. 4, pp. 425–45.

Marshall, T.H. (1950) *Citizenship and Social Class* (Cambridge: Cambridge University Press).

Martin, J.M. and Romano, A.T. (1992) *Multinational Crime, Terrorism, Espionage, Drug and Arms Trafficking* (London: Sage).

Martin, P. and Rogers, C.A. (1996) 'Trade Effects of Regional Aid', in R. Baldwin, P. Haaparanta and J. Kiander (eds), *Expanding the Membership of the European Union* (Cambridge: Cambridge University Press).

Martiniello, M. (ed.) (1995) *Migration, Citizenship and Ethno-National Identity in the European Union* (Aldershot: Avebury).

Martinotti, G. and Stefanizzi, S. (1995) 'Europeans and the Nation State', in O. Niedermayer and R. Sinnott (eds), *Public Opinion and Internationalized Governance* (Oxford: Oxford University Press).

Mattli, W. and Slaughter, A.-M. (1995) 'Law and Politics in the European Union: A Reply to Garrett', *International Organization*, vol. 49, no. 1, pp. 183–90.

Mattli, W. and Slaughter, A.-M. (1998a) 'The Role of National Courts in the Process of European Integration: Accounting for Judicial Preferences and Constraints', in A.-M. Slaughter, A. Stone Sweet and J.H.H. Weiler (eds), *The European Court and National Courts – Doctrine and Jurisprudence: Legal Change in Its Social Context* (Oxford: Hart Publishing).

Mattli, W. and Slaughter, A.-M. (1998b) 'Revisiting the European Court of Justice', *International Organization*, vol. 52, no. 1, pp. 177–209.

Mayhew, D. (1974) *Congress: The Electoral Connection* (New Haven: Yale University Press).

Mazey, S. (1998) 'The European Union and Women's Rights: From the Europeanisation of National Agendas to the Nationalisation of a European Agenda?', in D. Hine and H. Kassim (eds), *Beyond the Market: The EU and National Social Policy* (London: Routledge).

Mazey, S. and Richardson, J. (eds) (1993) *Lobbying in the European Community* (Oxford: Oxford University Press).

Mazey, S. and Richardson, J. (1997) 'The Commission and the Lobby', in G. Edwards and D. Spence (eds), *The European Commission*, 2nd edn (London: Catermill).

McAllister, R. (1997) *From EC to EU: An Historical and Political Survey* (London: Macmillan).

McCracken, P. (1977) *Towards Full Employment and Price Stability* (McCracken Report) Paris: Organisation for Economic Co-operation and Development.

McCubbins, M.D., Noll, R.G. and Weingast, B.R. (1990) 'Positive and Normative Models of Procedural Rights: An Integrative Approach to Administrative Procedures', *Journal of Law, Economics, and Organization*, vol. 6, pp. 307–32.

McCubbins, M.D. and Schwartz, T. (1984) 'Congressional Oversight Overlooked: Police Patrols versus Fire Alarms', *American Journal of Political Science*, vol. 28, no. 1, pp. 165–79.

McDougall, D. (1977) *Report of the Study Group on the Role of Public Finance in European Integration*, Vols. 1 and 2 (Brussels: European Commission).

McKay, D. (1996) *Rush to Union: Understanding the European Federal Bargain* (Oxford: Clarendon).

McKelvey, R. (1976) 'Intransitivities in Multidimensional Voting Models and Some Implications for Agenda-Control', *Journal of Economic Theory*, vol. 12, no. 3, pp. 472–82.

McKeown, T. J. (1991) 'A Liberal Trade Order: The Long-Run Pattern of Imports to the Advanced Capitalist States', *International Studies Quarterly*, vol. 35, no. 2, pp. 151–72.

McKinnon, R. (1963) 'Optimum Currency Areas', *American Economic Review*, vol. 53, pp. 717–25.

McLaughlin, A. M. and Greenwood, J. (1995) 'The Management of Interest Representation in the European Union', *Journal of Common Market Studies*, 33, 1, 143–56.

McNamara, K. R. (1998) *The Currency of Ideas: Monetary Politics in the European Union* (Ithaca: Cornell University Press).

Meehan, E. (1993) *Citizenship and the European Community* (London: Sage).

Meijers, H. *et al.* (1997) *Democracy, Migrants and Police in the European Union: The 1996 IGC and Beyond* (Utrecht: Standing Committee of Experts in International Immigration, Refugee and Criminal Law).

Meltzer, A. H. and Richard, S. F. (1981) 'A Rational Theory of the Size of Government', *Journal of Political Economy*, vol. 89, pp. 914–27.

Meunier, S. (1998) 'Divided but United: European Trade Policy Integration and EU-U.S. Agricultural Negotiations in the Uruguay Round', in C. Rhodes (ed.), *The European Community in the World Community* (Boulder: Lynne Reiner).

Migration Policy Group (1996) *The Comparative Approaches to Societal Integration Project: Final Report* (Brussels: Migration Policy Group).

Miller, G. (1995) 'Post-Maastricht Legislative Procedures: Is the Council "Institutionally Challenged?"', paper presented at the Fourth Biennial Conference of the European Community Studies Association, April, Charleston.

Miller, G. J. and Hammond, T. H. (1989) 'Stability and Efficiency in a Separation-of-Powers Constitutional System', in B. Grofman and D. Wittman (eds), *The Federalist Papers and the New Institutionalism* (New York: Agathon).

Milner, H. V. (1997) *Interests, Institutions, and Information: Domestic Politics and International Relations* (Princeton: Princeton University Press).

Milner, H. V. and Keohane, R. O. (1996) 'Internationalization and Domestic Politics: An Introduction', in R. O. Keohane and H. V. Milner (eds), *Internationalization and Domestic Politics* (Cambridge: Cambridge University Press).

Minford, P. (1996) 'The Price of Monetary Unification', in M. Holmes (ed.), *The Eurosceptical Reader* (London: Macmillan).

Minority Rights Group (ed.) (1997) *World Directory of Minorities* (London: Minority Rights Group).

Mitnick, B. M. (1980) *The Political Economy of Regulation: Creating, Designing and Removing Regulatory Forms* (New York: Columbia University Press).

Moe, T. (1987) 'Interests, Institutions and Positive Theory: The Politics of the NLRB', *Studies in American Political Development*, vol. 2, pp. 236–99.

Moe, T. (1989) 'The Politics of Bureaucratic Structure', in J. Chubb and P. Peterson (eds), *Can Government Govern?* (Washington, D.C.: The Brookings Institution).

Moe, T. (1990) 'The Politics of Structural Choice: Towards a Theory of Public Bureaucracy', in O. E. Williamson (ed.), *Organizational Theory: From Chester Barnard to the Present and Beyond* (Oxford: Oxford University Press).

Monar, J. (1995) 'Democratic Control of Justice and Home Affairs: The European Parliament and National Parliaments', in R. Bieber and J. Monar (eds), *Justice and Home Affairs in the European Union: The Development of the Third Pillar* (Brussels: Interuniversity Press).

Monar, J. (1997) 'European Union – Justice and Home Affairs: A Balance Sheet and an Agenda for Reform', in G. Edwards and A. Pijpers (eds), *The Politics of European Treaty Reform: The 1996 Intergovernmental Conference and Beyond* (London: Pinter).

Monar, J. and Morgan, R. (eds) (1994) *The Third Pillar of the European Union: Cooperation in the Fields of Justice and Home Affairs* (Brussels: Interuniversity Press).

Monnet, J. (1978) *Memoirs*, Doubleday: Garden City.

Montanari, I. J. (1995) 'Hamonization of Social Policies and Social Regulation in the European Community', *European Journal of Political Research*, vol. 27, no. 1, pp. 21–45.

Moore, B. (1967) *Social Origins of Dictatorship and Democracy: Lord and Peasant in the Making of the Modern World* (Harmondsworth:, Penguin).

Moravcsik, A. (1991) 'Negotiating the Single European Act: National Interests and Conventional Statecraft in the European Community', *International Organization*, vol. 45, no. 1, pp. 19–56.

Moravcsik, A. (1993) 'Preferences and Power in the European Community: A Liberal Intergovernmanetalist Approach', *Journal of Common Market Studies*, vol. 31, no. 4, pp. 473–524.

Moravcsik, A. (1997) 'Taking Preferences Seriously: A Liberal Theory of International Politics', *International Organization*, vol. 51, no. 4, pp. 513–53.

Moravcsik, A. (1998) *The Choice for Europe: Social Purpose and State Power from Messina to Maastricht* (Ithaca: Cornell University Press).

Moravcsik, A. and Nicolaïdis, K. (1998) 'Keynote Article: Federal Ideals and Constitutional Realities in the Treaty of Amsterdam', *Journal of Common Market Studies: Annual Review*, vol. 36, pp. 13–38.

Morgenthau, H. J. (1948) *Politics Among Nations: The Struggle for Power and Peace* (New York: Knopf).

Morriss, P. (1996) 'QMV and Power Indices: A Further Comment to Johnston', *British Journal of Political Science*, vol. 26, pp. 595–97.

Moser P. (1996) 'The European Parliament as a Conditional Agenda-Setter: What Are the Conditions? A Critique of Tsebelis (1994)', *American Political Science Review*, vol. 90, no. 4, pp. 834–8.

Moser, P. (1997) 'The Benefits of the Conciliation Procedure for the European Parliament: Comment to George Tsebelis', *Aussenwirtschaft*, vol. 52, no's 1/2, pp. 57–62.

Mueller, D. C. (1989) *Public Choice II* (Cambridge: Cambridge University Press).

Munchau, W. (1998) 'Emu's First Boom and Bust', *The Financial Times*, 8 October 1998.

Mundell, R. (1961) 'A Theory of Optimal Currency Areas', *American Economic Review*, vol. 51, pp. 657–65.

Musgrave, R. A. (1959) *Public Finance in Theory and Practice* (New York: McGraw-Hill).

Myrdal, G. (1957) *Economic Theory and the Underdeveloped Regions* (London: Duckworth).

Nanetti, R. Y. (1996) 'EU Cohesion and Territorial Restructuring in the Member States', in L. Hooghe (ed.), *Cohesion Policy and European Integration: Building Multi-Level Governance* (Oxford: Oxford University Press).

Nedergaard, P. (1995) 'The Political Economy of CAP Reform', in F. Laursen (ed.), *The Political Economy of European Integration* (The Hague: Kluwer).

Neuwahl, N. A. E. M. (1995) 'Judicial Control in Matters of Justice and Home Affairs: What Role for the Court of Justice?', in R. Bieber and J. Monar (eds), *Justice and Home Affairs in the European Union: The Development of the Third Pillar* (Brussels: Interuniversity Press).

Neven, D. J. (1992) 'Regulatory Reform in the European Community', *American Economic Review*, vol. 82, pp. 98–108.

Nicolaides, P. (1995) 'The Effect of Regional Integration on Trade Policy: Lessons from the European Community', in F. Laursen (ed.), *The Political Economy of European Integration* (The Hague: Kluwer).

Niedermayer, O. (1991) 'Public Opinion and the European Parliament', in K. Reif and R. Inglehart (eds), *Eurobarometer: The Dynamics of European Public Opinion – Essays in Honour of Jacques-René Rabier* (London: Macmillan).

Niedermayer, O. (1995a) 'Trends and Contrasts', in O. Niedermayer and R. Sinnott (eds), *Public Opinion and Internationalized Governance* (Oxford: Oxford University Press).

Niedermayer, O. (1995b) 'Trust and Sense of Community', in O. Niedermayer and R. Sinnott (eds), *Public Opinion and Internationalized Governance* (Oxford: Oxford University Press).

Niedermayer, O. and Sinnott, R. (1995) 'Democratic Legitimacy and the European Parliament', in O. Niedermayer and R. Sinnott (eds), *Public Opinion and Internationalized Governance* (Oxford: Oxford University Press).

Niessen, J. and Guild, E. (1996) *The Developing Immigration and Asylum Policies of the European Union: Adopted Conventions, Resolutions, Recommendations, Decisions and Conclusion* (The Hague: Kluwer).

Niskanen, W. A. (1971) *Bureaucracy and Representative Government* (Chicago: Aldine, Atherton).

Norman, P. (1998) 'Productivity Study Shows Dangers of Euro Wage Claims', *The Financial Times*, 7 July 1998.

Norris, P. and Franklin, M. (1997) 'Social Representation', in M. Marsh and P. Norris (eds), *Political Representation in the European Parliament*, special issue of *European Journal of Political Research*, vol. 32, no. 2.

North, D. C. (1990) *Institutions, Institutional Change and Economic Performance* (Cambridge: Cambridge University Press).

Nurmi, H. (1997) 'The Representation of Voter Groups in the European

Parliament: A Penrose-Banzhaf Index Analysis', *Electoral Studies*, vol. 16, no. 3, pp. 317–27.

Nuttall. S. (1996) 'The Commission: The Struggle for Legitimacy', in C. Hill (ed.), *The Actors in Europe's Foreign Policy* (London: Routledge).

Nuttall, S. (1997) 'The Commission and Foreign Policy-Making', in G. Edwards and D. Spence (eds), *The European Commission*, 2nd edn (London: Catermill).

Obradovic, D. (1996) 'Prospects for Corporatist Decision-Making in the European Union: the Social Policy Agreement', *Journal of European Public Policy*, vol. 2, no. 2, pp. 261–83.

O'Leary, S. (1995) *The Evolving Concept of Community Citizenship: From the Free Movement of Persons to Union Citizenship* (The Hague: Kluwer).

Olson, M. (1965) *The Logic of Collective Action* (Cambridge: Harvard University Press).

O'Nuallain, C. (ed.) (1985) *The Presidency of the European Council of Ministers* (London: Croom Helm).

Oppenhuis, E, van der Eijk, C. and Franklin, M. (1996) 'The Party Context: Outcomes', in van der Eijk, C. and Franklin, M. (eds), *Choosing Europe? The European Electorate and National Politics in the Face of Union* (Ann Arbor: University of Michigan Press).

Ordeshook, P. C. (1992) *A Political Theory Primer* (London: Routledge).

Ostner, I. and Lewis, J. (1995) 'Gender and the Evolution of European Social Policies', in S. Leibfried and P. Pierson (eds), *European Social Policy: Between Fragmentation and Integration* (Washington, D.C.: The Brookings Institution).

Ostrom, E. (1990) *Governing the Commons: The Evolution of Institutions of Collective Action* (Cambridge: Cambridge University Press).

Østrup, F. (1995) 'Economic and Monetary Union', in F. Laursen (ed.), *The Political Economy of European Integration* (The Hague: Kluwer).

van Oudenhave, G. (1965) *Political Parties in the European Parliament: The First Ten Years, September 1952–September 1962* (Leyden: A.W. Sijthoff).

Page, E. (1997) *People Who Run Europe* (Oxford: Clarendon).

Papademetriou, D. G. and Hamilton, K. A. (1996) *Converging Paths to Restriction: French, Italian, and British Responses to Immigration*, International Migration Policy Program 3 (Washington, D.C.: Carnegie Endowment for International Peace).

Patterson, L. A. (1997) 'Agricultural Policy Reform in the European Community: A Three-Level Game Analysis', *International Organization*, vol. 51, no. 1, pp. 135–65.

Pedlar, R. and Van Schendelen, M. P. C. M. (eds) (1994) *Lobbying the European Union: Companies, Trade Associations and Interest Groups* (Aldershot: Dartmouth).

Pelkmans, J. (1990) 'Regulation and the Single Market: An Economic Perspective', in H. Siebert (ed.), *The Completion of the Internal Market* (Tübingen: Mohr).

Pelkmans, J. and Winters, L. A. (1988) *Europe's Domestic Market* (London: Royal Institute of International Affairs).

Peltzman, S. (1976) 'Toward a More General Theory of Regulation', *Journal of Law and Economics*, vol. 19, no. 2, pp. 211–40.

Peltzman, S. (1989) 'The Theory of Economic Regulation after a Decade of Deregulation', *Brookings Papers on Economic Activity – Microeconomics* (Washington, D.C.: The Brookings Institution).

Peters, B. G. (1992) 'Bureaucratic Politics and the Institutions of the European Community', in A. M. Sbragia (ed.), *Euro-Politics: Institutions and Policy-making in the "New" Europe* (Washington, D.C.: The Brookings Institution).

Peters, B. G. (1994) 'Agenda-Setting in the European Community', *Journal of European Public Policy*, vol. 1, no. 1, pp. 9–26.

Peterson, J. (1991) 'Technology Policy in Europe: Explaining the Framework Programme and Eureka in Theory and Practice', *Journal of Common Market Studies*, vol. 29, no. 3, pp. 269–90.

Peterson, J. (1995a) 'EU Research Policy: The Politics of Expertise', in C. Rhodes and S. Mazey (eds), *The State of the European Union, vol. 3* (London: Longman).

Peterson, J. (1995b) 'Playing the Transparency Game: Consultation and Policy-Making in the European Commission', *Public Administration*, vol. 73, no. 3, pp. 473–92.

Petracca, M. P. (ed.) (1994) *The Politics of Interests: Interest Groups Transformed* (Boulder: Westview).

Pfetsch, F. (1994) 'Tensions in Sovereignty: Foreign Policies of the EC Members Compared', in W. Carlsnaes and S. Smith (eds), *European Foreign Policy: The EC and Changing Perspectives in Europe* (London: Sage).

Piening, C. (1997) *Global Europe: The European Union in World Affairs* (Boulder: Lynne Rienner).

Pierson, P. (1996) 'The Path to European Integration: A Historical Institutionalist Analysis', *Comparative Political Studies*, vol. 29, no. 2, pp. 123–63.

Piner Tank, G. (1998) 'The CFSP and the nation-state', in K. A. Eliassen (ed.), *Foreign and Security Policy in the European Union* (London: Sage).

Plötner, J. (1998) 'Report on France', in A.-M. Slaughter, A. Stone Sweet and J. H. H. Weiler (eds), *The European Court and National Courts – Doctrine and Jurisprudence: Legal Change in Its Social Context* (Oxford: Hart Publishing).

Pollack, M. A. (1995a) 'Creeping Competence: The Expanding Agenda of the European Community', *Journal of Public Policy*, vol. 14, no. 1, pp. 97–143.

Pollack, M. A. (1995b) 'Regional Actors in an Intergovernmental Play: The Making and Implementation of EC Structural Policy', in C. Rhodes and S. Mazey (eds), *The State of the European Union, vol. 3* (London: Longman).

Pollack, M. A. (1996) 'The New Institutionalism and EC Governance: The Promise and Limits of Institutional Analysis', *Governance*, vol. 9, no. 4, pp. 429–58.

Pollack, M. A. (1997a) 'Delegation, Agency and Agenda Setting in the European Community', *International Organization*, vol. 51, no. 1, pp. 99–134.

Pollack, M. A. (1997b) 'Representing Diffuse Interests in EC Policy-Making', *Journal of European Public Policy*, vol. 4, no. 4, pp. 572–90.

Pollack, M. A. (1997c) 'The Commission as an Agent', in N. Nugent (ed.), *At the Heart of the Union: Studies of the European Commission* (London: Macmillan).

Poole, W. (1990) 'Optimal Choice of Monetary Policy Instruments in a Simple Stochastic Macro Model', *Quarterly Journal of Economics*, vol. 85.

Portes, R. and Rey, H. (1998) 'The Emergence of the Euro as an International

Currency', in D. Begg *et al.* (eds), *EMU: Prospects and Challenges for the Euro* (Oxford: Blackwell).

Praet, P. (1987) 'Economic Objectives in European Foreign Policy Making', in J. K. de Vree, P. Coffey and R. H. Lauwaars (eds), *Towards a European Foreign Policy: Legal, Economic and Political Dimensions* (Dordrecht: Martinus Nijhoff).

Pridham, G. and Pridham, P. (1979) 'The New Party Federations and Direct Elections', *The World Today*, vol. 35, no. 2, pp. 62–70.

Quanjel, M. and Wolters, M. (1993) 'Growing Cohesion in the European Parliament', Paper presented at the Annual Joint Sessions of the European Consortium for Political Research, April 1993, Leiden.

Quermonne, J. (1994) *La Système politique de l'Union européene*, Paris: Montchrétien.

Radaelli, C. M. (1996) 'Fiscal Federalism as a Catalyst for Policy Development? In Search of a Framework for European Direct Tax Harmonisation', *Journal of European Public Policy*, vol. 3, no. 3, pp. 402–20.

Rasmussen, H. (1986) *On Law and Policy in the European Court of Justice* (Dordrecht: Martinus Nijhoff).

Raunio, T. (1996a) *Party Group Behaviour in the European Parliament* (Tampere: University of Tampere).

Raunio, T. (1996b) 'Parliamentary Questions in the European Parliament: Representation, Information and Control', *Journal of Legislative Studies*, vol. 2, no. 4, pp. 356–82.

Rawls, J. (1971) *A Theory of Justice* (Cambridge: Harvard University Press).

Reif, K. (1984) 'National Election Cycles and European Elections, 1979 and 1984', *Electoral Studies*, vol. 3, no. 3, pp. 244–55.

Reif, K. (1997) 'Reflections: European Elections as Member State Second-Order Elections Revisited', *European Journal of Political Research*, vol. 31, no. 1, pp. 115–24.

Reif, K. and Schmitt, H. (1980) 'Nine Second-Order National Elections: A Conceptual Framework for the Analysis of European Election Results', *European Journal of Political Research*, vol. 8, no. 1, pp. 3–45.

Rhodes, M. (1995) 'A Regulatory Conundrum: Industrial Relations and the Social Dimension', in S. Leibfried and P. Pierson (eds), *European Social Policy: Between Fragmentation and Integration* (Washington, D.C.: The Brookings Institution).

Rhodes, M. and van Apeldoorn, B. (1997) 'Capitalism versus Capitalism in Western Europe', in M. Rhodes, P. Heywood and V. Wright (eds), *Developments in West European Politics* (London: Macmillan).

Rhodes, R. A. W. and Dunleavy, P. (eds) (1995) *Prime Minister, Cabinet and Core Executive* (London: Macmillan).

Richardson, J. (1996) 'Actor-Based Models of National and EU Policy Making', in H. Kassim and A. Menon (eds), *The EU and National Industrial Policy* (London: Routledge).

Riker, W. H. (1962) *The Theory of Political Coalitions* (New Haven: Yale University Press).

Riker, W. H. (1980) 'Implications from the Disequilibrium of Majority Rule for the Study of Institutions', *American Political Science Review*, vol. 74, no. 2, pp. 432–46.

Riker, W. H. (1986) *The Art of Political Manipulation* (New Haven: Yale University Press).

Riker, W. H. (1992) 'The Merits of Bicameralism', *International Review of Law and Economics*, vol. 12, no. 2, pp. 166–68.

Rokkan, S. (1973) 'Cities, States, and Nations: A Dimensional Model for the Study of Contrasts in Development', in S. N. Eisenstadt and S. Rokkan (eds), *Building States and Nations: Models and Data Resources, vol. 1* (London: Sage).

Rosecrance, R. (1986) *The Rise of the Trading State* (New York: Basic Books).

Ross, G. (1994) *Jacques Delors and European Integration* (Cambridge: Polity).

Sala-i-Martin, X. and Sachs, J. (1991) 'Fiscal Federalism and Optimum Currency Areas: Evidence for Europe from the United States', Working Paper no. 3855 (Cambridge: National Bureau of Economic Research).

Sandholtz, W. (1992) 'ESPRIT and the Politics of International Collective Action', *Journal of Common Market Studies*, vol. 30, no. 1, pp. 1–39.

Sandholtz, W. (1993) 'Choosing Union: Monetary Politics and Maastricht', *International Organization*, vol. 47, no. 1, pp. 1–39.

Sandholtz, W. (1996) 'Money Troubles: Europe's Rough Road to Monetary Union', *Journal of European Public Policy*, vol. 3, no. 1, pp. 84–101.

Sandholtz, W. and Stone Sweet, A. (1997) 'European Integration and Supranational Governance', *Journal of European Public Policy*, vol. 4, no. 3, pp. 297–317.

Sandholtz, W. and Stone Sweet, A. (eds) (1998) *European Integration and Supranational Governance* (Oxford: Oxford University Press).

Sandholtz, W. and Zysman, J. (1989) '1992: Recasting the European Bargain', *World Politics*, vol. 42, no. 1, pp. 95–128.

Sbragia, A. M. (ed.) (1992) *Euro-Politics: Institutions and Policymaking in the 'New' European Community* (Washington: The Brookings Institution).

Sbragia, A. M. (1996) 'Environment Policy', in H. Wallace and W. Wallace (eds), *Policy-Making in the European Union*, 3rd edn (Oxford: Oxford University Press).

Scarrow, S. (1997) 'Political Career Paths and the European Parliament', *Legislative Studies Quarterly*, vol. 22, no. 2, pp. 253–63.

Scharpf, F. W. (1988) 'The Joint-Decision Trap: Lessons from German Federalism and European Integration', *Public Administration*, vol. 66, no. 3, pp. 277–304.

Scharpf, F. W. (1996) 'Negative and Positive Integration in the Political Economy of European Welfare States', in G. Marks, F. W. Scharpf, P. C. Schmitter and W. Streeck (eds), *Governance in the European Union* (London: Sage).

Scharpf, F. W. (1997a) 'Economic Integration, Democracy and the Welfare State', *Journal of European Public Policy*, vol. 4, no. 1, pp. 18–36.

Scharpf, F. W. (1997b) 'Introduction: The Problem-Solving Capacity of Multi-Level Governance', *Journal of European Public Policy*, vol. 4, no. 4, pp. 520–38.

Schattschneider, E. E. (1960) *The Semi-Sovereign People: A Realist's View of Democracy in America* (New York: Holt, Rinehart and Winston.

Schendelen, M. P. C. M. van (1996) ' "The Council Decides": Does the Council Decide?', *Journal of Common Market Studies*, vol. 34, no. 4, pp. 531–48.

Schmidt, S. K. (1998) 'Commission Activism: Subsuming Telecommunications and Electricity under European Competition Law', *Journal of European Public Policy*, vol. 5, no. 1, pp. 169–84.

Schmitter, P. C. (1974) 'Still the Century of Corporatism?', *Review of Politics*, vol. 36, no. 1, pp. 85–131.

Schmitter, P. C. (1996) 'How to Democratize the Emerging Euro-polity: Citizenship, Representation, Decision-making', unpublished mimeo.

Schmitter, P. C. and Lehmbruch, G. (eds) (1979) *Trends Towards Corporatist Intermediation* (London: Sage).

Schneider, G. and Weitsman, P. A. (1996) 'The Punishment Trap: Integration Referendums as Popularity Contests', *Comparative Political Studies*, vol. 28, no. 4, pp. 582–607.

Schumpeter, J. (1943) *Capitalism, Socialism and Democracy* (London: Allen and Unwin).

Scully, R. M. (1997a) 'Policy Influence and Participation in the European Parliament', *Legislative Studies Quarterly*, vol. 22, no. 2, pp. 233–52.

Scully, R. M. (1997b) 'The EP and the Co-Decision Procedure: A Reassessment', *Journal of Legislative Studies*, vol. 3, no. 3, pp. 58–73.

Scully, R. M. (1997c) 'The EP and Co-Decision: A Rejoinder to Tsebelis and Garrett', *Journal of Legislative Studies*, vol. 3, no. 3, pp. 93–103.

Scully, R. M. (1997d) 'Positively My Last Words on Co-Decision', *Journal of Legislative Studies*, vol. 3, no. 4, pp. 144–46.

Shapiro, M. J. (1981) *Courts: A Comparative and Political Analysis* (Chicago: University of Chicago Press).

Shapiro, M. J. (1992) 'The European Court of Justice', in A. M. Sbragia (ed.), *Euro-Politics: Institutions and Policymaking in the 'New' European Community* (Washington, D.C.: The Brookings Institution).

Shapiro, M. J. and Stone, A. (eds) (1994) *The New Constitutional Politics of Europe*, special issue of *Comparative Political Studies*, vol. 26, no. 4.

Shapley, L. S. and Shubik, M. (1954) 'A Method for Evaluating the Distribution of Power in a Committee System', *American Political Science Review*, vol. 48, N. 4, pp. 787–92.

Sharp, M. and Pavitt, K. (1993) 'Technology Policy in the 1990s: Old Trends and New Realities', *Journal of Common Market Studies*, vol. 31, no. 2, pp. 131–51.

Shaw, J. (1996) *Law of the European Union*, 2nd edn (London: Macmillan).

Shaw, J. (1997) 'Citizenship of the Union: Towards Post-National Membership?', Harvard Law School Jean Monnet Working Paper Series no. 6/97.

Shepsle, K. A. (1979) 'Institutional Arrangements and Equilibria in Multi-dimensional Voting Models', *American Journal of Political Science*, vol. 23, no. 1, pp. 27–59.

Shepsle, K. A. (1979) 'Institutional Arrangements and Equilibrium in Multi-dimensional Voting Models', *American Journal of Political Science*, vol. 23, no. 1, pp. 27–59.

Shepsle, K. A. (1986) 'Institutional Equilibrium and Equilibrium Institutions', in H. F. Weinberg (ed.), *Political Science: The Science of Politics* (New York: Agathon).

Shepsle, K. A. (1989) 'Studying Institutions: Some Lessons from the Rational Choice Approach', *Journal of Theoretical Politics*, vol. 1, pp. 131–47.

Shepsle, K. A. and Weingast, B. (1987) 'Why are Congressional Committees Powerful?', *American Political Science Review*, vol. 81, no. 4, pp. 935–45.

Shepsle, K. A. and Weingast, B. (1994) 'Positive Theories of Congressional Institutions', *Legislative Studies Quarterly*, vol. 19, no. 2, pp. 149–79.

Shonfield, S. (1973) *Europe: Journey to an Unknown Destination* (London: Allen Lane.

Siebert, H. (1990) 'The Harmonization Issue in Europe: Prior Arrangement or a Competitive Process?', in H. Siebert (ed.), *The Completion of the Internal Market* (Tübingen: Mohr).

Sinnott, R. (1995) 'Policy, Subsidiarity, and Legitimacy', in O. Niedermayer and R. Sinnott (eds), *Public Opinion and Internationalized Governance* (Oxford: Oxford University Press).

Skowronek, S. (1982) *Building a New American State: The Expansion of National Administrative Capacities* (Cambridge: Cambridge University Press).

Slater, M. (1982) 'Political Elites, Popular Indifference and Community Building', *Journal of Common Market Studies*, vol. 21, no's 1/2, pp. 69–87.

Smith, A. D. (1991) *National Identity* (London: Penguin).

Smith, D. L. and Wanke, J. (1993) 'Completing the Single European Market: An Analysis of the Impact on the Member States', *American Journal of Political Science*, vol. 37, no. 2, pp. 529–54.

Smith, M. (1996) 'The European Union and a Changing Europe: establishing the Boundaries of Order', *Journal of Common Market Studies*, vol. 34, no. 1, pp. 5–28.

Smith, M. (1997a) 'The Commission and External Relations', in G. Edwards and D. Spence (eds), *The European Commission*, 2nd edn (London: Catermill).

Smith, M. (1997b) 'The Commission Made Me Do It: The European Commission as a Strategic Asset in Domestic Politics', in N. Nugent (ed.), *At the Heart of the Union: Studies of the European Commission* (London: Macmillan).

Smith, M. (1998a) 'Does the Flag Follow Trade?: "Politicisation" and the Emergence of a European Foreign Policy', in J. Peterson and H. Sjursen (eds), *A Common Foreign Policy for Europe? Competing Visions of the CFSP* (London: Routledge).

Smith, M. (1998b) 'Rules, Transgovernmentalism, and the Expansion of European Political Co-operation', in W. Sandholtz and A. Stone Sweet (eds), *European Integration and Supranational Governance* (Oxford: Oxford University Press).

Smith, M. and Sandholtz, W. (1995) 'Institutions and Leadership: Germany, Maastricht and the ERM Crisis', in C. Rhodes and S. Mazey (eds), *The State of the European Union*, vol. 3 (London: Longman).

Soysal, Y. (1994) *Limits of Citizenship: Migrants and Postnational Membership in Europe* (Chicago: University of Chicago Press).

Spence, D. (1997) 'Staff and Personnel Policy in the Commission', in G. Edwards and D. Spence (eds), *The European Commission*, 2nd edn (London: Catermill).

Sperling, J. and Kirchner, E. (1997) 'The Security Architectures and Institutional Features of Post–1989 Europe', *Journal of European Public Policy*, vol. 4, no. 2, pp. 155–70.

van Staden, A. (1994) 'After Maastricht: Explaining the Movement towards a Common European Defence Policy', in W. Carlsnaes and S. Smith (eds), *European Foreign Policy: The EC and Changing Perspectives in Europe* (London: Sage).

Stavridis, S. (1997) 'The Common Security Policy of the European Union: Why Institutional Arrangements Are Not Enough', in S. Stavridis, E. Mossialos, R. Morgan and H. Machin (eds), *New Challenges to the European Union: Policies and Policy-Making* (Aldershot: Dartmouth).

Stein, E. (1981) 'Lawyers, Judges and the Making of a Transnational Constitution', *American Journal of International Law*, vol. 75, no. 1, pp. 1–27.

Steinle, W. J. (1992) 'Regional Competitiveness in the Single Market', *Regional Studies*, vol. 26, no. 4, pp. 307–18.

Steunenberg, B. (1994) 'Decision-making under different institutional arrangements: Legislation by the European Community', *Journal of Institutional and Theoretical Economics*, vol. 150, no. 4, pp. 642–69.

Steunenberg, B. (1997) 'Codecision and its Reform: A Comparative Analysis of Decision-Making Rules in the European Union', in B. Steunenberg and F. van Vught (eds), *Political Institutions and Public Policy* (Amsterdam: Kluwer).

Steunenberg, B., Koboldt, C. and Schmidtchen, D. (1996) 'Policymaking, Comitology, and the Balance of Power in The European Union', *International Review of Law and Economics*, vol. 16, no. 2, pp. 329–44.

Stigler, G. J. (1970) 'Director's Law of Public Income Redistribution', *Journal of Law and Economics*, vol. 13, no. 1, pp. 1–10.

Stigler, G. J. (1971) 'The Theory of Economic Regulation', *Bell Journal of Economics and Management Science*, vol. 6, no. 2, pp. 3–21.

Stigler, G. J. and Friedland, C. (1962) 'What Can Regulators Regulate? The Case of Electricity', *Journal of Law and Economics*, vol. 5, no. 1, pp. 1–16.

Stone, A. (1992) *The Birth of Judicial Politics in France: The Constitutional Council in Comparative Perspective* (Oxford: Oxford University Press).

Stone, A. (1993) 'Where Judicial Politics Are Legislative Politics: The French Constitutional Council', in M. L. Volcansek (ed.), *Judicial Politics and Policy-Making in Western Europe* (London: Frank Cass).

Stone Sweet, A. (1998) 'Constitutional Dialogues in the European Community', in A.-M. Slaughter, A. Stone Sweet and J. H. H. Weiler (eds), *The European Court and National Courts – Doctrine and Jurisprudence: Legal Change in Its Social Context* (Oxford: Hart Publishing).

Stone Sweet, A. and Brunell, T. L. (1998a) 'Constructing a Supranational Constitution: Dispute Resolution and Governance in the European Community', *American Political Science Review*, vol. 92, no. 1, pp. 63–81.

Stone Sweet, A. and Brunell, T. L. (1998b) 'The European Court and National Courts: A Statistical Analysis of Preliminary References, 1961–95', *Journal of European Public Policy*, vol. 5, no. 1, pp. 66–97.

Stone Sweet, A. and Sandholtz, W. (1997) 'European Integration and Supranational Governance', *Journal of European Public Policy*, vol. 4, no. 3, pp. 297–317.

Story, J. (1996) 'Strategy, Ideology and Politics: The Relaunch of Social Europe, 1987–1989', in O. Cadot, L. Gabel, J. Story and D. Webber (eds), *European Casebook on Industrial and Trade Policy* (Hemel Hempstead: Prentice-Hall).

Streeck, W. (1995) 'From Market Making to State Building? Reflections on the Political Economy of European Social Policy', in S. Leibfried and P. Pierson (eds), *European Social Policy: Between Fragmentation and Integration* (Washington, D.C.: The Brookings Institution).

Streeck, W. (1996) 'Neo-Voluntarism: A European Social Policy Regime?', in G. Marks, F. W. Scharpf, P. C. Schmitter and W. Streeck (eds), *Governance in the European Union* (London: Sage).

Streeck, W. (1997) 'Industrial Citizenship under Regime Competition: The Case of the European Works Councils', *Journal of European Public Policy*, vol. 4, no. 4, pp. 643–64.

Streeck, W. and Schmitter, P. C. (1991) 'From National Corporatism to Transnational Pluralism: Organized Interests in the Single European Market', *Politics and Society*, vol. 19, no. 2, pp. 133–64.

Streit, M. E. and Mussler, W. (1995) 'The Economic Constitution of the European Community: From "Rome" to "Maastricht"', *European Law Journal*, vol. 1, no. 3, pp. 5–30.

Strom, K. (1990) 'A Behavioural Theory of Competitive Political Parties', *American Journal of Political Science*, vol. 34, no. 2, pp. 565–98.

Sun, J.-M. and Pelkmans, J. (1995) 'Regulatory Competition and the Single Market', *Journal of Common Market Studies*, vol. 33, no. 1, pp. 67–89.

Sunstein, C. R. (1990) *After the Rights Revolution: Reconsidering the Regulatory State* (Cambridge: Harvard University Press).

Sutherland, P. *et al.* (High Level Group on the Operation of the Internal Market) (1992) *The Internal Market After 1992: Meeting the Challenge* (Luxembourg: Office of Official Publications of the European Communities).

Tarrow, S. (1995) 'The Europeanisation of Conflict: Reflections from a Social Movement Perspective', *West European Politics*, vol. 18, no. 2, pp. 223–51.

Taylor, M. (1976) *Anarchy and Cooperation* (New York: Wiley).

Taylor, P. (1982) 'Intergovernmentalism in the European Communities in the 1970s: Patterns and Perspectives', *International Organization*, vol. 36, no. 4, pp. 741–66.

Taylor, P (1989) 'The European Community and the State: Assumptions, Theories and Propositions', *Review of International Studies*, vol. 17, no. 4, pp. 567–79.

Taylor, P. (1991) 'The European Community and the State: Assumptions, Theories and Propositions', *Review of International Studies*, vol. 17, no. 2, pp. 109–25.

Taylor, P. (1996) *The European Union in the 1990s* (Oxford: Oxford University Press).

Teague, P. (1994) 'Between New Keynesianism and Deregulation: Employment Policy in the European Union', *Journal of European Public Policy*, vol. 1, no. 3, pp. 315–45.

Teasdale, A. L. (1993) 'The Life and Death of the Luxembourg Compromise', *Journal of Common Market Studies*, vol. 31, no. 4, pp. 567–79.

Thelen, K. and Steinmo, S. (1992) 'Historical Institutionalism in Comparative Politics', in S. Steinmo, K. Thelen and F. Longstreth (eds), *Structuring Politics: Historical Institutionalism in Comparative Politics* (Cambridge: Cambridge University Press).

Tilly, C. (1990) *Coercion, Capital and European States, 990–1990* (Oxford: Blackwell).

Tinbergen, J. (1965) *International Economic Integration*, 2nd edn (Amsterdam; Elsevier).

Titmus, R. M. (1974) *Social Policy* (London: Allen and Unwin).

Torres, F. (1998) 'Portugal Toward EMU: A Political Economy Perspective', in E. Jones, J. Frieden and F. Torres (eds), *Joining Europe's Monetary Club: The Challenges for Smaller Member States* (London: Macmillan).

Truman, D. (1951) *The Process of Government* (New York: Knopf Press).

Tsebelis, G. (1990) *Nested Games: Rational Choice in Comparative Politics* (Berkeley: University of California Press).

Tsebelis, G. (1994) 'The Power of the European Parliament as a Conditional Agenda-Setter', *American Political Science Review*, vol. 88, no. 1, pp. 128–42.

Tsebelis, G. (1995a) 'Conditional Agenda-Setting and Decision-Making *Inside* the European Parliament', *Journal of Legislative Studies*, vol. 1, no. 1, pp. 65–93.

Tsebelis, G. (1995b) 'Will Maastricht Reduce the "Democratic Deficit?" ', *APSA-Comparative Politics Newsletter*, vol. 6, no. 1, pp. 4–6.

Tsebelis, G. (1995c) 'Decision Making in Political Systems: Veto Players in Presidentialism, Parliamentarism, Multicameralism and Multipartyism', *British Journal of Political Science*, vol. 25, no. 2, pp. 289–325.

Tsebelis, G. (1996) 'Maastricht and the Democratic Deficit', *Aussenwirtschaft*, vol. 52, no's 1/2, pp. 29–56.

Tsebelis, G. and Garrett, G. (1996) 'An Institutional Critique of Intergovernmentalism', *International Organization*, vol. 50, no. 2, pp. 269–99.

Tsebelis, G. and Garrett, G. (1997a) 'Agenda Setting, Vetoes and the European Union's Co-decision Procedure', *Journal of Legislative Studies*, vol. 3, no. 3, pp. 74–92.

Tsebelis, G. and Garrett, G. (1997b) 'More on the Co-Decision Endgame', *Journal of Legislative Studies*, vol. 3, no. 4, pp. 139–43.

Tsebelis, G. and Kreppel, A. (1998) 'The History of Conditional Agenda-Setting in European Institutions', *European Journal of Political Research*, vol. 33, no. 1, pp. 41–71.

Tsebelis, G. and Money, J. (1997) *Bicameralism* (Cambridge: Cambridge University Press).

Tsoukalis, L . (1997) *The New European Economy Revisited* (Oxford: Oxford University Press).

Tullock, G. (1971) 'The Charity of the Uncharitable', *Western Economic Journal*, vol. 9, pp. 379–92.

Turner, P. (1991) *Capital Flows in the 1980s*, BIS Economic Papers, no. 30, Basle: Bank of International Settlements.

Tversky, A. and Kahneman, T. (1981) 'The Framing of Decisions', *Science*, vol. 211, no. 3, pp. 453–8.

Ugar, M. (1995) 'Freedom of Movement vs. Exclusion: A Reinterpretation of the 'Insider' – 'Outsider' Divide in the European Union', *International Migration Review*, vol. 29, no. 4, pp. 964–99.

Ullrich, H. (1998) 'Transatlantic Relations in the Post-Cold War Era', *Journal of European Public Policy*, vol. 5, no. 1, pp/. 200–205.

Vanberg, G. (1998) 'Abstract Judicial Review, Legislative Bargaining, and Policy Compromise', *Journal of Theoretical Politics*, vol. 10, no. 3, pp. 299–326.

Visser, J. and Ebbinghaus, B. (1992) 'Making the Most of Diversity? European Integration and Transnational Organization of Labour', in J. Greenwood, J. R. Grote and K. Ronit (eds), *Organized Interests and the European Community* (London: Sage).

Vogel, D. (1995) *Trading Up: Consumer and Environmental Regulation in a Global Economy* (Cambridge: Harvard University Press).

Vogel, D. (1997) 'Trading Up and Governing Across: Transnational Governance and Environmental Protection', *Journal of European Public Policy*, vol. 4, no. 4, pp. 556–71.

Volcansek, M. L. (1986) *Judicial Politics in Europe: An Impact Analysis* (New York: Peter Lang).

Volcansek, M. L. (1993a) 'The European Court of Justice: Supranational Policy-Making', in M. L. Volcansek (ed.), *Judicial Politics and Policy-Making in Western Europe* (London: Frank Cass).

Volcansek, M. L. (ed.) (1993b) *Judicial Politics and Policy-Making in Western Europe* (London: Frank Cass).

Vos, E. (1997) 'The Rise of Committees', *European Law Journal*, vol. 3, no. 3, pp. 210–29.

Waever, O. (1996) 'European Security Identities', *Journal of Common Market Studies*, vol. 34, no. 1, pp. 103–32.

Waltz, K. N. (1979) *Theory of International Politics* (New York: McGraw-Hill).

Walzer, M. (1983) *Spheres of Justice: A Defense of Pluralism and Equality* (New York: Basic Books).

Weale, A. (1996) 'Environmental Rules and Rule-Making in the European Union', *Journal of European Public Policy*, vol. 3, no. 4, pp. 594–611.

Weatherill, S. and Beaumont, S. (1995) *EC Law: The Essential Guide to the Legal Workings of the European Community*, 2nd edn (London: Penguin).

Weber, M. (1946 [1919]) 'Politics as a Vocation', in H. H. Gerth and C. Wright Mills (eds), *From Max Weber: Essays in Sociology* (New York: Oxford University Press).

Webster, R. (1998) 'Environmental Collective Action: Stable Patterns of Co-operation and Issue Alliances at the European Level', in J. Greenwood and M. Aspinwall (eds), *Collective Action in the European Union* (London: Routledge).

Weiler, J. H. H. (1981) 'The Community System: The Dual Character of Supranationalism', *Yearbook of European Law*, vol. 1, pp. 268–306.

Weiler, J. H. H. (1991) 'The Transformation of Europe', *Yale Law Journal*, vol. 100, pp. 2403–83.

Weiler, J. H. H. (1993) 'Journey to an Unknown Destination: A Retrospective and Prospective of the European Court of Justice in the Area of Political Integration', *Journal of Common Market Studies*, vol. 31, no. 4, pp. 417–46.

Weiler, J. H. H. (1994) 'A Quiet Revolution: The European Court of Justice and Its Interlocutors', *Comparative Political Studies*, vol. 26, no. 4, pp. 510–34.

Weiler, J. H. H. (1995) 'Does Europe Need a Constitution? Reflections on Demos, Telos and the German Maastricht Decision', *European Law Journal*, vol. 1, no. 3, pp. 219–58.

Weiler, J.H.H. (1997a) 'The Reformation of European Constitutionalism', *Journal of Common Market Studies*, vol. 35, no. 1, pp. 97–131.

Weiler, J.H.H. (1997b) 'The European Union Belongs to the Citizens: Three Immodest Proposals', *European Law Review*, vol. 22, pp. 150–156.

Weiler, J.H.H. (1997c) 'To Be a European Citizen – Eros and Civilization', *Journal of European Public Policy*, vol. 4, no. 4, pp. 495–519.

Weiler, J.H.H. and Haltern, U.R. (1998) 'Constitutional or International? The Foundations of the Community Legal Order and the Question of Judicial *Kompetenz-Kompetenz*', in A.-M. Slaughter, A. Stone Sweet and J.H.H. Weiler (eds), *The European Court and National Courts – Doctrine and Jurisprudence: Legal Change in Its Social Context* (Oxford: Hart Publishing).

Weingast, B.R. (1996) 'Political Institutions: Rational Choice Perspectives', in R.E. Goodin and H.-D. Klingeman (eds), *A New Handbook of Political Science* (Oxford: Oxford University Press).

Weingast, B.R. and Moran, M. (1983) 'Bureaucratic Discretion or Congressional Control? Regulatory Policymaking by the Federal Trade Commission', *Journal of Political Economy*, vol. 91, no. 4, pp. 775–800.

Weingast, B.R., Shepsle, K.A. and Johnson, C. (1981) 'The Political Economy of Benefits and Costs: A Neoclassical Approach to Distributive Politics', *Journal of Political Economy*, vol. 89, pp. 642–64.

Werts, J. (1992) *The European Council* (Amsterdam: North Holland).

Wessels, B. (1995a) 'Development of Support: Diffusion or Demographic Replacement?', in O. Niedermayer and R. Sinnott (eds), *Public Opinion and Internationalized Governance* (Oxford: Oxford University Press).

Wessels, B. (1995b) 'Evaluations of the EC: Élite or Mass-Driven?', in O. Niedermayer and R. Sinnott (eds), *Public Opinion and Internationalized Governance* (Oxford: Oxford University Press).

Wessels, W. (1991) 'The EC Council: The Community's Decisionmaking Center', in R.O. Keohane and S. Hoffmann (eds), *The New European Community: Decisionmaking and Institutional Change* (Boulder: Westview).

Wessels, W. (1992) 'Staat und (west-europäische) Integration, Die Fusionsthese', in M. Kreile (ed.), *Die Integration Europas*, PVS Sonderheft no. 23, pp. 36–61.

Wessels, W. (1996) 'German Administration Interaction and European Union: The Fusion of Public Policies', in Y. Mény, P. Muller and J.-L. Quermonne (eds), *Adjusting to Europe: The Impact of the European Union on National Institutions and Policies* (London: Routledge).

Wessels, W. (1997a) 'An Ever Closer Fusion? A Dynamic Macropolitical View on Integration Processes', *Journal of Common Market Studies*, vol. 35, no. 2, pp. 267–99.

Wessels, W. (1997b) 'The Growth and Differentiation of Multi-Level Networks: A Corporatist Mega-Bureaucracy or Open City?', in H. Wallace and A.R. Young (eds), *Participation and Policy-Making in the European Union* (Oxford: Clarendon).

Wessels, W. and Rometsch, D. (1996) 'Conclusion: European Union and National Institutions', in D. Rometsch and W. Wessels (eds), *The European Union and Member States: Towards Institutional Fusion?* (Manchester: Manchester University Press).

Westlake, M. (1994) *A Modern Guide to the European Parliament* (London: Pinter).

Westlake, M. (1995) *The Council of the European Union* (London: Catermill).

Whitten, G., Gabel, M. and Palmer, H. (1998) ' "Euro-Pork": How Fiscal Policy Influences Public Support for European Integration', unpublished mimeo.

Widgrén, M. (1995) 'Probabilistic voting power in the EU Council: The cases of trade policy and social regulation', *Scandinavian Journal of Economics*, vol. 97, pp. 345–56.

Wiener, A. (1997) *Building Institutions: The Developing Practice of European Citizenship* (Boulder: Westview).

Wilensky, H. (1975) *The Welfare State and Equality* (Berkeley: University of California Press).

Wilks, S. and McGowan, L. (1995) 'Disarming the Commission: The Debate over a European Cartel Office', *Journal of Common Market Studies*, vol. 32, no. 2, pp. 259–73.

Wincott, D. (1995) 'The Role of Law or the Rule of the Court of Justice? An 'Institutional' Account of Judicial Politics in the European Community', *Journal of European Public Policy*, vol. 2, no. 4, pp. 583–602.

Winkler, B. (1996) 'Towards a Strategic View on EMU: A Critical Survey', *Journal of Public Policy*, vol. 16, no. 1, pp. 1–28.

Witte, B. de (1998) 'Sovereignty and European Integration: The Weight of Legal Tradition', in A.-M. Slaughter, A. Stone Sweet and J. H. H. Weiler (eds), *The European Court and National Courts – Doctrine and Jurisprudence: Legal Change in Its Social Context* (Oxford: Hart Publishing).

Wolf, M. (1998) 'Euro's World Test', *The Financial Times*, 7 July 1998.

Woods, N. (1996) 'The Use of Theory in the Study of International Relations', in N. Woods (ed.), *Explaining International Relations Since 1945* (Oxford: Oxford University Press).

Woolcock, S. (1994) *The Single European Market: Centralization or Competition Among National Rules?* (London: Royal Institute of International Affairs).

Woolley, J. T. (1994) 'Linking Political and Monetary Union: The Maastricht Agenda and German Domestic Politics', in B. Eichengreen and J. Frieden (eds), *The Political Economy of European Monetary Unification* (Boulder: Westview).

Wright, V. (1996) 'The National Co-ordination of European Policy-Making: Negotiating the Quagmire', in J. Richardson (ed.), *European Union: Power and Policy-Making* (London: Routledge).

Wyatt-Walker, A. (1995) 'Globalization, Corporate Identity and European Technology Policy', *Journal of European Public Policy*, vol. 2, no. 3, pp. 427–46.

Young, A. R. (1997) 'Consumption Without Representation? Consumers in the Single Market', in H. Wallace and A. R. Young (eds), *Participation and Policy-Making in the European Union* (Oxford: Clarendon).

Young, A. R. (1998) 'European Consumer Groups: Multiple Levels of Governance and Multiple Logics of Collective Action', in J. Greenwood and M. Aspinwall (eds), *Collective Action in the European Union* (London: Routledge).

Zwaan, J. W. de (1995) *The Permanent Representatives Committee* (Amsterdam: Elsvier).

Index